BLUEPRINT
to
WEALTH

Powerful Time-tested
Investing Strategies to
Grow Your Nest Egg

GARY STONE

Published by Share Wealth Publishing
Suite 101, 75 Tulip Street
Cheltenham, VIC, 3193, Australia

Company and product names mentioned herein are the trademarks or registered trademarks of their respective owners.

The SPIVA® Scorecards and Persistence Scorecards are proprietary to and are published and distributed by S&P Opco, LLC (a subsidiary of S&P Dow Jones Indices LLC), its affiliates and/or its licensors and portions thereof have been licensed for use hereunder. S&P®, S&P 500®. S&P MidCap 400®, S&P SmallCap 600®, S&P Composite 1500®, S&P Europe 350® and SPIVA®, among other famous marks, are registered trademarks of Standard & Poor's Financial Services LLC; Dow Jones® is a registered trademark of Dow Jones Trademark Holdings LLC; TSX® is a registered trademark of TSX, Inc.; ASX® is a registered trademark of ASX Operations Pty Limited; and IFCI® is a registered trademark of International Finance Corporation. © 2016 S&P Dow Jones Indices LLC, its affiliates and/or its licensors. All rights reserved."

Index data is provided with permission from Norgate Investor Services ("Premium Data").

Mutual fund data is provided with permission from Barchart.com, Inc.

ISBN: 978-0-9945967-1-0 (Paperback)
ISBN: 978-0-9945967-2-7 (eBook)
ISBN: 978-0-9945967-4-1 (Color Paperback)
ISBN: 978-0-9945967-3-4 (Color Hardback)

First Edition

Printed by IngramSpark in the United States and Australia.

Cover and interior design by Jerry Dorris, AuthorSupport.com

Library of Congress Cataloguing-in-Publication is available upon request.

www.blueprinttowealth.com

Contents

Acknowledgments

This book represents two and half decades of research and experience on investing ideas and practices that have culminated in the compilation of the simple and efficient investing approaches in this book, which anybody can use.

I am indebted to many who have contributed to my thinking, research, and experience. Thank you to Mark Douglas, a mentor and friend, who provided the first inspiration more than twelve years ago for me to write a book. Mark's unique understanding and articulation of the nature of investing and trading in his one-on-one mentorship over many long conversations and in his books has had a huge influence on me confirming and improving my investing processes and those that my clients use.

I would like to thank my colleagues in the Share Wealth Systems team while I have been writing this book: Shane Archer, Milton Behrendorff, David Sayer, Campbell Sinclair and Karl Stanguts. Thank you for taking care of business while I was mostly absent getting this book completed.

Thanks to Steve Harrison's Quantum Leap Program and the entire team at Bradley Communications Corp, who have taken my mindset to a whole new level about writing a book and letting the world know about it.

I would like to acknowledge and thank the many women and men whom have been clients over the last two plus decades. Their journeys and the many conversations that I have had with dozens of them confirmed to me that successful do-it-yourself investing truly can be learned and executed by busy everyday people. I have written this book also in response to the infrequent but ongoing prompting by many clients over the last one and a half decades.

Finally, I'd like to thank my wife and life partner, Heather, who has been a stalwart in every venture that I have undertaken over the last thirty years, including this book. Your trust and belief in me continues to be a rock in my life.

Gary Stone
Melbourne

Preface

In days long gone retirees relied on company pension schemes. These were 'defined benefit' structures where the corporation, in collaboration with active mutual fund managers, took the full risk for the growth of their employees' retirement savings and ongoing payment of a pension right through the employee's retirement years. The company took the entire risk for ensuring that their pension fund did not run out of money to continue paying their ex-employees' pensions. Otherwise, the company had to pay the ex-employees' pensions out of the company's annual profits.

On the surface, this seemed effective to everyday people because they took no risk and spent little time managing their retirement savings. It wasn't better; the fees, mostly hidden, and excessive caution ate into returns. Also actuarially, the company and collaborating mutual funds ensured that they weren't short-changed by paying out more pension than had been accumulated over time; meaning that the only people losing out were the employees through a potentially lower monthly pension and who had sacrificed salary in foregoing raises over the years.

If the worst happened and the company failed, the odds were that the company pension 'defined benefit' scheme collapsed with the enterprise. In this sense maybe the risks were bigger for retirees! Of course, government 'defined benefit' pensions don't face this latter risk. Or do they, as deficits and debt continue to rise?

Since the 1990's, saving and investing for retirement has moved from being mainly 'defined benefit' to being majority 'defined contribution' where the employee now takes the full risk to save for and grow their retirement nest egg. But employees can also reap rewards from this change through minimizing costs and using better performing investing approaches to accumulate a far larger nest egg.

Both 'defined benefit' and 'defined contribution' methods have been and continue to be supplemented by the promise of government Social Security payments when employees reach retirement. However, Social Security has limits, and there are plenty of ongoing discussions and doubts about the level of Social Security payments in the future. It is possible they will not even survive in the future given both government debt levels around the world and the investment needed by governments to support aging and longer living populations.

The bottom line is that workers today just cannot plan to rely on their Social Security being sufficient to fund a comfortable retirement in years to come.

More than ever, employees need to take responsibility early for saving and investing for their retirement. Some have, but most have not. This book has been written to cut through the jargon and confusion of investing alternatives to provide specific solutions for investors who may even have no prior investing knowledge and who want to provide for a comfortable retirement, or even better, to achieve financial freedom. These solutions are also very applicable to those investing for reasons other than retirement.

For decades, many large mutual fund institutions and their distribution networks have preyed on would-be investors and scared them into believing that it is too risky and too difficult to be a do-it-yourself (DIY) investor.

The independent everyday investor CAN manage and control their own financial resources, invest them confidently and do much better than the active mutual funds.

[A term I will frequently use in this book is 'active mutual funds'. These are large mutual funds that invest in one or more investment classes with ongoing re-balancing in and between asset classes and investing strategies in trying to *perform better than a benchmark index*. They can include active equity mutual funds, balanced funds of some sort, bond funds or money market funds. In many countries, they are called 'managed funds.' By contrast, 'passive index funds' attempt to *match, or track, a benchmark index*.]

One of the most glaring misrepresentations of the active mutual fund industry is to advise investors that the *only* way to profit in the stock market is by "time in the market." They expound a long-term buy-and-hold strategy in their fund as the only way to invest capital for retirement, or any other goal. And as a result, fund managers have benefited greatly by keeping ordinary people financially confused by marketing *their* 'investment philosophies'.

Fund managers use the ups and downs of the financial markets, stock trading jargon and the need for a steep learning curve to investment literacy as evidence that the independent investor would soon fail if they did it themselves. Some of their catch cries include buy-and-hold active mutual funds forever otherwise missing the ten best days every ten years could wipe out all your ten-year gains; risk management through diversification; professional portfolio management; streamlined administration; accountability and transparency through regulation; and others.

For example, *diversification across different asset classes is an essential risk management technique used by active balanced and target date mutual funds.*

It is a valid method, but for investment horizons of three to seven years, or maybe ten at a push. But not for twenty, thirty or forty year horizons.

The average time to retirement for all working people investing for retirement is thirty-three years! This average is getting longer as more young workers start their 'defined contribution' retirement savings journey, and older workers retire later.

There is a mismatch between the risk management technique and the investment horizon of their customers. I will expose the poor performance that results from long-term diversification that also doesn't deliver as much risk minimization as it is supposed to do.

These and other distortions are myths, and in this book, I will show you how false marketing tactics should not sway people from investing successfully using alternative approaches.

It is evident also that *percentage based commissions and fees computed on 'funds under management' (FuM)* motivates fund managers to build their fund size as much as possible through raising capital and incentivizing advisors, with secondary regard for growing their customers' wealth.

This book will help you learn simple, well-researched strategies to do it yourself (DIY). For those with many years before retirement, your strategy may be a type of 'buy-and-hold', but not individual stocks or active mutual funds.

You can learn much better strategies in a few hours with this book, and spend less time managing and executing them than it takes to watch just half an hour of TV a week.

You will then be able to create wealth faster than those who don't know these simple secrets of successful investing, and faster than leaving your nest egg invested in active mutual funds. I will explain the advantages of being an active, agile and savvy do it yourself (DIY) investor with a defined strategy and Investment Plan.

Of course, DIY may not be acceptable to 100% of investors. I accept that. Some will be skeptical, some apathetic. Some will say that it is just not for them. Most will justify their current strategy as appropriate for their goals which, hopefully, will provide for their years of retirement when they get there.

Better technology means populations are living longer nowadays but also need more access to costly health and medical care. Supporting this assertion, in 2015 there was a 70% chance that one of a sixty-five-year-old couple would reach age ninety; suggesting the need to provide for even longer retirement. And all the statistics show that collectively most people simply will not have enough and nor will Social Security help make up the shortfall.

To make retirement far more satisfying, comfortable and efficient, each of us will have to take carefully considered decisions to achieve the most effective investment outcomes for our money. We will either need to contribute more to our retirement savings, achieve better growth for our savings before and during retirement, or both.

This book contains the necessary solutions and tools for you to become an empowered investor. For retirement, or other goals. I sincerely trust that by discovering and using these strategies over the long term you will create wealth for a retirement that is happy, secure and comfortable, and you will be financially free to do what you want with your money.

My mission, through this book and my business, Share Wealth Systems, is to empower and skill everyday people just like you to achieve a better life and retirement nest egg through simple stock market investing.

I wish you enjoyable learning and effective investing.

Gary Stone
July 2016

Introduction

*"Employ your time in improving yourself by other men's writings,
so that you shall gain easily what others have labored hard for."*

SOCRATES

If you are responsible for managing your retirement portfolio, then this book is for you.

If you think that you are NOT responsible for your retirement portfolio, this book is also for you! You'll discover why it's essential for you to take responsibility for your wealth and how you can accumulate it far better than the active mutual funds.

This book is the culmination of my research, experiences, personal investment journey, mentoring and interaction with thousands of ordinary investors for more than twenty-five years, especially in Australia, the United States, and South Africa.

Through supporting and educating thousands of 'do it yourself' (DIY) investors since 1995, I have gained deep insight into the problems that everyday investors struggle with and how to overcome them through simple and efficient strategies and, very importantly, investor psychology.

The combination of this empathy and a quarter of a century of experience through extensive execution and research has crystallized in my mind straightforward approaches that everyday people can easily fit into their already busy lives to achieve much better growth of their investment nest eggs. Over the two decades that I've been working with clients, frequently they have said, "I wish I had known this years ago and started then."

The investing industry continually distributes marketing materials to re-enforce the inaccuracy that everyday investors don't and can't have the necessary investing skills and must rely on the professionals' expertise to grow their nest eggs. Beware of this message; it is part of the misinformation that is broadcast by the investing industry.

I have discovered that the majority of investors (everyone who contributes to a retirement fund is an investor) would be far better off over the long term managing their retirement funds than allowing their money to be managed by active mutual funds. By the time you finish this book, I am sure you will agree with me.

The problem is that so few people in this fast paced 24/7 world take the time to seek to understand. They are confused by the jargon and overwhelmed with the complexity of the instruments and investment alternatives available. I see why many investors are confused, and that's one of the reasons I have written this book.

I will expose myths that are broadcast by the financial industry. I will demonstrate how poorly the active mutual funds actually perform, particularly the fastest growing categories of Balanced Funds and Target Date funds.

When you finish this book, you will come away with a few straightforward and focused strategies that will liberate you from feeling unconfident or inadequate when it comes to investing for your retirement, or any other goal. You will be a transformed investor that can rapidly move to investing maturity.

There are four core IDEAS in this book that will help you transform the way you think about the stock market.

IDEA 1 – EVERYBODY CAN BEAT NEARLY EVERY ACTIVE MUTUAL FUND

The performance that the market indices achieve, plus dividends, is available for everyone who invests for any reason, and especially for those that have a defined contribution retirement plan such as a 401(k), IRA, Superannuation fund or invested pension plan of any variety, anywhere in the world.

EVERY person who is saving for retirement, and hence investing, can achieve this index-type performance. Why would they want to do this? *Because just matching the index does better over time than nearly EVERY actively managed retirement fund in which everyday people invest their retirement monies.* Much more money in your retirement years leads to a more secure and comfortable financial future, free from worry and anxiety, to do whatever you want to do.

The investing instrument that can help everyone achieve this goal is the index Exchange Traded Fund or index ETF. Index ETFs have revolutionized investing and are rapidly growing investment instruments due to their simplicity and access to index type returns that outperform nearly all active mutual funds.

IDEA 2 – EVERYDAY INVESTORS CAN BEAT THE STOCK MARKET BENCHMARK INDEX

There is a myth circulating that states that **ordinary investors cannot beat the stock exchange indices,** or put another way, cannot beat the market. It simply is not so. They can. I will expose this myth in this book with evidence-based research and ongoing live execution in the market.

Beating the market is far simpler than the financial services industry wants you to know. Whether you are age eighteen or age eighty, or you have $500 or $5,000,000 to invest, you can do it yourself, and do it well.

This myth implies that the investing professionals, the active mutual funds, can beat the market. However, some 85% of all active mutual funds in the United States don't beat the market year after year, and almost none do over six years or more. I will debunk both with factual, evidence-based research.

IDEA 3 – YOUR CUSTOMIZED INVESTMENT PROCESS

The DIY approach builds assets through the structure and rigor of clear, researched investment *processes*. The approach is tailored to each's investing requirements and implemented using a simple framework. Each person's requirements depend on investing objectives, tolerance for risk, capital to invest and time available to execute a simple strategy.

The simple processes can be systematically and easily applied, and can be implemented efficiently in as little as fifteen minutes a quarter to fifteen minutes a week depending on the processes deployed. It is the equivalent of following a recipe with a known outcome.

IDEA 4 – THE MARKET CAN BE TIMED

I contend that the market can be timed. However, according to the investing industry, the market cannot be timed. I will debunk this myth too.

The experts may say it's "time in the market" not "timing the market" and may use sleight of hand tools to try to prove to unsuspecting investors that staying in the market in active mutual funds is the ordinary investor's only option to achieve nest egg growth and reduce risk.

In this book, you will discover how to "time the market" with very little effort, potentially doing fewer than three trades a year, and reap far better rewards than the market benchmark indices offer over the long term. Using timing, your time commitment, on average, will be only fifteen minutes a week, maybe less.

WHAT TO DO?

This book is about *why* you should do it yourself, and *how* to do it yourself. It provides concrete step by step solutions that can be started immediately so you can begin the journey to achieving much improved long-term investment returns for a better life and a better retirement.

Investors can implement an **initial simple strategy** *immediately based on the first and third core ideas that requires as little as fifteen minutes a quarter.* **Other simple strategies use the combination of all four core ideas** *and are provided to deliver a means for you to become a consistently successful investor over the long term and achieve even better results than the first simple strategy.*

Reading the book alone will not achieve these results. All results only come from taking action. In other words, after finishing this book you will know exactly what to do, but **there is a huge difference between knowing what to do and doing what you know**.

Although the strategies are simple, a transition to doing what you know will still be needed, as with any new process in your life. For this, a transition exercise is provided in the last chapter of the book.

If you want your returns to improve when the markets are rising and to protect your investment capital during market declines, then YOU must change the way that you think about your investments.

Changing the way that you do something begins with an idea but implementing that idea and turning it into reality starts with DESIRE.

Do you desire to retire securely and comfortably with more money

than you otherwise would have had if you left your funds invested with the active mutual funds for your whole life?

Most won't even be able to answer this question because they don't know what their returns have been or whether they've matched or beaten the markets. When you do find out, I guarantee that you will be shocked!

Around 80% of all retirement savings in the U.S. are invested in active mutual funds, whether the money is in a 401(k), an IRA, Target Date fund, or company retirement plan. And this trend is not abating; it is strengthening. Despite the massive amount of discussion that has occurred for many years about the merits of index investing.

This book will:

- Demonstrate how you can outperform the active mutual funds, the so-called investing professionals.
- Inspire you to overcome the apathy or confusion you may have about investing.
- Stir your desire to do better.
- Provide perspective on the different investment choices.
- Position simple solutions on how to invest smarter.
- Provide specific out-of-the-box step-by-step actions and tools documented in a completed Investment Plan to implement these solutions.
- Inspire you to transition to becoming a consistently successful investor.

My hope is that your investing journey will be as satisfying as mine has been, but also easier because you are benefiting from the experiences, mistakes, and successes of my journey, my mentors, and those of many others I have coached. **My hope is that not having to 're-invent the wheel' for yourself is a massive shortcut to you achieving financial freedom.**

You've probably read other books about investing, and the jargon can be confusing. That's not the kind of book I've written. I will be taking you on a mentoring journey, just as I took Iain[1] on his journey. I'm including his typical questions along with my responses to assist you in discovering and transforming to a better way to invest.

You may get eager and want to take action before you understand all

---

1   Iain is a composite of the many everyday people who have become clients over the last twenty-one years.

the principles that I discuss, just as Iain occasionally did. As I advised Iain, you need to be patient. And since this is such an important journey, I urge you also to read the book carefully. You may have to re-read a particular chapter or take some time to absorb the content. After all, I'm asking you to suspend much that you've heard from the active mutual fund industry, financial media and possibly your personal financial planner or adviser. I know you will find the challenge well worth it.

If you're a baby boomer who is approaching or in retirement and worried about another big stock market decline, this book is definitely for you. But, if you've recently entered the workforce and concerned about how you will create wealth, you should also read this book. (My twenty-seven-year-old daughter started using the most straightforward strategy in 2015.)

Reading the book will take longer than actually implementing the plan. When I say you can execute the strategies in fifteen minutes a quarter, or week, I'm not exaggerating. I've done all the research, testing, and analysis for you, so you only have to focus on following simple steps to achieve your goals.

Hopefully, when you've read the entire book, you will be able to create your customized blueprint to financial freedom; and you won't have to spend much time doing so as I have done all the preparation, planning and research for you. Embrace and enjoy the journey...

PART 1

HIDDEN TRUTHS ABOUT MUTUAL FUNDS

CHALLENGING THE ESTABLISHMENT

For as long as anyone can remember, human beings have made progress by their willingness to challenge the status quo. Curiosity and the desire to do better drive us to seek a better way and to uncover the truth from myth. Sometimes the status quo is a good option but not always, and discerning the difference requires some knowledge and motivation to identify another way, a better way of reaching a goal. Often the better way already exists, but we just aren't aware of it.

Also, things change; innovators invent new instruments and gadgets. What was a great way to do things a few years ago may not be the best way now, or in the foreseeable future. We have to keep questioning "What if..." and not merely accept the status quo just because everybody else does things a certain way, or the establishment says so.

Part 1 of this book challenges the status quo of the financial establishment through curiosity-driven research that reveals massive underperformance by the active mutual funds; in the very place where most people invest their retirement savings.

CHAPTER 1

Active Mutual Funds and the Everyday Investor

"The man who removes a mountain begins by carrying away small stones."

CHINESE PROVERB

Iain developed an interest in do it yourself (DIY) investing to take control of his financial future when he realized that the money he would need to last through his retirement years would be in the hands of the active mutual funds; at least for another twenty working years and then even longer during his retirement. At that point, a worried Iain broke into a cold sweat.

Nearly every employee in the western world is an investor by default through some direct or indirect exposure to at least one mutual fund.

According to the Investment Company Institute (ICI) 2016 Fact Book, as at December 2015, 88.6% of U.S. mutual fund assets were invested in active equity mutual funds, balanced funds of some sort, such as a target date fund, bond funds or money market funds. The remaining 11.4% of mutual fund assets were invested in index equity mutual funds that track a stock exchange index.

Combine these statistics with the fact that 91% of American households invest in mutual funds of all kinds for retirement, with 72% as their

3

primary reason[1], and it tells us just how important a role mutual funds, both active mutual funds, and passive index mutual funds, play in the futures of Americans.

From these statistics, we can deduce that more than **80% of America's retirement savings are invested in active mutual funds.**

Why did Iain's realization cause him to break into a cold sweat? Well, Iain had read an article about the performance of the very funds in which he had chosen to invest nearly all of his retirement savings, and he didn't like what he read. It made him realize that he may not have enough savings to last his retirement years. It was a frightening thought that invigorated him to take action.

As Iain explained to me shortly after we first met, this was the catalyst for him to make a choice. "Was I going to do something about it or be apathetic like millions of other people in the same boat? After all, if just about everybody invests this way then I should be alright, shouldn't I?" asked Iain.

"Wrong! It's the old 'safety in numbers' myth!" I exclaimed. "Just because active mutual funds dominate the market with billions and billions of dollars of investors' retirement savings invested with them, it doesn't mean that you will automatically have enough to retire on time."

The article that Iain had read was written by Jeff Sommer in *The New York Times* on March 14, 2015[2].

How Many Mutual Funds Routinely Rout the Market? Zero

"The bull market in stocks turned six last Monday, and despite some rocky stretches — like last week, when the market fell — it has generally been a very pleasant time for money managers, who have often posted good numbers.

Look more closely at those gaudy returns, however, and you may see something startling. The truth is that very few professional investors have actually managed to outperform the rising market consistently over those years.

In fact, based on the updated findings and definitions of a particular study, it appears that no mutual fund managers have.

---

1   page 120 ICI 2016 Fact Book, www.ici.org
2   http://www.nytimes.com/2015/03/15/your-money/how-many-mutual-funds-routinely-rout-the-market-zero.html?_r=0

I wrote about the initial findings of that study last summer. It is called "Does Past Performance Matter? The Persistence Scorecard," and it is conducted by S&P Dow Jones Indices twice a year. The edition of the study that I focused on began in March 2009, the start of the bull market.

It included 2,862 broad, actively managed domestic stock mutual funds that were in operation for the 12 months through 2010. The S&P Dow Jones team winnowed the funds based on performance. It selected the 25 percent of funds with the best returns over those 12 months — and then asked how many of those funds actually remained in the top quarter in each of the four succeeding 12-month periods through March 2014.

The answer was remarkably low: two.

Just two funds — the Hodges Small Cap fund and the AMG SouthernSun Small Cap fund — managed to hold on to their berths in the top quarter every year for five years running. And for the 2,862 funds as a whole, that record is even a little worse than you would have expected from random chance alone.

In other words, if all of the managers of the 2,862 funds hadn't bothered to try to pick stocks at all — if they had merely flipped coins — they would, as a group, probably have produced better numbers. Instead of two funds at the end of five years, basic probability theory tells us there should have been three.

The study seemed to support the considerable body of evidence suggesting that most people shouldn't even try to beat the market: Just pick low-cost index funds, assemble a balanced and appropriate portfolio for your specific needs, and give up on active fund management.

The data in the study didn't prove that the mutual fund managers lacked talent or that you couldn't beat the market. But, as Keith Loggie, the senior director of global research and design at S&P Dow Jones Indices, said in an interview last week, the evidence certainly didn't bolster the case for investing with active fund managers.

"Looking at the numbers, you can't tell whether there is skill involved in what they do or whether their performance is just a matter of luck," Mr. Loggie said. "I believe that many of them do have skill. But even if they do have it, based on how they've done in the past you really can't predict how they will perform in the future."

Still, those two funds did manage to perform splendidly in that

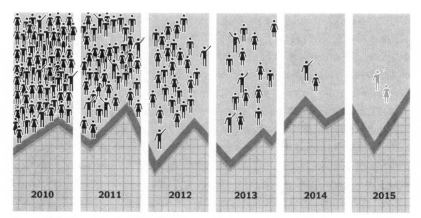

Credit Minh Uong/The New York Times   Figure 1-1

study. Their stubborn persistence at the top of the heap over that five-year period suggested that there was some hope for active fund managers. If they could do it, after all, others could, too.

But we're now about two weeks away from the completion of another 12 months since the end of that study, and it's been a mediocre stretch, at best, for those two mutual funds. When the month is over, to borrow from Agatha Christie, it looks as though we'll be saying: And then there were none.

Here are the dismal statistics: The SouthernSun Small Cap fund has actually lost money for investors over the 12 months through Thursday. It was down 3.2 percent, according to Morningstar, and for the nine months through December, it was in the bottom quartile of funds in the S&P Dow Jones study.

The Hodges Small Cap fund has done better, gaining almost 6 percent through Thursday. S&P Dow Jones Indices says that put it in the third quartile — or second-to-worst one — through December. While it's mathematically possible, it is highly unlikely that either will climb to the top quartile in the next few weeks, Mr. Loggie said."

After reading the article, Iain chose to do something about it.

I found myself summarizing the main point of the article, as I've done countless times over the years in presentations, webinars, calls with clients and prospective clients, discussions with friends over the dinner table, and in rounds of golf with friends and strangers.

"Not only do more than 80% of active mutual funds underperform their benchmark indices over one to ten years, as I will show you shortly, but the 20% of the funds that outperform are *not the same funds*, year on year. Making it almost impossible for an ordinary investor to select an active mutual fund, or two, in advance, that will match, let alone, outperform the market indices over, say, six years or more. Just as in Figure 1.1, the number of funds that outperform each and every year moves towards ZERO over six years!"

"I say 'almost impossible' because I don't believe in probabilities of zero and one, but the chances are so small that it might as well be no chance!"

"So what! What does this actually mean for everyday people?" asked Iain.

"It means that choosing to invest their 401(k) or IRA contributions, or any other investments, in active mutual funds of any kind, it is almost certain they will end up with a significantly smaller nest egg when they retire. They will accumulate a nest egg that is unlikely to support an independent and comfortable retirement."

"Is there another way?" asked Iain.

"There certainly is. A very simple way for these same everyday investors with no previous investing experience to achieve much better investment growth that will put them on a path to fix their nest egg."

"What are the studies that Jeff Somers in *The New York Times* is talking about and why are they so important?" asked Iain.

"Have you looked up the S&P Dow Jones Indices studies, which they call their SPIVA* Scorecard, mentioned in the article?" I asked Iain. "SPIVA being S&P Indices Versus Active."

"No," he said.

"Well you aren't alone," I said. "I have been following the scorecard report for some years now, and I'm amazed at how few investors are even aware of them, let alone read them."

Having run an investing education and coaching business for more than two decades, I speak with everyday investors regularly. Despite the coverage in financial pages about SPIVA Reports, most people have no idea what they are.

After our initial discussion, I helped Iain research the SPIVA Scorecard reports so he could see that somewhere between 75% and 89%, but seldom less than 70%, of active mutual funds, do indeed underperform the market indices, for any given report, over the years.

This motivated Iain to calculate roughly how much their

underperformance could cost him in lost retirement money over the next twenty plus years compared to just matching the market indices, let alone beat them.

We looked at the difference between the annual returns in the S&P MidCap 400 Total Return index and Iain's active 'balanced' mutual fund over the previous twenty years. It revealed that over the remaining twenty or so working years that Iain had left until retirement, he could end up more than **$800,000 *worse off*** if he continued to contribute his monthly 401(k) savings to his current active 'balanced' fund.

On the other hand, ***by significantly reducing fees with a simple strategy*** and spending a few minutes each month investing his same monthly 401(k) contribution in a different way, he could ***end up with around 76% more in his retirement nest egg***.

I continued, "The difference could be ***as much as one and a half to two million dollars, for others with more time on their side or more already saved***. By doing nothing more than putting in a little bit of effort, just fifteen minutes a month, or using the IDEA of timing the market, spending just fifteen minutes a week, to ensure avoiding most of any severe market falls."

Now Iain was really startled! "It's unbelievable," he said, "***why do people continue handing their money over to the active mutual funds and pay them fees to do worse than the stock market benchmarks?***"

"I'll be answering this question in some detail. It's even more unbelievable when you realize that stock market index returns are at least on offer from the stock market for EVERYONE over the long term," I said. "You can do even better than straight index returns," I added. "Together we'll look at some more deeply researched comparisons between active mutual funds and stock market indices."

Iain's question about why people don't take action to change their investing path is one that we discussed and researched together as we worked to discover why the active mutual funds underperform their respective market benchmarks so dramatically and how everyday investors can grow their nest egg by taking a different but simple path from the herd.

As we researched, the more misrepresentations that we found, the more frustrated Iain grew with the financial industry and the more determined he became to find a better path to break free from the poor relative performance. Now in his mid-forties, Iain had come to the obvious conclusion that he needed to maximize his nest egg growth potential to make certain he and his wife had the necessary funds to secure their retirement.

I explained, "Iain, it's not just people in the twenty years before retirement who are so severely affected by active mutual funds underperformance to the stock market indices, it's everybody!"

"Think about the sixty-year-old who has to survive financially until he is eighty-five or even ninety, or the twenty-somethings who have time on their side. Whatever age, every investor is faced with this underperformance problem. What matters is what the person does about it."

Iain concluded, "If these strategies can work for me then maybe I can use the same strategies for other investing capital such as saving for my children's college and even teaching my kids' this strategy for when they start working."

"Sure, the investing professionals may appear to have the same objective—to get the best returns that they can within their chosen charter. However, the investing problem that they have to solve is very different than the one that you as an individual has to solve."

I continued, "They have to find a home for hundreds of millions of dollars and even tens of billions of dollars. They are forced to deploy strategies that have advantages but also have limitations compared to what the agile individual investor can do with tiny, in comparison, sums of investment capital. One of the funds' biggest problems is not being able to sell all their holdings in the market when it falls severely. Doing so would lead to a self-perpetuating greater decline in the stock market if their total sell-off was during a downturn."

"This means that active and passive index mutual funds alike have to keep their allocated capital mostly or entirely invested during stock market downturns. And because active mutual funds can't totally exit from the market they have to find other ways of lessening the blow during severe market downturns which force them to invest in less volatile but lower return investment classes, or to over-diversify."

Herein is one of the greatest advantages that an individual DIY investor has over the investing professional. ***Individual investors can move their entire investment portfolio into cash*** if they want to. This is crucial. In fact, ***it is one of the profound principles that favors the individual investor*** that we will examine in some detail as one of the investing paths that can be followed by everyday investors.

LAST WORD

- Doing it yourself (DIY) has the potential to add hundreds of thousands of dollars to your retirement nest egg over the long term.
- Investors with horizons of longer than six years have a very low probability of matching, let alone outperforming, market indices when investing in an active diversified mutual fund of any kind.
- Individual investors have more advantages than professional investors in the financial markets; they just need a little knowledge and confidence in their skills.

CHAPTER 2

Spotlight—Active Mutual Fund Performance

"Genius ain't anything more than elegant common sense."

JOSH BILLINGS

"Right Iain," I exclaimed, "We will start this session off with a simple question."

"What is *the* most well-known and proven investment plan for stocks; and one of the most successful too?"

He thought for a while, searching for an answer.

I offered some clues.

"Just about everybody in the world who has watched the finance segment on the evening news would be aware of it. It uses a simple process. It requires no payment of exorbitant bonuses to investment teams. No advertising to market it. No stock selection is required using fundamental analysis, value investing, or even technical analysis. It knows what assets to include in and exclude from its portfolio and when. It also knows how much of each stock to hold. And it takes the tiny team a very short period, from time to time, to execute the process."

I added, "By the way, I'll explain what fundamental and technical analyses are in a future session."

11

Iain tried a number of answers including, "Warren Buffett's process that he uses for Berkshire Hathaway."

"No, that fails by not being the most well-known. Also, Buffett uses fundamental analysis and value investing criteria," I rallied back.

"Then I don't know," Iain said. "In fact, how am I supposed to know? I don't have much investing experience."

I have asked this question to hundreds of attendees at numerous live presentations. On almost every occasion, everyone in the audience has failed to get the answer.

"Well, you do know, and when I mention the name you will recognize it, but you will be surprised that it is the most well-known and proven system."

"What is it?" Iain surrendered.

"The S&P500 index on the New York Stock Exchange," I said.

"Really!" said Iain. "Don't I have to buy a subset of individual stocks so I can't invest in it unless I have millions to buy all 500 stocks!"

"Not correct," I said. "You can buy the S&P500 *index* right now on the stock exchange. In fact, anyone anywhere in the world can buy it almost instantly. All you need is an account with any stock broker-dealer."

"What's more, it will cost you less than $10 in fees to buy the S&P500 index," I added.

"So even if it is *the* most well-known investing process, why should I invest in it?" asked Iain. "It's just an index. Surely individual stocks and stock mutual funds can do better."

"It's not just an index," I replied. "It's a system in its own right that is uninfluenced by emotion, surmise or opinion. Recall that we discussed the SPIVA Scorecard and how many actively managed domestic stock mutual funds underperform the S&P500 Total Return index."

I pointed out that the difference between the S&P500 index and S&P500 Total Return index is that the Total Return index includes dividends in the calculation of the S&P500 index. Table 2-1 shows the Scorecard Performance to December 31, 2015, for U.S. Equity Funds. The phrase 'U.S. Equity Funds' is used where the word 'equity' (or equities) can be utilized interchangeably with 'stock' (or stocks).

It shows emphatically that the vast majority of U.S. Equity Funds do worse than their benchmark total return indices.

Table 2-1[1]

Report 1: Percentage of U.S. Equity Funds Outperformed by Benchmarks					
Fund Category	Comparison Index	One-Year (%)	Three-Year (%)	Five-Year (%)	Ten-Year (%)
All Domestic Equity Funds	S&P Composite 1500	74.81	80.85	88.43	83.18
All Large-Cap Funds	S&P 500	66.11	75.81	84.15	82.14
All Mid-Cap Funds	S&P MidCap 400	56.81	61.64	76.69	87.61
All Small-Cap Funds	S&P SmallCap 600	72.20	81.73	90.13	88.42
All Multi-Cap Funds	S&P Composite 1500	73.64	79.61	88.56	88.32
Large-Cap Growth Funds	S&P 500 Growth	49.30	76.34	86.54	93.63
Large-Cap Core Funds	S&P 500	73.82	83.70	88.26	82.84
Large-Cap Value Funds	S&P 500 Value	59.16	78.70	82.17	61.00
Mid-Cap Growth Funds	S&P MidCap 400 Growth	79.89	65.91	81.48	91.23
Mid-Cap Core Funds	S&P MidCap 400	67.88	62.59	76.51	87.76
Mid-Cap Value Funds	S&P MidCap 400 Value	32.35	48.68	70.27	82.56
Small-Cap Growth Funds	S&P SmallCap 600 Growth	88.43	85.59	91.89	92.39
Small-Cap Core Funds	S&P SmallCap 600	77.62	86.62	91.44	89.16
Small-Cap Value Funds	S&P SmallCap 600 Value	46.56	79.51	92.31	86.36
Multi-Cap Growth Funds	S&P Composite 1500 Growth	68.02	79.00	90.57	90.44
Multi-Cap Core Funds	S&P Composite 1500	86.68	86.81	91.16	88.25
Multi-Cap Value Funds	S&P Composite 1500 Value	52.42	61.24	76.87	77.71
Real Estate Funds	S&P US Real Estate Investment Trust	61.90	76.22	82.64	86.08

Source: S&P Dow Jones Indices LLC, CRSP. Data as of Dec. 31, 2015. Table is provided for illustrative purposes. Past performance is no guarantee of future results.

I highlighted the second line in Table 2-1 with the *Fund Category* of 'All Large-Cap Funds' and *Comparison Index* of 'S&P 500'; the **percentages of active equity mutual funds that underperformed the S&P500 Total Return index over five and ten years were 84.15% and 82.14%, respectively**.

Scanning down the 'Ten-Year (%)' column reveals that just two categories of funds had percentages less than 82%; the S&P500 Value index outperformed 61% of 'Large-Cap Value Funds,' and the S&P Composite 1500 Value index outperformed 77.71% of 'Multi-Cap Value Funds.'

Iain said, "It's amazing how locked-in I am to my old ways. Even though I had just committed to investigating a better way to invest, I still back-tracked to the status quo of thinking that active mutual funds are the way to get the best growth and protection for my investments."

"I have seen this in hundreds of investors," I said. "And I know from my experience in the active investing industry that millions of investors must share this difficulty. I have noted that only enduring action changes one's old beliefs to a renewed way of thinking. But before that can happen a personal decision must be made to change and to seek

---

1   https://us.spindices.com/documents/spiva/spiva-us-yearend-2015.pdf

evidence that confirms the new direction will work better compared to the previous path."

I continued, "You have started in the right direction. You have the desire to change caused by realizing how much money you could forfeit if you take an apathetic investing path and leave your money with active mutual funds over the next twenty or so years while still working. You now seek evidence to confirm this and to discover how you can do it."

Standard & Poor's Dow Jones Indices update their SPIVA˚ Scorecard bi-annually to show how well the U.S. active equity mutual funds have performed compared to the S&P500 Total Return index. They also track performance for other regions including Canada, Europe, Australia, Japan, South Africa, India and South America.

The theme is the same: a large majority of active equity mutual funds the world over underperform their respective benchmark indices. Refer to Tables 2-1 to 2-7; please take careful note of the Report headings as they are not identical in all tables.

In Australia, as shown in Table 2-2, two-thirds of actively managed funds underperformed the ASX200 Accumulation index over five years to December 31, 2015.

Table 2-2[2]

Report 1: Percentage of Funds Outperformed by the Index				
Fund Category	Comparison Index	One-Year (%)	Three-Year (%)	Five-Year (%)
Australian Equity General	S&P/ASX 200	36.22	44.82	67.16
Australian Equity Mid- and Small-Cap	S&P/ASX Mid-Small Index	27.27	29.90	28.87
International Equity General	S&P Developed Ex-Australia LargeMidCap	72.27	86.70	88.24
Australian Bonds	S&P/ASX Australian Fixed Interest 0+ Index	85.71	86.00	87.04
Australian Equity A-REIT	S&P/ASX 200 A-REIT	84.06	89.04	85.00

Source: S&P Dow Jones Indices LLC, Morningstar. Data as of Dec. 31, 2015. Table is provided for illustrative purposes. Past performance is no guarantee of future results.

In Canada, as shown in Table 2-3, 77% of active equity mutual funds underperformed the TSX60 Total Return index over five years to June 30, 2015.

---

2   https://au.spindices.com/documents/spiva/spiva-australia-year-end-2015.pdf

Table 2-3[3]

Report 1: Percentage of Funds Outperforming the Index				
Fund Category	Comparison Index	One-Year (%)	Three-Year (%)	Five-Year (%)
Canadian Equity	S&P/TSX Composite	39.62	41.79	22.97
	S&P/TSX Capped Composite	39.62	41.79	22.97
Canadian Small-/Mid-Cap Equity	S&P/TSX Completion	72.73	67.65	42.86
Canadian Dividend & Income Equity	S&P/TSX Canadian Dividend Aristocrats	27.50	42.86	2.27
U.S. Equity	S&P 500 (CAD)	16.67	7.41	3.16
International Equity	S&P EPAC LargeMidCap (CAD)	37.84	9.52	4.44
Global Equity	S&P Developed LargeMidCap (CAD)	17.54	9.52	4.20
Canadian Focused Equity	50% S&P/TSX Composite + 25% S&P 500 (CAD) + 25% S&P EPAC LargeMidCap	9.84	9.46	6.33

Source: S&P Dow Jones Indices LLC, Fundata. Data as of June 30, 2015. CIFSC categorizations are used. Financial information provided by Fundata Canada Inc. Table is provided for illustrative purposes. Past performance is no guarantee of future results. Benchmarks used are total return indices.

In South Africa, nearly 91% of active equity mutual funds underperformed the South African benchmark index over five years to June 30, 2015, as shown in Table 2-4.

Table 2-4[4]

Report 1: Percentage of South African Funds Outperformed by Benchmarks				
Fund Category	Comparison Index	One-Year (%)	Three-Year (%)	Five-Year (%)
South African Equity	S&P South Africa DSW	80.95	80.16	90.91
Global Equity	S&P Global 1200	68.97	80.77	96.43
Short-Term Bond	STeFI Composite	58.54	26.83	21.05
Diversified/Aggregate Bond	JSE/ASSA ALBI	86.84	39.66	74.07

Source: S&P Dow Jones Indices LLC, Morningstar. Data for periods ending June 30, 2015. Outperformance is based on equal-weighted fund counts. Index performance is based on total return in South African rands. Past performance is no guarantee of future results. Table is provided for illustrative purposes.

As shown in Table 2-5, Japan seems to be a country with better performance but over 60% of the active mutual funds still underperform the Large-Cap benchmark index.

---

3   http://au.spindices.com/documents/spiva/spiva-canada-scorecard-midyear-2015.pdf
4   http://au.spindices.com/documents/spiva/spiva-south-africa-mid-year-2015.pdf

Table 2-5[5]

Report 1: Percentage of Funds Outperformed by the Index				
Fund Category	Comparison Index	One-Year (%)	Three-Year (%)	Five-Year (%)
Japanese Large-Cap Funds	S&P/TOPIX 150	71.62	67.92	65.89
Japanese Mid-Cap Funds	S&P Japan Mid Cap 100	55.17	56.36	52.63
Japanese Small-Cap Funds	S&P Japan Small Cap 250	81.25	42.86	49.50
All Japanese Equity Funds	S&P Japan 500	71.89	65.60	63.24
U.S. Equity Funds	S&P 500	87.79	74.07	90.63
Global Equity Funds	S&P Global 1200	81.53	82.94	90.91
International Equity Funds	S&P Global 1200 Ex Japan	62.96	61.11	90.00
Emerging Equity Funds	S&P Emerging BMI	61.14	60.49	65.60

Source: S&P Dow Jones Indices LLC, Morningstar. Data as of June 30, 2015. Table is provided for illustrative purposes. Past performance is no guarantee of future results.

In Europe, equity mutual funds underperformance of European indices ranges between 73% and 87% over five years to June 30, 2015, as shown in Table 2-6; underperformance is even worse over ten years.

Table 2-6[6]

Report 1: Percentage of European Equity Funds Outperformed by Benchmarks					
Fund Category	Comparison Index	One-Year	Three-Year	Five-Year	Ten-Year
Data in EUR					
Europe Equity	S&P Europe 350®	55.03	70.59	82.79	87.31
Eurozone Equity	S&P Eurozone BMI	59.01	84.62	87.46	91.95
France Equity	S&P France BMI	63.44	80.88	86.42	86.32
Germany Equity	S&P Germany BMI	63.83	65.91	73.63	83.33
Global Equity	S&P Global 1200	82.48	87.92	97.09	97.96
Emerging Markets Equity	S&P/IFCI	83.39	85.91	92.50	97.47
U.S. Equity	S&P 500	83.56	90.61	96.84	98.38
Data in GBP					
Europe Equity	S&P Europe 350	24.24	43.75	52.58	69.35
Europe Ex-U.K. Equity	S&P Europe Ex-U.K. BMI	32.77	51.20	57.69	72.00
U.K. Equity	S&P United Kingdom BMI	18.01	33.33	52.34	72.86
U.K. Large-/Mid-Cap Equity	S&P United Kingdom LargeMidCap	8.04	25.66	45.59	72.67
U.K. Small-Cap Equity	S&P United Kingdom SmallCap	84.85	79.41	72.22	84.62
Global Equity	S&P Global 1200	65.45	72.63	88.95	88.28
Emerging Markets Equity	S&P/IFCI	79.25	71.90	77.91	86.05
U.S. Equity	S&P 500	72.08	70.86	90.57	89.13

Source: S&P Dow Jones Indices LLC, Morningstar. Data for periods ending June 30, 2015. Outperformance is based on equal-weighted fund counts Index performance based on total return. Past performance is no guarantee of future results. Table is provided for illustrative purposes.

The same underperformance by active equity mutual funds holds true in South America, as shown in Table 2-7, where 88% of Large-Cap Funds underperformed the index over five years.

---

5   http://au.spindices.com/documents/spiva/spiva-japan-midyear-2015.pdf
6   http://au.spindices.com/documents/spiva/spiva-europe-mid-year-2015.pdf

Table 2-7[7]

Report 1: Percentage of Funds Outperformed by the Benchmark				
Fund Category	Comparison Index	One-Year (%)	Three-Year (%)	Five-Year (%)
Brazil Equity Funds	S&P Brazil BMI	56.84	69.83	62.86
Brazil Large-Cap Funds	S&P Brazil LargeCap	80.49	96.59	88.73
Brazil Mid-/Small-Cap Funds	S&P Brazil MidSmallCap	80.46	73.33	78.57
Brazil Corporate Bond Funds	Anbima Debentures Index (IDA)	28.35	63.01	91.67
Brazil Government Bond Funds	Anbima Market Index (IMA)	56.67	55.91	80.63
Chile Equity Funds	S&P Chile BMI	55.81	84.78	97.56
Mexico Equity Funds	S&P Mexico BMI	86.67	52.38	83.33

Source: S&P Dow Jones Indices LLC, Morningstar. Data for periods ending June 30, 2015. Outperformance is based on equal-weighted fund counts Index performance based on total return in local country currency. Table is provided for illustrative purposes. Past performance is no guarantee of future results.

"Okay, I get the point," said Iain, "If I invest in an active equity mutual fund or other active mutual funds, there is an excellent chance that they will underperform their respective stock market benchmark indices; only about 11% to 25% of funds outperform their Total Return indices."

"Is there a service that will tell me which are the best performing active equity mutual funds? Then I could find the outperforming active equity funds and invest in them," he said.

"I guess you could put in a lot of time looking for a paid service or you could do it yourself by scanning the financial pages for free. I've been there and done that! It merely changes you into someone trying to do active equity mutual fund timing rather than stock market timing."

"You now know that stock market indices outperform active mutual funds so why would anybody waste their time trying to time a lesser performing instrument?"

I continued, "None of that enormous effort would help you because *it's not always the **same** 11% to 25% of active mutual funds that outperform*. How do I know this? By reviewing another piece of relevant research, the SPIVA® Scorecard Performance Persistence Report."

"Remember the illustration in the *New York Times* in Chapter 1 showing the two remaining active equity funds that were outperforming after five years and none after six years? That's what this Persistence Report in Table 2-8 tells us in numbers instead of a picture."

---

7   http://au.spindices.com/documents/spiva/spiva-latin-america-midyear-2015.pdf

Table 2-8[8]

Exhibit 2: Performance Persistence of Domesitc Equity Funds Over Five Consecutive 12-Month Periods					
Mutual Fund Category	Fund Count at Start (September 2011)	Percentage Remaining in Top Quartile			
		September 2012	September 2013	September 2014	September 2015
Top Quartile					
All Domestic Funds	703	20.77	6.97	1.85	0.28
Large-Cap Funds	268	16.04	5.22	0.75	0
Mid-Cap Funds	98	19.39	10.2	2.04	0
Small-Cap Funds	148	21.62	8.11	1.35	0.68
Multi-Cap Funds	189	27.51	6.88	3.7	0.53
Mutual Fund Category	Fund Count at Start (September 2011)	Percentage Remaining in Top Half			
		September 2012	September 2013	September 2014	September 2015
Top Half					
All Domestic Funds	1406	43.53	22.48	12.94	7.82
Large-Cap Funds	535	39.81	19.63	12.34	7.48
Mid-Cap Funds	196	36.22	19.39	8.67	3.06
Small-Cap Funds	296	48.31	26.69	11.49	7.43
Multi-Cap Funds	379	48.81	24.8	17.15	11.08

Source: S&P Dow Jones Indices LLC. Data for periods ending Sept. 30, 2015. Past performance is no guarantee of future results. Table is provided for illustrative purposes.

I continued, "Looking at the top line in Table 2-8 entitled 'Top Quartile, All Domestic Funds,' it shows 703 under the September 2011 column. Meaning that after the twelve months ending September 2011, 703 funds were in the top 25% of funds; by the definition of quartile, there were 4 x 703 = 2812 active funds in the study. A year later, 20.77% of the 703 were still in the Top Quartile. Then another year later 6.97% survived in the Top Quartile and by the fifth year just 0.28%, or only eight, of the original top quartile 703 funds from the first twelve months were still in the Top Quartile."

"Look at the second line of Table 2-8, 'Large-Cap Funds,' not a single Large-Cap Fund remained in the top quartile! Nor in the third line for 'Mid-Cap Funds'!"

"This means that not a single active U.S. Equity Fund was able to persist and match, let alone beat, the S&P500 and S&P400 Total Return indices over five years."

"And it's not just the Top 25%! The heading 'Top Half, All Domestic Funds' in the lower portion of Table 2 shows that 1296 of the 1406 funds that were in the top 50% performers fall into the bottom 50% of performers over five years. Leaving just 110, or 7.82% ('September 2015' column), that remain in the top half!"

"This is strong evidence for not selecting mutual funds based on past performance."

---

8   http://au.spindices.com/documents/spiva/persistence-scorecard-january-2016.pdf

"Yet what does everybody do when searching for an active mutual fund in which to invest?"

Iain responded, "They scan the financial pages or the internet for the best-performing mutual funds over one, three or five years!"

"Exactly!" I exclaimed. "What a futile waste of time! Here's a quote from the SPIVA Scorecard Performance Persistence Report."

"When it comes to the active versus passive debate, the true measurement of successful active management lies in the ability of a manager or a strategy to deliver above-average returns consistently over multiple periods. Demonstrating the ability to outperform repeatedly is the only proven way to differentiate a manager's luck from skill." [9]

"So Iain, we know from the SPIVA Scorecard in Table 2-1 that 66.1% of 'All Large-Cap Funds' underperformed the S&P500 Total Return index over one year and that over three, five and ten years, 75.8%, 84.2% and 82.1% underperformed the S&P500 Total Return index, respectively. The percentages are similar for the other categories of active mutual funds."

"Bringing the Persistence Report into the reckoning demonstrates that those outperforming over these periods are NOT the same active funds and for periods longer than five years almost none of those funds that were performing at the start of the five years were still doing so at the end. Their performance falters and does not persist."

---

*"To summarize, if your **investing horizon is longer than six years**, there is only a tiny probability that you can choose in advance an active equity mutual fund in which to invest to grow your retirement savings that will even match, let alone outperform, its stock market benchmark index."*

But Iain responded, "So why shouldn't active mutual fund investors scan the bottom 50% of funds to find those that are likely to rise into the top half or even top quartile?"

"Ah, try to pick the currently underperforming funds," I said. "This might sound like a logical step to take, but it's not that simple; it never

---

9   December 11, 2014 SPIVA® Scorecard Persistence Report.

is. There are probably good reasons why they are currently underperforming. But look what happens to the bottom 50%," I said showing Iain the SPIVA Scorecard Performance Persistence Report comments about these, "About a third to a half of them do not survive."

"The transition matrices are designed to track the performance of top and bottom-quintile performers over subsequent time periods...

Our research also suggests consistency in the death rate of bottom-quartile funds. Across all market cap categories and all periods studied, fourth-quartile funds had a much higher rate of being merged or liquidated. The five-year transition matrix illustrates that 36.13% of large-cap funds, 29.51% of mid-cap funds, and 32.32% of small-cap funds in the fourth quartile disappeared." [10]

"So what are my chances of picking a performing active equity mutual fund for the long term?" Iain queried. "I, or anybody, even a 401(k) Plan provider, would have to do so much research to find one that it goes against the whole reason for investing in mutual funds – to be a passive investor!"

"Getting back to where we started this discussion, we might conclude conversely that not only is the S&P500 the most well-known investing 'system' for the stock market but it is also the best long-term performing large-cap 'system' when measured against active equity mutual funds."

In fact, there is further historical evidence of this principle. In the book *Winning the Loser's Game,* Charles D Ellis states: *"The historical record is that in the 25 years ending with 1997, on a cumulative basis, over three-quarters of professionally managed funds underperformed the S&P500 Market Stock Average."* [11]

In his book *The Little Book of Common Sense Investing,* John Bogle and his team found that over a twenty-five-year period from 1980 to 2005 that the majority of active mutual funds in the United States could **not** beat the S&P500 index, let alone the S&P500 Total Return index.

These two research periods cover two separate twenty-five year periods. One from 1972 to 1997 and another from 1980 to 2005 and both conclude with the same findings. Even worse, their findings also showed that active mutual fund **investors** did worse than the active mutual fund

---

10   Source: SPIVA® Scorecard Performance Persistence Report January 2016.
11   Page 5, Winning the Loser's Game, 3rd edition, by Charles D Ellis.

managers. Through making mistakes in timing their switches into and between various active mutual funds driven by chasing performance into funds just as their performance slowed, leaving them with returns that averaged 40% below those of the S&P500 Total Return index.

In his book, *The Little Book of Common Sense Investing* John Bogle states: *"During the quarter century from 1980 to 2005, the return on the stock market (measured by the S&P500 Total Return index) averaged 12.5 percent per year. The return on the average mutual fund averaged just 10.0 percent."* [12]

In the same book John Bogle then states: *"When we compare tradition-ally calculated fund returns with returns actually earned by the investors, it turns out that the average [mutual] fund investor earned, not the 10.0 percent reported by the average fund, but 7.3 percent – an annual return fully 2.7 percentage points per year less than that of the fund."* [13]

This research means that active mutual funds averaged the same return as the S&P500 index that excludes dividends, even though, naturally, the funds receive dividends, also meaning they could not match the S&P500 Total Return index, falling 2.5% per year below, on average. I will demon-strate in detail just how many hundreds of thousands of dollars 2.5% per year of underperforming amounts to over twenty-five years, and even shorter periods.

In case he needed further evidence of not investing in active mutual funds I handed Iain a quote from Warren Buffett [14]:

"Most investors, of course, have not made the study of business pros-pects a priority in their lives. If wise, they will conclude that they do not know enough about specific businesses to predict their future earning power. **I have good news for these non-professionals: The typical investor doesn't need this skill.** *In aggregate, American business has done wonderfully over time and will continue to do so (though, most assuredly, in unpredictable fits and starts). In the 20th Century, the Dow Jones Industrials index advanced from 66 to 11,497, paying a rising stream of dividends to boot. The 21st Century will witness further gains, almost certain to be substantial. The goal of the non-professional should not be to pick winners – neither he nor his "helpers"*

---

12   Page 44, The Little Book of Common Sense Investing by John Bogle.
13   Page 50, The Little Book of Common Sense Investing by John Bogle.
14   Page 20, February 2014 Letter to Berkshire Hathaway Shareholders by Warren Buffett.

*can do that – but should rather be to **own a cross-section of businesses that in aggregate are bound to do well. A low-cost S&P 500 index fund will achieve this goal.***

*My money, I should add, is where my mouth is: What I advise here is essentially identical to certain instructions I've laid out in my will. One bequest provides that cash will be delivered to a trustee for my wife's benefit. (I have to use cash for individual bequests, because all of my Berkshire shares will be fully distributed to certain philanthropic organizations over the ten years following the closing of my estate.) My advice to the trustee could not be more simple: Put 10% of the cash in short-term government bonds and **90% in a very low-cost S&P 500 index fund. (I suggest Vanguard's.) I believe the trust's long-term results from this policy will be superior to those attained by most investors – whether pension funds, institutions or individuals – who employ high-fee managers.***"

"Quote, unquote. Emphasis added by me," I said to Iain as he finished reading what Warren Buffett had said to his shareholders.

Iain replied, "After taking me through the SPIVA˙ material I can understand why he has said this."

"Before we move on I must clarify the difference between active equity mutual funds and active balanced, or diversified, mutual funds. Equity mutual funds only invest in a single asset class, stocks. Balanced funds diversify their investments across multiple asset classes, such as stocks, bonds, and fixed interest accounts; and maybe private equity and property. Typically, as we'll see, active equity funds perform better than active balanced funds."

"In which active mutual funds do you think most people invest their retirement savings?" I asked Iain.

"Active equity mutual funds, or probably where I did, in Balanced Funds with a 401(k) provider that manages their retirement savings," he answered.

"And what chance do you think they have of matching - let alone beating - the stock market indices over many years based on the SPIVA˙ research?" I asked.

"Close to zero chance!" exclaimed Iain in a pivotal moment of realization that investing with active mutual funds probably won't achieve an acceptable outcome let alone the best outcome, which is available to all ordinary investors.

"The bottom line is that defaulting to an active equity mutual fund, Balanced, Diversified, Target Date or Superannuation Fund by merely checking a box on a form, which unbelievably, but best describes how most people make their retirement investment decision, will just not suffice."

"If you are even only mildly interested in growing your retirement investments, and others, so that you'll have enough money to provide you with a comfortable lifestyle of your choice right through retirement – and provide financial freedom – you will need to make a better decision than using active mutual funds. I'll show you what decisions to make and why."

Last Word

- Up to 75% of active equity mutual funds (see the 'All Domestic Equity Funds' in Table 2-1) underperform their benchmark indices every year, and 88% and 83% over periods of five and ten years, respectively.
- It's not the same 25% that outperforms their benchmark indices each year.
- **For periods longer than five to six years, the number that outperforms is only a handful or zero, according to the SPIVA Performance Persistence Report, in Table 2-8.**
- Even if a few active mutual funds match, or even outperform, the stock market indices over six years or more, how can an everyday investor, or even a financial advisor, find them in advance? How much research and time would it take?
  ◊ It would be like finding a needle in a haystack.
- Rather invest in the whole haystack! That is the index.
- Even Warren Buffett, arguably the world's greatest investor, recommends that ordinary investors and professional advisers should NOT use active mutual funds!

CHAPTER 3

How do the Active Mutual Funds Invest and Perform?

*"Do not go where the path may lead, go instead
where there is no path and leave a trail."*

RALPH WALDO EMERSON

In a word, the active mutual funds **diversify**. They diversify across asset classes and within a single asset class. A little diversification can be good, but diversify too much and returns can be retarded, at least with respect to the objective that is trying to be achieved.

"The strategy we've adopted precludes our following (of) standard diversification dogma. Many pundits would, therefore, say the strategy must be riskier than that employed by more conventional investors. We disagree. We believe that a policy of portfolio concentration may well decrease risk." [1]

---

1   Warren Buffett in his 1993 Letter to Shareholders of Berkshire Hathaway.

In fact, Warren Buffett has often used the word 'diworsification' when referring to 'diversification' in investing.

'Diworsification' is a word invented by famous investor Peter Lynch in his book, *One Up On Wall Street*.

Investopedia, an online 'investing encyclopedia', defines 'Diworsification' as such:

"The process of adding investments to one's portfolio in such a way that the risk/return trade-off is worsened. Diworsification occurs where risk is at its lowest level, and additional assets reduce potential portfolio returns, as well as the chances of outperforming a benchmark."

Logic dictates that diversifying across more stocks or more asset classes will reduce volatility, that is the degree of up and down price movement, and therefore, reduce risk. While it *may* do so, it *will* also reduce returns. This explains the ongoing arm-wrestle between risk and return. How much of each of reward and risk is required to achieve your retirement investing objective?

The problem with diversification is that it won't necessarily achieve its primary aim which is to protect investors in all stock market declines. During the stock market decline from October 2007 to March 2009, the S&P500 fell nearly -56% and almost every sector, and asset class was affected by the carnage on the markets.

While pundits claimed that 2008 was a once in a lifetime event, the fact is that virtually every asset class declined in value. Even Gold dropped -30%. Cash was the only asset class that didn't fall in value, except for the small effect of inflation over the relatively short period.

Owning too many active mutual funds, too many asset classes or too many stocks ensures mediocre results and does not necessarily provide the protection that you might expect.

William N Goetzmann, in his hypertext book, *An Introduction to Investment Theory*[2], explains diversification well:

---

*"Ex post [based on actual results rather than forecast], some assets will do better than others; but since one does not know **in advance***

---

which assets will perform better, this fact cannot be exploited in advance.

The ex post return on a diversified portfolio can never exceed that of the top-performing investment, and indeed will always be lower than the highest return *(unless all returns are ex post identical). Conversely, the diversified portfolio's return will always be higher than that of the worst-performing investment.*

So by diversifying, one loses the chance of having invested solely in the single asset that comes out best, but one also avoids having invested solely in the asset that comes out worst.

That is the role of diversification: it narrows the range of possible outcomes. Diversification need not either help or hurt expected returns, unless the alternative non-diversified portfolio has a higher expected return."

On diversification, Warren Buffett is quoted as having said, "*Diversification is protection against ignorance, it makes little sense for those who know what they're doing.*" [3] "I guess what he is saying, besides that diversification is not necessarily a positive thing over the long term, as Peter Lynch also said, is that investors shouldn't be ignorant and should know what they are doing. It is their responsibility to discover what to do and to achieve some focus."

"Well, there appear to be cases for and against diversification. Which do you support?" Iain asked.

"I lean mostly towards the 'against' camp, but not totally. As with all things, there are degrees. An investor's circumstances and investing objectives should be taken into account but only after the necessary information has been gathered to know what is possible."

I continued, "The everyday investor's perceived need for diversification across asset classes stems from the lack of, or insufficient, focus and priority on their investing, particularly for retirement."

"I think most investors make the choice for diversification without fully considering or understanding the potentially dire long-term consequences or the potentially better returns from an alternative approach."

"The need for diversification by active mutual funds is seen as the funds doing the right thing to please uneducated investors by protecting their

---

3   Page 80 of the book The Tao of Warren Buffett.

savings. In fact, the active mutual funds also diversify for their own protection. They reduce volatility so that their customers don't withdraw their money and move to another fund, thereby reducing the funds' fees income."

"There appears to be more emphasis on reducing volatility than getting the best returns, particularly by Balanced Funds and Target Date funds (which we'll soon discuss in detail). Unfortunately, in many cases, volatility is not reduced by as much as it should, which compares badly to the benefits that are lost by the investor. I'll show you this graphically and statistically."

"The way I see it then," Iain said, "is that there can be a cost to diversifying and a cost to not diversifying."

"Agreed," I said, "but they are different types of cost. One is the **cost of profits not gained, and the other is the cost of gained profits not kept and hence lost.**"

"I think I get it," said Iain. "You are saying that in the first scenario *with diversification*, there is less growth, hence less profit, because the diversified fund invests in asset classes that do not perform as well as the stock market when it is rising strongly. In this case, most investors wouldn't be aware of what they didn't have. When the stock market falls, the diversified fund falls, but from a lower value and by a smaller amount because it invested in other non-stock market asset classes that don't fall by as much."

He continued, "In the second scenario *without diversification* across other asset classes, there is more profit, but when the market falls, the non-diversified stock market fund falls by a greater amount from a higher value."

"You've got it. Understanding this distinction is key," I said. "I'll show you this in pictures shortly."

Iain continued, asking, "What is the actual opportunity cost that stems from diversification? I mean, *what are the actual profits not gained? And what is the dollar differential between the diversified and non-diversified approaches at their peaks and after a big market fall?*"

"Surely all that matters is which approach gets me the best return up to when I need the money. At any time, even at the end of a big fall?"

I responded, "To answer these questions with the necessary detail, I will demonstrate the principles at play, and we'll compare the performance of particular balanced active mutual funds to what is offered by the leading indices. And then I'll define the precise effort required to take the most advantage of diversifying, and of not diversifying by achieving investing focus."

I continued, "***My purpose is to help you resolve the conflict between managing risk and delivering returns to achieve a better life and***

retirement in just a few minutes a week. I'm going to do that by using diversification within a single asset class rather than into more but potentially worse performing asset classes. I will also show you a simple and efficient risk management technique of market timing where we will alternate between two asset classes, the stock market, and cash."

"It might sound complicated right now to your unfamiliar ear, but the execution will be simple, I promise. I'm using terminology that the active mutual funds use, but we won't need the jargon when it comes to actually doing this."

"But first, let's look at how the active fund managers manage their invested money to achieve returns while managing risk. We need to know this to explain why they underperform so that we understand what not to do so we can do better."

HOW DOES AN ACTIVE EQUITY MUTUAL FUND INVEST MY MONEY?

"At the highest level, there are four broad categories of active mutual funds; equity (stocks only) mutual funds, Balanced Funds (also referred to as 'hybrid' funds), bond funds and money market funds. Target Date funds are a subset of Balanced Funds, but I am going to cover both of them separately in a little detail because they are the fastest growing category of active mutual funds."

"Which of these mutual fund categories do they include in the SPIVA Scorecard research?" asked Iain.

"Only the equity mutual funds, which invest only in stocks," I replied. "Using the SPIVA Scorecard research, I have shown how the category of active equity mutual funds performs compared to the stock market benchmark indices and that the odds are stacked against using active equity mutual funds to try to do better than stock market total return indices over the long term. Also, this stocks-only category of active mutual funds typically performs better than Balanced Funds, and hence Target Date funds."

"According to the ICI 2016 Fact Book, $15.7 trillion was invested in all mutual funds in the U.S. as at the end of 2015. 52%, 9%, 21.5%, and 17.5% was invested in the four categories of equity, balanced, bond and money market mutual funds, respectively."

I continued, "Of the 52% invested in equity mutual funds, 22% is invested in *index* equity mutual funds, meaning that 11.44%, or $1.8

trillion, of all mutual fund investments, are invested in index equity mutual funds. 11.44% is a relatively small portion. I will be talking about index funds a lot more in future discussions."

"How do active equity mutual funds invest?" asked Iain.

"There is a vast array of investing approaches and far too many to cover here. Sector focus is common where funds will concentrate more than 50%, or nearly all of their investable funds, in market sectors such as Consumer Discretionary, Utilities, Energy, Health, Technology or Finance. Another approach is to focus on high dividend yield stocks or high shareholder yield. Then there are those that focus on small-caps, mid-caps, and large-caps, and then 'value' or 'growth' for each of the small, mid and large-caps, as per the categories listed in the left-hand column of Table 2-1 in Chapter 2. There is also stock picking based on individual stock analysis using varying analysis techniques."

I concluded, "The research conducted by the SPIVA Scorecard and by investing legends, John Bogle and Charles Ellis, shows that there is a very low chance of selecting one or a few equity mutual funds in advance that match, let alone beat, stock market indices over the long term."

How does a 'Balanced' mutual fund invest my money?

"So remind me, how did your retirement funds get to be invested where they are?" I asked Iain.

"I selected the 'Balanced' option with the 401(k) Plan provider linked to my workplace at the time, and I think that nearly all of my retirement investments are invested with a single active mutual fund and are in the stock market," Iain volunteered.

"Well, I don't think you know that," I said.

"What do you mean?" asked Iain, "Balanced is balanced, isn't it?"

"Have you researched what the breakdown in asset classes is for YOUR 'Balanced' Fund? Do you know what the split is for other 401(k) Plan 'Balanced' Funds?"

"Not really," said Iain.

I continued, "We'll look at some examples of the research I have done and it shows that 'Balanced' to one provider means something different to another."

"Typically the argument for investors to invest in a Balanced Fund is that these funds are usually not the worst performers. But nor are they the best performers. The argument continues that if you are not interested in getting some focus and spending a little time to achieve higher returns for your retirement or other investments, then go for the active mutual funds that won't do the worst; the Balanced Funds!"

"That sounds perfect for the apathetic!" said Iain. "Like I was!"

"I agree," I said. "Investing for retirement is just too important for you to be apathetic about it. Most retirement investment returns end up around the median of a wide range which can be substantially less than what is available from a stock market index benchmark. Despite this Balanced Funds and Target Date funds, which we'll investigate next, are what most new hires are selecting to invest their retirement savings."

I continued, "Let's look at specific cases to give you a flavor of how these mutual funds operate and perform."

As at mid-2015, three of the top performing Balanced Funds in the U.S., as measured by their combined five and ten-year returns, were:

- American Century One Choice Aggressive Fund (AOGIX), $1.1 billion net assets.
- Vanguard LifeStrategy Growth Fund (VASGX), $11.2 billion net assets.
- Wells Fargo Advantage Index Asset Allocation Fund (SFAAX), $950 million net assets.

Their respective asset allocations were:

- AOGIX[4]: Equities U.S. and International 79%, Bonds & Fixed Interest 21%.
- VASGX[5]: Equities U.S. and International 79.9%, Bonds & Fixed Interest 20.1%.
- SFAAX: Equities U.S. and International 59.43%, Bonds & Fixed Interest 40.57%.

Notice how different the asset allocation is for SFAAX.

Their respective annual fees, excluding entry and exit fees, are:

---

4   https://www.americancentury.com/content/americancentury/direct/en/investment-products/
    mutual-funds/mutual-fund-details/holdings-attributes/one-choice-portfolio-aggressive.
    html#AOGIX

5   https://personal.vanguard.com/us/funds/snapshot?FundId=0122&FundIntExt=INT#tab=2

- AOGIX: 0.98%.
- VASGX: 0.17%.
- SFAAX: 1.15%.

Vanguard is famous for keeping their annual fees much lower than other mutual fund managers.

Their respective performances over five and ten years to June 30, 2015, including fees, were:

- AOGIX: 12.82% and 7.46% compounded per year.
- VASGX: 12.36% and 6.47% compounded per year.
- SFAAX: 14.79% and 6.96% compounded per year.

Over the same periods *the S&P500 Total Return index* achieved:

- *17.34% and 7.89% compounded per year*.

I concluded, "All three underperformed the S&P500 Total Return index which isn't a surprise after seeing the SPIVA˙ Scorecard. Typically, Balanced Funds will underperform stocks-only active equity mutual funds. *However, their underperformance of two other indices that I will be referring to often, the S&P500 Equal Weight Total Return and S&P MidCap 400 Total Return indices, was even greater.* The S&P500 Equal Weight index tracks exactly the same stocks as the S&P500 except it equally weights all of the 500 constituents rather than weighting more to the larger cap stocks and less to the small-cap stocks in the list of 500."

The AOGIX One Choice fund and the VASGX Vanguard fund are 'funds of funds' with Vanguard holding just four funds and AOGIX eighteen funds. These Balanced Funds may pay layered fees, i.e. fees on fees. Three of the funds in which AOGIX invests are from its own stable:

- American Century U.S. Equity Growth, BEQGX, $3.26B net assets with annual fees of 0.67%.
- American Century Large Company Value, ALVIX, $0.871B net assets with annual fees of 0.84%.
- American Century International Growth stocks, TWIEX, $1.61B net assets with annual fees of 1.17%.

The SFAAX Wells Fargo Advantage Index Asset Allocation Fund invests directly in stocks and bonds.

Another, the American Balanced Fund, ABALX[6], has total assets of $83.5 billion making it one of the largest Balanced Funds in the United States. Started in July 1975, as at mid-2015 ABALX's asset allocation was:

- Domestic and International Equities 64.3%,
- Bonds and fixed interest/cash 35.7%.

Again, different to SFAAX, AOGIX, and VASGX.

ABALX has achieved 12.93% and 6.99% returns, respectively, over the last five and ten years to June 30, 2015. Both well below the S&P500 Total Return index. Its annual fees are 0.59%.

A discussion on Balanced Funds just cannot omit Balanced Funds offered by Fidelity or Vanguard, two of the biggest mutual fund companies in the world.

As at July 2015 the $29.2 billion FBALX[7] Fidelity Balanced Fund has yet a different asset allocation:

- Domestic Equities 60.57%,
- International Equities 5.85%,
- Bonds 32.04%,
- Cash & Net Other Assets 1.54%.

With annual fees of 0.56% it's five and ten-year returns through June 30, 2015, were 12.57% and 7.49%, respectively. Both worse than the S&P500 Total Return index.

And the $26.5 billion Vanguard Balanced Fund, VBINX[8], is different again, with its asset allocation as at July 31, 2015, having less in stocks than any of the other funds considered so far:

- Domestic Equities 57.57%,
- Bonds 39.48%,
- Cash & Net Other Assets 2.95%.

Its returns reflect this, with lower returns over the five years to June 30, 2015, at 11.71%, and 6.95% over ten years despite its annual fees being among the lowest at 0.23%.

The last Balanced Fund we will look at in Figure 3-1 is the $2.6 billion

---

6   https://www.americanfunds.com/individual/investments/fund/abalx
7   https://fundresearch.fidelity.com/mutual-funds/composition/316345206
8   https://finance.yahoo.com/q/hl?s=VBINX

IVY Balanced Fund IBNAX that was started on November 16, 1987, and has an annual management fee of 1.11%.

It has 68.2% of its funds invested in stocks and the rest in bonds and cash as at June 30, 2015.

All these asset mixes change from time to time. It just goes to show how different each 'balanced' is from another 'balanced'.

Figure 3-1[9]

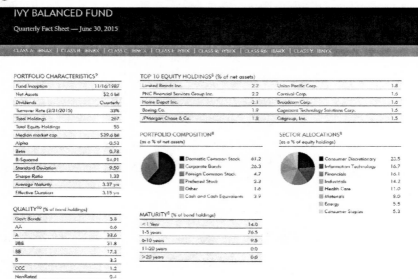

I said to Iain, "IBNAX was one of the *best* performing Balanced Funds in the U.S. over recent years with its five and ten-year returns through June 30, 2015, coming in at 16.6% and 7.98%, respectively. The ten-year return is actually better than the S&P500 Total Return index!"

"But did it do better than the two indices that we will use as part of our strategies going forward–the S&P500 Equal Weight Total Return index and the S&P MidCap 400 Total Return index? It did not, wait and see!"

"I have repeated this research for Australian balanced funds and the findings are similar, showing that mutual fund operators are similar the world over." (For this analysis, please see the *Appendix for Australian Readers* in this book and visit the Resources page on the website www. blueprinttowealth.com for further research).

"Why do these funds diversify into other asset classes?" asked Iain.

"Great question," I said. "Indirectly, funds are forced to by their customers, the investors!"

I continued, "Fund managers all want to do as well as they can over the long term. If returns were *only* how their success was measured, I'm sure they would invest 100% in a fund that tracks a stock market index because over the long-term stock market indices outperform all other asset classes."

"But the stock market is also considered the most volatile asset class and the managers have to minimize volatility during adverse periods, which can occur at any time. They do this to prevent their investors from pulling out all their money and putting it elsewhere if the funds don't hold up well during these negative periods. It's almost as if their primary motivation is to perform the least-worst during volatile times than the best over the long term."

"Volatility can mean big swings in performance, particularly to the downside. Balanced funds invest in asset classes that don't move up and down by as much as the stock market to reduce volatility. In return for less volatility, there is less growth, thereby putting a brake on long-term returns."

Iain responded, "When the stock market is rising, every dollar that is not invested in the stock market will hold back a fund's performance. But when the stock market has significant declines, the fund will have smaller falls because the worse performing asset classes typically don't fall by as much as the stock market."

"Correct," I said. "But over the long term, the overall performance will be much lower because there is less exposure to the stock market."

"So they use asset class diversification as a method to manage risk. Why don't the funds just time the market as a risk management technique, as you mentioned?" asked Iain.

I had hoped Iain would ask this question.

"Due to the amount of capital that mutual funds manage they cannot sell all their stock market holdings. Active mutual funds all simultaneously selling would force the market down even more so the managers have to stay invested with most, if not all, of their stock market exposure and let their investors ride out the market fall."

"Most funds will sell some of their stock market investments, but they cannot use market timing as a risk management technique in the same way that an individual can and move 100% into cash. **This is one of the reasons that the active mutual fund industry propagates the myth that the market cannot be timed.**"

I showed Iain Figure 3-2 that depicts the typical volatility of the different asset classes by showing the best and worst single calendar year returns over the twenty-five-year period to the end of 2015. This illustrates the reward-to-risk trade-off that exists between these asset classes.

The right side of Figure 3.2 shows asset classes that are less volatile over periods of a single year that can lack the ability, due to low volatility, to grow retirement savings to exceed inflation over the long term.

At the other end of the spectrum on the left side of Figure 3-2 are the more volatile asset classes that have greater potential for substantial short-term and long-term growth but also for more short-term volatility.

The white cross-bar in each column marks the compounded annual growth. Don't be fooled, the 1.36% compounded per year difference between U.S. Shares and U.S. Investment Grade Bonds is a huge difference in absolute dollars over twenty-five years; as we will see in a moment.

Figure 3-2[10]

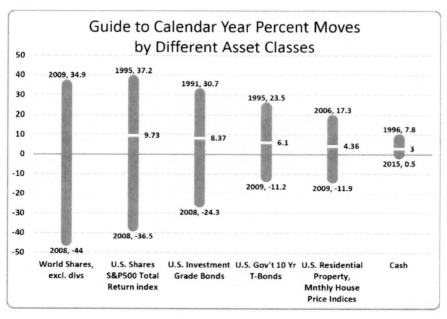

I explained, "The rule of thumb is that the less volatile the asset class, the worse that asset class will perform over the long term. In the diagram,

10   "Monthly House Price Indexes Report for Census Divisions and U.S." for U.S. Residential Property

the bigger the top-to-bottom range, the more volatile the asset class, but the higher the potential returns over the long term."

I continued, "The issue is that downside volatility in the stock market occurs over short periods that arise suddenly and may last from a few weeks to a few months or up to a year or so. However, the diversified, balanced portfolio has to carry the burden of diversifying away from the stock market for the *whole life of the portfolio*, which, for retirement investing, could be decades for many investors."

I continued, "Balanced Funds may be appropriate for three to seven year investing horizons and for those who are happy to put absolutely no effort or focus into their non-retirement investments, for whatever reason, and blindly trust how a third party diversifies their funds. Which is fine provided you can live with the consequence of less growth."

"For long-term investing beyond six years it doesn't make sense to invest in Balanced Funds, especially when a stock market focused instrument is available for everybody to use, such as an index, that is engineered to have a long-term upward bias."

"I get it," said Iain. "Why didn't anybody explain this to me when I chose to invest in the Balanced Fund? And, what do you mean by 'engineered to have an upward bias'?" he asked.

"I'll answer both questions later," I replied.

Then I continued, "It's a sad fact that few investors spend more than a few minutes in choosing which fund to select from their 401(k) Plan's list. The new employee typically checks a box on a form, submits it and forgets about it for years, maybe even decades. Research by the EBRI (Employee Benefit Research Institute) shows that the majority of new hires are doing just this, selecting balanced fund options for their 401(k) contributions. That simple action will cost most investors hundreds of thousands of dollars over many years in lost compounding of returns."

How have Balanced Funds performed compared to stock market indices?

"To illustrate the dramatically forfeited compounding of returns, I'll use the example of a large-cap growth active equity mutual fund (i.e. stocks only), which is focused on growth without much consideration for reducing volatility, and compare it to two Balanced Funds."

I continued, "It has performed very well over three decades. What we don't know is whether it will continue to do so since it seems to have achieved most of its growth from market leading health and technology stocks, the two best performing but most volatile sectors over the last thirty years, as we know now with the benefit of hindsight. But the managers chose this strategy many years ago and fortunately, or through great analysis, they were right. Does it matter that the level of volatility, and hence risk, is high?"

The fund is Fidelity's Large-Cap Growth Fund, FDGRX, an equity mutual fund. Table 3-1 shows its comparative compounded annual return performance at five-year intervals through June 30, 2015. At every five-year interval, FDGRX has outperformed the S&P500 Total Return index, $SPXTR, and the Ivy Balanced Fund, IBNAX, one of the best of the Balanced Funds over the last ten years, and the Wells Fargo Growth Fund, SFAAX, except at the fifteen-year interval.

Table 3-1

Mutual Fund Symbol	Fees	FuM	Jun 30 2010 5 Yrs	Jun 30 2005 10 Yrs	Jun 30 2000 15 Yrs	Jun 30 1995 20 Yrs	Jun 30 1990 25 Yrs	Jun 30 1985 30 Yrs
FDGRX	0.82%	40.7B	20.73%	11.63%	4.85%	10.91%	11.89%	11.58%
SFAAX	1.15%	937M	14.79%	6.96%	4.98%	7.72%	8.19%	
IBNAX	1.11%	2.6B	16.60%	7.98%	3.35%	5.01%	5.46%	5.64%
$SPXTR			17.34%	7.89%	4.36%	8.91%	9.54%	10.29%

FDGRX has been one of the best performing active equity mutual funds in the U.S. as measured purely by returns. It was accessible to any investor with only a minimum $2,500 investment before closing it to new investors in April 2006. (Some health sector only focused funds, such as Vanguard's Health Care Fund VGHCX, which is also an equity mutual fund, have also performed well.)

Despite this excellent performance by FDGRX, both the S&P500 Equal Weight Total Return and S&P MidCap 400 Total Return indices both performed better over thirty years than FDGRX at 12.04% and 12.51% compounded per year, respectively. These are two indices on which we will focus in coming sessions.

Dividends and distributions are included in Table 3-1, but taxes excluded in the returns. If invested via a traditional 401(k) or IRA, no taxes would be due anyway on a yearly basis until after retirement so these are like-for-like comparisons.

The asset allocation of FDGRX is weighted almost entirely towards U.S. stocks with 0% in bonds and 0.21% cash as of July 31, 2015.

Asset Allocation of FDGRX[11]:

- Domestic Equities: 93.38%
- International Equities: 6.41%
- Developed Markets: 4.69%
- Emerging Markets: 1.72%
- Tax-Advantaged Domiciles: 0.00%
- Bonds: 0.00%
- Cash & Net Other Assets: 0.21%

Allocation of Domestic Equities:

- Information Technology   34.17%
- Health Care   24.92%
- Consumer Discretionary   17.49%
- Consumer Staples   8.74%
- Industrials   8.28%
- Financials   3.18%
- Energy   1.55%
- Materials   0.98%
- Telecommunication Services   0.48%
- Utilities   0.00%

The asset allocation means FDGRX is not a Balanced Fund; it is an active equity mutual fund that focuses on a single asset class, the stock market. In fact, it focuses primarily on just three sectors within the stock market— Information Technology, Health Care and Consumer Discretionary.

This is the sort of stock market focus that an active mutual fund needs to stand a chance of beating, or even matching, a stock market index.

What Table 3-1 doesn't show is the long-term journey of the funds' performance along the way. To do this, we'll look at the life journey of these funds compared to the S&P500 Total Return index over twenty-five years in graph form to determine from a picture how volatile each was.

---

11   https://fundresearch.fidelity.com/mutual-funds/composition/316200104

The three twenty-five-year semi-logarithmic equity curves in Chart 3-1 all started with $100,000 on June 29, 1990, through to June 30, 2015, with no 401(k) contributions added during the period. They are in the same order as the legend, in descending order of the S&P500 Total Return index (S&P500TR), SFAAX then IBNAX, two Balanced Funds that I have already introduced.

"What is a semi-logarithmic equity curve?" asked Iain.

"An equity curve is the plotting of the end-of-day value or 'price' of a portfolio on a day to day basis. It allows you to view the long-term day by day journey of the price of an index or stock or value of a portfolio," I replied.

"Semi-logarithmic plotting is used when the range of a price move has been large, which typically occurs over long-term equity curves. Think of it as plotting and displaying the equity curve in percentage movements rather than absolute dollars. Semi-logarithmic plotting normalizes the movement of prices for more accurate comparison over the long term."

Chart 3-1

From the SPIVA Scorecard you should expect that these two Balanced Funds will underperform the S&P500TR ($SPXTR in Table 3-1). However, the magnitude of difference in dollars between the respective Balanced Funds is not expected nor would you expect such a big difference between the Balanced Funds and the S&P500 Total Return index.

Even though IBNAX has performed really well over the last five years, it still lags the long-term performance of the S&P500TR by a considerable amount over twenty-five years. And remember, it is long-term performance that we are seeking for all or part of our retirement savings, even for those aged over sixty-years-old.

In Chart 3-1, the ending capital amounts after twenty-five years, each starting with $100,000 on June 29, 1990, were:

- S&P500TR: $1,004,047.
- SFAAX : $716,002.
  - ◊ This is **$288,045 less** than the S&P500TR index for the seemingly small 1.35% compounded per year less return (9.54–8.19, from Table 3-1). Overall this leads to 32% less profit.
- IBNAX : $376,663.
  - ◊ This is **$627,384 less** than the S&P500TR index! That's what 4.08% compounded per year less return (9.54 – 5.46, from Table 3-1) over 25 years looks like! Or overall 69.4% less money at the end of twenty-five years!

These differences are serious amounts of money. Think of what you have lost by simply checking a box without considering alternative approaches.

This comparison, with a starting capital of $100,000 in 1990, might emulate a forty to forty-five-year-old who has twenty-five years left before retirement. Note that this comparison excludes any 401(k) contributions made over that period. With ongoing 401(k) contributions, the relative, absolute differences between the outcomes would be larger through the additional compounding on a larger amount of ongoing contributed capital.

Now let's add the equity curve of the FDGRX Fidelity Large-cap Growth Fund. From the **25 Years** column in Table 3-1, we expect this fund to finish with more money than the other two funds and more than the S&P500 Total Return index.

Chart 3-2 shows FRGRX added to the other three equity curves. From the same starting date and amount of capital, FRDRX ended the twenty-five years with $1,660,316.72 or:

- $656,270, or 65.36%, more than the S&P500TR,
- $944,314, or 131.89%, more than the SFAAX, and
- $1,283,654, or 340.8%, more than IBNAX.

Again, these differences are significant amounts of money and clearly demonstrate why it is important to spend a little more time and focus deciding how to invest for retirement.

These amounts of dollars can be the potential cost of apathy and pushing retirement goals down the list of priorities when they should be near the top. That's all it is really, everyday investors deciding NOT to put a once-off higher priority and focus on how to invest for their retirement. If they did, they would discover the type of information presented here.

In the semi-logarithmic Chart 3-2, the FDGRX equity curve has been added to the equity curves in Chart 3-1.

Chart 3-2

Iain found the huge differences in outcomes spectacular.

"There was a big dollar difference between the FDGRX peak and the S&P500TR peak in 2000. What was it?" Iain asked next.

"FDGRX reached $1,048,404 and was $509,272 ahead of the S&P500TR. SFAAX was $688,006 behind FDGRX and IBNAX was $804,492 behind FDGRX" I answered.

"Wow, that's a big difference when starting with the same amount of capital just ten years earlier. How could an investor protect some of that huge difference?" he asked.

"Well, I think you know the answer to that—by timing the market and going into cash at some stage soon after reaching the peak and before FDGRX started giving a lot of profit back to the market."

"So the amount that is given back to the market is a way of measuring the tolerance for risk by the fund manager who is not able to revert to cash?" asked Iain.

"Correct," I said.

"What risk was taken to achieve the excellent long-term outcome that FDGRX achieved?" asked Iain.

"Let's explore that right now," I replied.

The next metric that I will introduce after annual compounded growth, is **maximum drawdown**. This tells us what the maximum decline in the equity curve was from the previous highest equity curve peak that the fund reached. It is typically most meaningful during severe market declines.

The two columns at the extreme right in Table 3-2 show the **maximum drawdown (Max DD)** during the two major bear markets over the twenty-five years to June 30 2015. These were the bear markets that occurred in 2000 to 2002 and 2007 to 2009, where FDGRX declined -69.35% and -53.9%, respectively.

The propensity for FDGRX to have a substantial drawdown exists and this plays a major role in defining the riskiness of the strategy that the fund uses. Conversely, the annual compounded return shows the propensity for FDGRX to outperform; as it did IBNAX by 340.8%, or $1,283,654, over twenty-five years, starting with $100,000.

Such reward and risk outcomes give investors an insight into the characteristics not only of the individual funds but also of the strategy of using a near 100% of capital directly into specific volatile sectors of stocks.

Table 3-2

Fund/ Index Symbol	Fund/ Index Name	5 Yrs	10 Yrs	15 Yrs	20 Yrs	25 Yrs	Max DD Mar-00 Oct-02	Max DD Oct-07 Mar-09
FDGRX	Fidelity	20.73%	11.63%	4.85%	10.91%	11.89%	-69.35%	-53.90%
SFAAX	Wells Fargo	14.79%	6.96%	4.98%	7.72%	8.19%	-32.49%	-49.89%
IBNAX	Ivy Balanced	16.60%	7.98%	3.35%	5.01%	5.46%	-47.41%	-32.14%
$SPXTR	S&P500 Tot.Ret.	17.34%	7.89%	4.36%	8.91%	9.54%	-47.37%	-55.25%

Note that even the more conservative Balanced Fund, SFAAX, which roughly has a 60/40 split between stocks and bonds, respectively, still had a serious drawdown of -49.89% in 2007 to 2009. To forfeit significantly higher returns by diversifying into lower performing asset classes outside the stock market, someone investing for retirement might have expected to have less drawdown in SFAAX.

My point is that drawdown is unavoidable unless you are in cash 100% all the time which will not achieve the necessary returns and retirement nest egg you'll need to retire at all, let alone comfortably.

The question then becomes not whether there will be drawdown, but rather how much reduction in capital, or risk, are you prepared to tolerate with your retirement savings? And the risk has to be greater than zero.

Are you prepared to wear a -70% drawdown such as nearly occurred with FDGRX in the 2000 to 2002 technology bear market? This fall was more than double the drawdown, or maximum risk, of SFAAX and 46% worse than the S&P500TR ($SPXTR) drawdown. How would you react if this occurs with your retirement savings in the future?

Iain's first comment was, "I think I would struggle but would probably accept it as long as the -69% or -53% drawdown doesn't occur within a few years of my retirement starting, or even during retirement!"

I replied, "That's where low-effort near-passive timing comes to the fore. More on timing later."

"I can see the dilemma," said Iain.

"Retirement savers need to invest in the stock market to get higher returns that aren't possible in other asset classes over the long term. But by doing so are vulnerable to bigger drawdowns that could be

devastating if they occur at the wrong time, such as when income has ceased, and they are drawing down their retirement nest egg."

"Well stated," I replied. "This is called **sequence-of-returns risk**, which we'll address later."

"Looking at Chart 3-2, the two *troughs* achieved by FDGRX in 2002 and 2008 were well above the *peaks* reached by IBNAX at the same time. In fact, at all times after starting in 1990, the retirement investor would have had more money by investing in FDGRX, even at the troughs of the two big bear markets."

I continued, "So maybe being able to endure a -69.35% drawdown is fine if you:

- are mentally prepared for the drawdown,
- know that the fund will continue to perform as it has in the past and recover lost ground after a significant drawdown occurs, and
- will have more money at the bottom of a major bear market than you otherwise would have had in another fund."

"This may be so, but what if I had started investing in FDGRX at the peak of the equity curve in 2000?" asked Iain. "I would have had a -70% drawdown straight from the get go."

"While that is an absolute worst case scenario, it is worth investigating the potential outcomes. Rather than do this exercise now I'll return to it when we discuss low-effort near-passive timing," I replied.

"Okay," Iain agreed. "You mentioned that two other indices–the S&P500 Equal Weight and S&P MidCap 400 indices–have performed better than FDGRX over 30 years. Can you show me their performances over the five-year snapshots compared to active Balanced Funds?" asked Iain.

I showed Iain Table 3-3, which shows a list of Balanced Funds (without the $ prefix), which invest in stocks and bonds, compared to a number of mainstream stock market indices (with the $ prefix). Table 3-3 shows the compounded percentage returns over thirty years at five-year intervals.

I informed Iain, "The bold typed indices are the Total Return indices of their respective 'base' index. Remember, the Total Return indices include the reinvestment of dividends into the index calculation."

Table 3-3

Mutual Fund Symbol	Mutual Fund Index Name	Fees	FuM	Jun 30 2010 5 Yrs	Jun 30 2005 10 Yrs	Jun 30 2000 15 Yrs	Jun 30 1995 20 Yrs	Jun 29 1990 25 Yrs	Jun 28 1985 30 Yrs
AOGIX	American Century	0.96%	1.1B	12.82%	7.46%				
VASGX	Vanguard LifeSta	0.17%	11.5B	12.36%	6.47%	4.55%	7.65%		
SFAAX	Wells Fargo Adv	1.15%	937M	14.79%	6.96%	4.98%	7.72%	8.19%	
LKBAX	LKCM Balanced	0.80%	375M	12.17%	7.69%	5.80%			
IBNAX	Ivy Balanced	1.11%	2.6B	16.60%	7.98%	3.35%	5.01%	5.46%	5.64%
WAGRX	InvestEd Growth	1.05%	150M	12.09%	7.85%				
ABALX	American Balanc	0.59%	83.6B	12.93%	6.99%	7.48%	8.54%	8.65%	
FBALX	Fidelity Balanced	0.56%	29.2B	12.57%	7.49%	7.43%	8.97%	9.32%	
FPURX	Fidelity Puritan	0.55%	25.2B	12.73%	7.41%	6.74%	8.35%	9.29%	9.33%
VBINX	Vanguard Balanc	0.23%	26.5B	11.71%	6.95%	5.40%	7.91%		
VWELX	Vanguard Welling	0.26%	86.8B	12.08%	7.89%	7.94%	8.91%	9.78%	10.07%
RPBAX	T. Rowe Price Bal	0.60%	4B	11.78%	7.02%	5.87%	7.84%	8.00%	6.94%
$W5000	Wilshire 5000			15.08%	6.28%	3.20%	7.29%	7.69%	8.34%
$SPX	S&P500			14.89%	5.65%	2.36%	6.88%	7.26%	8.24%
$SPXTR	**S&P500 Total Return**			**17.34%**	**7.89%**	**4.36%**	**8.91%**	**9.54%**	**10.29%**
$SPXEW	S&P500 Equal Weight			16.20%	7.63%	7.29%	8.98%	9.33%	10.09%
$SPXEWTR	**S&P500 Equal Weight Total Ret**			**18.42%**	**9.63%**	**9.18%**	**10.93%**	**11.48%**	**12.04%**
$NDX	NASDAQ 100			20.38%	11.40%	1.04%	11.07%	12.36%	12.83%
$NDXTR	**NASDAQ 100 Total Return**			**21.81%**	**12.41%**	**1.59%**	**11.62%**	**12.91%**	**13.38%**
$MID	S&P400 Mid Cap			16.11%	8.17%	7.88%	10.68%	11.03%	11.31%
$MIDTR	**S&P400 Mid Cap Total Return**			**17.82%**	**9.74%**	**9.08%**	**11.88%**	**12.23%**	**12.51%**
$SML	S&P600 Small Cap			17.00%	8.00%	8.53%	9.97%		
$SMLTR	**S&P600 Small Cap Total Return**			**18.44%**	**9.28%**	**9.53%**	**10.97%**		

*The dotted outlined numbers are computed using an assumed conservative differential from previous years' dividend yields or computed from an associated ETF.

Iain scanned his eyes over the table. "What am I looking for?" he asked. "Besides Vanguard having by far the lowest fees?"

"You tell me," I said.

"Probably the most consistently higher returns amongst the indices and then finding and comparing them to the highest Balanced Fund returns," he ventured.

"That'll do," I replied.

After a few minutes, Iain summarized his findings, "The best performing indices are S&P500 Equal Weight Total Return index, S&P MidCap 400 Total Return index, and the NASDAQ100 Total Return index except for the **15 Years** column for the NASDAQ100."

"The S&P600 Small-cap Total Return index also compares favorably," he added.

"Precisely," I said, "these indices beat all the active Balanced Funds shown in Table 3-3, as we would expect from the SPIVA™ Scorecard because active stocks-only mutual funds tend to outperform Balanced Funds. You have highlighted the main ones. The twenty-year period covers two decent bear markets and the thirty-year period from 1985 includes three decent bear markets, with two experiencing at least -50% declines in 1987 and in 2008 making this a great period for comparing performances."

I continued, "There is one other thing that I would like to highlight. The percentage returns shown here are compounded annual returns and small differences in compounding over an extended period make huge differences in the final outcomes. I will emphasize the power of compounding over and over again."

"Okay," said Iain, changing his focus. "How did they go with their drawdowns compared to the active Balanced Funds?" asked Iain.

"We will look at a couple of charts right now to answer that question," I replied. "I'll now introduce the S&P500 Equal Weight Total Return index ($SPXEWTR) into our analysis."

Chart 3-3

I showed Iain Chart 3-3 with four line graphs over twenty years comparing the S&P500 Equal Weight Total Return index ($SPXEWTR) to three of the largest U.S. Balanced Funds; the $83 billion ABALX American Balanced Fund, the $29 billion FBALX Fidelity Balanced Fund and the $26 billion VBINX Vanguard Balanced Fund.

The line graphs, or equity curves, are in the descending order of the legend. The start date of September 28, 1992, is the inception date of Vanguard's VBINX Balanced Fund.

I made the first comment, "At no stage over the twenty-three years did the S&P500 Equal Weight Total Return index have a lower value than any of the other three Balanced Funds!"

"But still," said Iain, "that drawdown in the $SP500EWTR looks frightening compared to the three Balanced Funds!"

"It does," I agreed showing Iain Table 3-4, "but look at the maximum drawdown percentages in 2008 in the column headed **Drawdown**. The Balanced Funds still had significant drawdowns. A lot more than most investors would think would occur for a fund that is supposed to reduce volatility through diversification. -43.6% and -40.2% for two of the biggest Balanced Funds, Fidelity and American, respectively."

Table 3-4

Index / Fund	Peak Date	Peak Price	Trough Date	Trough Price	Draw Down	Nov 09 '15	$ > VBINX	% Growth
$SP500EWTR	Jul 13 '07	$667,327	Mar 09 '09	$270,442	-59.5%	$1,201,431	$602,550	11.36%
FBALX	Oct 09 '07	$456,075	Mar 09 '09	$257,356	-43.6%	$683,934	$85,053	8.68%
VBINX	Oct 12 '07	$380,599	Mar 09 '09	$243,697	-36.0%	$598,881	$0	8.06%
ABALX	Oct 12 '07	$406,155	Mar 09 '09	$242,863	-40.2%	$648,064	$49,182	8.43%

I showed Iain Chart 3-4. "To normalize the percentage movements over the twenty-five-year period here is a semi-logarithmic scaled version of Chart 3-3 which visually puts the drawdown into better perspective."

Chart 3-4

I continued, "Over twenty-three years the seemingly insignificant extra 3.3% compounded per year in growth starting from $100,000 equals more than double the final value of VBINX, in fact, $602,550 more, as of November 9, 2015, when I prepared the numbers! And that's excluding any ongoing 401(k) contributions over that period which would make the absolute difference even wider."

"Two questions," said Iain. "How would I invest into the S&P500 Equal Weight Total Return index and how did it perform compared to the brilliant performing FDGRX that we looked at a little earlier?"

"There is an index fund listed on the New York Stock Exchange (NYSE) whose charter in life is to track the S&P500 Equal Weight index as closely as possible. It pays dividends on a quarterly basis which can then be re-invested back into the fund to mimic the S&P500 Equal Weight Total Return index. We'll discuss that it more detail later."

"It's that simple?" exclaimed Iain.

"Absolutely, just like buying a single stock" I replied, showing Iain Chart 3-5 to answer his second question. "This chart now adds the Fidelity Large-cap Growth mutual fund, FDGRX, to the picture."

Chart 3-5

"It has somewhat similar performance regarding the final outcome, except for the massive run-up and run-down in tech stocks before and after the year 2000, but over the twenty-three-year period it would be $141,000 ahead of the S&P500 Equal Weight Total Return index," I said.

"I'm not sure whether that would be worth the extra volatility for me," said Iain, "but I do understand that for other people, it might be. It provides an excellent example of the potential difference between a stocks-only active mutual fund, a balanced active mutual fund, and a stock market index."

I replied, "The other risk with using an active stock-only mutual fund is that it is dependent on the skill of individual fund managers, who retire or change jobs, or on the skill of the team maintaining the same theme and investment plan of their predecessors. On the other hand, an index fund merely tracks the index and is not dependent on the skills of individuals or investment teams."

"How does this chart look with a semi-logarithmic scale?" asked Iain.

We quickly made the adjustment and perused Chart 3-6.

Chart 3-6

I concluded, "I'll finish off this discussion on Balanced Funds by saying that you can achieve even better returns than merely buying and holding the S&P500 Equal Weight Total Return index or the Fidelity Large-cap Growth fund, FDGRX. By being a little diligent and mostly avoiding the severe drawdown periods–which you said looked frightening–by low-effort near-passive timing. We will come to timing in a later session."

"But first I need to cover the rapidly growing and very popular area of Target Date funds."

LAST WORD

- Diversification may be a valid strategy over certain investment horizons. However, it will not necessarily protect investors' money as well as it is supposed to during major stock market declines.
- Balanced Funds are all 'balanced' differently and hence the performance can vary significantly from one Balanced Fund to another.
- If your investment horizon is six years or longer, actively managed mutual funds are not likely to match, let alone exceed, the major stock market benchmark indices.
- Investing in Balanced Funds over the long term can make the significant difference of having hundreds of thousands of dollars less in a retirement nest egg compared to investing to achieve returns similar to a stock market index.

Excerpt from an interview[12] with John Bogle, with emphasis on the last two statements:

[Interviewer question] ... I imagine there's another thing that they think, some of these executives, and that is that this is a game about making money, and I'm much more successful than Jack Bogle. I'm a billionaire; Jack Bogle's not.

[John Bogle] ... If that's their objective in life, more power to them.

[Interviewer question] ... But that's how success is measured on Wall Street.

[John Bogle] ... That's how success is measured all over America.

[Interviewer question] ... In the financial sector.

[John Bogle] ... Everywhere. Corporate executives get paid a lot of money. Success is making more than your peers. If that's a remedy for a great society, then I'm just on the wrong track. I don't think it is. ...

[Interviewer question] ... But you had a simple idea a long time ago that has proven right.

---

12   Interview with John Bogle, Founder of Vanguard, in November 2012. Source: http://www.pbs.org/wgbh/frontline/article/john-bogle-the-train-wreck-awaiting-american-retirement/

*[**John Bogle**] ... It has been proven right year after year after year because it can't be proven wrong. It's a mathematical certainty — a tautology, if you will.*

*[**Interviewer question**] ... What's happened? Why has greed at this time in our history taken such a firm hold on the American ethos, the business ethos in America?*

*[**John Bogle**] ... I think we have a whole lot of false idols out there, number one of which is money. And you know, [there's] nothing the matter with trying to make more money for your family, that kind of thing. That's the American way, and it's the right way.*

But there is such a thing as a difference between degree and kind, difference of [the] kind when it's the building of that mountain of money that just gets out of hand. People are going to tell you as they tell me, greed is everywhere; it's always been with us. I think it's worse now.

A lot of it is built on a bad financial system. An awful lot of the greed is encapsulated in what Wall Street does, and I think part of that is a change in [the] compensation system. Executives get paid by the price of their stock and not the value of their company.

It's the easiest thing in the world to make the price of your stock go up for a little while and the most difficult thing in the world to build the intrinsic value of your company over time. ...

*[**Interviewer question**] ... Now, this wouldn't be so bad except that **the money that they're making money on is retirement money.***

*[**John Bogle**] ... **Other people's money. And it's not run the way you would run your own money.***

Author's emphasis added in last two comments.

CHAPTER 4

The trendy choice–
Target Date funds

"The measure of intelligence is the ability to change."
ALBERT EINSTEIN

Target Date funds appear at first glance to most investors to be an ideal solution. However, they are actually a solution to a different problem, that of helping the mutual fund industry prolong charging high fees.

The real problem to fix is to assist **more people to retire on time with enough of a nest egg to last their retirement years comfortably**. The risk of not having enough is called *longevity risk*.

Target Date funds are products that auto-rebalance between asset classes based on the time between your current age and when you plan to retire so that as you approach retirement your capital is exposed to less investment risk and more protection.

For auto-rebalancing between asset classes over the years, you will be locked into paying higher fees than through other ways of investing that have lower costs, potentially less risk, and higher returns.

Target Date funds' defense, as with Balanced Funds, is that stock market volatility is dangerous, and diversification is the only solution.

There are other ways of solving the problem of reducing exposure to market volatility. One way is to totally embrace the volatility early in your investing career because with volatility comes far better long-term returns. Another strategy is to use simple low-effort near-passive market timing around two to three times a year, on average, to swap into cash to avoid severe bear markets. More on these approaches later.

Investors see volatility as 'downside risk' or the risk of decimating their savings due to stock market falls. Diversifying into other lower performing asset classes may reduce drawdown, but it does **NOT remove** downside risk. You might think that diversification solves the problem if you listen to the messages from the active mutual fund industry.

It doesn't! And not only does it not remove downside risk; as we have seen with Balanced Funds there is a significant cost in diversifying across asset classes! *The cost is a long-term reduction in returns which is far too costly for the benefit that diversification is supposed to deliver, a benefit that is overstated.*

The strong evidence from personal research and the careful scrutiny of the research of others verifies this perspective.

Ultimately, the outcome of a Target Date fund approach is to swap the risk of your nest egg falling in value–due to a decline in the stock market–for the risk of not having sufficient retirement savings.

Put another way; evidence shows that *the size of the longevity risk is greater than the size of the downside risk* over the long term.

Let's first understand how Target Date funds work. They automatically rebalance exposure between the stock market and bonds to reduce downside risk as you get older and approach your retirement 'target date'. They use a 'glide path' to achieve this.

The following schematics show how an example 'glide path' rebalances the asset allocation.

If your retirement is more than twenty-five years in the future, your current mix could be 90% stocks and 10% fixed income, as shown in Figure 4-1.

Stocks can be a combination of domestic and international or just domestic. Fixed income can be any combination of cash, term deposits, Treasury Inflation Protection Securities (TIPS), domestic bonds and international bonds. Bonds can be government bonds and/or corporate bonds.

Figure 4-1

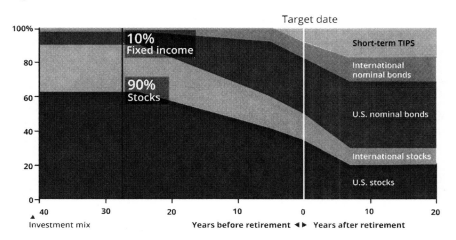

With twenty years to retirement, the mix could be 85% stocks and 15% fixed income, as shown in Figure 4-2. As the fixed income portion increases, returns should gradually decline compared to being totally invested in stocks. However, volatility or downside risk should also improve gradually.

The risk of having insufficient retirement nest egg increases as downside risk decreases because the returns of the fund also decrease.

Target Date funds promoters don't stress this and, in fact, ignore this reality.

Figure 4-2

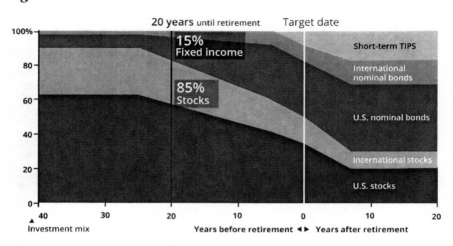

With fifteen years to retirement, Figure 4-3 shows that the mix could be 76% stocks and 24% fixed income.

Figure 4-3

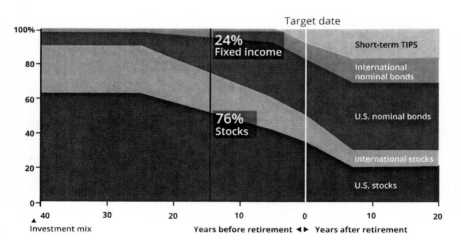

With about two years to retirement, as shown in Figure 4-4, the mix could be 55% stocks and 45% fixed income.

Figure 4-4

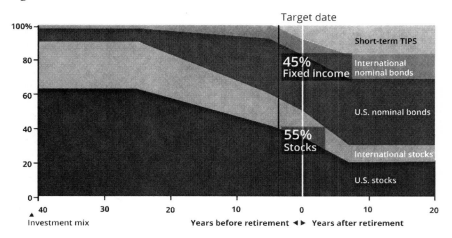

When the fund reaches the target retirement date, the mix could become 50% stocks and 50% fixed income, as shown in Figure 4-5.

Figure 4-5

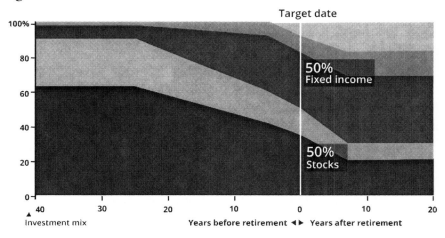

But the glide path doesn't have to stop there, assuming you stay invested during retirement. The exposure to stocks could continue to decline, depending on the Target Date fund provider, and could reach a minimum of 30% stocks and 70% fixed income and bonds, as shown in Figure 4-6, or even a 20%/80% mix.

Figure 4-6

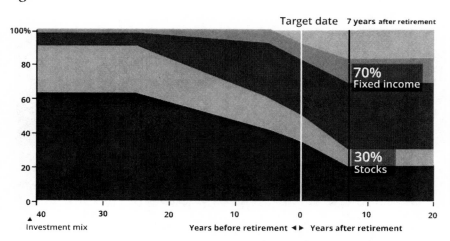

It is worth noting that a glide path exercises the lowest potential for growth during the few years just before retirement. During this period the pre-retirement nest egg has the highest potential for compounding into a larger nest egg.

Some financial commentators vehemently refute that this makes a glide path a weak concept while others claim it to be its weakest point. If people that live and breathe investing debate this, how are everyday people supposed to know? After all, it is only their lifetime retirement savings.

Ultimately, it depends on your tolerance for risk and your appetite for reward. But most people do not fully understand their risk profile nor, due to so many different offerings and complexity, do they invest the necessary time and focus on working out how one fund executes its glide path compared to another.

To resolve this question, we'll use a practical approach and analyze how various glide paths have performed in the markets. First, we need to know what type of asset class mix is used by various Target Date funds.

ASSET CLASS MIX OF SOME TARGET DATE FUNDS

Most Target Date funds are funds of equity funds, and of bond funds, rather than direct investments in stocks and bonds; that is, they are 'funds of funds.'

Some examples of Target Date funds, and their respective asset class mixes, as at Q3 2015, show that they are similar to Balanced Funds, except for their automatic rebalancing of asset class mix.

The glide paths are not consistent from one fund manager to another, nor are the asset class mixes between U.S. and international stocks and bonds, meaning that performance will differ from one Target Date fund manager to the next for the same target date.

Figure 4-7 shows the different glide paths used by three high-profile Target Date fund managers. It doesn't show what the glide paths do after the target date is reached. For example, Vanguard continues to reduce the exposure to stocks, but other fund managers don't necessarily do so. What is the glide path for your Target Date fund?

Figure 4-7

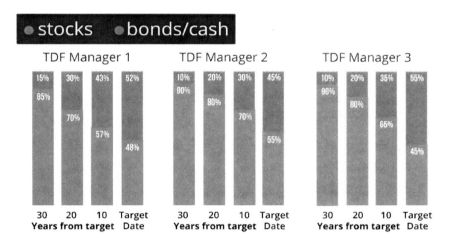

A mixture of the American, Fidelity and Vanguard 2020, 2030 and 2045 Target Date funds below clearly shows that all these are *funds of funds, and they have different mixes of asset classes.* Unless you know the asset allocation of each of the lower level funds, you will struggle to understand how your Target Date fund allocates its assets. Even if you did when you first invested in them, they could change their asset allocation glide path during your retirement investing lifetime.

AAHTX American 2045 Target Date Retirement Fund

As at July 31, 2015, the asset mix for AAHTX was:

- U.S. Equities: 57.7%.
- Non-U.S. Equities: 26.8%.
- U.S. Bonds: 7.2%.
- Non-U.S. Bonds: 1.4%.
- Cash & Equivalents: 6.9%.

AAETX American 2030 Target Date Retirement Fund

As at July 31, 2015, the asset mix for AAETX was:

- U.S. Equities: 51.7%.
- Non-U.S. Equities: 24.4%.
- U.S. Bonds: 15.0%.
- Non-U.S. Bonds: 2.2%.
- Cash & Equivalents: 6.7%.

FFFDX Fidelity Freedom 2020 Target Date Fund

As at May 31, 2016, the asset mix for FFFDX was:

- Domestic Equity Funds: 44.06%.
- International Equity Funds: 20.08%.
- Bond Funds: 29.76%.
- Short-Term Funds: 6.1%.

VTIVX Vanguard Target Retirement 2045 Fund

As at July 31, 2015, the asset mix for VTIVX was:

- Vanguard Total Stock Market Index Fund Investor Shares: 55.4%.
- Vanguard Total International Stock Market Index Fund Investor Shares: 34.4%.
- Vanguard Total Bond Market II Index Fund Investor Shares: 7.0%.
- Vanguard Total International Bond Market Index Fund Investor Shares: 3.2%.

VTWNX Vanguard Target Retirement 2020 Fund

As at July 31, 2015, the asset mix for VTWNX was:

- Vanguard Total Stock Market Index Fund Investor Shares: 37.2%.
- Vanguard Total International Stock Market Index Fund Investor Shares: 22.3%.

- Vanguard Total Bond Market II Index Fund Investor Shares: 28.1%.
- Vanguard Total International Bond Market Index Fund Investor Shares: 12.0%.
- Vanguard Short-term Inflation Protected Securities Index Fund Inv. Shares: 0.4%.

TARGET DATE FUNDS' PERFORMANCE COMPARED TO STOCK MARKET INDICES

"How well did the glide path concept work for various Target Date funds over the last ten to fifteen years and, in particular, during the 2002 and 2008 stock market bear markets?" I asked Iain this question as I handed him Table 4-1 showing the returns up to June 30, 2015, of the primary Target Date funds spanning target dates from 2010 to 2045.

The four columns on the right side of Table 4-1 show the compounded annual returns for each of the Target Date funds and each of the stock market Total Return indices over the respective periods of five, ten, fifteen and twenty years. Where there is a blank in the Table, it means that the fund didn't exist at that time.

Table 4-1

TDF/ Index Symbol	Target Date Fund / Index Name	Fees	FuM	Yrs since Incept to Jun 30 '15	Jun 30 2010 5 Yrs	Jun 30 2005 10 Yrs	Jun 30 2000 15 Yrs	Jun 30 1995 20 Yrs
AAHTX	American 2045	0.99%	2.4B	8.4	12.35%			
AAETX	American 2030	0.99%	6.1B	8.4	12.01%			
AACTX	American 2020	0.71%	6.1B	8.4	10.84%			
AABTX	American 2015	0.71%	2.9B	8.4	9.64%			
AAATX	American 2010	0.69%	1.8B	8.4				
LPHIX	BlackRock LifePth 2045	0.69%	35M	5.0	12.20%			
STLDX	BlackRock LifePth 2030	1.08%	580M	21.3	10.09%	5.29%	3.60%	6.94%
STLCX	BlackRock LifePth 2020	1.08%	630M	21.3	8.52%	5.09%	3.60%	6.40%
FFFGX	Fidelity Feedom 2045	0.75%	2.9B	9.1	12.37%			
FFTHX	Fidelity Feedom 2035	0.75%	6.1B	11.6	12.06%	6.11%		
FFFEX	Fidelity Feedom 2030	0.74%	11B	18.7	11.35%	6.01%	3.67%	
FFFDX	Fidelity Feedom 2020	0.66%	11.9B	18.7	9.62%	5.68%	3.84%	
FFVFX	Fidelity Feedom 2015	0.63%	5.93B	12.5	8.77%	5.61%		
FFFCX	Fidelity Feedom 2010	0.60%	4.77B	18.7	8.39%	5.35%	4.18%	
VTIVX	Vanguard 2045	0.18%	15.1B	11.7	13.51%	7.10%		
VTTHX	Vanguard 2035	0.18%	22.7B	11.7	13.16%	6.76%		
VTHRX	Vanguard 2030	0.17%	22.6B	9.1	12.35%			
VTWNX	Vanguard 2020	0.16%	26.2B	9.1	10.70%			
VTXVX	Vanguard 2015	0.16%	18.1B	11.7	9.68%	5.95%		
VTENX	Vanguard 2010	0.16%	5.8B	9.1	8.37%			
TRRKX	T. Rowe Price 2045	0.75%	7.9B	10.1	14.33%	7.73%		
TRRJX	T. Rowe Price 2035	0.74%	13.6B	11.3	14.05%	7.59%		
TRRCX	T. Rowe Price 2030	0.72%	24.7B	12.7	13.50%	7.50%		
TRRBX	T. Rowe Price 2020	0.66%	25.2B	12.7	11.71%	6.95%		
TRRGX	T. Rowe Price 2015	0.62%	9.8B	11.3	10.53%	6.61%		
TRRAX	T. Rowe Price 2010	0.58%	6.0B	12.7	9.29%	6.22%		
$SPXTR	**S&P500 Total Return**				**17.34%**	**7.89%**	**4.36%**	**8.91%**
$SPXEWTR	**S&P500 Equal Weight Total Return**				**18.42%**	**9.63%**	**9.18%**	**10.93%**
$NDXTR	**NASDAQ 100 Total Return**				**21.81%**	**12.41%**	**1.59%**	**11.62%**
$MIDTR	**S&P400 Mid Cap Total Return**				**17.82%**	**9.74%**	**9.08%**	**11.88%**
$SMLTR	**S&P600 Small Cap Total Return**				**18.44%**	**9.28%**	**9.53%**	**10.97%**
$IXBT	NASDAQ Biotech Index				37.03%	18.80%	8.01%	15.91%

He briefly looked at the percentage returns and then answered my question, "In a word, poorly! Target Date funds returns for all target dates have been woeful compared to the stock market indices."

"On which stock market index are you basing your quick analysis?" I asked.

"The S&P500 Equal Weight Total Return and the S&P MidCap 400 Total Return indices over all four periods of five, ten, fifteen and twenty years."

"Good," I replied, "These two indices will play a major role in the suggested approaches that I will show you."

Iain continued, "For example, over the five-year and ten-year periods *the best performing Target Date fund in Table 4-1 was T. Rowe Price Retirement 2045 Fund at 14.33% and 7.73% compounded per year, respectively. However, this was way behind the S&P MidCap 400 Total Return index* which achieved 17.82% and 9.74% compounded per year, respectively."

He exclaimed, "Especially the fifteen-year returns for the two 2030 Target Date funds which would have been thirty years out from their target dates fifteen years ago. They were about 5.4% compounded per year behind the S&P MidCap 400 Total Return index over fifteen years!"

I responded, "The most disappointing returns are the 2045 Target Date funds over five years for which should have been at least 85% invested in stock mutual funds until 2015, thirty years to the target date, but are 4% to 6% compounded per year worse than the stock market indices."

Table 4-2 shows a sample of Target Date funds' declines when the stock market declined in 2002 and 2008, compared to the S&P500 Total Return index, the S&P MidCap 400 Total Return index and the S&P500 Equal Weight Total Return index.

Only a few Target Date funds were around during the 2000 to 2003 bear market, but most were around during the 2008 market decline.

Table 4-2

Target Date fund	Code	Bear Market Performance	
		2002	**2008**
T. Rowe Price Retirement 2045	TRRKX	Pre Inception	-53.5%
Fidelity Freedom 2035	FFTHX	Pre Inception	-52.7%
Vanguard Target Retirement 2035	VTTHX	Pre Inception	-51.8%
Fidelity Freedom 2030	FFFEX	-42.5%	-51.8%
BlackRock LifePath 2030	STLDX	-38.9%	-48.4%
Fidelity Freedom 2020	FFFDX	-36.1%	-45.5%
BlackRock LifePath 2020	STLCX	-31.5%	-40.6%
Fidelity Freedom 2015	FFVFX	Pre Inception	-39.0%
Vanguard Target Retirement 2015	VTXVX	Pre Inception	-45.5%
Fidelity Freedom 2010	FFFCX	-22.1%	-36.8%
Vanguard Target Retirement 2010	VTENX	Pre Inception	-33.3%
S&P500 Total Return	**$SPXTR**	**-47.4%**	**-55.2%**
S&P500 Equal Weight Tot Return	**$SPXEWTR**	**-39.1%**	**-59.5%**
S&P400 Mid Cap Total Return	**$MIDTR**	**-32.2%**	**-55.2%**

"It just does not seem worth investing in Target Date funds if you're subject to only slightly less drawdown than that of the stock market indices while achieving far lower returns. Potentially you can lose many dollars when there is not much reduction in risk."

"I agree!" said Iain. "I'm surprised because I had the impression from all the hype and claims of safety of Target Date funds that the declines would be nowhere near as large as those that have occurred. You might as well fully invest in the stock market."

"Investors in Target Date funds should get greater benefit from automatically rebalancing more into bonds as this should significantly reduce the risk of a deep drawdown as they get closer to retirement. Further, if this doesn't lower the risk they should seek a different method with better performance."

"The cost of investing in Target Date funds and Balanced Funds is a long-term reduction in returns which is too costly for the benefit that being 'balanced' is supposed to deliver."

Effectively, the outcome of a Target Date fund approach is to *swap the risk of your nest egg falling in value–due to a decline in the stock market–for the longevity risk of not having sufficient retirement savings*.

Iain continued, asking, "Why did the Fidelity Freedom 2010 fund, FFFCX, have smaller declines than the other target date funds in Table 4-2 during the two bear markets in 2002 and 2008 at -22.1% and -36.8%, respectively. And similarly, how did the Vanguard Target Retirement 2010 fund, VTENX, have less of a decline than the others in 2008 at -33.3%?"

I answered, "Because they were closer to their target dates and therefore had less money invested in the stock market according to the glide path auto-rebalancing between stocks and bonds. Even so, a -36.8% decline within two years of the target retirement date is a significant drawdown for a fund that is supposed to reduce drawdown significantly by being nearly 50% invested in bonds."

"Okay then," said Iain, "during 2008 the Fidelity 2020 Target Date fund, FFFDX, which was some twelve years away from its target date, had a -45.5% drawdown. Surely this would imply that FFFDX contained some volatile investments that would have subsequently lead to some decent growth to make up for the risk taken in 2008?"

"You would think and hope so," I said. "Let's check."

"We'll graph all the data from the inception date for FFFDX in 1996 and compare it to the S&P500 Equal Weight Total Return index." I said.

I showed Iain Chart 4-1 plotted on a daily basis.

Chart 4-1

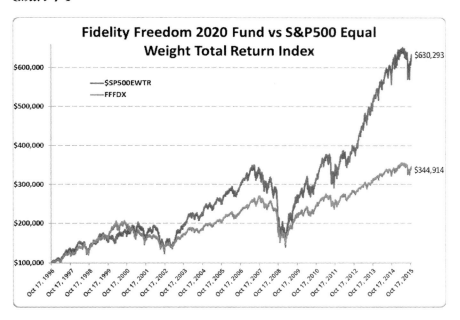

Iain asked the obvious question, "Why do the Target Date funds have such large drawdowns relative to their long-term growth? I understand that they are effectively a type of Balanced Fund, but they seem to have deeper drawdowns than the Balanced Funds that we have already looked at that also use a mix of stocks and bonds."

"Great question, Iain. It seems from my research that Target Date funds have included a higher mix of 'investment grade' bonds than government bonds in their asset class mix. Investment grade bonds are mainly corporate bonds which tend to provide higher fixed income returns than government treasury bonds but are also riskier than government bonds and hence a lot more volatile."

I continued, "For instance, take the Fidelity Freedom 2020 Target Date fund. It currently has 27.7% of its total investments in 'investment grade' bonds and the Fidelity Freedom 2015 fund has 31.3% in the same fund, called the Fidelity Series Investment Grade Bond Fund, FSIGX. The Fidelity Freedom 2010 fund has slightly more at 34% in the same 'investment grade' bond fund."

"Why is that not good?" asked Iain.

"Because 'investment grade' bond funds had relatively big falls during the 2002 and 2008 bear markets compared to other bond funds that invested mainly in government bonds," I answered.

I continued, "The Fidelity Series Investment Grade Bond Fund, FSIGX, invests over 50% of its funds in corporate bonds."

"How big were the falls?" asked Iain.

"There is no data for the FSIGX Series fund because its inception date of October 2008 is after most of the damage had occurred in the 2008 bear market. The 2010, 2015, 2020, 2030 Fidelity Target Date funds pre-date the FSIGX bond fund so they must have been invested in a different 'investment grade' bond fund at the time. The question begs why Fidelity changed the bond fund in which these Target Date funds were initially investing. However, I can show you a chart of a similar Fidelity 'investment grade' bond fund, SPHIX, to show how Fidelity 'investment grade' bond funds performed during 2002 and 2008."

Iain confirmed, "Okay, I get the idea. So we'll look at how other investment grade bond funds performed during the two bigger bear markets to try to establish a principle on how they may potentially perform in similar stock market declines in the future."

"Correct," I said, as I handed Iain Chart 4-2 of the Fidelity High Income Fund, SPHIX, charted over twenty years from June 30, 1995. It is important to understand this because it helps explain a major difference in performance between Target Date funds and Balanced Funds–it depends on the type of bonds that they use.

Chart 4-2

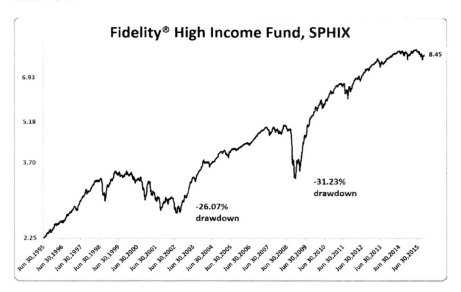

Fidelity® High Income Fund, SPHIX

-26.07% drawdown

-31.23% drawdown

"Those are pretty deep drawdowns for a bond fund," said Iain. "What kind of corporate bonds do they invest in?" he asked.

We found SPHIX on the Fidelity website.

"As at September 2015, 86% of its $4.7 billion is invested in corporate bonds and of that 86%, 30.4% is invested in BB-rated corporate bonds, 46.2% in B-rated bonds and 17.8% in CCC and below."

"I don't know much about bond Bs and Cs," said Iain, "but I have heard the ratings mentioned on TV news shows which I think scales from AAA down to C or D."

"They are bond credit ratings," I replied.

The scale differs between the three leading credit rating agencies Standard and Poor's, Moody's and Fitch. It has about twenty levels of grading with slightly different naming conventions starting at AAA as the best down to AA, A, BBB, BB, B, CCC, CC, C, DDD, DD, D.

"Well Iain, it looks like BB-rated bonds are hardly even investment grade bonds and are called 'non-investment, highly speculative' down to 'extremely speculative' by the credit rating agencies. I guess there is your answer!"

Another 'investment grade' bond fund is PRHYX, the $8.6 billion T.

Rowe Price High Yield Bond used by T. Rowe Price Target Date funds. It was down -30.76% during 2008.

Some bond funds, amongst others, with more than 50% invested in investment grade corporate bonds that performed poorly during recent stock market declines, include:

- FAGIX, the $10.2 billion Fidelity Capital and Income Fund was down -37.2% in 2008 and down -29.9% in 2002.
- VWEHX, the $17 billion Vanguard High Yield bond fund was down -30.17% during the 2008 bear market.

I added, "I can't find any evidence that any of the Vanguard Target Date funds currently use the VWEHX bond fund in their 'fund of funds' Target Date funds. Meaning that Vanguard probably uses a higher weighting of government grade bonds in their Target Date funds."

"You were going to show me the chart of how the various Target Date funds performed compared to the indices," said Iain.

"Well, here they are," I said showing Iain Chart 4-3 plotted on a daily basis.

"Chart 4-3 shows the S&P MidCap 400 Total Return index ($MIDTR) and the S&P 500 Equal Weight Total Return index ($SPXEWTR) compared to five Target Date funds all starting with $100,000 in October 1996."

The five funds in order of decreasing performance are:

- FFFDX, Fidelity Freedom 2020
- FFFEX, Fidelity Freedom 2030
- FFFCX, Fidelity Freedom 2010
- STLDX, BlackRock LifePath 2030
- STLCX, BlackRock LifePath 2020.

Chart 4-3

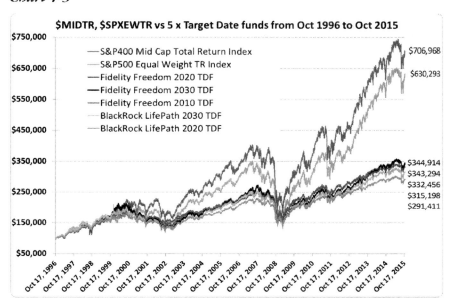

$MIDTR, $SPXEWTR vs 5 x Target Date funds from Oct 1996 to Oct 2015

Legend:
- S&P400 Mid Cap Total Return Index
- S&P500 Equal Weight TR Index
- Fidelity Freedom 2020 TDF
- Fidelity Freedom 2030 TDF
- Fidelity Freedom 2010 TDF
- BlackRock LifePath 2030 TDF
- BlackRock LifePath 2020 TDF

End values: $706,968 · $630,293 · $344,914 · $343,294 · $332,456 · $315,198 · $291,411

"There's a significant difference between the two stock market indices and the Target Date funds," said Iain. "The two 2030 Target Date funds, FFFDX and STLDX, which still have nearly fifteen years to run to their target date, are at least $285,000 behind the $SPXEWTR and at least $360,000 behind the $MIDTR!" he exclaimed.

"This is **way less than half the growth**," I said. "Starting from $100,000 the two 2030 Target Date funds generated $235,000 and $215,000 in profits, respectively, over nineteen years whereas the $SPXEWTR generated $530,000 profit and the $MIDTR $607,000 profit."

I continued, "At no time after 2000, four years from the start, did any of the Target Date funds have a value greater than either of the two stock market indices. *Meaning that an investor that retired at the bottom of the 2008 bear market, would still have been better off investing in a stock market index fund with its additional volatility than investing in a Target Date fund*."

"I get it," said Iain. "Why did you start the chart in October 1996?" asked Iain.

"That's the inception date of the three Fidelity Target Date funds," I replied.

"What about the other Target Date funds that started after these five? What do their graphs look like?" asked Iain.

I showed Chart 4-4 to Iain. The chart starts in February 2004, the inception date of TRRGX.

Chart 4-4

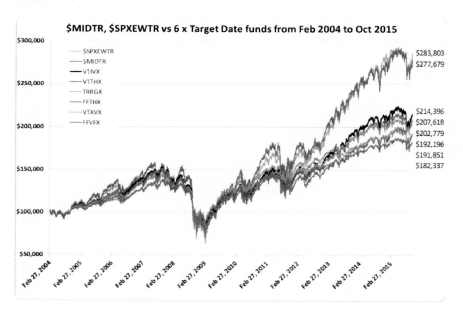

The six funds, all starting with $100,000, in order of decreasing performance after eleven years are:

- VTIVX, Vanguard Retirement 2045
- VTTHX, Vanguard Retirement 2035
- TRRGX, T. Rowe Price Retirement 2015
- FFTHX, Fidelity Freedom 2035
- VTXHX, Vanguard Retirement 2015
- FFVFX, Fidelity Freedom 2015.

"The pictures say it all," said Iain, "the Target Date funds fall way behind the stock market indices and certainly don't offer enough protection during large market declines that I was led to believe they did."

Iain continued, "And the long dated Target Date funds have performed poorly even though they have 90% of their capital invested in stocks! Look at FFTHX, with a 2035 target date. It has made just $92,196 in profit compared to the $SPXEWTR making $183,803 in profits over just eleven years. **That's as good as double!**"

VARIATION IN PERFORMANCE OF TARGET DATE FUNDS

There is another point that I would like to make about Target Date funds, and this applies to active Balanced Funds too. *There is a wide variation between the best and the worst funds.*

The more that I research Target Date funds and active Balanced Funds, the combination of the two being where the bulk of the world's new retirement savers are investing, the more I realize that for investment periods of longer than six years, these funds are like a lottery. Investors with their retirement nest eggs in these funds may be gambling with their future. The quality of retirement people will have, is almost entirely dependent on how well their retirement nest eggs grow pre-retirement.

The trend in population growth and other competing issues means that governments around the world probably will not be able to afford to pay for people's retirements as they did in the past. People are living longer, and many western governments are debt ridden.

As a result, individuals must take responsibility for their retirement savings and investments. As noted before, checking off a box on a form without doing any preparation or research, is NOT taking responsibility!

To get an idea of how much of a lottery it is choosing these funds, take note of the variation in returns of these near and longer dated Target Date funds.

Figure 4.8

Over the five years through June 30, 2015, the difference between the best and worst-performing **2015** Target Date funds was 5.2% (10.52%–5.32%) compounded per year; all the other compounded per year returns were somewhere in between:

- T. Rowe Price Retirement 2015 (TRRGX) achieved 10.52%, and
- Wells Fargo Advantage DJ Target 2015 (WFFFX) achieved 5.32%.

Imagine two investors back in 2010, each with five years left before retirement. One invests in the T. Rowe Price Retirement 2015 (TRRGX) Target Date fund and the other in the Wells Fargo Advantage DJ Target 2015 (WFFFX) Target Date fund. Each invests $400,000, which they amassed by saving and investing for retirement for the forty years leading up to 2010.

The first investor in TRRGX will retire with $659,530 and the second invested in WFFFX will retire with $518,321, a staggering difference of $141,209 in just five years from the same start!

Over the five years to June 30, 2015, the difference between the best and worst-performing **2030** Target Date funds was 7.66% (13.5%–5.84%) compounded annual return:

- T. Rowe Price Retirement 2030 (TRRCX) achieved 13.5%, and
- Pimco RealPath 2030 A (PEHAX) achieved 5.84%.

Imagine again two different everyday people invested in each of these funds in 2015 with fifteen years before retirement in 2030 and assume that these two funds maintain their same growth rates each starting with $220,000, which is an assumed average retirement savings balance for someone currently aged fifty.

The TRRCX investor would start retirement with $1,454,720 and the PEHAX investor with $512,995, *a massive difference of $941,725!*

It is unlikely that these two funds will maintain their growth rate as their respective glide paths edge closer to their target dates and depending on stock market conditions, but this does show what a massive difference there can be between the best and the worst performing Target Date funds. There will always be a best and worst; there will be a sizeable difference between the best and the worst; there will be millions of everyday people in the worst Target Date fund and in the many funds that are in the bottom half of performing Target Date funds.

How will your Target Date fund perform? Can you afford to be unaware and possibly end up in the worst one?

Counting on the returns of a Target Date fund over six years and longer to grow your retirement nest egg optimally is a low probability option.

On the other hand, a stock market index is a stock market index. There is no variation. There is no best or worst performance; the worst equals the best.

It will be what it will be, and there is a low probability that the stock market index will be outperformed by any Target Date fund or Balanced Fund over periods longer than seven years or more.

Go with the probabilities!

THE RETIREMENT INVESTING TREND – A DISTURBING PICTURE!

In the U.S., more people than ever before are choosing a Balanced Fund or Target Date fund when they sign up for their employer's 401(k) Plan.

Table 4-3 shows the enormous increase over a sixteen-year period in the number of recently hired 401(k) Plan participants with two years or less of tenure who are investing their retirement savings in Balanced Funds. (This is the most recently available data at time of writing.)

Table 4-3[1]

	Age group					
Many Recently Hired 401(k) Plan Participants Hold Balanced Funds						
Percentage of recently hired participants[1] holding balanced funds.[2] 1998–2014						
Year	20s	30s	40s	50s	60s	All
1998	27.0	29.0	30.5	30.9	28.4	28.9
1999	28.3	31.0	33.6	34.9	34.9	31.3
2000	27.1	28.3	30.8	32.1	33.2	29.1
2001	27.3	26.5	27.9	29.2	29.1	27.4
2002	32.7	33.1	33.7	33.9	30.2	33.0
2003	35.1	36.2	35.7	35.5	30.7	35.4
2004	38.9	39.8	39.8	40.3	36.3	39.3
2005	43.5	42.8	42.1	43.3	41.6	42.8
2006	48.5	47.9	46.6	47.8	45.5	47.6
2007	51.1	54.2	52.8	53.4	50.1	52.7
2008	63.6	59.6	57.8	58.0	53.9	59.9
2009	64.1	61.2	59.3	58.7	53.6	60.9
2010	69.6	63.0	59.9	59.1	55.2	63.0
2011	72.0	68.1	65.0	64.2	60.7	67.5
2012	70.8	69.5	67.2	66.7	63.9	68.6
2013	67.6	67.8	65.6	64.5	60.6	66.3
2014	68.1	67.5	67.6	65.6	63.9	67.2

Table 4-3 confirms that the movement to Balanced Funds *has more than doubled across every age group* from 1998 to 2014 and continues to increase.

However, Table 4-4 shows that the **rate of growth in new hires signing up for Target Date funds more than doubled from 2006 to 2014, in half the time that it took for the selection of Balanced Funds to double!** The middle section of Table 4-4 headed 'Holding target date funds*' shows this.

Further data that confirms this vigorous and growing trend is shown in the bottom section of Table 4-4, that there has been a corresponding

---

1   Figure 35, Page 38 of the *ICI Research Perspective, 401(k) Plan Asset Allocation Account Balances and Loan Activity in 2014* (ICI is the Investment Company Institute). Source website: https://www.ici.org/pdf/per22-03.pdf

decrease over the same period in those that select non-target-date balanced funds, which are mostly active equity mutual funds.

Table 4-4[2]

Many Recently Hired 401(k) Plan Participants Hold Target Date Funds
Percentage of recently hired participants, 2006–2014

| | Holding balanced funds | | | | | | | | |
Age group	2006	2007	2008	2009	2010	2011	2012	2013	2014
20s	48.5	51.1	63.6	64.1	69.6	72.0	70.8	67.6	68.1
30s	47.9	54.2	59.6	61.2	63.0	68.1	69.5	67.8	67.5
40s	46.6	52.8	57.8	59.3	59.9	65.0	67.2	65.6	67.6
50s	47.8	53.4	58.0	58.7	59.1	64.2	66.7	64.5	65.6
60s	45.5	50.1	53.9	53.6	55.2	60.7	63.9	60.6	63.9
All	47.6	52.7	59.9	60.9	63.0	67.5	68.6	66.3	67.2

| | Holding target date funds* | | | | | | | | |
Age group	2006	2007	2008	2009	2010	2011	2012	2013	2014
20s	29.4	32.4	47.5	50.5	55.3	59.3	59.4	58.6	60.6
30s	28.5	35.5	44.3	48.3	49.8	55.9	58.7	58.2	59.7
40s	27.4	34.6	42.6	46.6	47.2	52.8	55.8	54.8	57.7
50s	28.1	35.3	42.7	46.2	46.8	52.4	55.5	53.6	57.0
60s	26.1	32.3	39.1	41.8	43.1	49.0	51.5	48.9	55.4
All	28.3	34.3	44.4	47.9	49.8	55.2	57.3	56.3	58.9

| | Holding non–target date balanced funds | | | | | | | | |
Age group	2006	2007	2008	2009	2010	2011	2012	2013	2014
20s	22.5	21.2	18.5	16.7	15.8	14.0	12.8	10.1	8.6
30s	22.5	21.9	18.2	16.2	15.1	14.0	12.6	11.2	11.9
40s	21.3	21.1	17.7	15.8	14.4	13.9	13.3	12.4	14.8
50s	21.4	20.9	17.6	15.4	13.8	13.5	13.0	12.4	13.3
60s	19.8	20.1	16.7	14.0	13.2	13.1	13.9	13.0	13.1
All	21.9	21.3	18.0	16.1	14.8	13.9	13.0	11.4	11.8

Together Tables 4-3 and 4-4 show that two-thirds of new hires are choosing Balanced Funds, and nearly 60% of those choosing Balanced

---

2   Figure 36, *ICI Research Perspective, 401(k) Plan Asset Allocation Account Balances and Loan Activity in 2014* (ICI is the Investment Company Institute). Source website: https://www.ici.org/pdf/per22-03.pdf

Funds are checking the Target Date fund box on their employment forms! More people in their twenties, thirties, and forties, **who should be the least concerned with short-term market volatility**, are signing up for Balanced Funds and its principal subset, Target Date funds.

Evidence presented so far shows that active equity mutual funds have the potential to perform better than Balanced Funds and Target Date funds – although worse than stock market indices, as per the SPIVA ScoreCard. The majority of active mutual investing is currently in active equity mutual funds, but these tables tell us that is changing rapidly. **To the category of Balanced Funds and Target Date funds**.

Table 4-5 shows that not only are new hires selecting Target Date funds and Balanced Funds, but they are **investing *most* of their retirement nest eggs in these funds**.

These decisions will have dramatic ramifications for their long-term returns and consequently, their retirement. And, YES, it is their choice and their responsibility, not their employers or the 410(k) Plan provider.

Table 4-5[3]

Many Recently Hired 401(k) Participants Hold High Concentrations in Target Date Funds			
Percentage of recently hired participants holding the type of fund indicated,[1,2] 2014			
Percentage of account balance invested in balanced funds			
Age group	>0 to 50 percent	>50 to 90 percent	>90 percent
20s	10.4	7.5	82.1
30s	13.4	8.7	77.9
40s	14.4	8.2	77.4
50s	14.7	7.4	77.8
60s	13.9	6.7	79.4
All	12.9	7.9	79.2
Percentage of account balance invested in target date funds[3]			
Age group	>0 to 50 percent	>50 to 90 percent	>90 percent
20s	8.6	7.6	83.8
30s	11.7	12.0	76.4
40s	13.0	12.5	74.6
50s	12.8	11.9	75.4
60s	11.7	11.8	76.5
All	11.1	10.7	78.2
Percentage of account balance invested in non-target date balanced funds			
Age group	>0 to 50 percent	>50 to 90 percent	>90 percent
20s	37.5	8.4	54.1
30s	38.9	25.1	35.9
40s	34.7	25.2	40.1
50s	37.3	27.2	35.5
60s	33.4	30.1	36.5
All	36.7	22.0	41.2

Table 4-6 sums up the change in the retirement investing trend from 1998 to 2014 for new hires across all age groups but especially those aged

---

3   Figure 38, *ICI Research Perspective, 401(k) Plan Asset Allocation Account Balances and Loan Activity in 2014* (ICI is the Investment Company Institute). Source website: https://www.ici.org/pdf/per22-03.pdf

in their twenties. The move from electing active equity mutual funds to electing Balanced Funds, the majority of which are Target Date funds, is gathering pace.

Table 4-6[4]

Average Asset Allocation of 401(k) Plan Accounts by Participant Age Among Recently Hired[1] 401(k) Plan Participants
Percentage of account balances,[2] *1998 and 2014*

Age group	Equity funds 1998	Equity funds 2014	Balanced funds Total 1998	Balanced funds Total 2014	Target date funds[3] 2014	Non-target date balanced funds 2014
20s	66.9	29.7	7.4	55.0	47.0	8.0
30s	67.8	37.1	8.0	46.9	39.6	7.3
40s	64.5	39.6	9.7	41.6	34.3	7.3
50s	60.5	37.8	11.3	36.9	31.1	5.8
60s	50.0	34.7	12.1	31.9	27.1	4.8
All	64.8	36.9	9.1	41.5	34.9	6.6

Age group	Bond funds 1998	Bond funds 2014	Money funds 1998	Money funds 2014	GICs[4] and other stable value funds 1998	GICs[4] and other stable value funds 2014	Company stock 1998	Company stock 2014
20s	5.1	4.2	4.0	1.0	3.7	1.2	10.5	3.6
30s	5.1	5.7	4.1	1.2	3.2	1.6	9.4	2.6
40s	5.9	7.3	5.1	1.6	4.4	1.7	8.0	2.6
50s	6.6	10.6	5.9	1.9	6.7	3.5	6.5	2.6
60s	8.7	15.7	7.8	2.3	13.3	3.7	5.7	2.0
All	5.7	8.6	4.9	1.6	4.6	2.4	8.6	2.6

4   Figure 40, *ICI Research Perspective, 401(k) Plan Asset Allocation Account Balances and Loan Activity in 2014* (ICI is the Investment Company Institute). Source website: https://www.ici.org/pdf/per22-03.pdf

This trend isn't just a concern for the people who could potentially forego more than a million dollars in retirement savings. It poses a significant problem for the future government pension finances of the U.S. and other countries that will have to provide for underfinanced retirees. In Australia, the trend towards Balanced Funds and Cohort funds (similar to Target Date funds) for retirement investing is equally as strong.

"Wow," said Iain, "it appears that the trend is that the majority of those investing for retirement for decades to come are investing in the poorer long-term performers, the Balanced Funds, and Target Date funds. That is incredible. Why?"

Iain ventured after I decided not to answer, "Maybe investors just don't know the facts? They don't understand? They don't care? They merely accept the status quo without questioning it. Maybe it's the ongoing indoctrination through advertising and publicity by the financial industry that a managed diversified portfolio is the only way to go? It seems that if investors took some time to find out about the returns on these types of funds over the long term, they might reconsider."

Iain continued, "And this even flies in the face of what the world's most successful investor ever has committed that he will do with his estate. As you showed me earlier in the extract from Warren Buffett's letter to his shareholders in 2014 he won't be diversifying into other asset classes, just investing in a stock market index fund with 90% of his estate capital."

"It seems unstoppable," Iain added.

I replied, "It does! I concede that the majority of investors will remain disengaged and uninformed until it is too late to catch up. But a few, with a little effort and focus, can learn about a far more effective but simple strategy that will have a hugely positive effect on the security of their financial futures and hence their level of comfort both pre and post retiring."

"If everyday investors who are currently financially disengaged decide to embark on a savvier investing journey for their future, they will propel themselves ahead of the herd, and their efforts to understand this book and act on it will be worth it."

ROBO-ADVICE

"What is all this talk I hear about robo-advice?" asked Iain.

"Robo-advice is growing in popularity and even being fueled by the big end of town who are buying existing robo-advice businesses or establishing their own because it is a way to charge fees to do extra work on behalf of their clients."

"What is it and why is it growing?" asked Iain.

"The two main differentiators of robo-advice are the online capture of requirements instead of face-to-face meetings with an advisor, and then automatically, or robotically, rebalancing allocations of capital across different asset classes according to one's risk profile determined from the online capture of one's requirements."

"It is growing mainly because of its novelty of lower fees compared to face-to-face financial advice, and perception of being yet another disruptive technology. However, *robo-advice merely uses a Balanced Fund approach* camouflaged in different terminology and technology."

I continued, "Robo-advice does offer a solution for those who:

- Have small investment accounts and want to pay lower fees than they would pay to an actual financial advisor who would charge a minimum 'schedule' fee that could be a large percentage of the investor's total investment capital.
  - ◊ For example, an investor **with less than $10,000 to invest** who pays 0% to 0.35% in annual fees to a robo-advisor with no minimum fee. Compared to using a 'face-to-face' investment advisor who might charge a minimum $500 initial fee (=5% of $10,000), or larger, and then 1.0% of FuM (Funds under Management) per year after that.
- Have no interest in researching, developing and executing their own investment plan, that is, the investing apathetic.

Most robo-advisors use index mutual funds and index ETFs in nearly all their principle products that everyday investors could invest in directly themselves without any additional advice fees; robo-advice or otherwise.

Iain summarized, "So robo-advisors spread capital across stocks, bonds and other asset classes using index funds and ETFs? If that's the case, wouldn't a low-cost active Balanced Fund such as Vanguard's VBINX at 0.23% fees per year, **without any additional robo-advice fees**, offer much the same returns and drawdown for a lower cost?"

"Correct, you noticed it immediately," I said. "Besides them delivering their service online and using proprietary computer algorithms to rebalance automatically between index ETFs, there is no conceptual investing difference to an active balanced mutual fund."

I emphasized, "The huge point to make here is that ***robo-advisers diversify across asset classes, and this makes them very similar to the whole category of active balanced funds***. Meaning that all the analysis of returns and drawdowns that we have seen for Balanced Funds and Target Date funds so far applies to robo-advisers too in the same way."

I continued, "In fact, because robo-advisers spread their investments across funds rather than investing directly in stocks and bonds, they are most similar to lifestyle mutual funds. These are mostly 'funds of funds' that provide a choice of aggressive, moderate or conservative approaches, which differ widely in their mix of asset classes."

"Based on this, robo-advice will still underperform stock market indices by large margins over the long term. And there will be a huge variation in returns from one robo-advisor to the next, and from one robo-advice theme to another; just like Target Date funds."

"Still, I have no doubt that due to their novelty and acceptance by the large fund managers, like Vanguard and Fidelity, which will legitimize and endorse them, many investors will use them. However, this does not make them the best investing solution from a return or a risk perspective over the long term; particularly for retirement nest eggs."

"***The best alternative solution for those with small investment balances, who typically are those in their twenties and thirties that would consider robo-advice, is to invest in a low-fee index fund.*** For example, a Vanguard S&P500 fund, which can charge fees as low as 0.07% per year with no additional 'advice' fees, robo or otherwise; or for better long-term performance, in an S&P400 index fund that charges fees of 0.12% per year."

LAST WORD

- Over the long term, diversification retards growth. It is like driving a car with one foot ALWAYS on the brake in case a crash situation arises, instead of applying the brake only when it is required.
- Nearly 70% of newly hired Americans are investing their retirement nest eggs in Balanced Funds or Target Date funds.
- The funds that have low diversification, and focus nearly all of their capital on the single asset class of stocks, experience larger drawdowns but far better returns over the long term than those that diversify into other asset classes.
- Balanced Funds and Target Date funds will always under-perform the market indices over the long term because of their diversification into lower performing asset classes.
- Diversifying into poorer performing asset classes may improve returns over investing timeframes of less than seven years, but not over the long term.
- The same principles apply to robo-advisers who also diversify across asset classes and rebalance using computer algorithms. They are merely doing the same task as Balanced Funds for a slightly lower fee, but maybe not.
   ◊ Automated technology CANNOT make the poor performing asset classes exceed the top performing asset class and therefore their performance will still lag stock market indices over the long term.

CHAPTER 5

Nest egg Alert! Will you have enough?

"Compound interest is the eighth wonder of the world. He who understands it, earns it... he who doesn't... pays it."

ALBERT EINSTEIN

There are many methods to estimate how much money you need to retire comfortably and independently; some of them are used in a variety of retirement calculators available online many of which are relatively sophisticated.

Two simple methods that approximate the more advanced calculators that determine how much is required by a retired couple are:

- Annual income during retirement: 70% of the salary earned in their final year of working, indexed annually for inflation.
- Lump sum retirement nest egg: ten to twelve times the salary earned in their final year of working.

Neither method is perfect but will provide a good estimate, particularly if you're relatively close to retirement and can calculate your ending salary with some accuracy. However, if you're much younger and have many years until retirement, your salary in your final year of working would be a guess at best.

Your current salary can also be used to determine how much you should have accumulated at various points in your working life to be on target to have sufficient savings to live a comfortable and independent retirement. Investment firms use as guidelines the following multipliers of your current annual salary that you should have saved:

- By age thirty-five: 1x to 1.5x.
- By age forty-five: about 3x.
- By age fifty-five: 5x to 7x.
- At retirement: 10x to 12x your final annual salary.

Research shows that very few people achieve these milestones. What is more important is having a plan, regardless of your age, to focus on the amount you need when you stop working and no longer earn a regular salary; and then execute that plan.

To formulate such a plan, ensure critical assumptions are applied. For instance, an ***independent retirement*** means ***not relying*** on Social Security or any form of government 'age pension' during retirement. You may still receive this but not need it to survive financially.

Regardless, it's advisable to plan for a future without a government pension to avoid the worst case scenario. It's also prudent to assume that government assistance may not be available or be far more limited than it is today.

Furthermore, ***financial freedom,*** *by definition, means having enough money to do what you wish* ***without having to rely on any third party for your finances.***

Let's first deal with annual income during retirement, then determine the size of the nest egg lump-sum required to last a comfortable independent retirement; and thereby eliminate longevity risk.

After much research, I have concluded that ***$60,000*** per year, after taxes and rent or mortgage payments, is required for a **couple** to live a comfortable retirement in 2016 dollars in the U.S., Canada or Australia[1]. An **individual** retiree will need around 70% of what a couple needs, about ***$42,000*** annually, after taxes.

Your definition of 'comfortable' will differ from that of your next door

---

1   The Association of Superannuation Funds of Australia Limited, ASFA Retirement Standard

neighbor's description. Perhaps you would want to afford decent health insurance, travel regularly locally and overseas, own and maintain a car and motorhome, be a member of a sporting club, dine out regularly, not have to skimp on your grandchildren, not rely on your children for support, etc. On the other hand, you might be content with a more modest lifestyle where you don't travel, own a car or enjoy fee-based leisure activities, but that will be considered 'comfortable' for you.

Adjust the annual $60000/$42000 according to the discretionary amount that you will need to support the target retirement lifestyle that you will desire. You can also use 70% of *your* projected final annual salary to adjust the $60,000 upwards.

Remember too; most governments are using more stringent asset tests for retirees to qualify for state pensions so the chances are that any additional money you will require will have to come through your personal financial arrangements.

REQUIRED NEST EGG SIZE IN 2016 FOR AN INDEPENDENT RETIREMENT

For a **couple** to have sufficient independent retirement savings to last twenty years[2] in a comfortable lifestyle from age, say, sixty-five to eighty-five, using *all* savings over that period, would require a retirement nest egg of *$965,000 in 2016 dollars if retirement started in 2016.*

Assuming 2.5% per year inflation, to make this lump sum last will also require the annually declining nest egg, as it is drawn down for retirement income, to be grown 5% annually during the twenty years of retirement. The $60,000, in 2016 dollars, will increase to $98,317 at the beginning of 2036 in twenty years' time because of the 2.5% per year inflation.

Table 5-1 shows a twenty-year period of drawing down steadily rising retirement income, adjusted for inflation, from a retirement nest egg that must achieve a **Growth Rate** of an average of 5% per year to support this level of lifestyle. The annual income starts at $60,000, and the retirement nest egg starts with $965,000.

The $965,000 assumes that the retiree does not need to pay any monthly rent or mortgage repayments. It also factors in a reduction in spending by $5,000 in 2016 dollars, (i.e. $7,065 after fifteen years in 2031 dollars) when you reach age eighty, and another $5,000 in 2016 dollars

---

2   Current life expectancy is 83 for men and 85 for woman

when you reach age eighty-five. This is why the **Inflation** column in Table 5-1 ends with $82,330 in the last row and not $98,317.

Table 5-1

No. of Years	End of Year:	Age	$60,000 $965,000	Growth Rate 5.00%	Inflation 2.50%
1	2016	66	903,500	948,675	61,500
2	2017	67	885,638	929,919	63,038
3	2018	68	865,306	908,571	64,613
4	2019	69	842,342	884,460	66,229
5	2020	70	816,575	857,404	67,884
6	2021	71	787,822	827,213	69,582
7	2022	72	755,892	793,687	71,321
8	2023	73	720,583	756,612	73,104
9	2024	74	681,680	715,764	74,932
10	2025	75	638,959	670,907	76,805
11	2026	76	592,182	621,791	78,725
12	2027	77	541,097	568,152	80,693
13	2028	78	485,442	509,714	82,711
14	2029	79	424,935	446,182	84,778
15	2030	80	366,349	384,666	79,833
16	2031	81	302,838	317,980	81,829
17	2032	82	234,105	245,810	83,875
18	2033	83	159,839	167,831	85,971
19	2034	84	79,710	83,695	88,121
20	2035	85	1,365	1,433	82,330

At these rates of investment growth, inflation and drawing down annual income from the retirement nest egg, Table 5-1 shows that $965,000 will run out after twenty years.

Table 5-2 indicates that the shortfall could be $487,285 if the couple both live five years longer than twenty years in retirement and require the same level of income indexed for inflation at 2.5% per year.

Table 5-2

No. of Years	End of Year:	Age	$60,000 $965,000	Growth Rate 5.00%	Inflation 2.50%
19	2034	84	79,710	83,695	88,121
20	**2035**	**85**	**1,365**	1,433	**82,330**
21	2036	86	-82,955	-87,103	84,389
22	2037	87	-173,602	-182,282	86,498
23	2038	88	-270,943	-284,490	88,661
24	2039	89	-375,367	-394,136	90,877
25	2040	90	-487,285	-511,649	93,149

The assumed projected inflation rate of 2.5% per year is lower than the average inflation rate of 3.94%[3] over the past forty years. However, inflation has remained low, averaging 1.39%[4] since 2009, and many economists forecast that it will continue to be low for many years to come; unless a hyperinflation scenario comes to pass.

Incidentally, **at 4% per year inflation,** the $60,000 per year in 2016 dollars will have increased to $131,467 per year in the year 2036!

In reality, inflation won't be a steady 2.5% per year nor will investment growth be a steady 5% per year during your retirement years. Meaning that drawing down a constant equivalent of $60,000 per year probably won't be entirely realistic either.

The bottom line is that no one knows what the future holds regarding inflation and investment growth, so it makes sense to err on the safe side and do three things:

- Set a higher target for your retirement nest egg than those discussed in this chapter.

---

3   U.S. Bureau of Labor Statistics
4   U.S. Bureau of Labor Statistics

- Save more and start saving earlier in your working career.
- Use investing techniques that have a higher probability of providing a better return on your retirement savings than other investment avenues, both before and after retirement starts.

To compensate for possible higher inflation, lower investment growth, more comfort, less worry, contingencies for living expense shocks, health-care issues and potentially a longer life, it would have been prudent for a couple to have aimed higher than $965,000 by the time their retirement started in 2016.

For example, if a retirement nest egg *grows at just 2.5% annually instead of 5% annually*, as it is drawn down over the next twenty years during retirement, and inflation remains at 2.5%, then:

1. The indexed annual income could only start at $48,750 instead of $60,000 to ensure the nest egg lasts the full twenty years. That could lead to an uncomfortable retirement with two people having to live off what might be comfortable for just one!
2. Conversely, to be able to afford an indexed $60,000 per year, *$1,195,000 would need to have been saved* by the start of retirement in 2016 instead of $965,000; an additional $230,000.

However, the retiree can't know in advance that a lower growth rate will occur. Table 5-3 shows that continuing to spend $60,000 per year with 2.5% inflation and 2.5% growth would result in running out of money in the sixteenth year or retirement. Another $345,000 would be needed at that stage to last the twenty years, spending at the same rate.

Table 5-3

No. of Years	End of Year:	Age	$60,000 $965,000	Growth Rate 2.5%	Inflation 2.50%
1	2036	66	903,500	926,088	61,500
2	2037	67	863,050	884,626	63,038
3	2038	68	820,013	840,513	64,613
4	2039	69	774,284	793,641	66,229
5	2040	70	725,757	743,901	67,884
6	2041	71	674,319	691,177	69,582
7	2042	72	619,856	635,353	71,321
8	2043	73	562,248	576,305	73,104
9	2044	74	501,373	513,907	74,932
10	2045	75	437,102	448,030	76,805
11	2046	76	369,304	378,537	78,725
12	2047	77	297,844	305,290	80,693
13	2048	78	222,579	228,144	82,711
14	2049	79	143,365	146,949	84,778
15	2050	80	70,034	71,785	**76,915**
16	2051	81	-7,053	-7,230	78,838
17	2052	82	-88,039	-90,240	80,809
18	2053	83	-173,069	-177,396	82,829
19	2054	84	-262,296	-268,853	84,900
20	**2055**	**85**	**-344,581**	-353,196	**75,728**
21	2056	86	-430,817	-441,587	77,621
22	2057	87	-521,149	-534,178	79,562
23	2058	88	-615,729	-631,122	81,551
24	2059	89	-714,711	-732,579	83,590
25	2060	90	-818,259	-838,715	85,679

Another $818,000 would be needed in their sixteenth year for the couple to both enjoy a *twenty-five-year* retirement if they continued to spend at the same rate. (Note the growth rate becomes an interest paid rate–a very low one at 2.5%–when the negative red numbers start!) You can't spend what you don't have, unless these are borrowings, possibly against the equity in an existing asset such as an unmortgaged property.

Emphatically showing that having a little more at the start of retirement makes it easier to adjust to living longer and to different economic conditions during retirement. Rather than trying to come up with more money when you, or your family, least want to worry about it, in the last few years of your life.

This scenario is not exhaustive, but it does help to position and understand the target nest egg to accumulate and what expenses to allow for. It would be prudent to aim to build a contingency of an additional twenty percent for your retirement nest egg.

An **individual** retiring in 2016 requiring an inflation-indexed $42,000 per year **would need $668,130** to last the full twenty years, assuming 5% growth and 2.5% inflation during the retirement years.

Table 5-4 shows the necessary size of retirement nest egg, after taxes, at the time of retirement for couples and individuals retiring in 2016 given these four scenarios, starting from the left of the Table:

- 7% compounded growth and 2.5% inflation during the twenty years of retirement,
- 5% growth and 2.5% inflation,
- 2.5% of each growth and inflation, and
- 0% growth and 2.5% inflation.

The **bold** numbers in the two middle columns are the suggested range to have aimed at for twenty years of retirement. Achieving 5% per year compounded growth during retirement will require investing at least 40% to 50% of retirement capital in assets such as stocks. Achieving 7% per year compounded growth will require well over 50% invested in stocks, maybe as much as 80%, depending on the stocks investing approach used and stock market performance during retirement. Achieving 0% is investing wholly in cash deposits, although there would be some return for doing this.

Table 5-4

Retiring in 2016 for 20 years, no tax

	Annual Income	Savings required at retirement			
		7% & 2.5%	5% & 2.5%	2.5% & 2.5%	0% & 2.5%
Couple	$60,000	$826,100	**$964,460**	**$1,195,000**	$1,517,900
Individual	$42,000	$573,165	**$668,130**	**$826,000**	$1,046,600

In the U.S., retirees pay taxes on withdrawals from traditional 401(k) and IRA Plans, which assumes the contributions to the plan were tax-exempt. However, there are significant tax benefits for retirees receiving dividend income from stock market investments, though taxes will vary from State to State.

Table 5-5 assumes an annual average net tax rate of 10% on retirement income and provides an idea of how much more you would need to have saved to allow for this net tax rate.

Table 5-5

Retiring in 2016 for 20 years, 10% per year tax

	Annual Income	Savings required at retirement			
		7% & 2.5%	5% & 2.5%	2.5% & 2.5%	0% & 2.5%
Couple	$60,000	$908,710	**$1,060,920**	**$1,314,500**	$1,669,700
Individual	$42,000	$630,480	**$734,950**	**$908,600**	$1,151,250

Remember that both Tables 5-4 and 5-5 do not account for needing income for longer than twenty years and also assume that both of a couple reach age eighty-five, assuming retirement started for both at sixty-five.

HOW MUCH ARE AMERICANS SAVING FOR RETIREMENT?

Table 5-6 shows that the longer participants contribute to a 401(k) Plan, the more money they will have in retirement. This goes without saying, but much more importantly, Table 5-6 shows that the average retirement saver in the U.S. will NOT have sufficient retirement savings if 401(k) contributions and growth occur at their current rate.

Table 5-6[5]

401(k) Plan Account Balances Increase With Participant Age and Tenure						
Average 401(k) plan account balance, by age and tenure, 2014						
	Tenure (years)					
Age Group	0–2	>2–5	>5–10	>10–20	>20–30	>30
20s	$4,940	$11,597	$18,789			
30s	$12,438	$24,269	$44,727	$67,416		
40s	$19,697	$37,199	$66,173	$114,997	$159,118	
50s	$27,091	$47,040	$73,857	$131,749	$222,887	$272.399
60s	$34,673	$49,775	$68,792	$113,062	$189,341	$274,043

Source: Tabulations from EBRI/ICI Participant-Directed Retirement Plan Data Collection Project.
Note: At year-end 2014, the average account balance among all 24.9 million 401(k) participants was $76,293; the median account balance was $18,127. Account balances are participant account balances held in 401(k) plans at the participants' current employers and are net of plan loans. Retirement savings held in plans at previous employers or rolled over into IRAs are not included. The tenure variable is generally years working at current employer, and thus may overstate years of participation in the 401(k) plan.

Note to Table 5-6: The average account balance among all 24.9 million 401(k) plan participants was $76,293; the median account balance was $18,127. Account balances are participant account balances held in 401(k) plans at the participants' current employers and are net of plan loans. Retirement savings held in plans at previous employers or rolled over into IRAs are not included. The tenure variable is generally years working at current employer, and thus may overstate years of participation in the 401(k) plan.

Source: Tabulations from EBRI/ICI Participant-Directed Retirement Plan Data Collection Project

This paints a distressing picture, even taking into account that these are averages and that they don't include savings from previous employment– see the Note contained in Table 5-6.

Chart 5-1 shows the savings in IRAs by age group, which can provide a close approximation of how much has been saved for retirement from previous employment, assuming that these 401(k) balances have been rolled over into an IRA. These include all the different categories of IRA accounts, viz., Traditional, ROTH, SEP, and SIMPLE. (Chapter 13 discusses these entities).

Combining the data in Table 5-6 and Chart 5-1 shows that sixty-year-olds approaching retirement with greater than thirty years' tenure have an *average* of $274,043 + $188,976 = $463,019 (188,976 = [165,139

---

5   EBRI Issue Brief, No 423, Page 17, 401(k) Plan Asset Allocation Account Balances and Loan Activity in 2014, April 2016

+ 212,812] ÷ 2). Comparing this to Table 5-4 there is an average ***short-fall of $205,000 (or 31%) for individuals and $502,000 (or 52%) for couples*** where there has been a single income earner in the household. This excludes the twenty percent contingency.

Chart 5-1[6]

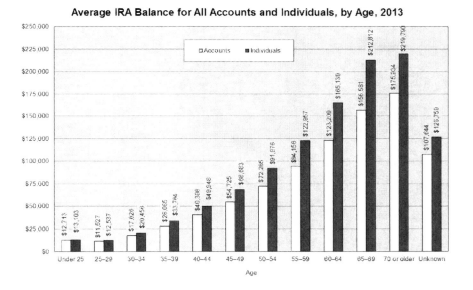

Average IRA Balance for All Accounts and Individuals, by Age, 2013

Averages do not indicate ***how many people*** would have saved these amounts for retirement. Let's look at further data to ascertain the level of accumulated retirement savings by around ***half of the population***. To do this, we will look at the percentage of sixty-year-olds that have saved over $100,000 in their 410(k) Plan accounts. A statistic called the ***median***, which indicates the status of half the population, is used to determine this.

Chart 5-2 shows that 55% of those in their sixties with a savings tenure of greater than thirty years would have 401(k) Plan account balances of greater than $100,000 at the end of 2014. Or conversely, that 45% would have 401(k) Plan account balances of less than or equal to $100,000.

---

6   EBRI Issue Brief, No 414, Page 9, IRA Balances, Contributions, and Rollovers, 2013; With Longitudinal Results 2010–2013: The EBRI IRA Database. This is the latest data available as at May 2016.

Chart 5-2[7]

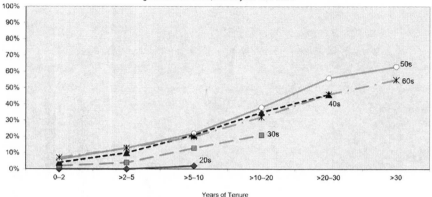

**401(k) Plan Account Balances Greater Than $100,000,
by Participant Age and Tenure**

Percentage of participants with account balances
greater than $100,000 at year-end 2014

Years of Tenure

Source: Tabulations from EBRI/ICI Participant-Directed Retirement Plan Data Collection Project.
Note: Account balances are participant account balances held in 401(k) plans at the participants' current employers and are net of plan loans. Retirement savings held in plans at previous employers or rolled over into IRAs are not included. The tenure variable is generally years working at current employer, and thus may overstate years of participation in the 401(k) plan.

Chart 5-3 shows the *medians* for IRA balances, which means that fifty percent, or half, of retirement investors, would have IRA balances of equal to or less than the amounts shown in Chart 5-3.

For **65-69**-year-olds, fifty percent (the median), or half, have IRA balances of $75,277 or less.

7   EBRI Issue Brief, No 423, Page 18, 401(k) Plan Asset Allocation Account Balances and Loan
      Activity in 2014, April 2016.

Chart 5-3[8]

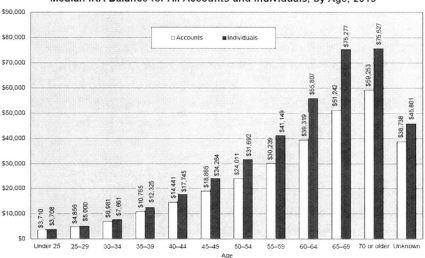

Median IRA Balance for All Accounts and Individuals, by Age, 2013

From Charts 5-2 and 5-3, it can be concluded that fifty percent of sixty-year-olds with greater than thirty years' tenure have $175,000 or less saved for their retirement. From Table 5-4, $175,000 is *around $493,000 (or 74%) short for individuals* with longer than thirty years' tenure and even worse for people who have been contributing to a 401(k) for less time. If these people had been the only breadwinners *for a couple, then $175,000 is around $790,000 (or 82%) short* of a comfortable independent retirement!

Social Security even at current levels – which is more likely to decrease than increase–is just not going to make up the shortfall for a comfortable retirement for well over fifty percent, the vast majority, of current sixty-year-olds nearing retirement.

Also, it is worth nothing that Table 5-6 and Charts 5-1 to 5-3 only include people who actually contribute to their retirement savings. If the statistics included non-contributors, the averages and medians would be much lower than the already low figures shown.

Note how much the EBRI/ICI researched balances in Table 5-6 and

8   EBRI Issue Brief, No 414, Page 9, IRA Balances, Contributions, and Rollovers, 2013; With Longitudinal Results 2010–2013: The EBRI IRA Database. This is the latest data available as at May 2016.

Charts 5-1 to 5-3 are below those in Table 5-4, even adjusting slightly for the delay of the research data by sixteen months.

Assume that *both of a couple have saved for retirement* to some degree. Assume, too, that women currently have 33%[9] less retirement savings than men across all age groups, which means that men have 50% more.

Using the *median to determine the situation of half, at most,* of those approaching retirement, a couple in this situation would have $175,000 + $115,500 = $290,500. This is *a shortfall of $674,500 (or 70%)* of what is required to retire comfortably and independent of a government-provided Social Security in 2016. Half of the population nearing retirement will be worse off than this.

Using the *averages*, which would cover a lot less than fifty percent of people approaching retirement in 2016, a *couple* who had both contributed to their 401(k)s would have $275,000 + $184,000 = $459,000. This is a *shortfall of $506,000, (or 53%)* of what is required to retire comfortably and independent of a government-provided Social Security in 2016 for twenty years.

What would this couple's indexed annual expenditure not need to exceed to ensure that their money lasts twenty years without a government pension? Answer: just $29,980 per year or $2,498 per month. This definitely would have required a large top up from Social Security.

Lastly, looking at Table 5-6 and Charts 5-1 to 5-3, *the evidence clearly shows that all those aged less than sixty will NOT be any better off than the scenarios that I just described.* Combine that with nearly 70% of all new hires, especially the younger generations, electing Balanced Funds and Target Date funds, and *you have a recipe for disaster brewing over the next few decades* that will only put more pressure on government deficits and debt.

Of course, in the immediate future, Social Security in the U.S. and state 'age pensions' in other countries won't go to $0, but there is a high probability they will be limited by more stringent asset tests and constrained by what governments can afford.

So if you are not planning to retire for, perhaps, another twenty years, how can you avoid the precarious position of people currently in their sixties in the U.S. approaching retirement? You have three options:

---

9   EBRI Issue Brief, No 414, Page 12, IRA Balances, Contributions, and Rollovers, 2013; With Longitudinal Results 2010–2013: The EBRI IRA Database.

- You can save more for retirement by making higher regular 401(k) and IRA contributions into direct contribution accounts that you control.
- You can achieve higher returns for the money that is accumulating in your retirement nest egg.
- Or do both.

You could also delay retirement and work longer, thereby continuing to contribute to your retirement nest egg and reducing the time you will be drawing down on these funds. Delaying retirement could also increase the amount of Social Security that you receive.

TWENTY YEARS FROM NOW...

To avoid an uncomfortable retirement and eliminate longevity risk, what size nest egg would mid-forty-year-olds with around two decades to retirement need in 2036 at the start of retirement to live a comfortable independent retirement?

$60,000 per year in 2016 dollars will be $98,317 per year in 2036, assuming a 2.5% inflation rate between now and then. The $98,317 would then continue to inflate for twenty years at 2.5% per year until 2056.

Table 5-7 shows the same columns as Table 5-4 with the same assumptions, except the annual income starts at $98,317 in 2036. Using the column with 5% per year compounded growth and 2.5% inflation rate per year during retirement, the ***target retirement nest egg in 2036 is $1,585,700.***

Table 5-7

Retiring in 2036 for 20 years, no tax					
	Annual Income	Savings required at retirement			
		7% & 2.5%	5% & 2.5%	2.5% & 2.5%	0% & 2.5%
Couple	$98,317	$1,357,700	**$1,585,700**	**$1,966,100**	$2,500,000
Individual	$68,822	$943,100	**$1,100,100**	**$1,362,000**	$1,727,000

Table 5-8, which is similar to Table 5-1 for 2016 dollars, shows the retirement income in 2036 dollars, being drawn down over twenty years, indexed for 2.5% inflation and the remaining balance each year growing at 5% per year.

Table 5-8

No. of Years	End of Year:	Age	$98,317 $1,585,700	Growth Rate 5.0%	Inflation 2.50%
1	2036	66	1,484,925	1,559,171	100,775
2	2037	67	1,455,877	1,528,671	103,294
3	2038	68	1,422,794	1,493,934	105,877
4	2039	69	1,385,410	1,454,681	108,524
5	2040	70	1,343,444	1,410,616	111,237
6	2041	71	1,296,599	1,361,429	114,018
7	2042	72	1,244,561	1,306,789	116,868
8	2043	73	1,186,999	1,246,349	119,790
9	2044	74	1,123,565	1,179,743	122,784
10	2045	75	1,053,889	1,106,583	125,854
11	2046	76	977,583	1,026,462	129,000
12	2047	77	894,236	938,948	132,225
13	2048	78	803,417	843,588	135,531
14	2049	79	704,669	739,902	138,919
15	2050	80	607,493	637,867	**132,410**
16	2051	81	502,147	527,255	135,720
17	2052	82	388,142	407,549	139,113
18	2053	83	264,958	278,206	142,591
19	2054	84	132,050	138,653	146,156
20	**2055**	**85**	**138**	**145**	**138,515**

What does a mid-forty-year-old need to do between now and then to achieve sufficient retirement savings by 2036 to afford $60,000 per year in 2016 dollars, therefore $98,317 in 2036 dollars?

Firstly, how much would such a person currently have saved for retirement?

Chart 5-2 shows that around 55% of people aged in their forties with a savings tenure of between twenty and thirty years would have a 401(k) Plan account balance of less than or equal to $100,000 at the end of 2014. Those with less tenure would obviously have less saved.

From Chart 5-1, mid-forty-year-olds have an *average* of $59,316

[(49,948 + 68,683) ÷ 2], say $60,000, rolled over or contributed into IRAs from previous employers at the end of 2013.

From Chart 5-3, mid-forty-year-olds have a *median* of $29,877 [(17,745 + 24,264) ÷ 2], say $30,000, in IRAs from previous employers, meaning that half would have $30,000 or less in an IRA.

From this latest available data as at May 2016, it would be safe to conclude that at least half of mid-forty-year-olds would have a maximum of $130,000 saved for retirement.

How might their balance have reached $130,000 in the first place? Starting with $0 at, say, age 25, a twenty-year contribution period with zero growth would require contributions of $6,500 per annum (20 x 6,500 = 130,000).

Allowing for growth similar to Target Date funds of 6.4% compounded per year over the last twenty years, unindexed annual 401(k) contributions would need to have averaged around $3,850, or $320.83 monthly. Or allowing for an average of 2.5% per year increase in contributions, they could have started at $2,665 per year, $222.08 monthly, and risen to $4,358 per year, $363.17 monthly, over twenty years.

These contributions are reasonable and realistic for up to half of the workers in this age bracket. It is, however, probably less than 3x the average forty-five-year-old's annual salary.

Let's assume a forty-five-year-old who is a single breadwinner for a family begins a revised retirement investment plan in 2016 with savings of $130,000. Is it possible to reach the retirement nest egg target of $1,585,700 by 2036 and if so, how?

CALCULATIONS FOR FURTHER SCENARIOS OF RETIREMENT NEST EGG TARGETS

Please visit the Resources page on the website www.blueprinttowealth.com to access the following scenarios for other age groups:

- Fifty-seven-year-old with ten years to retirement.
- Fifty-two-year-old with fifteen years to retirement.
- Forty-two-year-old with twenty-five years to retirement.
- Thirty-seven-year-old with thirty years to retirement.
- Thirty-two-year-old with thirty-five years to retirement.
- Twenty-seven-year-old with forty years to retirement.

The website provides other scenarios with differing income amounts, retirement periods, inflation rates and growth rates.

Remember to add contingencies of around twenty percent. The website provides scenario planning for these.

Reaching a 2036 independent retirement target

The more planning and effort that an everyday investor puts into maximizing nest egg growth returns while working and earning an income, the less financial pressure there will be during retirement.

Investing in a Target Date fund

As Target Date funds are the highest growth investing area for new hires contributing to 401(k) Plans, I'll use them for the first scenario.

To start with, we need to understand what sort of returns Target Date funds achieve in the twenty years before their target date? To get an idea, we can look at the relative returns achieved by currently available Target Date funds with a 2015 target date. Then we can at least determine how well the glide path worked by comparing the Target Date funds to the S&P500 Total Return index, $SPXTR, as is done in Table 5-9.

The biggest determinant of Target Date fund returns, and all other Balanced Funds for that matter, will be how well the stock market performs; because greater than 50% of the asset allocation of all these mutual funds will always be invested in the stock market, until the target date or close to it.

However, Target Date funds have not been around long enough to have a twenty-year track record. In fact, I couldn't find any 2015 Target Date funds and just one 2020, STLCX, and one 2030, STLDX, Target Date fund with twenty-year track records to June 30, 2015. Table 5-9 shows their performance.

Table 5-9

TDF/ Index Symbol	Target Date Fund / Index Name	Fees	FuM	Jun 30 2010 5 Yrs	Jun 30 2005 10 Yrs	Jun 30 2000 15 Yrs	Jun 30 1995 20 Yrs
STLDX	BlackRock LifePath 2030	1.08%	580M	10.09%	5.29%	3.60%	6.94%
STLCX	BlackRock LifePath 2020	1.08%	630M	8.52%	5.09%	3.60%	6.40%
FFFEX	Fidelity Feedom 2030	0.74%	11B	11.35%	6.01%	3.67%	
FFFDX	Fidelity Feedom 2020	0.66%	11.9B	9.62%	5.68%	3.84%	
FFVFX	Fidelity Feedom 2015	0.63%	5.93B	8.77%	5.61%		
FFFCX	Fidelity Feedom 2010	0.60%	4.77B	8.39%	5.35%	4.18%	
VTHRX	Vanguard 2030	0.17%	22.6B	12.35%			
VTWNX	Vanguard 2020	0.16%	26.2B	10.70%			
VTXVX	Vanguard 2015	0.16%	18.1B	9.68%	5.95%		
VTENX	Vanguard 2010	0.16%	5.8B	8.37%			
TRRCX	T. Rowe Price 2030	0.72%	24.7B	13.50%	7.50%		
TRRBX	T. Rowe Price 2020	0.66%	25.2B	11.71%	6.95%		
TRRGX	T. Rowe Price 2015	0.62%	9.8B	10.53%	6.61%		
TRRAX	T. Rowe Price 2010	0.58%	6.0B	9.29%	6.22%		
$SPXTR	**S&P500 Total Return**			17.34%	7.89%	4.36%	8.91%
$SPXEWTR	**S&P500 Equal Weight Total Return**			18.42%	9.63%	9.18%	10.93%
$NDXTR	**NASDAQ 100 Total Return**			21.81%	12.41%	1.59%	11.62%
$MIDTR	**S&P400 Mid Cap Total Return**			17.82%	9.74%	9.08%	11.88%
$SMLTR	**S&P600 Small Cap Total Return**			18.44%	9.28%	9.53%	10.97%
$IXBT	NASDAQ Biotech Index			37.03%	18.80%	8.01%	15.91%

Using the BlackRock LifePath 2020 Target Date fund, STLCX, we will use an average 6.4% compounded annual return, which includes distributions, as a guide for the twenty years leading up to the target date of 2036.

We will assume that monthly 401(k) contributions to the Target Date fund started at $363.17, being $4,358 per year, over exactly two decades, indexed at 2.5% for inflation. Contributions in the final year would have risen to $593.66 monthly and $7,046.36 annually, averaging $5,353 per year over the twenty years.

This level of growth and contributions would have left a retiree in 2036 with $659,891, some $440,109 less than the amount of $1,100,100 required for a comfortable independent retirement for **individuals** and $925,809 less than the amount of $1,585,700 required by **couples**.

This $659,891 would allow only $42,080 annual spending money in 2036 dollars when $98,317 will be necessary for couples and $68,822 by individuals (all three increasing with inflation) to ensure that the money does not run out before twenty years of a comfortable independent retirement without Social Security. Again, it is unlikely that Social Security will make up the shortfall for a *comfortable dependent* retirement, let alone a comfortable independent retirement.

Not having enough to last your retirement years is **longevity risk**.

WHAT 401(K) CONTRIBUTION IS REQUIRED?

So just how much would a *single person* have needed to contribute to a Target Date fund via a 401(k) or IRA that achieved 6.4% annual growth, starting with $130,000, to reach the required target of $1,100,100 (see Table 5-7) over twenty years?

The answer is $16,435 per year, unindexed for inflation, for twenty years. Or start with $13,380 per year ($1,115 monthly) which will rise to $21,634 ($1,823.30 monthly) in 2036 just before retirement, assuming a 2.5% per year increase.

Only you know what percentage of your salary $16,435 per year would be right now and whether you could afford to contribute that amount – but for the vast majority of individuals, this probably would not be affordable.

[Note: contributing that sum is possible in the U.S. since a maximum pre-tax contribution of $18,000 per year is allowed into a traditional or Roth 401(k) until age fifty, and then $24,000 per year after age fifty. For IRAs, the limits are much lower at $5,500 until age fifty and then $6,500 per year. The government should continue to index these maximums in the future. Multiple plans are permissible.]

Here is another interesting, but frightening, scenario. If there had been just *one breadwinner in a household* and therefore just one 401(k) account needing to achieve $1,585,700 (see Table 5-7), then what annual contributions would have been required to reach this amount?

At the currently permissible annual maximum 401(k) contribution amounts, if the breadwinner could afford them unindexed for inflation over twenty years, it would *not be possible to get past $1,311,208* by investing in a fund of any sort that achieved 6.4% compounded growth per year. The maximum contributions would leave the retirees around $274,492 or 17.3% short of the required $1,585,700.

Assuming raising the contribution limits by 2.5% per year on average, the retiree would still not be able to reach $1,585,700.

Finally, in these calculations, we are assuming that no tax is payable on investment profits during accumulation of retirement savings and that there is no major stock market decline in the period immediately before the date of retirement. We'll examine this potential problem and solution in Chapter 14.

INVESTING IN THE S&P500 EQUAL WEIGHT TOTAL RETURN INDEX

I have demonstrated that Target Date funds will not satisfy most retirement needs over the long term.

On the other hand, what if future returns similar to that of the S&P500 Equal Weight Total Return index – the 10.93% of $SPXEWTR–shown in Table 5-9, could be achieved over the next twenty years?

Answer: the investor could invest $9,426 per year, unindexed for inflation, and reach the necessary target for a couple to enjoy a comfortable independent twenty-year retirement.

What a huge difference a few compounded percent per year makes; 10.93% compared to 6.4%! Nearly half (47%) per year less in contributions are required over twenty years than the maximum allowable of $18,000 to reach the necessary target that a lower performing Target Date fund could not reach.

Chart 5-4, plotted monthly, shows the difference between achieving returns similar to a Target Date fund (lower line) and making S&P500 Equal Weight Total Return index type returns (upper line) while contributing $9,426 per year, on a monthly basis, and re-investing dividends in the twenty years leading up to retirement.

Chart 5-4

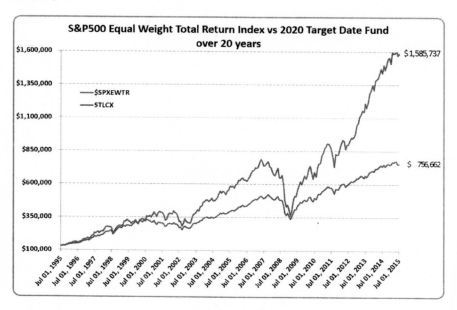

Investing via a Target Date fund *would have achieved* **less than half** of the ending balance that would have been achieved by the S&P500 Equal Weight Total Return index to June 30, 2015.

At no point during this period would the S&P500 Equal Weight index investor have received a monthly statement with a balance of less than that of the Target Date fund investor. Even at the bottom of both major bear markets during 2002 and 2008, despite the S&P500 Equal Weight Total Return index having greater falls than the Target Date funds.

What if a retirement investing journey was started in May 2007 at the worst possible time right at the peak of the $SPXEWTR equity curve in Chart 5-4 just before the stock market fell -56%? With $130,000 and investing $9,426 per year, which is $785.50 monthly.

Chart 5-5 shows that the S&P500 Equal Weight Total Return index investor would have increased their 401(k) Plan account by $248,823 to $378,823 after eight years. The Target Date fund investor achieving much lower returns would have grown their 401(k) Plan account by $135,153 to $265,153, or just 54% of the profit.

Chart 5-5

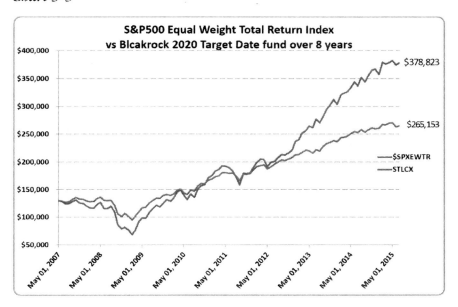

S&P500 Equal Weight Total Return Index
vs Blcakrock 2020 Target Date fund over 8 years

Alternatively, for an even better return, the S&P MidCap 400 Total Return index at 11.88% compounded per year performed nearly 1% compounded per year better than the S&P500 Equal Weight Total Return index over the twenty-year period. Unindexed annual contributions of $7,112 could reach the target nest egg of $1,585,700, which is $2,314 less than the $9,426 required per year for the S&P500 Equal Weight Total Return index.

Finally, actuaries are now saying that there is a 70% chance of one spouse of a sixty-five-year-old couple living to age ninety. So retirees should probably be factoring in living to age ninety when doing their sums. Today's sixty-five-year-olds should probably plan for their retirement nest egg to last twenty-five years instead of twenty!

The Principles at Play

Iain had been listening intently to my analysis of retirement needs. I summarized, "However you look at it, not changing the investment path for your retirement savings away from Balanced Funds or Target Date funds can make a massive difference to the type of retirement that you will enjoy."

"The principles at play here are:

- The stock market performs better than all other asset classes over the long term.
- Drawdowns in the stock market are larger than drawdowns in other asset classes in which active Balanced Funds and Target Date funds diversify but the odds are that returns in these funds over the long term are simply not good enough to achieve a comfortable independent retirement.
- Diversified asset classes have drawdowns that don't necessarily provide the protection for longer term retirement objectives that they are purported to have.
- Over the long term, the growth achieved in the stock market more than makes up for the higher volatility it experiences.
- All avenues of retirement investing are dependent on stock market performance to some degree."

"I get it," said Iain.

"Do you really get it?" I asked. "Are you prepared to make the switch from keeping your retirement nest egg invested in diversified active mutual funds, either in Balanced Funds or Target Date funds, to 100% invested in the stock market all, or nearly all, of the time?"

DECISION TIME

Iain said, "It would take days of repeated research to choose the right active equity fund, Balanced Fund or another active fund such as a Target Date fund if I was going to continue with active mutual funds."

"You have already shown me that the spread of different returns across various active mutual funds **makes the choice equivalent to a lottery**. Whether they are equity, balanced or Target Date funds. If my findings showed that my current 401(k) Plan's 'balanced' was too conservative compared to another that I prefer, I would have to do all the research to find another active mutual fund. And then do the paperwork to change funds within my 401(k) Plan, if they permit it. After doing all that, how do I know that the new fund wouldn't change its 'balanced' asset class mix in the future or perform worse than if I hadn't changed balanced funds? I would have to keep checking! Or pay somebody else to do it for me."

"What is your point?" I asked.

"That huge effort would be required regardless; to use what is supposedly a passive strategy via active mutual funds! I would need to do all the initial research and then keep redoing it, even though I am not supposed to do anything myself," replied Iain.

"Otherwise, I could easily end up at the bottom end of the spectrum of outcomes that the various equity funds, Balanced Funds, and Target Date funds achieve. That's a risk in itself! And I remember what John Bogle said about investors that keep switching between different active mutual funds; they end up performing even worse than the average active mutual fund."

He continued, "Actually I would be paying them fees to invest for me, but I would have to put in all this effort anyway."

"Well, you could do nothing! Just leave things the way they are," I said, pausing to allow this suggestion to sink in.

Eventually, he continued as if he had just experienced a big moment of realization,

---

"I guess it's my money, and my wife's and my future so I am going to have to take responsibility for it and be accountable for my decisions one way or the other."

He continued, "Either I decide to let somebody else attempt to grow my investments and build my nest-egg on my behalf, or I choose to do it myself and go with the probabilities. There is a high probability that if I continue on my current path, we will not have enough with which to retire comfortably; which would make our golden years stressful. ***Ultimately the fund managers are not accountable for the size of my nest egg when I reach my retirement. I am!*** Whether I choose to use them or not!"

"What criteria are you going to use to help you make this decision?" I asked.

Iain looked at me and said, "It's now or never, isn't it?"

I didn't reply. This moment could be profound in Iain's investing journey, or it could just slip away and be a nothing moment. It was his turn to consider seriously and decide what he was going to do about his investing future.

A few more moments of silence passed. I could sense that besides trying to answer my question, Iain was also trying to work out what he would need to give up to become a do-it-yourself (DIY) investor and what priority fixing his nest egg held compared to his other responsibilities.

Despite the overwhelming evidence to not use Balanced Funds or Target Date funds, I could see that Iain was still battling to bring himself to take responsibility. His hesitation may have been due to not wanting to be different to everyone else, heightened by the power of the financial industry's marketing.

To illustrate, participants in a study chose products that were clearly inferior merely because they were copying the people around them. The authors of the study concluded[10], *"Our research demonstrates that automatic forms of social influence are more pervasive than previously thought. The automatic processes that underlie behavioral mimicry appear to not only influence nonverbal communication, emotions, and behavior when people interact, but they adopt the same preferences as other consumers."*

This research shows that when people don't have a strong opinion or understanding about the choices presented to them, they simply mimic the people around them, regardless of their level of education or worldly experience. Rather than asking questions, or spending time understanding the choices open to them, people simply deferred to the "social default."

Iain had enough information to be motivated to decide to do it himself, but he might not be confident enough of his knowledge and skills. I could teach him what he needed to know, but I couldn't teach him to make the decision to do it himself. He had to make that on his own. If he didn't, then I knew that my ongoing mentoring would mostly be a waste of time.

Iain analyzed his situation: "That article that I read in the *New York Times* is fact. It startled me then. And you have since shown me that there is a very low probability that active equity mutual funds, 401(k) fund providers, who support Balanced Funds and Target Date funds, themselves will ever match let alone beat the indices over the long term. And the longer the investing period is, the bigger the gap between the potential outcomes."

"And we did that quick spreadsheet exercise soon after we met comparing the Balanced Fund in which I invest, with merely moving to a single index fund. Which demonstrated that I could have at least $800,000 less in my nest egg when I retire if I change nothing and remain with the status quo, the investing herd."

He continued answering my question about his decision criteria, "Fixing and growing our retirement nest-egg is the key principle."

---

10   Source: http://careymorewedge.com/papers/SocialDefaults.pdf

"Another would be whether I even need to match the indices. Maybe underperforming the indices will be okay if we could save enough money to see us through a ***dependent*** retirement with what we save in our nest egg and receive in Social Security. But this may still not be sufficient as we have no idea what will happen with Social Security in the future. What's more, this would ***not achieve financial freedom*** to allow us to have enough to do with our money what we want when we stop working for a living."

"Anything else?" I asked.

"Other criteria include how much time I would need to manage an ongoing investing process that I currently don't do. What tools, knowledge and skills I would need; how long it would take to learn the process; what the chances are of me not making any really big mistakes that could unravel the whole strategy, and what if there was a significant market fall just before I retire?"

"All great questions," I said.

"Another is whether I will be able to accept the additional volatility that comes with being:

- totally invested in the stock market compared to having my retirement savings 'balanced' across multiple asset classes,
- 'tuned-in' to how my investments are performing on a regular basis compared to being 'tuned-out' when invested in an active mutual fund."

I responded to this question, "From a purely objective financial point of view you should be able to achieve this perspective now that you have seen the evidence. As I showed you, even with the greater drawdowns that the stock market indices experience, the active diversified mutual funds still experience drawdowns of their own and nearly all people invested in them have a lower account balance over the long term than they would have achieved with a stock market index."

I continued, "However, I am acutely aware that few people have an objective big picture perspective and get emotionally sucked into negative market periods and react irrationally. It takes effort to learn to think objectively and to achieve big picture perspective. Our sessions still to come will help you gain these skills."

Iain voiced a last concern. "Will putting in additional effort be worth the extra returns that I will achieve compared to what I would have made by doing nothing and outsourcing the process and just letting an active Balanced Fund run it's course?"

"Those are great criteria," I said. "Hopefully, we have already partially answered this last question from a financial viewpoint. But there is more to it than just money. The additional effort will also gain other skills; life skills that I will cover in a later session, which may be as beneficial as the financial gain."

"Wait," said Iain, "before we move on to addressing those questions. I understand from previous discussions why the Balanced Funds perform worse than an index, but why do the mutual funds continue to invest in other asset classes? And if I do this investing thing myself should I also consider those other asset classes?"

He added one more question, "Why should I or anybody use the share market indices as the benchmark against which to measure performance?"

"Raising these issues shows that you are already engaged in this discovery process," I replied, "We'll cover the last two questions first as they are at the heart of why investors should do-it-yourself and *why* the active mutual funds underperform the market benchmarks. Then, if you are satisfied, we will get to *how* you do this investing thing yourself."

LAST WORD

- A lot more than half of all everyday investors of any age don't currently have sufficient retirement savings to fund a comfortable independent retirement.
- If these people continue contributing to and growing their retirement nest egg at the same rate, most will fall a long way short of what is required to fund a comfortable, let alone independent, retirement.
  - ◊ Financial freedom is most probably completely out of reach for these people.
- Planning for and using a different investing approach to that used by 80% of retirement investors with their nest eggs invested in active equity and Balanced Funds is necessary if they want to retire at their chosen retirement age with enough savings for a comfortable and independent retirement.
  - ◊ And maybe even financial freedom.

CHAPTER 6

Why the Stock Market?

"... the real risks in the long run are the risks of inflation and excessive caution."

CHARLES D ELLIS[1]

Iain asked, "Before you answer those questions about asset classes, let's discuss the most basic level of investing so I can understand why I don't just leave my money in the bank to earn interest. Why take on the risk of investing in the stock market or any other asset classes?"

He continued, "Nearly every week I read how much riskier the stock market is whether it is in the doldrums or is rocketing upward. When it's down, everybody points out the billions that have been wiped out in losses, and when it's up, most commentary is about how it can't keep going up and big losses are just around the corner!"

"You have summed it up well," I said, "As the sayings go, 'bear markets slide down a slope of hope.' and 'bull markets climb a wall of worry.' But you won't improve your lot by swaying with the opinions of commentators on a day by day basis. You need to keep a big picture perspective based on facts and research, not biased opinions or un-researched views from those who need to fill their columns with content and who know that bad news sells."

---

1   Charles D Ellis, page 52 of his book "Winning the Loser's Game"

"Firstly we'll discuss why the active mutual funds continue to use other asset classes then we'll look at the asset classes in which an everyday investor can invest directly."

In the interests of brevity of what is supportive background information to my main messages, I will précis and summarize the material for this session. You can follow up this summary in a more detailed Chapter 6 on the Resources page of the website for this book www.blueprinttowealth.com.

DIVERSIFYING ACROSS DIFFERENT ASSET CLASSES

Diversification can be used within a *single* asset class of, say, the stock market, by holding many stocks to spread risk across various businesses and different sectors so that if some fall others may rise to neutralize those that fell. Active equity mutual funds do this.

A stock market index does this too. However, one of the biggest problems with diversifying across one asset class is that it doesn't address **market risk;** also called systematic risk. When the market has a big fall, nearly all stocks decline, regardless of an individual stock's fundamental strength. ***Market risk is one of, if not, THE biggest risks that investors face with their investing*.**

In 2008, the stock market decline was -56%. Target Date funds declined between -20% and -45% and some large bond funds fell between -30% and -37%.

Primarily active balanced mutual funds use ***diversifying across multiple asset classes as a risk management tool*** to limit the fall in the value of their fund if a bear market occurs in the foreseeable future.

An analogy for diversification would be driving a motor car with one foot on the brake ALL the time in case a 'crash' situation arises instead of ***only*** applying the footbrake when needed.

So why do active mutual funds diversify into other asset classes? To put it bluntly, because their core revenue comes from fees. And fleeing customers due to large falls in the value of their fund during severe stock market declines is not good for fee revenue.

If growth were genuinely the sole purpose for all mutual funds, they would merely become a fund that tracks indices. Because, as we have seen in Chapter 1 with the *New York Times* article and Chapter 2 with the SPIVA ScoreCard, stock market indices outperform nearly ALL active mutual funds over rolling periods of around six years and more.

Active mutual funds have to put more importance on buffering declines than maximizing rises and therefore returns.

CHOICES OF ASSET CLASS

There are four main categories—or asset classes—open to the everyday investor; they include the stock market and related financial markets, property, bonds, and fixed interest from cash in the bank. Typically, cash is seen as the safest and the stock market is considered the riskiest, as shown in Figure 3.2 in Chapter 3.

Cash and Fixed Interest

Cash is perceived to be the least risky form of investing, but in fact, I believe it can be the opposite. Investing the majority of your retirement nest egg in cash pre-retirement could actually be the highest risk asset class for long-term investing because it will reduce your buying power over the years and it simply will not grow your nest egg by enough to last through your retirement. The risk I'm referring to here is **longevity risk**."

Even the world's best-acknowledged investor, Warren Buffett, says so. His words should convince you if mine don't. Here's what he said to his shareholders[2]:

"Stock prices will always be far more volatile than cash-equivalent holdings. Over the long term, however, currency-denominated instruments are riskier investments – far riskier investments – than widely diversified stock portfolios that are bought over time and that are owned in a manner invoking only token fees and commissions."

"[The long-term investor's] focus should remain fixed on attaining significant gains in purchasing power over their investing lifetime. For them, a diversified equity portfolio bought over time, will prove far less risky than dollar-based securities."

Not only does he dispel cash as a long-term asset class for investing, but he also says that stocks are less risky than cash over the long term!

The first objective of investing over the long term for retirement is

---

2   Warren Buffett, 2015 Letter to Berkshire Hathaway Shareholders, page 17

to grow your existing investments at least **at the rate than inflation, net of tax** *so that you can overcome the declining value of your dollars over time.*

The second and more important objective is to accumulate a nest egg for the future that grows by a **lot more than inflation to have enough to last multiple years** *of supporting what you want to do when you have no outside income beyond what you can draw from your retirement nest egg.* **That's the challenge.**

Longevity risk rises rapidly when mainly investing in cash over the long term.

Bonds

Bond prices move in the opposite direction to bond yields (the percent return realized on a bond).

When bond yields rise, bond prices fall meaning that the initial investment capital will fall in value if the bond is sold before maturity. And vice versa. Most everyday investors are invested in bonds via bond mutual funds in their 401(k) Plans.

Table 6-1 shows the performance of a list of popular bond mutual funds that have a history of at least twenty-five years to June 30, 2015, compared to the mainstream stock market Total Return indices.

Table 6-1

Mutual Fund Symbol	Mutual Fund Name / Index Name	Fees	FuM	Turn-over	Yrs since Incept to Jun 30 '15	Jun 30 2010 5 Yrs	June 30 2005 10 Yrs	Jun 30 2000 15 Yrs	Jun 30 1995 20 Yrs	Jun 29 1990 25 Yrs
FAGIX	Fidelity Capital & Income	0.72%	10.2B	41%	37.7	9.77%	8.87%	8.38%	8.76%	10.21%
SPHIX	Fidelity High Income Fund	0.72%	4.7B	37%	24.8	7.79%	7.23%	6.21%	6.80%	
FSIGX	Fidelity Series Investmnt Grde	0.45%	24B	157%	6.7	3.71%				
FBIDX	Fidelity Spartan US Bond Fnd	0.22%	20.5B	75%	25.3	3.14%	4.00%	5.05%	5.34%	6.07%
FTBFX	Fidelity Total Bond Fund	0.45%	23B	140%	12.7	3.14%	5.59%			
PRHYX	T. Rowe Price High Yield	0.74%	8.6B	59%	30.5	8.64%	7.45%	7.49%	7.64%	8.27%
VWEHX	Vanguard High Yield	0.23%	17B	35%	36.5	8.20%	6.55%	6.20%	6.53%	7.61%
VFICX	Vanguard Intermediate Term	0.20%	20.9B	88%	21.7	4.94%	5.21%	6.21%	6.06%	
VIPSX	Vanguard Inflation-Protected	0.20%	22.8B	39%	15.0	3.07%	3.89%	5.13%		
VBMFX	Vanguard Total Bond Market	0.20%	147.9B	72%	28.6	3.14%	4.30%	5.18%	5.44%	6.20%
$SPXTR	**S&P500 Total Return**					17.34%	7.89%	4.36%	8.91%	9.54%
$SPXEWTR	**S&P500 Equal Weight Total Return**					18.42%	9.63%	9.18%	10.93%	11.48%
$NDXTR	**NASDAQ 100 Total Return**					21.81%	12.41%	1.59%	11.62%	12.91%
$MIDTR	**S&P400 Mid Cap Total Return**					17.82%	9.74%	9.08%	11.88%	12.23%
$SMLTR	**S&P600 Small Cap Total Return**					18.44%	9.28%	9.53%	10.97%	
$SPXATR	**S&P500 Health Care Total Return**					23.84%	11.27%	7.08%	12.19%	11.45%

The two total U.S. bond market funds in Table 6-1 are VBMFX and FBIDX that predominantly invest in government bonds (65% to 75%), with the balance in varying ratings of corporate bonds. VIPSX invests 100% in government bonds, particularly in TIPS, which are inflation-protected government bonds. The high-income bond funds invest predominantly in corporate bonds. These are SPHIX, PRHYX, VWEHX and VFICX in Table 6-1.

Chart 6-1 is a long-term graph comparing bond fund returns over twenty-five years from June 1990 to those of two stock market indices, the S&P500 Total Return index ($SPXTR) and the S&P500 Equal Weight Total Return index ($SPXEWTR).

As you might expect, the two predominantly corporate bond funds, PRHYX and VWEHX, have outperformed the two predominantly government bond funds, and the stock market indices have handsomely beaten all four bond funds from June 1990 to June 2015.

Chart 6-1

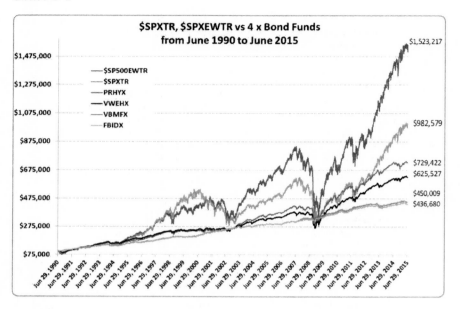

$SPXTR, $SPXEWTR vs 4 x Bond Funds from June 1990 to June 2015

Property

Investing in residential property is another option for people saving for retirement.

The points made in this section on property investment do not apply to the family primary residence as part of investing for retirement. The reason is that the $60,000 per year required for a comfortable independent retirement assumes that the retiree owns their home outright, lives in it and does not pay for it or receive rent from it by the time retirement is reached.

When all the expenditure of the full life cycle of investing in residential property is added up, it will be discovered that property investing expenses are much higher than expected. So, the first point is that gross annual residential property returns may match, or even slightly better the stock market in absolute growth performance, but underperforms the stock market indices in net return over the long term.

These are important considerations when considering investing in residential property:

1. A property investor requires a relatively large amount of starting capital for a down payment and initial costs, typically around 20% to 50% of the value of the property.
2. Investing in residential property is typically a highly leveraged venture.
3. There is leverage risk; property investors borrow anywhere between 50% and 80% to invest in residential property. If property prices fall dramatically, as occurred in 2008 in the U.S., all of the investor's equity can be wiped out.
4. A major drawback to investing in property is the high entry and exit cost. Entry costs can range from *4% to 8% of the property value*.
5. There are also ***ongoing costs*** for residential property investment such as mortgage interest, insurance, rates, tenant management fees and additional land taxes in some countries and states.
6. Residential property investing can also be high maintenance which can consume a lot of personal time.
7. Then there is occupancy risk, meaning the investor may not have tenants on the property for periods of time, which would reduce income that would otherwise cover some of the costs.
8. Property is illiquid; meaning it can take extended periods of time to find and buy the right property that meets an investor's investing requirements, which also consumes plenty of an investor's time.
9. Residential property is not divisible, meaning that you can't sell a part of a house. Hence, property investment ties up large chunks of investing capital.

Holding a full-time job and managing multiple properties is challenging because you need to spend lots of time executing real estate investing – very few, if any, cost the huge amount time into their property investment returns. Many everyday investors have done it successfully and amassed wealth through residential property investing but also typically carry significant debt; meaning that success generally comes on the back of considerable leverage, and hence relatively high risk.

Stocks

The three previous asset classes are avenues that investors use because they don't know how to overcome the supposed risks of investing in the stock market and are bamboozled by the jargon and perceived complexity. This is a fundamental point that I want to stress. All of the risks involved with investing in the stock market and the reasons that people might diversify into cash, property, or bonds, can be overcome with tactics and strategies to minimize these risks.

The foremost approach is to adopt a long-term view and never sell. You do this by investing in a ***very low-cost instrument*** that will ***always recover*** from large stock market declines and you continually re-invest ***all dividends*** until you need them for income.

The second approach is to use timing. Timing becomes your key ***risk management technique*** against large stock market declines, so you don't have to diversify and venture into these other asset classes that reduce growth.

There are degrees of timing the market. For instance, trying to time the market on an intraday basis is tremendously challenging and is more than a full-time job. The majority of intraday timers lose money until they hone multiple skills which can take years, perhaps even decades.

Timing on a daily basis is also tough, ***but over longer term periods of a few months to many months, the probability of successfully timing the market increases significantly***.

The advantages of stock market investing are:

1. It's highly liquid, which makes it very efficient to buy and sell.
2. It's easy to access. All that is needed is access to the internet.
3. It has a low cost of entry and exit of around 0.1%, 0.2%, 0.3%, or even commission-free for certain instruments.
4. It outperforms all mainstream asset classes over time when you realistically take in account all costs.

For those more interested in bricks and mortar, it is interesting to make an overall comparison between investing in the stock market and investing in residential property – I provide more detail in Chapter 6 on the Resources page of the website for this book www.blueprinttowealth.com:

- Stocks are liquid. Investors can buy them in a matter of seconds.
  - ◊ Residential property is illiquid and can take weeks or even months to find and buy, and just as long to sell.
- Stock dividends are paid on a bi-annual or quarterly basis and can be reinvested to achieve a compounding effect over many years by using the dividends to buy more stock.
  - ◊ Compounding rent in a residential investment property isn't as

simple because rent is mostly used to cover costs for the investment property itself.

- Stocks incur one-time, extremely low commission fees to buy and sell. And have no ongoing costs for insurance, maintenance or agent fees.
- Factor in the investor's time into maintaining an investment property and returns can fall well behind stocks.
- Stocks are massively divisible and flexible; you can buy a thousand and sell one for a few hundred dollars, but you can't sell one room of a house and use the cash elsewhere.

Stock market index returns are what are possible and are within everybody's reach. The gains achieved by the index are what they are, without variation. Index type returns with reinvested dividends net of ALL costs outperform all other asset classes over time.

LAST WORD
- The stock market, as measured by index performance, with reinvested dividends net of all costs and without using leverage has been the best performing asset class for decades.
- Residential property investment net returns are much lower than the gross returns when all the costs are factored in, especially including the value of the investor's time.
- Interest returns from cash probably won't maintain the buying power of your investments over the long term.
- Active mutual funds are caught between a rock and a hard place:
  ◊ People perceive the stock market as volatile, causing random short-term up and down swings in investors' nest eggs.
  ◊ Investors are heavily influenced to fear and avoid volatility.
  ◊ So active mutual funds:
    · Can't be totally out of the market when it falls because

their holdings are so large that selling would cause stock markets to fall even more.

- Diversify capital across other less volatile asset classes, which reduces returns.

◊ Other asset classes all provide returns below that of the stock market with dividends reinvested.

◊ Active mutual funds try to time the market by rebalancing between asset classes or within the same asset class, which consumes massive effort and leads to:

- Increased research & analysis costs, which reduces long-term returns.
- Mistakes, which reduces long-term returns.
- The inability to make up the difference to at least match the stock market index for periods longer than six years, as proven by S&P Dow Jones SPIVA Scorecards.

• Investors are caught between a rock and a hard place:

◊ Cash is perceived to be the lowest risk because volatility is non-existent.

◊ Cash is the worst performing asset class and erodes buying power over time.

◊ Individuals need to take some risk but fear the volatility of the stock market.

◊ Individuals default to the common middle ground and invest in active mutual funds.

You might want to read what Warren Buffett says on these points in a more detailed Chapter 6 on the Resources page of the website for this book: www.blueprinttowealth.com.

PART 2

Discovering A Better Way

BUSTING A MYTH AND VERIFYING THE BETTER WAY

This section will start by debunking the myth that the stock market cannot be timed. The mutual fund fraternity keeps propagating this fabrication which is a complete falsehood.

Fund managers say it is "time in the market, not timing the market." I say it is "time in the market AND timing the market."

We'll examine a well-publicised misinformation that will show emphatically that investors can and should time the market.

CHAPTER 7

The "market cannot be timed" Myth

"You have to do what others won't, to achieve what others don't."

ANONYMOUS

The spreadsheet analysis that Iain and I had conducted showing that he would be worse off by more than $800,000 by not changing his investing path inspired him to find a way to do better.

He was now passionate about doing something new, in much the same way kids feel about taking up a new sport or a hobby. You just can't get enough of it. You want to discover more and improve your skills. The learning bug has bitten you. It consumes you in every waking moment; you yearn to spend more of your time engrossed in discovering more.

Iain's mind was racing ahead, "How will I know when to move my investment capital into cash if I time the market? Everything I've read and heard says that it's impossible to time the market and know when to move into cash."

I responded, "You've just asked a crucial question, but before I answer it I need to ask you a question. Are you open to the possibility that the market can be timed? Or is your mind closed before we start?"

It was important to address this issue up front because one of the main reasons individual investors can do so much better than their professional counterparts is that they can move 100% into cash during market downturns whereas nearly all active mutual funds, except for relatively small boutique funds, cannot.

Iain said, "I'll try to be objective as I learn since there's a lot at stake if the market can be timed consistently and I *assume incorrectly without at least seeking some understanding*. I still remember how much my mutual fund and my few stock investments fell in the 2008 bear market. That was painful. It kept me awake many nights. And I know friends whose funds declined even more than mine. Some removed their money when the pain become too great and never re-invested again, missing the whole upturn from 2009 to present, increasing their pain even more."

I explained that the pain that Iain felt was emotional pain, which is as unpleasant to the subconscious mind as physical pain. The subconscious can't tell the difference between emotional and physical pain; all it knows and does is try to avoid a recurrence of the same pain in the future. To this end, it uses our senses to poll and scan the environment to find associated conditions similar to those that caused the emotional pain previously. If there is a match, a process automatically triggers the mind and body to try to avoid the same painful feeling.

To be clear, once etched into the subconscious with a high degree of energy, such pain avoidance could be triggered by the slightest fall in the financial markets causing short-term over-reaction by the investor. Sound familiar?

To avoid the emotional pain experienced during a past large bear market, you have two choices:

- One is to remove yourself entirely from the environment in which you experienced the pain, thereby also removing the possibility of achieving the rewards that can come from the very same environment.
- The other is to engage the environment and find a way to deal with a potential reoccurrence by circumventing, in a positive way, the conditions that caused the emotional pain the first time. You eliminate or substantially reduce the pain, but you also open up the possibility of inducing pleasure that the same environment can offer when it provides positive outcomes.

The first is 'flight,' the second is 'fight.' In caveman terms: do you want to flee and starve and avoid the pain you felt in your previous clash with the saber tooth tiger or do you want to overcome your previous painful experience to get dinner and feel the pleasure of a full belly?

In all cases, if death is a low probability, 'fight' potentially leads to future confidence and significantly improved skill. But it is not guaranteed – that's the risk. However, taking flight guarantees no discovery, future growth or confidence.

"Do you still want to test yourself and discover?" I asked Iain.

"Absolutely," said Iain as the passion that had built up over our time overcame the weight of fear, uncertainty, and doubt that years of TV advertising had sown into his mind, from media articles, books by academics and active mutual fund marketing.

To get past his belief system about investing that has been pre-programmed by previous untrue propaganda, Iain will need more than raw passion, which will come as he gains new evidence-based knowledge and skills.

BE WARY OF MARKETING MESSAGES FROM LARGE ACTIVE MUTUAL FUNDS

Active mutual funds have potentially subjected Iain and all unsuspecting everyday investors to marketing message misinformation. Part of the billions of dollars in the form of fees collected from their customers by most of the active mutual fund industry are used to disseminate information and misinformation about investing.

I asked Iain, "I assume that you've heard the saying: 'time in the market, not timing the market'?"

"Yes."

"What does that statement mean to you?" I asked.

"That trying to time the market won't work and that remaining invested in the stock market through all its rallies and falls is the only approach that will work."

"I'll go with that," I said.

I showed Iain Figure 7-1. "Take a look at this schematic distributed as a one-page flyer by one of the largest fund managers in the world, Fidelity, under the heading, you guessed it, 'Time in the market, not timing the market.' I'll use this flyer as an example of the type of marketing messages to be wary of right across the financial industry."

Figure 7-1[1]

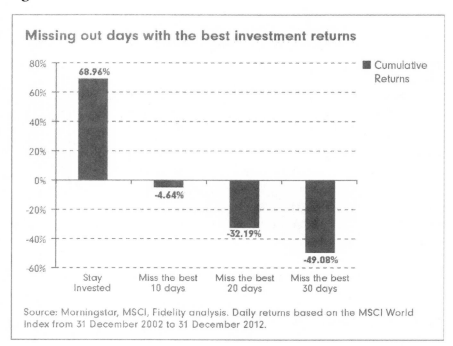

The caption read:

"It is very, very difficult to predict when is the best time to enter or exit the market. The speed at which markets react to news means stock prices have already absorbed the impact of new developments. When markets turn, they turn quickly.

Those trying to time their entry and exit may actually miss the bounce. The chart above highlights the impact of an investor in global stocks missing out on returns on the market's best days over the past 10 years. Missing out on just the 10 best days in the market since 2002 will have left your assets in negative territory."

"Iain," I said, "this quick exercise requires some concentration. But once you understand it, I know that it will change your view of active

---

mutual funds forever. In fact, it may be exactly the clincher that overcomes some of the doubt that you may still have about the possibility of finding a better way."

I asked, "At first glance without thinking much about it, what conclusion do you draw from Figure 7-1?"

"Miss the ten best days at your peril! If I try to time the stock market, there is a good chance that I would miss those ten best days and ten years of cumulative investment returns would go down the drain."

The message from the flyer is this: if investors miss ONLY the best ten days in the stock market over an entire ten-year period, then their total accumulated returns will drop from a total of 68.96% absolute return to -4.64%, a total turnaround of -73.6%. That is, just for missing a miserly ten days, ALL the profits will be given back to the market, plus more. And it gets worse if investors miss the best twenty and thirty days through trying to time the market!

Ten years is around 2,500 trading days, making ten days just 0.4% of the total period!

In other words, the message is: trying to time the market is impossible to do successfully because you almost certainly would miss the ten best days.

Conclusion: be fearful of trying to do it yourself, give up on that idea and invest long-term in a Fidelity mutual fund!

Most investors would take this at face value and not think about it any further, especially as the information comes from a credible big name in the industry. And, if someone questioned Fidelity's pitch with any friends or relatives, no doubt they could be laughed at because everyone assumes investors cannot time the market successfully!

I said to Iain, "Let's put Figure 7-1 into more tangible monetary terms with which you can identify. Let's say that you invested $100,000 on December 31, 2002, and in one scenario you stayed invested until December 31, 2012, and achieved a 68.96% return. And in a second scenario, you tried to time the market and missed the twenty best days."

"What Fidelity is saying is that in the first scenario, you would end up with $168,960 and in the second scenario, you would end up with $67,810. That's a $101,150 difference! For missing just twenty days!"

"How do you feel now?"

Iain replied, "I'm favoring the 'stay invested' approach at this stage in case any timing efforts missed the best days. But I know you've got something coming that I haven't thought of yet. I'm still all ears."

I explained to Iain that I did the same exercise of missing the best days on the S&P500 index in the U.S., and the All Ordinaries index in Australia, using two other indices, for slightly different ten-year periods, because I'm always wary of a sample of one.

The outcomes for both were similar to the MSCI World index used in the Fidelity column chart. I went further and checked what would happen if an investor missed the forty best days.

Figure 7-2

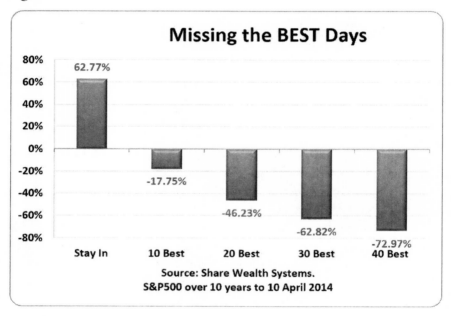

Figure 7-2 shows that the case for not missing the ten best days on the S&P500 index was even stronger than on the MSCI World index with the turnaround in total absolute cumulative returns of 80.52% (62.77 minus -17.75).

The ASX All Ordinaries index wasn't quite as bad as the S&P500 and MSCI World indices, but the point that Fidelity is trying to make still holds if an investor misses the ten best days.

Figure 7-3

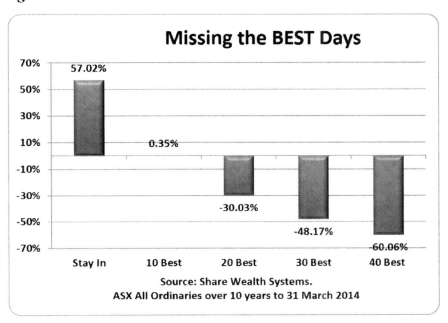

In the investing world, as in all other walks of life, it pays to be as objective as possible. Meaning apply a neutral mindset and also look at the flipside of any scenario.

It also means that investors should maintain a curious mindset and ask, "What if…?" Thinking this way opens the mind to other possibilities and potentially better alternatives.

The first question to ask in this situation is, "What if we missed the ten worst days?"

So I investigated the outcomes if an investor missed the ten worst days on both the S&P500 and ASX All Ordinaries index. Figure 7-4 and Figure 7-5, respectively, show this.

Figure 7-4

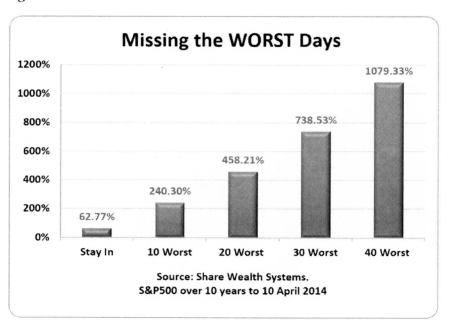

Figure 7-5

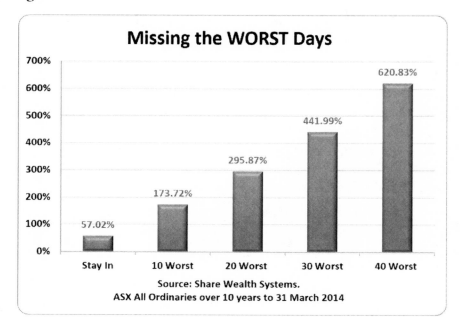

Figures 7-4 and 7-5 show a massive increase in returns if investors miss the ten worst days, nearly a fourfold better outcome (240.3%) on the S&P500 in Figure 7-4 compared to staying in (62.7%).

While he looked at the two charts of **Missing the WORST Days** Iain gasped, "There's definitely a case for trying to miss the worst days."

However, there is one small problem with the comparison–missing the worst days had the best days included in the outcome. Just as missing the best days had the worst days included in the results.

To get a logical answer on which was better on a net basis, I needed to do the exercise to determine what the outcomes would be if an investor missed both the best and worst days.

The two graphs in Figure 7-6 and Figure 7-7 show that the net return is better if BOTH the best and worst days were missed compared to merely **Stay In**, regardless of whether the duration was ten, twenty, thirty or forty days.

Figure 7-6

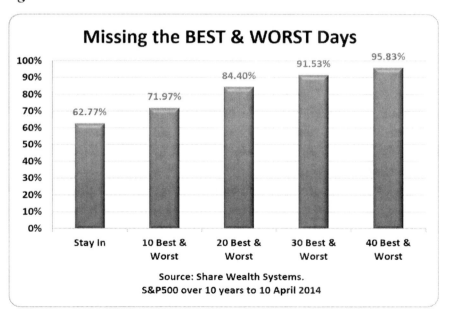

Figure 7-7

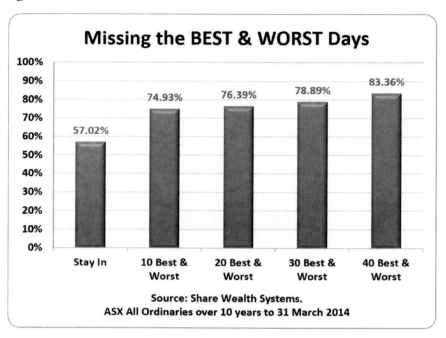

**Source: Share Wealth Systems.
ASX All Ordinaries over 10 years to 31 March 2014**

"Now listen carefully to my next statement," I said to Iain. "This is fundamental to any investor seeking a better way than just defaulting to active mutual funds managing their money."

I stated, *"There is more to be gained by missing the ten worst days over a ten-year period than there is by being in the market for the ten best days during the same period."*

Perhaps the brochure should make some reference to this fact, but I couldn't find it. This finding certainly doesn't support the hypothesis of 'time *in* the market.' In fact, it supports the exact opposite of the theory–find a way to spend 'time *out of* the market' to miss the worst days!

I said to Iain, "That's the first profound point, but it doesn't actually destroy the 'market cannot be timed' myth that missing the ten best days tries to substantiate. To do that, there's more discovery to be done and another question to be asked: *WHEN* did the best and worst days occur over the ten-year period?"

"I'll start with the worst days because, as you've seen, missing them has a bigger net positive impact than missing the best days."

To determine this is not a difficult exercise. Merely access ten years of daily data for the S&P500 from Yahoo Finance, or elsewhere. Using a spreadsheet, calculate the daily percentage move, then sort the **% Move** column from smallest to largest to get the worst days, and vice versa to get the best days.

Table 7-1 shows the forty worst days. The 'YES' in the **2008 Bear?** column denotes whether the down day occurred during the 2008/2009 bear market, or not. The column headed **S&P500** is the 'close' value of the S&P500 index on the date in the **Date** column.

I have used April 2, 2009, to mark the end of the 2008 bear market on the S&P500. Even though May 4, 2009, would probably have been the first day that more conservative analysts might have called the end of the bear market since this was the first day that the S&P500 achieved a new ten-day swing higher close. Calling it any earlier would have been a gamble since the exact top and bottom of the market cannot be picked with any consistency. The precise bottom was March 9, 2009, which became evident a few months after.

Notice for the S&P500 that nine of the ten worst days and seventeen of the twenty worst days occurred during the 2008 bear market. This is not that surprising.

Table 7-2 shows the forty worst days for the ASX All Ordinaries index (XAO) with the YES in the **2008 Bear?** This means the same as YES in Table 7-1.

Table 7-1

Date	S&P500	% Move	2008 Bear?
Oct-15-2008	907.8	-9.03%	YES
Dec-01-2008	816.2	-8.93%	YES
Sep-29-2008	1106.4	-8.81%	YES
Oct-09-2008	909.9	-7.62%	YES
Nov-20-2008	752.4	-6.71%	YES
Aug-08-2011	1119.5	-6.66%	
Nov-19-2008	806.6	-6.12%	YES
Oct-22-2008	896.8	-6.10%	YES
Oct-07-2008	996.2	-5.74%	YES
Jan-20-2009	805.2	-5.28%	YES
Nov-05-2008	952.8	-5.27%	YES
Nov-12-2008	852.3	-5.19%	YES
Nov-06-2008	904.9	-5.03%	YES
Feb-10-2009	827.2	-4.91%	YES
Aug-04-2011	1200.1	-4.78%	
Sep-17-2008	1156.4	-4.71%	YES
Sep-15-2008	1192.7	-4.71%	YES
Mar-02-2009	700.8	-4.66%	YES
Feb-17-2009	789.2	-4.56%	YES
Aug-18-2011	1140.7	-4.46%	
Aug-10-2011	1120.8	-4.42%	
Apr-20-2009	832.4	-4.28%	
Mar-05-2009	682.5	-4.25%	YES
Nov-14-2008	873.3	-4.17%	YES
Oct-02-2008	1114.3	-4.03%	YES
May-20-2010	1071.6	-3.90%	
Oct-06-2008	1056.9	-3.85%	YES
Sep-22-2008	1207.1	-3.82%	YES
Nov-09-2011	1229.1	-3.67%	
Mar-30-2009	787.5	-3.48%	YES
Feb-27-2007	1399.0	-3.47%	
Feb-23-2009	743.3	-3.47%	YES
Oct-24-2008	876.8	-3.45%	YES
Jun-04-2010	1064.9	-3.44%	
Sep-09-2008	1224.5	-3.41%	YES
Jan-14-2009	842.6	-3.35%	YES
Jan-29-2009	845.1	-3.31%	YES
May-06-2010	1128.2	-3.24%	
Feb-05-2008	1336.6	-3.20%	YES
Sep-22-2011	1129.6	-3.19%	

Table 7-2

Date	XAO Close	% Move	2008 Bear?
Oct-10-2008	3939.46	-8.20%	YES
Jan-22-2008	5221.97	-7.26%	YES
Oct-16-2008	3988.11	-6.66%	YES
Nov-13-2008	3672.36	-5.44%	YES
Oct-08-2008	4369.78	-4.96%	YES
Oct-23-2008	3939.32	-4.39%	YES
Nov-20-2008	3332.60	-4.32%	YES
Sep-30-2008	4631.28	-4.30%	YES
Nov-06-2008	4106.52	-4.22%	YES
Aug-05-2011	4169.68	-4.21%	
Jan-15-2009	3476.77	-4.07%	YES
Dec-02-2008	3473.42	-4.02%	YES
Jan-23-2009	3300.25	-3.83%	YES
Aug-10-2007	5965.21	-3.59%	
Sep-12-2011	4125.12	-3.56%	
Nov-18-2008	3513.12	-3.47%	YES
May-14-2009	3710.77	-3.43%	
Dec-17-2007	6331.79	-3.42%	YES
Aug-19-2011	4171.90	-3.41%	
Nov-11-2008	3921.79	-3.40%	YES
Oct-06-2008	4544.68	-3.36%	YES
Aug-01-2007	5989.36	-3.20%	
Mar-20-2008	5182.41	-3.12%	YES
Oct-22-2008	4120.14	-3.09%	YES
Jul-25-2008	5028.92	-3.07%	YES
May-17-2010	4500.74	-3.06%	
Aug-15-2007	5801.47	-3.03%	
Jun-23-2009	3792.99	-3.01%	
Jan-20-2009	3425.04	-3.00%	YES
Feb-06-2008	5677.63	-2.98%	YES
Mar-07-2008	5368.94	-2.95%	YES
Jan-21-2008	5630.94	-2.90%	YES
Mar-03-2008	5510.74	-2.89%	YES
May-25-2010	4286.31	-2.87%	
Mar-02-2009	3203.81	-2.82%	YES
Jul-27-2007	6127.33	-2.76%	
Nov-27-2009	4597.23	-2.76%	
Oct-24-2008	3831.62	-2.73%	YES
Jun-07-2010	4350.67	-2.72%	
Aug-08-2011	4056.74	-2.71%	

Table 7-3

Date	S&P500	% Move	2008 Bear?
Oct-13-2008	1003.3	11.58%	YES
Oct-28-2008	940.5	10.79%	YES
Mar-23-2009	822.9	7.08%	YES
Nov-13-2008	911.3	6.92%	YES
Nov-24-2008	851.8	6.47%	YES
Mar-10-2009	719.6	6.37%	YES
Nov-21-2008	800.0	6.32%	YES
Sep-30-2008	1166.4	5.42%	YES
Dec-16-2008	913.2	5.14%	YES
Oct-20-2008	985.4	4.77%	YES
Aug-09-2011	1172.5	4.74%	
Aug-11-2011	1172.6	4.63%	
May-10-2010	1159.7	4.40%	
Jan-21-2009	840.2	4.35%	YES
Sep-18-2008	1206.5	4.33%	YES
Nov-30-2011	1247.0	4.33%	
Oct-16-2008	946.4	4.25%	YES
Mar-18-2008	1330.7	4.24%	YES
Nov-04-2008	1005.8	4.08%	YES
Mar-12-2009	750.7	4.07%	YES
Sep-19-2008	1255.1	4.03%	YES
Feb-24-2009	773.1	4.01%	YES
Dec-02-2008	848.8	3.99%	YES
Dec-08-2008	909.7	3.84%	YES
Apr-09-2009	856.6	3.81%	
Mar-11-2008	1320.7	3.71%	YES
Dec-05-2008	876.1	3.65%	YES
Apr-01-2008	1370.2	3.59%	YES
Nov-26-2008	887.7	3.53%	YES
Oct-27-2011	1284.6	3.43%	
Aug-23-2011	1162.3	3.43%	
Oct-10-2011	1194.9	3.41%	
May-04-2009	907.2	3.39%	
Jan-28-2009	874.1	3.36%	YES
May-27-2010	1103.1	3.29%	
Mar-17-2009	778.1	3.21%	YES
Jan-02-2009	931.8	3.16%	YES
Jul-07-2010	1060.3	3.13%	
May-18-2009	909.7	3.04%	
Dec-20-2011	1241.3	2.98%	

For the ASX All Ordinaries index, nine of the ten worst days and fifteen of the twenty worst days occurred during the 2008 bear market.

Iain wanted to race ahead. "Quickly," he said, "the suspense is killing me, when did the best days occur?"

He may even have suspected the outcome. Table 7-3 shows the best days for the S&P500.

For the S&P500, ten of the ten best days and sixteen of the twenty best days over the same ten-year period occurred during, you guessed it, the 2008 bear market!

And it wasn't that much different for the ASX All Ordinaries index (XAO), as shown in Table 7-4, where nine of the ten best days and seventeen of the twenty best days occurred during the 2008 bear market!

"This is the clincher that busts the 'time in the market only' myth propagated in this flyer," I said. "Let me break it down further. Follow these few trading days over a single month during the ten-year period covered in the flyer."

Table 7-4

Date	XAO Close	% Move	2008 Bear?
Nov-25-2008	3575.411	5.51%	YES
Oct-13-2008	4141.9	5.14%	YES
Jan-25-2008	5886.258	5.00%	YES
Nov-03-2008	4172.967	4.78%	YES
Aug-20-2007	5926.456	4.52%	
Sep-22-2008	5050.139	4.33%	YES
Jan-23-2008	5445.637	4.28%	YES
Oct-14-2008	4311.543	4.10%	YES
Nov-28-2008	3672.668	4.10%	YES
Sep-19-2008	4840.723	4.06%	YES
Oct-30-2008	3957.332	3.98%	YES
Oct-01-2008	4814.491	3.96%	YES
Oct-20-2008	4098.735	3.90%	YES
Oct-21-2008	4251.367	3.72%	YES
Dec-08-2008	3553.845	3.70%	YES
Mar-19-2008	5349.245	3.59%	YES
Sep-08-2008	5126.296	3.57%	YES
Oct-06-2011	4132.129	3.50%	
Sep-27-2011	4063.473	3.46%	
Mar-25-2008	5355.702	3.34%	YES
Mar-13-2009	3294.685	3.27%	YES
Jul-21-2008	5075.418	3.26%	YES
Feb-01-2008	5882.306	3.25%	YES
Jul-14-2009	3858.774	3.23%	
Aug-24-2009	4434.186	2.98%	
Jan-24-2008	5605.759	2.94%	YES
Mar-17-2009	3393.353	2.91%	YES
Apr-21-2008	5664.238	2.91%	YES
May-04-2009	3846.018	2.89%	
Nov-05-2008	4287.319	2.82%	YES
Jan-27-2009	3392.31	2.79%	YES
Aug-06-2008	5018.051	2.79%	YES
Aug-10-2011	4207.354	2.70%	
Apr-02-2009	3622.156	2.69%	YES
Oct-24-2011	4313.644	2.62%	
Nov-30-2009	4715.481	2.57%	
Jul-02-2013	4810.252	2.57%	
Aug-15-2011	4346.784	2.57%	
May-10-2010	4622.182	2.55%	
Aug-23-2007	6149.747	2.54%	

- September 29, 2008, the S&P500's third **worst day** over the ten-year period, down -8.81%.
- September 30, the next day, the eighth **best day** occurred, up 5.42%.
- October 2, two days later, the twenty-fifth **worst day** occurred, down -4.03%.

- October 6, two trading days later, the twenty-seventh **worst day** occurred, down -3.85%.
- October 7, the next day, the ninth **worst day** occurred, down -5.74%.
- October 9, two days later, the fourth **worst day** occurred, down -7.62%.
- October 13, two trading days later, the **best day** occurred, up 11.58%.
- October 15, two days later, the **worst day** occurred, down -9.03%.
- October 16, the next day, the seventeenth **best day** occurred, up 4.25%.
- October 20, two trading days later, the tenth **best day** occurred, up 4.77%
- October 22, two days later, the eighth **worst day** occurred, down -6.1%.
- October 28, four trading days later, the second **best day** occurred, up 10.79%

I summarized, "Note that during the entire ten-year period *the two biggest single day moves of more than 10% were UP days, not down days, and they occurred in the worst month over the ten years where the total move for the month was -22.48%!*"

I explained, "This shows unequivocally that the best and the worst days occur in the *same market conditions* and in very close proximity to each other. Meaning that *it is almost impossible to miss ONLY the best days without also missing most of the worst days; if you tried to time the market.*"

I continued, "And *missing BOTH the best and worst days would have a better outcome than staying in the market for all the best and worst days!* Why don't active mutual funds tell us this?"

"In reality, the opposite is true to what is suggested will happen if an investor missed the ten best days through attempting to time the market. Returns would actually improve by missing the ten best days; because an investor would also miss the worst days! And when both are missed the outcome is better than if both are not missed!"

Myth destroyed. Debunked.

Iain exclaimed, "This makes an excellent case for doing the exact opposite to what the example flyer says. An investor should, in fact, try to time the market rather than be in the market all the time through all market conditions!"

"Correct," I said, "Active mutual funds appear to withhold the worst days' data from their marketing material, which some might argue can mislead or confuse investors, or are they incapable of doing the simple research that I have done in this exercise."

Active mutual funds must surely have this same data given the size of their research teams. More disturbing is that the same teams probably conduct sophisticated research to select stocks for their active mutual funds. Or is it simply the marketing departments, funded by investors' fees, which choose to omit the worst days' data so that they can push the 'time in the market' message in their favor?

I said to Iain, "Remember this profound stock market principle: ***The most important task for active investors that want to improve returns in any investing timeframe is to ensure that they miss the worst days in the market.***"

I continued, "In fact, the data shows that if investors specifically ***target to miss the best days,*** they will actually achieve their goal of missing the worst days and improve their returns quite dramatically."

To emphasize and summarize this discussion, active mutual funds say that investors must ensure they do not miss the best days. In fact, the target action for investors is to do the exact opposite, to do all that they can to **ENSURE THAT THEY DO MISS THE BEST DAYS**, meaning that they will also then miss the worst days and be far better off.

Yet another paradox in the stock market – there are many showing that the truth can often be the exact opposite of common belief and what many commentators say.

As at the date of publication, the following web page has a calculator that shows graphically the equity curve impact of missing the BEST days.

http://www.fidelity.com.au/tools/investment-tools1/timing-the-mark/

Of course, it only removes the BEST days and leaves in the WORST days.

As you now appreciate, to provide a complete picture, this calculation should remove BOTH the best and worst days to represent the data accurately. I have shown that missing one without missing the other is virtually impossible as they are so close together. The web page mentions this proximity on their website *but doesn't include the calculations of missing the worst days.* If it did, we now know that it would show a better result than it currently shows on the web page.

I have used this flyer as an example of the type of marketing messages that everyday investors should be wary of across the financial industry.

What else do all types of active mutual funds know and withhold from their fee-paying customers?

BEWARE THE SAMPLE OF ONE

"What do you mean by beware the sample of one?" asked Iain.

"A researcher needs to demonstrate a hypothesis with more than just a sample of one or two to support it. In the October 2008 sample, the data is quite clear, but we need to use a few more periods to be certain this is a market principle," I explained.

"Let's look at another completely different period with different economic conditions. How about the period 1981 to 1991? This period was mostly during a secular[2] bull market that started in October 1982 whereas 2008 was during a secular bear market."

We spent a few minutes accessing the data for this period from Yahoo Finance and did the necessary spreadsheets to calculate the daily moves for the period and then sorted them first from smallest to largest to get the worst days, and then from largest to smallest to get the best days. We then recorded a period that included the first and second best and worst days. Sure enough, during the period surrounding these days, there were plenty of top forty best and worst days.

- September 22, 1987, the fifteenth best day for the S&P500 over this period, up 2.89%.
- October 6, ten trading days later, the nineteenth worst day occurred, down −2.7%.
- October 14, six trading days later, the fifteenth worst day occurred, down −2.95%.
- October 15, the next day, the twenty-ninth worst day occurred, down -2.34%.
- October 16, the next day, the fifth **worst day** occurred, down -5.16%.
- October 19, the next trading day, the **worst day** occurred, down -20.47%.
- October 20, the next day, the second **best day** occurred, up 5.33%.
- October 21, the next day, the **best day** occurred, up 9.1%.

---

2   'Secular' in this context means 'long term' over many years, typically greater than ten years.

- October 22, the next day, the tenth **worst day** occurred, down -3.92%.
- October 26, two trading days later, the second **worst day** occurred, down -8.28%.
- October 27, the next day, the thirty-fourth best day occurred, up 2.44%.
- October 29, the next day, the third **best day** occurred, up 4.93%.
- October 30, the next day, the sixteenth best day occurred, up 2.87%.

"What was the total move for the month of October in 1987?" asked Iain.

"*Down -21.76% for the month. And* **note that the three best days of the entire ten-year period occurred within ten calendar days of the worst day** *in that entire period of ten years, a -20.47% down day,* **all in the same month** *of October 1987. In fact,* **the two best days of the whole period of ten years were the next two trading days straight after this worst day of -20.47%!**"

"Convinced now?" I asked.

"Yes," said Iain. "I understand that the best way to achieve improved returns in the market is not 'time in the market,' potentially it is to 'time the market.' And that *'time in the market' when the best days occur is indeed a gigantic myth because that forces the investor also to be in when the worst days occur and that makes returns worse, not better.*"

"Great explanation. Do you still want to be in the market for the best ten days as active mutual funds say that you should be?" I asked.

Iain smiled, "But how do I time the market?" he asked.

"Patience," I said, "you are not ready for that yet. I have to take you through a few more steps of discovery before you're ready for that part of the journey."

IS THERE AN EASIER WAY TO SPOT THESE PERIODS?

Once Iain had accepted that the revelations on timing were to come, he expanded on his question, "Is there a way that I can look at a ten-year period on a single page and determine when these periods occur?"

"Of course, there is," I said. "It's simple if you have an inexpensive technical analysis software tool, such as Beyond Charts, which I use (www.beyondcharts.com). Hundreds of thousands of individual DIY investors use tools such as this to analyze the financial markets. There is a calculation called Average True Range, which measures the range of price movement from one day to the next and then averages it over a selected number of days. I typically use a fifteen-day average and divide it by the 'price' of the index to get a percent volatility result. Chart 7-1 shows the percent volatility in the lower graph for the ten-year period from 1981 to 1991 for the S&P500."

Chart 7-1 [Printed with permission from Beyond Charts]

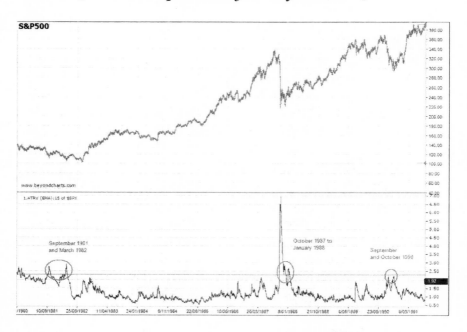

I explained, "The ellipses show the high volatility periods where the worst and best days' cluster, viz. September 1981, March 1982, October 1987 to January 1988 and September and October 1990. Typically, high volatility periods will be grouped at market troughs during and after a decline in the market, but not always."

I continued, "Chart 7-2 shows the S&P500 and its volatility in the lower graph over the ten-year period from 2004 to 2014. Note the October 2008 period that we researched earlier."

Chart 7-2 [Printed with permission from Beyond Charts]

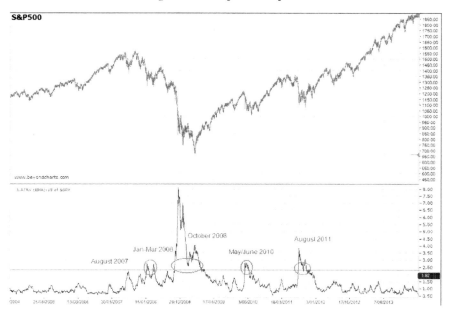

"Even without a trained eye, it is simple to spot these periods with the benefit of hindsight. The real challenge to be able to avoid these periods *before* they occur, or as the market enters a period of higher than usual volatility."

"Some might call this predicting. In fact, it has nothing to do with predicting, it has to do with understanding and focusing on probabilities, which I will show you."

"And a simple process can be used to avoid most of these periods before and as they occur. For example, here is a sneak preview of timing on the S&P500 index to whet your appetite."

I showed Iain Chart 7-3 of the S&P500 from March 2007 to March 2009. I explained that the periods where the red stepped timing line is *below* the 'price' of the S&P500 were periods to be in the market; and periods when the red stepped timing line was above the 'price' of the S&P500, were periods to be out of the market.

The beginning and end of each of the periods to be in the market are signaled with a buy and a sell signal, respectively. Meaning that there is always an objective, unambiguous alert to exit the market before the market really starts falling with increasing volatility. Note that the exit signal does not occur at the peak of a market rise but after the market has already rolled over and started falling.

Likewise, an alert to re-enter the market occurs near the trough of a decline but after the market has started rising.

Chart 7-3 [Printed with permission from Beyond Charts]

Notice that the entire period in October 2008 when the best and worst days occurred, an everyday investor using simple timing such as this would have been out of the stock market and 100% in cash. This is the benefit of longer term timing which is very different to the sort of timing that active mutual funds infer everyday investors might try to do – to time the market on a day by day basis.

A FURTHER FLAW IN ACTIVE MUTUAL FUNDS' PROPAGANDA

Do mutual funds buy, hold and never sell the stocks that they include in their active funds, or do they time the market?

I contend that the moment that any approach or method sells a stock and buys another, timing is taking place. Some criteria will be used to determine what to buy and sell, and when.

Apparently, the very thing that active mutual funds say you mustn't do, they actually do themselves. Wait! I thought that their catchcry to everyday investors is 'time in the market, not timing the market.'

Why is it that other professions promote timing and try to use it the best that they can? But the financial industry promotes the opposite – that investors can't time the market, and shouldn't even attempt it.

In many other walks of life, the better the timing, the better the outcome. In any sport or stand-up comedy or storytelling or medicine, achieving great timing is crucial for maximum accomplishment.

But we are all told that somehow this doesn't apply in the financial world. The gurus of Wall Street want you to go to them to do the timing. They insist you can only achieve high returns through *their* timing? The rest of us should only heed their relentless misrepresentation.

I know that timing works, but I also know that timing can burden investors with unnecessary risk. The problem that I have with the active mutual funds spreading the myth that timing can't be done is simple. Firstly, it can be done. Secondly, the reason *they* say it can't be done is:

"It is very, very difficult to predict when is the best time to enter or exit the market. The speed at which markets react to news means stock prices have already absorbed the impact of new developments. When markets turn, they turn quickly.

Those trying to time their entry and exit may actually miss the bounce."

While this statement is true, stating that everyday investors in large numbers will attempt this with their long-term retirement investments is not necessarily true.

The reason that it can be dangerous has a lot more to do with things that are in the control of the investor, such as:

- The preparation involved in creating an Investment Plan.
- The discipline and consistency to adhere to the plan regardless of what the market is doing.
- The basic psychology needed to be consistent and objective over the long term in the face of random short-term volatility that cannot be foreseen by anyone.

The introduction paragraphs in the flyer make more sense that anything else in it:

"Understandably, it can be difficult to invest with confidence while markets are volatile. However, you should not let short-term market movements alter your investment discipline.

On the contrary, keeping calm and adopting a consistent and disciplined investment approach could help you ride out volatility."

Iain said, "But what does all this mean? Even a large mutual fund makes confusing statements like this on a flyer. I just want to know what to do, and I'll do it."

"All will be revealed soon. Have patience."

"Great," he said, "I had thought that this was going to be easy."

"Nothing worthwhile is easy when you first start, but it will become simple to understand and simple to execute when you see it alongside other investing alternatives, especially those followed by uninformed investors. In fact, I'll leave you with an Investment Plan that maps out exactly what to do that will provide returns far better than active mutual funds of all kinds over time and will take you less time to follow and execute than you spend brushing your teeth each week."

LAST WORD

- Your aim should not be to ensure that your money is in the market for the best days; your aim should be the exact opposite.
- You want to be out of the market for the best days which will ensure that you also miss the worst days. Missing the best and worst days has a far greater positive impact on your returns than not missing any days.
- **"In reality, the opposite is true to what is suggested will happen if an investor missed the ten best days through attempting to time the market. Returns would actually improve by missing the ten best days; because an investor would also miss the worst days! And when both are missed the outcome is better than if both are not missed!"**
- The active mutual funds industry can and does propagate incomplete information, and average investors should be wary of this.
- Have a "What if...?" curiosity about investing concepts. Be prepared to do your own research to dispel or accept the theories.

A DIY INVESTOR'S STORY

[Author's note: Many clients provide positive feedback to Share Wealth Systems for the continuous systems research that we conduct and the products and services that we offer. This feedback humbles us but we are also grateful for it and for our customers. I felt that it would be remiss of me not to include some of our clients' investing journeys to give you an insight into other people's real experiences.]

An interest in growing my wealth through stocks and instruments that would perform better than leaving money in the bank or mutual funds is what led me to start doing my own investing. I was fortunate to have sold a very successful business and 'retired' from full-time nine-to-five work decades earlier than most.

I invested in the stock market, based on tips from broker-dealers and friends. I tried using professional options [Exchange Traded Options] traders that would manage a portfolio for me. I hired the services of a financial planner who put me into an assortment of managed investment products.

I had a huge emotional roller coaster ride investing in this way. I felt great and knowledgeable when performance was good and felt dull and out of control when the performance of my investments deteriorated.

I became very disillusioned with my own investment choices in the stock market and my lack of control over when and why I would either be successful or lose money. When I made money I would sometimes feel great, but I was still confused as to whether I had made any contribution or was just lucky this time.

Similarly, I became very disillusioned with the managed investment products in which my advisor invested my money. There seemed to be such a lack of nimbleness that would enable me to achieve better performance, and then, when first the tech crash happened in the year 2000 and then later crashes, my entire investments were just about wiped out.

The significant losses with an options trader and losses in the tech crash motivated me to make a determined effort to find a way that I could take control of my investment activities.

I attended investment seminars, read heaps of books and looked at lots of systems that would provide me with a framework for investing with the following elements:

- *Formalized processes that could be tested and would remove my emotions from decision-making.*
- *The ability to move in and out of the market, in total, as required.*
- *The capacity to control the amount of risk to which I will expose my capital.*
- *The ability to directly manage my own affairs.*
- *The capacity to measure my performance against an independent benchmark.*
- *Take control over my investments*
- *Minimize my costs.*
- *Manage my own Superannuation Fund [retirement nest egg such as an IRA or 401(k)].*

I bought several different systems, but it was not until a friend suggested that I look at Share Wealth Systems in the early 2000s that I finally saw in a product and a company that had most of the elements I wanted.

The Share Wealth Systems investing methods and organization provided a framework that was in harmony with how I thought and what I needed. It took away emotional and judgmental decisions. It enabled me to organize and structure my investments on a portfolio basis.

I learned how to think at the portfolio level, not only at the individual stock level.

I was also introduced to other markets and instruments, such as ETFs, and provided systems for these instruments.

I embarked on this investment journey over a decade and a half ago. I was able to transform a hobby into a business.

It still is a very rewarding activity for me; I can be in control at the macro level of all my investments.

KA

CHAPTER 8

Approaches to Utilize in the Stock Market

"If you don't know where you are going, you'll end up someplace else."

YOGI BERRA

"If the stock market is what it is going to be, what approach to stock investing should I use? I have heard of so many strategies. Where should I start?" asked Iain.

I responded, "I'll preface this session by saying that I will explain some stock market approaches for DIY investors and briefly explain their relevance to investing for retirement. I would like you to understand how realistic and practical, or not, these approaches are for everyday investors focused on sustained long-term investing in their busy lives."

"In the broad sense, active mutual funds can be viewed as a stock market approach. We have already dissected them and, clearly, we are looking for an alternative to investing in active mutual funds."

"I will discuss some instruments that are used in various investing strategies in the stock market so that you become aware of the scope of available methods. However, it is suggested that retirement capital is not used to invest with these strategies. I will suggest why, even though they are valid strategies to meet other investing objectives."

151

I continued, "Retirement investing requires a balance between return and risk to meet your retirement investing goals. This balance necessitates each investor to adopt and accept risk management techniques to meet the stated aims of an Investment Plan. We'll discuss the Investment Plan in due course."

"When investing for retirement we want to instill a strategy that doesn't take up much time, is preferably not leveraged and is a viable, practical and fruitful way to solve the problem of growing a retirement nest egg over the long term. Everyday investors require ***strategies that can be followed consistently for twenty to forty years, or even longer, to grow capital*** in a way that doesn't impact an everyday person's chosen lifestyle."

"Almost any strategy could be subjectively justified to meet these criteria, but in reality, only a minuscule number of investors working in a full-time job would be able to execute strategies successfully for decades with instruments that are leveraged or demand vigilance multiple times a day and frequent actions week in and week out."

"To help us determine whether any particular strategy is relevant to solving the retirement investing equation an everyday investor with a full-time job should ask this question: ***would I invest all, or a significant portion, of my retirement savings using strategies with leveraged instruments that require lots of vigilance and activity?***"

"The answer to this all-important question is an emphatic NO!"

I continued, "I understand that instruments which I suggest shouldn't be used for long-term nest egg investing many investors may use for short-term trading endeavors. However, the question then begs what action they are taking with their long-term nest egg investing. Hopefully it is not parked off out-or-mind in a Balanced Fund or Target Date fund under-performing the stock market benchmark while they ***trade*** with much smaller sums of money."

"That would be silly when the more important gains and protections should be made with their larger nest egg," agreed Iain.

In the interests of brevity of what is supportive background information to my main messages, I will précis and summarize the material for this session. You can follow up this summary in a more detailed Chapter 8 on the Resources page of the website for this book: www.blueprinttowealth.com.

The topics covered in the detailed Chapter 8 on my website cover:

- Investing Instruments to Avoid
- Stock Market Approaches
  - ◊ Long-term Buy-and-Hold
    - · Case Study Lehman Brothers
    - · Long-term Buy-and-Hold Volatility
  - ◊ Long-term Active Investing
    - · Fundamental Analysis and Technical Analysis
  - ◊ Medium-term Active Investing
  - ◊ Short-term Trading
  - ◊ Index Investing

INVESTING INSTRUMENTS TO AVOID

There is a vast array of investing approaches available, typically based on various investing instruments such as:

- Options,
- Futures,
- Forex,
- Spread betting, and
- Contracts for Difference, or CFDs.

"Valid trading strategies are available with all these instruments, however, the everyday investor shouldn't use them when investing for retirement. I use the word 'trading' because an ordinary investor would not be 'investing' when using these instruments."

"For example with stock options, an approach such as writing covered calls is a good strategy; potentially for generating income, but not as a core growth retirement investing strategy."

"All of these instruments have leverage built into their structure. Hence they are high risk and mainly lend themselves to short-term strategies with positions that are open from a day to a few weeks. They are time intensive to execute and better suited to generating income that achieving growth."

STOCK MARKET APPROACHES

"There are many timeframes in which stock market investing can occur, ranging from the intraday timing of stock price movement from a few minutes, even seconds, for each trade to using monthly prices and open positions lasting many years. Along with each approach comes a varying degree of difficulty, time requirement, knowledge, skill, temperament, mindset, attitude and capital requirement. A 'trade' is the round trip of entering a positon and then closing that same position."

"Why would I need to know about these different approaches?" asked Iain.

"You wouldn't if you accept the research that has been done by SPIVA Scorecard and merely implement an approach that mimics an index to achieve performance similar to a Total Return index. Thereby outperforming around 85% of all active equities funds over five years, including 401(k) providers and all types of balanced funds."

"However you may wish to put in a little extra effort and do better by 1%, 2%, 3%, 4% or even 5% compounded per year than the Total Return indices and in so doing achieve two important objectives:

1. Accumulate an even larger retirement nest egg that, due to the power of compounding, could mean hundreds of thousands of dollars more in savings and thereby potentially eliminate longevity risk and achieve complete financial freedom.
2. Remove the possibility of having your retirement capital exposed to a significant market fall just before or during retirement."

"How do I decide whether to put in a little extra effort and how much is a little extra?" asked Iain.

"Once you establish the process with the core solution that I will provide, the little extra effort shouldn't be more than fifteen minutes a quarter. However, a more active 'Core Satellite' investment approach will require more effort, around an average of fifteen minutes a week. For those that are interested, an even more active approach would require fifteen minutes a day."

LONG-TERM BUY-AND-HOLD

"The first area of stock market investing to discuss is a passive direct stock investing approach rather than 'active investing.' It is the long-term buy-and-hold approach."

"There are many brilliant examples of long-term buy-and-hold businesses. In hindsight, 3M, IBM, and Apple are three such businesses."

I provided some details to Iain showing the following:

- 3M (MMM), up 65,900% or 10.52% compounded per year from February 1950 to the March 2015 peak, excluding dividends.

◊ 3M became a Dow Jones component in August 1976 and is up 2,167% since, or 8.43% compounded per year to its peak in March 2015, excluding dividends.

- IBM, up 78,500% or 11.22% compounded per year from its trough in July 1950 to its last peak in March 2013 before writing, excluding dividends.
    ◊ IBM was a Dow Jones component from May 1932 to March 1939 and took a 40-year break before becoming a Dow component again on June 29, 1979. From this date to its peak in March 2013 IBM was up 1,076% or 7.58% compounded per year.
- Apple Inc. (AAPL), up 25,800% or 17.64% compounded per year from its initial listing date in December 1980 to its peak in May 2015, excluding dividends."

I continued, "Investors may have the stated intention to buy-and-hold, which means never sell. But when markets have dramatic downturns, most individual investors don't have the mental stamina to hold onto the stocks as they intended. Many sell most or all of their holdings. They do this when the pain becomes unbearable, not having a strong enough temperament, and that is typically when the market declines -30% to -55%. If they do manage to hold on, it is with many sleepless nights and lots of stress. Fear of losing more is usually the reason that investors battle to continue holding."

"And, of course, having been burnt and scarred mentally by the massive losses they take on the way down, they usually don't buy back in when the market starts rising again, fearing more pain from another potential fall should it occur. This ensures they don't participate in the rise after that, meaning they lock in the loss without ever making it up."

I continued, "In the rather severe bear market of 2008, we saw blue chip banking stocks in the U.S., including Bank of America and Citigroup, falling at least -90%. More than six years later these two are still down -67% and -89%, respectively, from their pre-2008 highs."

"Citigroup was a Dow Jones Industrial Average (DJIA) component before the 2008 bear market; it was dropped from the DJIA index in June 2009."

"Consider if stocks like Lehman Brothers, Freddie Mac, Fannie Mae or Bear Stearns that were delisted went to $0 in your portfolio. Enron was another firm whose share price fell from above $90 to twelve cents over eighteen months in the 2002 bear market before being delisted. So did WorldCom, in the same year. There are many more companies if you care to investigate. And many index constituents in other countries have also dropped out the index and delisted with shareholders losing all their money invested in the individual stock."

"***An index can never fall to a value of zero*** because the index custodians cull such stocks from the index as their market capitalization decreases before they reach $0 and a stock whose market capitalization is increasing replaces them. ***Meaning that indices are biased to increase over the long term.***"

"Wow," said Iain, "that's almost unprincipled!"

"It might appear that way, but that's how things work. We should ensure that we use this to our advantage. This bias is called *'survivorship bias'* where indices are biased towards survivors that continue to prosper relative to the laggards and underperformers that drop out of the index. The DJIA is a price-weighted index but market capitalization indices such as the S&P500 are weighted toward survivors, or, more precisely, against laggards."

CASE STUDY OF LEHMAN BROTHERS

To emulate 'living' through such an experience, I took Iain through the case study of Lehman Brothers. "I'm sure that many buy-and-hold portfolios and many active managed funds, both in the U.S. and elsewhere in the world, had positions in Lehman Brothers, given it was the fourth largest investment bank in the United States."

I started, "Over ten years from February 1997 to February 2007, [Chart 8-3 shows that] Lehman rose over 1000%, or 27% compounded per year, excluding dividends. Over the same period, the S&P500 rose 6.32% compounded per year. Massive outperformance, I'm sure you'll agree."

The rest of this Case Study can be accessed in the detailed Chapter 8 on the Resources page of the book website www.blueprinttowealth.com.

LONG-TERM BUY-AND-HOLD VOLATILITY

"Let's return to Apple, a household name whose stellar long-term growth we looked at earlier, to see how its journey panned out to achieve that brilliant growth of 17.47% compounded per year over many decades."

Chart 8-1 shows that Apple Inc. had eight periods of at least -40% falls in its stock price over thirty-four years:

- -69.4% from December 1980 to July 1982.
- -76.7% from June 1983 to August 1985.
- -57.8% from October 1987 to October 1990.
- -82.2% from April 1991 to December 1997.
- -81.8% from March 2000 to April 2003.
- -40.8% from January 2006 to July 2006.
- -60.8% from December 2007 to January 2009.
- -44% from September 2012 to April 2013.

I showed Iain a long-term semi-logarithmic chart of Apple's performance, highlighting their down periods. (3M and IBM are provided in the detailed Chapter 8 on the Resources webpage.)

Chart 8-1 [Printed with permission from Beyond Charts]

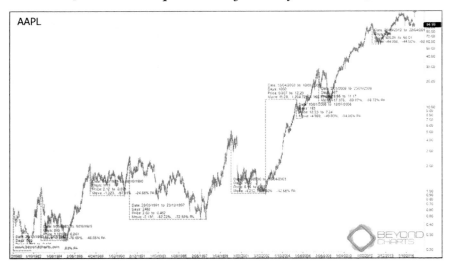

I added, "These stats are for at least -40% falls but if we counted falls of at least -15% there were more than 160 falls across all three stocks in up and down trends and around **100 in up trends only**."

Iain asked, "Apple had two -80% falls close to each other, within just over two years. How does somebody handle that? How much does the stock have to rise to get back to the price it was at before each of the -80% falls?"

"One divided by, one minus 80%, and then subtract one," I replied. "So, one divided by 0.2 equals five, then subtract one, equals four, represented as a percentage equals 400%."

"Did Apple rise by 400% twice within a few years after each of the 80% falls?" Iain asked.

"By more," I said. "By 998% from 47 cents in December 1997 to $5.15 in March 2000! And then by 1200% from 93 cents in April 2003 to $12.23 in January 2006!"

LONG-TERM ACTIVE INVESTING

"Explaining the buy-and-hold approach and how stocks move provides an excellent background to other stock portfolio approaches. The second category of managing a stock portfolio is what I call *long-term active investing.*"

"I haven't questioned what 'long-term' means so far as I have assumed it to be many years. But what do you mean by 'long-term' here?" asked Iain.

"I'm referring to the average hold period for each position in the market from entry to the exit of that position. Average hold periods longer than four months for each position are what I call *long-term active investing*; one to four-month average hold periods are *medium-term active investing*; average hold periods of less than one month I call *short-term trading.*"

"Looking at an example such as Apple, if you were a buy-and-hold investor how do you know that a stock will rise again when it is already -80% down?" asked Iain.

"You don't," I replied. "Lehman Brothers delisted and their shareholders lost their entire investment. If you are using active timing, then your predetermined technical analysis timing criteria will combine to provide you with a call to action to re-enter the stock when its price starts rising again, thereby taking a risk that the pre-tested entry criteria, based on probabilities, might be correct on this occasion. When you do re-enter you predefine the precise maximum risk to take at that time which is the exit that you will act on if the stock falls below that exact maximum-risk price."

"How do you determine the exact timing criteria?" asked Iain.

"With thousands of hours of research," I replied. "This is what we do at Share Wealth Systems in our systems and product development."

"But you still don't know whether the entry and exit will result in profit." said Iain.

"There is no certainty on *each* market entry," I said. "But with well researched precise entry and exit criteria you can determine the existence of an edge and thereby can create certainty over a large sample of trades. Again, more on that later."

"If you do so much research why can't every trade be a winner?" asked Iain.

"My, don't human beings crave certainty in an uncertain world. Look at it this way. There is a risk and reward equation that is continuously running within the markets. There are ***millions of variables, all out of your control and all interacting simultaneously*** within the financial markets. They ***impact each other and each financial instrument by varying degrees of magnitude at any given time. It can take just one of these many variables to affect your position in the market negatively at any given time, but you will never know in advance which variable that might be.*** This is one of the fundamental truisms of financial markets."

I continued, "And these variables don't even have to be in the financial arena to negatively affect your position. It could be a terrorist attack or a natural disaster. That's why one of the guiding principles that I use in my investing is 'anything can happen.' It was one of the key points in the book *Trading in the Zone* by Mark Douglas."

"***Each significant fall in a stock's price starts off being a small decline.*** Objective investors don't fall in love with individual stocks and treat each fall in each stock the same. They subscribe to the belief that 'anything can happen' and manage their investing in a consistent manner."

"My goal for doing the Lehman's case study and of looking at a few stocks' history is to provide a big picture perspective on how stock prices and indices can and do move. What we know from history is that stocks of all shapes and sizes will continue to experience big down periods from time to time for reasons that only become apparent after the fact. What we don't know in advance is what will cause these declines in any given situation, how big the declines will be and how long each down period will last."

I summarized, "That's why we have to ***create objective and consistent risk management processes that minimize the financial damage*** that comes from these negative periods in the market. While simultaneously taking risk to generate returns that outperform inflation, taxes, and other asset classes to meet our investing mission, goals, and objectives."

"However, hundreds of stocks also experience massive rises and hence present tremendous opportunities that are simply not available in other investing asset classes."

FUNDAMENTAL ANALYSIS AND TECHNICAL ANALYSIS

"Fundamental analysis is a method of determining the intrinsic value and strength of a listed stock by researching and analyzing many ratios from the current and historical Balance Sheets and Profit & Loss Statements of the stock. Based on this method an analyst will determine whether the current stock price of a listed company is under or overvalued compared to the company's intrinsic value."

I added, "Investors can also apply fundamental analysis to commodities and Forex, but would analyze a different set of fundamental data in these instances. Gold stocks require analysis of different ratios to industrial or financial stocks."

"Technical analysis, also called charting, is a method of determining what the probability is of the current stock price or security such as a commodity, rising or falling based on its recent and long-term price and volume movements. Patterns in price, volume and volatility form on charts, showing trends and support and resistance zones. These patterns allow the analyst to form a view on the probability of the direction of the security's price continuing or changing."

A more detailed insight into these two analyses techniques is provided in the detailed Chapter 8 on the Resources webpage of the book's website: www.blueprinttowealth.com.

MEDIUM-TERM ACTIVE INVESTING

"The next approach is *medium-term active investing* of a stock portfolio in which you could be managing between seven and twenty-five open positions."

Medium-term active investing requires more effort and time than longer term active investing, around one to two hours a week after you've mastered the core competencies. Daily attention is needed to manage an active medium-term portfolio."

"Why do people even embark on a medium-term active investing approach?" asked Iain.

"Because medium-term active investing turns over the same capital more often and hence achieves more compounding. Compounding is the holy grail of investing. Medium-term active investing compounding produces growth more quickly than long-term active investing. And this is where, with today's lower transaction costs, people who can execute medium-term active investing well, with method and mindset, can be very profitable and grow their capital at a much faster rate over the long term."

"I'll leave medium-term active investing alone for the time being," Iain said cautiously.

"That's exactly what I recommend you do, given your situation," I concluded.

[Note: Readers that are interested in medium-term active investing can refer to the Appendices in this book on more active investing strategies.]

SHORT-TERM TRADING

"The last area of stock market approaches that we will discuss is *short-term trading*. Note that I use the word 'trading' and not 'active investment' with short-term strategies. Short-term trading requires at least one to a few hours a day, and even sharper mental skills to consistently, objectively and successfully make profits. Gaining the necessary skills can take many years, and in fact, maybe even decades, depending on the level of activity and fervor with which you approach short-term trading."

"Short-term traders typically start moving towards using leverage, or margin, and margin instruments such as futures, Forex, CFDs and shorting. Everything that I said about the skills required for medium-term active investing grows exponentially the shorter the term of your trading, leading even into intraday trading."

I concluded, "All of these approaches work depending on the quality of research and criteria used to determine the timing of entry and exit. They also depend greatly on successfully applying two areas of active investing that I haven't even mentioned in any detail yet—risk management and trade size for each position opened in the market, also called money management or position sizing. Both of these are hugely important especially for medium-term and short-term active trading."

"My business, Share Wealth Systems, and I have invested heavily in researching and compiling robust risk and money management rules for medium-term active investing. We don't provide short-term trading strategies."

I continued, "These more active approaches are dependent ultimately on the time you have available, your skills and how much preparation you've done in creating or finding a method and then being able to repeatedly execute that strategy consistently and objectively."

"Now, with all of the instruments and active investing stock picking approaches out of the way, I'm going to get to the crux of the book; index investing."

INDEX INVESTING

"To put your mind at ease after covering these active approaches, which may appear to be rather onerous, I repeat, none of it is necessary to be able to match the market indices. And hence beat around 85% of active mutual funds over six years and more, and nearly all active mutual funds over longer investing horizons. The approach that we are going to cover now is the start of what we'll be discussing in our sessions from now on."

An index investing approach does not require the intense time require-ments or mental skills necessary with the more active strategies. All everyday investors should build the backbone of their retirement investing portfolios using index investing. Index investing should become the core component.

"Let's start by looking at what an index is. An index comprises a subset of stocks listed on a particular stock exchange that is deemed to be repre-sentative of how that whole stock exchange is performing."

I continued, "Index custodians calculate a stock market index by selecting a limited number of stocks whose total number is a subset of all the stocks listed on that stock exchange. They call these listed companies 'index constituents.' An index can consist of twenty to 3000 constituents. An index is typically used to provide an objective measurement of how the overall market is doing and, therefore, is a benchmark against which investors can compare the performance of active mutual funds, individual stocks and their portfolios."

"Like the S&P500, S&P MidCap 400, Dow Jones Industrial Average or NASDAQ 100," volunteered Iain.

I responded, "It's important to know that index custodians do not use a buy-and-hold approach in compiling, calculating and maintaining which stocks are constituents in a stock market index."

"Why is that important?" asked Iain.

"If the index custodians used a buy-and-hold approach, then every single stock that had ever been a constituent in an index would remain in the value calculation of the index, even those that are no longer listed or have fallen out of favor over the years."

An index may be made up of, say, the top 500 stocks. Broadly speaking, if one or a few of these stocks perform poorly over time and are 'punished' by investors selling them, their price and market capitalization will fall. If the capitalization falls far enough, it could fall below that of a stock outside the top 500. When this happens, they will change places.

"As we have discussed, this is called *'survivorship bias'* and gives stock market indices a long-term upward bias," I confirmed. "But over the long term, it would be possible for an index to have a downward bias if every past constituent was calculated into an index on a buy-and-hold basis (which it isn't). At the very best that index would probably not have risen at the same rate that it has and hence be below the current level of the S&P500."

"So the S&P500 is made up of the five hundred stocks that have the highest market capitalizations?" asked Iain.

"Essentially yes," I responded. "It's important to note that the removal and addition of stocks is not based on an intrinsic value of the listed company even though that may have played a role in the company's market capitalization rising."

"So it is based on the price movement of the stock, not fundamental analysis?" said Iain.

"Mostly yes," I replied. "And because businesses that are growing concerns that provide products and services make up an index, over the long term there is an upward bias in indices from the organic growth of growing populations and inflation."

Iain added, "And when you combine this with our other discussions about the SPIVA Scorecard, indices beat just about every active mutual fund over six years or more. *So why not just find a way to buy the index?*"

"Exactly," I said. "You've got it. Index investing is a bone fide simple alternative to selecting stocks in a portfolio or, more importantly, to investing in active mutual funds of any kind."

"Remember I asked you in an earlier session what is the most well-known and proven investment strategy available?"

"Yes," said Iain, "and the answer was the S&P500 index."

"Correct," I said. "This was recognized by a select few in the early 1970s and marked the start of index investing with index mutual funds. Their charter was to track an index, such as the S&P500 index, as closely as possible, to match the index, not to outperform it like active mutual funds try to do. A pioneer of index mutual funds was the founder of Vanguard, John Bogle, whom I have quoted a few times now."

I continued, "Then in the early 1990s, the concept of listing an index mutual fund on the stock exchange came to fruition. Rather than having to complete a prospectus and post it with money to an index mutual fund manager, the actual fund was listed on the stock exchange, meaning that anyone could invest in the index fund, in the same way as a stock is bought and sold on the stock market. These funds were named Exchange Traded Funds, or ETFs."

"An index ETF is an index mutual fund that is listed on the stock exchange."

"Is it that simple?" asked Iain.

"It certainly is. But be careful—there are many other ETFs listed on the stock exchange that are effectively boutique active mutual funds that don't try to track an index, they still try to outperform the indices. They are called 'active ETFs.' View these in the same way as those active mutual funds that the SPIVA˚ Scorecard measures against the indices and that underperform the indices over the long term."

"Index investing is one approach that I'm going to suggest you use. Primarily, we're going to use index investing strategies that can be executed in ten to fifteen minutes a quarter, a month or a week, depending on the strategy. This approach is far less time consuming than an active stock portfolio and way, way less than any of those other strategies that we have spoken of that use options, futures, foreign exchange, spread betting, etc."

"We will not only be able to match the index but outperform the indices that the active mutual funds cannot match, let alone beat, over the long term. And, we'll take less risk than the active mutual funds, Target Date funds, and Balanced Funds."

"We are going to discuss a few simple strategies that range *from purely buying and holding an index* and thereby nearly matching what an index achieves—such as the S&P500, S&P400 or S&P600—to *using timing to avoid sitting through steep bear markets. This way you can get ahead of the index by a substantial percentage each time that a major bear market occurs.*"

Iain replied, "I can see the benefits of buy-and-hold index investing, but I get the feeling that the way to make significant and lasting effects is to use timing if it only takes a few minutes each week to ensure that an investor misses a major portion of any declining market period."

"Correct," I said.

Last Word

- When considering a potential investing strategy for retirement, always ask, *"Would I invest all or most of my retirement monies with this method?"*
- If you are trading with leveraged instruments suited to time-intensive short-term trading, what strategies are you using for your more important long-term retirement nest egg?
- Index investing is a valid method for growing a retirement nest egg.
    ◊ Exchange Traded Funds (ETFs) are the easiest and most cost-effective way of deploying index investing.
    ◊ ETFs should be a core component of every investor's retirement nest egg.

CHAPTER 9

Accessing the Indices

"The role of genius is not to complicate the simple,
but to simplify the complicated."

CRISS JAMI, AUTHOR, AND SINGER.

One of the major deterrents of the stock market to the uninitiated is its apparent complexity. Another is its random short-term volatility. And another is the potential for significant percentage declines. These play havoc with the minds of investors who invest directly in the market and are the leading causes of the knee-jerk emotional reactions that can wreck an investor's long-term plan.

When investing in individual stocks, there is no guarantee that a stock will return to the price it was before a sharp, deep fall. There is a very high probability of a declining mainstream index returning to its previous high 'price'; this is not the case for an individual stock which may never do so.

Therefore, if you have invested for the long term in an index ETF (Exchange Traded Fund), then the risk of your investment never returning to its former price is all but removed. Especially if you do not need to sell; in which case there is no need to concern yourself at all about random short-term volatility.

*"The investor's best answer to short-term market riskiness is to
ignore the interim fluctuations and be a long-term investor."*

CHARLES D ELLIS[1]

Achieving what Charles Ellis states is far more easily done by accessing
the indices than worrying about the fortunes of individual stocks. I'll add
to Charles Ellis's quote, ".... in an index ETF." While the stock market is not
a simple place, using ETFs does greatly simplify the process of investing in
the stock market; and doing so successfully.

EXCHANGE TRADED FUNDS–ETFS

When index mutual funds were initially created in the early 1970s, many
people scoffed, wondering back then why any mutual fund would not try
to beat the index.

John Bogle, the founder of Vanguard, must have known something
that nobody else knew! **The SPIVA Scorecard shows quite conclusively
that over time the odds are much higher of an index fund outperforming
an active mutual fund than the other way around.**

Until January 1993, index investing could only be achieved through
index mutual funds, the pioneer of which was John Bogle's Vanguard.
You completed a form, mailed off a check to purchase the units in the
index fund, much as you did for an active mutual fund. The same process
was involved in exiting an index fund, mailing off a form. This is still the
process today.

In January 1993, the first ETF was listed by State Street on the stock
exchange in the U.S. to track the S&P500 index. Its stock exchange symbol
is SPY.

An ETF:

- Is listed on the stock exchange and can be invested in and sold via any
  broker-dealer account just like any listed stock.
- Tracks its underlying index as closely as possible.
- Charges much lower fees than active mutual funds.

Chart 9-1 shows how closely the SPY ETF has tracked the S&P500
since its inception in 1993. Believe it or not, there are two price charts

---

1   Charles D Ellis, "Winning the Loser's Game"

on that graph, one of the SPY ETF and the other of the S&P500 index (blue line).

This matching occurred despite the ETF having an annual Expense Ratio of 0.0945%, being the annual management fees. The ETF annual fee is deducted from dividends before they are distributed and hence doesn't affect the 'price' of the ETF.

The SPY *annual fee is in the order of seven to eight times less than the average annual management fee charged by active mutual funds* in 2015, and around fifteen to twenty times less than back in the mid-1990s.

Chart 9-1 [Printed with permission from Beyond Charts]

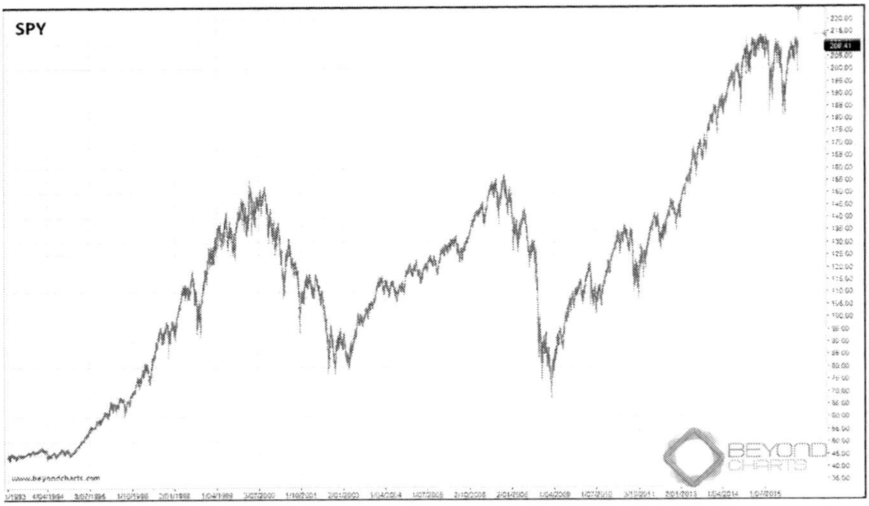

Up to the mid-1990s, the simple strategies provided in this book would not have been possible using index mutual funds, because they are not listed on the stock exchange. The accessibility of ETFs that closely track stock market indices that can be bought and sold in a few seconds on a stock exchange, not over a few days like an index mutual fund, has made the strategies possible.

Meaning that back in 1990 to 1995 investors saving and growing their retirement savings would not have had access to the flexible strategies that we are about to discuss. Back then, trying to execute strategies with an instrument that required days or even a week in which to open and close a position simply would have been less successful.

A word of caution, stick to the mainstream index ETFs when selecting an ETF and proceed with caution with ETFs that may just be masquerading as an index ETF but really are just an active mutual fund listed on the stock exchange. These are called 'active ETFs.'

As at the end of 2015[2]:

- $15.7 trillion was invested in mutual funds in the U.S.
- $1.79 trillion, or 11.4%, was invested in index mutual funds.
- $2.1 trillion was invested in ETFs, that is, index ETFs and active ETFs.

Assuming that half of the $2.1 trillion invested in ETFs was invested in index ETFs, the total for index investing in the U.S. at the end of 2015, ETF and mutual funds, was around $2.84 trillion (1.79 + 1.05). Out of a total of $17.8 trillion (15.7 + 2.1), or 15.96%.

About $2.84 trillion invested in both index mutual funds and index ETFs is certainly a sizeable amount. However, given the enormous amount of media coverage that index investing has received over the last two decades or so and the evidence presented in this book and by many others, including John Bogle and Warren Buffett, there should be much much more invested in index funds, mutual or ETF, than just 16%.

This relatively small amount is evidence that, together with their marketing and the distribution networks of potentially conflicted investment advisors, the *active mutual funds around the world are still winning the minds of unsuspecting investors.*

Furthermore, the *growth of new hires in the U.S., and other countries, selecting Balanced Funds and Target Date funds as their chosen vehicle for investing their 401(k) Plan contributions, or equivalent, is far greater than those electing index funds, mutual or ETF.* Given the evidence stated so far, I find this astonishing. Which is why I have written this book; hopefully, to expose the bleeding obvious as far and wide as possible.

ETFs EXPLAINED

If there was a way that you could invest in the companies that are currently the thirty largest listed companies in the U.S., or twenty largest Australian companies, for the rest of your life, do you think you would seriously consider this? And not just the thirty most major companies today but the thirty largest ... always?

---

2   ICI Fact Book 2016

How can you pick the thirty biggest companies always, without lifting a finger to buy and sell different stocks?

To answer this, it's worth asking these few simple questions to explain the importance of this approach.

Are the thirty biggest companies today the same thirty businesses that were the biggest two decades ago? Will they be the same in twenty years from now?

Do you think the thirty biggest companies are the biggest by accident or do you think they continually strive to reinvent themselves and continue growing?

If they fail to perform, do you think they will get knocked off their perch and another company that's doing better will replace them? That happened to Eastman Kodak, a long time Dow Jones Industrial Average index component, whose core business was decimated by technology changes to which it did not adapt.

If you had $30,000 and invested $1,000 *directly* into each of those thirty companies today, would you simply buy-and-hold onto those same thirty forever? If one of them started to fail and dropped off the list, would you keep holding it, hoping it came back into the list or would you prefer to exit that failing stock and put your money into the growing one that took its place?

That makes sense, doesn't it? The top thirty are always going to be the top thirty. Companies may come and go on the list, but the thirty biggest by market capitalization will always be the top thirty of the pile.

So how do you keep up to date with the thirty biggest and keep your money invested in them, whoever they may be, at all times, now and into the future?

An Exchange Traded Fund (ETF) can play this role that for you. The fund does the investing for you and the goal for this particular ETF is always to have your money in the thirty biggest U.S. companies, or twenty biggest Australian companies, or hundred biggest U.K. companies.

In the United States, DIA is the symbol of an ETF that mimics the index that comprises the thirty largest listed enterprises that make up the Dow Jones Industrial Average index, commonly called "the Dow Jones." In Australia, ILC is an ETF that mimics the index that comprises the twenty biggest listed companies in Australia, the S&P/ASX20 index. In the U.K., ISF is an ETF that tracks the FTSE100 index.

So if one company falls out of the top thirty or twenty in the index, the

DIA ETF or ILC ETF sells that stock and buys the one replacing it in the formal stock exchange index.

In essence by purchasing the one ETF, you are buying a little slice of each of the thirty or twenty biggest stocks, not just the thirty or twenty biggest stocks today, but the thirty or twenty biggest stocks... always.

Investing in an ETF all but eliminates the risk of one or a few listed companies decimating your portfolio because they are delisted or overtaken by a disruptive technology. And it also ensures that you will invest in businesses that are the disrupters when they grow to be one of the largest listed on their particular stock exchange.

Furthermore, you don't have to stick with a single index ETF since there are many index ETFs that each track a specific area of the stock market.

"There is more to how an ETF provider tracks its benchmark index – you can research this–but you don't need to know this if you focus on the mainstream index tracking ETFs only, and exclude all the other active ETFs," I said.

"That makes so much sense to me," said Iain. "You've already shown me by how much the S&P500 Equal Weight Total Return and S&P MidCap 400 Total Return indices smash the active Balanced Funds and Target Date funds over the long term. And the SPIVA˙ Scorecard shows that stock market indices outperform active equity mutual funds over six years and more."

RETURNS ON OFFER FROM STOCK INDICES

Table 9-1 shows the five to thirty year compounded annual returns from some mainstream U.S. indices. The consistent performers over all periods are the following:

- S&P MidCap 400 Index and its Total Return index.
- S&P500 Equal Weight index and its Total Return index.
- NASDAQ 100 and its Total Return index.
- Health Indices led by the NASDAQ Biotech Index. Many health indices such as the S&P500 Managed Health Care Index have done well over the periods examined.
- The S&P600 Small-cap index.

Table 9-1 *

Index	Index Name	Jun 30 2010 5 Yrs	Jun 30 2005 10 Yrs	Jun 30 2000 15 Yrs	Jun 30 1995 20 Yrs	Jun 29 1990 25 Yrs	Jun 28 1985 30 Yrs
$SPX	S&P500	14.89%	5.65%	2.36%	6.88%	7.26%	8.24%
$SPXTR	**S&P500 Total Return**	**17.34%**	**7.89%**	**4.36%**	**8.91%**	**9.54%**	**10.29%**
$SPXEW	S&P500 Equal Weight	16.20%	7.63%	7.29%	8.98%	9.33%	10.09%
$SPXEWTR	**S&P500 Equal Wght Tot Ret**	**18.42%**	**9.63%**	**9.18%**	**10.93%**	**11.48%**	12.04%
$NDX	NASDAQ 100	20.38%	11.40%	1.04%	11.07%	12.36%	12.83%
$NDXTR	**NASDAQ 100 Total Return**	**21.81%**	**12.41%**	1.59%	11.62%	12.91%	13.38%
$W5000	Wilshire 5000	15.08%	6.28%	3.20%	7.29%	7.69%	8.34%
$MID	S&P400 Mid Cap	16.11%	8.17%	7.88%	10.68%	11.03%	11.31%
$MIDTR	**S&P400 Mid Cap Total Ret**	**17.82%**	**9.74%**	9.08%	11.88%	12.23%	12.51%
$SML	S&P600 Small Cap	17.00%	8.00%	8.53%	9.97%		
$SMLTR	**S&P600 Small Cap Total Ret**	**18.44%**	**9.28%**	9.53%	10.97%		
$IXBT	NASDAQ Biotech Index	37.03%	18.80%	8.01%	15.91%		
$SPXA	S&P500 Health Care	21.38%	9.12%	5.22%	10.32%	9.95%	
$SPXATR	**S&P500 Health Care Tot Ret**	**23.84%**	**11.27%**	**7.08%**	**12.19%**	11.45%	

* *The dotted outlined numbers for the Total Return indices are computed using an assumed conservative differential from previous years' dividend yields or computed from an associated ETF.*

Not all indices are shown here, but these are the best performing indices over the long term that are tracked by mature index ETFs. In the future, there will be many more Industry Group ETFs that will mature as their liquidity increases and more than a few years of historical data is compiled. Their relative performance will provide additional research data for researchers and investors such as myself.

I have used the Total Return indices as comparative benchmarks against active mutual funds–such as active equities mutual funds, Balanced Funds, and Target Date funds. Total Return indices include the reinvestment of dividends.

"Total Return indices to consider for your investments that perform better than the S&P500 Total Return index include:

1. The S&P500 Equal Weight Total Return index, $SPXEWTR. This index consistently achieves at least more than 1%, sometimes nearly 2%, compounded per year better than the S&P500 Total

Return index, and as much as 4.82% compounded annually, in the **15 Years** column in Table 9-1.

2. The S&P MidCap 400 Total Return index, $MIDTR, which achieves at least 2% compounded per year better than the S&P500 Total Return index over most periods.
3. The NASDAQ Biotech index, $IXBT.
4. The NASDAQ100 Total Return index, $NDXTR."

Iain had scanned his eye over the Index Returns Table, "The NASDAQ100 **15 Years** performance doesn't look too good," he said.

"That was due to of the "tech wreck" of 2000 to 2002," I said. "This is where timing can really help. Some indices lend themselves to buying and holding and reinvesting of all dividends and others lend themselves to deploying some simple, efficient timing techniques."

I added, "Chart 9-2 of the indices shows the differences more clearly, excluding dividends and listed in descending order of performance, over twenty years to the end of 2015."

Chart 9-2 *[Printed with permission from Beyond Charts]*

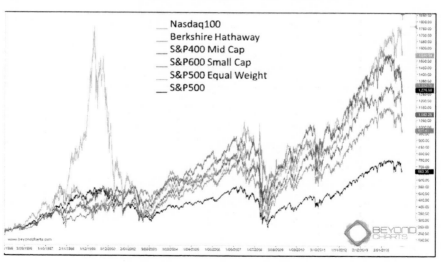

"The S&P500 does get left a long way behind," said Iain. "The Nasdaq Biotech index is not in Chart 9-2."

"The Biotech index dwarfed the others, so I charted it separately, as shown in Chart 93," I responded.

Chart 9-3 [Printed with permission from Beyond Charts]

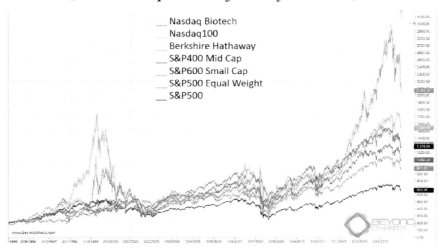

Nasdaq Biotech
Nasdaq100
Berkshire Hathaway
S&P400 Mid Cap
S&P600 Small Cap
S&P500 Equal Weight
S&P500

"If these are the main indices on which to focus how would I access them via an ETF?" asked Iain.

I provided Iain with the corresponding ETF symbols for each of the indices and their respective providers:

- NASDAQ Biotech: IBB. iShares.
- NASDAQ100: QQQ. Invesco PowerShares.
- S&P MidCap 400: MDY, IJH. State Street (SPDR) and iShares, respectively.
- S&P SmallCap 600: IJR. iShares.
- S&P500 Equal Weight: RSP. Guggenheim.
- S&P500: SPY, IVV, VOO. State Street (SPDR), iShares and Vanguard, respectively.

"Are these the only index ETFs that I will need to be aware of?" asked Iain.

"They could easily be," I said. "But a few more ETFs could be used depending on what simple strategies you would like to use. But, yes, you could actually focus on two or three of these for the rest of your investing career and should massively outperform the majority of active mutual funds. You should also ensure that you avoid, through long-term timing, most of any severe bear market that may come along."

"There are others that you can use that track other stock exchanges around the world. We will cover them later."

RETURNS ON OFFER FROM THE ETFS THAT TRACK THESE INDICES

I introduced Table 9-2, which shows the corresponding ETFs to those shown in Table 9-1, by telling Iain that there is no such thing as a Total Return ETF, hence the use of 'Total Return' in inverted commas in Table 9-2. The 'Total Return' ETF performances shown in Table 9-2 in bold are merely the ETF's historical price movement including the reinvestment of dividend distributions that ETFs pay to their investors in the same way that mutual funds pay distributions to their investors and stocks pay dividends.

*Table 9-2**

ETF Symbol	Index ETF Name	Fees	FuM	Yrs since Incept. to Jun 30 '15	Jun 30 2010 5 Yrs	Jun 30 2005 10 Yrs	Jun 30 2000 15 Yrs	Jun 30 1995 20 Yrs
SPY	SPDR S&P500	0.09%	182B	22.4	14.80%	5.62%	2.37%	6.91%
SPY	**SPDR S&P500 'Total Return'**				**17.17%**	**7.79%**	**4.29%**	**8.80%**
IVV	iShares S&P500	0.07%	70.3B	15.1	14.90%	5.69%	2.41%	
IVV	**iShares S&P500 'Total Return'**				**17.26%**	**7.83%**	**4.32%**	
VOO	Vanguard S&P500	0.05%	219B	4.8				
VOO	**Vanguard S&P500 'Total Ret'**							
RSP	S&P500 Equal Weight	0.40%	9.6B	12.2	16.12%	7.43%	6.89%	8.58%
RSP	**S&P500 Equal Weight 'Tot Ret'**				**17.92%**	**9.03%**	**8.78%**	**10.53%**
QQQ	PowerShares NASDAQ 100	0.20%	43B	16.3	20.28%	11.32%	0.96%	10.92%
QQQ	**NASDAQ 100 'Total Return'**				**21.51%**	**12.15%**	**1.51%**	**11.47%**
VTI	Vanguard Total US Market	0.05%	404.3B	14.1	15.28%	6.21%		
VTI	**Vanguard Total US Market 'TR'**				**17.57%**	**8.32%**		
MDY	SPDR S&P400 Mid Cap	0.25%	14.8B	20.2	16.17%	8.15%	7.82%	10.60%
MDY	**SPDR S&P400 Mid Cap 'Tot Ret'**				**17.48%**	**9.41%**	**8.98%**	**11.71%**
IJH	iShares S&P400 Mid Cap	0.12%	26.7B	15.1	16.09%	8.15%	7.84%	
IJH	**iShares S&P400 Mid Cap 'TR'**				**17.69%**	**9.60%**	**9.13%**	
MDYG	SPDR S&P400 Mid Cap Growth	0.21%	317M	9.6	16.99%			
MDYG	**S&P400 Mid Cap Growth 'TR'**	0.25%	.256B	9.6	**17.97%**			
IJR	iShares S&P600 Small Cap	0.13%	17B	15.1	16.84%	7.92%	8.48%	
IJR	**S&P600 Small Cap 'Total Ret'**				**18.37%**	**9.17%**	**9.57%**	
SLY	SPDR S&P600 Small Cap	0.20%	.413B	9.6	17.06%			
SLYG	SPDR S&P600 Small Cap Grwth	0.25%	.594B	14.8	18.98%	9.93%		
XLV	SPDR Health Care	0.15%	16.5B	16.5	21.42%	9.14%	6.35%	
XLV	**SPDR Health Care 'Total Ret'**				**23.61%**	**11.07%**	**7.88%**	
IBB	NASDAQ Biotech	0.48%	8.05B	14.4	36.62%	18.44%		
IBB	**NASDAQ Biotech 'Total Ret'**				**36.98%**	**18.64%**		
VHT	Vanguard Health Care	0.09%	6.7B	11.4	22.74%	10.33%		
VHT	**Vanguard Health Care 'Tot Ret'**				**24.28%**	**11.85%**		

* *The four dotted outlined numbers in the 20 Years column and the two in the 15 Years column are computed using assumed conservative differentials from previous years.*

"*So investing in an index and achieving the index type returns that you have shown me so far with Total Return indices really is possible?*" asked Iain.

"Absolutely," I replied. "It's amazing how often I have explained the concept of ETFs to ordinary investors, who struggle to grasp them."

I continued, "And even when they do get it, they're still more distrustful of the idea than I would have thought. I know everyone takes some time to warm to any novel idea, but I suspect that the distrust has less to do with the novelty of the concept to them than it has to do with the successful societal programming through advertising and marketing over decades by the active mutual fund fraternity. And to do with the network of advisors that gain no fees from recommending ETFs but do for supporting active mutual funds."

"I also suspect that very few people are aware of the facts that over periods of six years or more, very few active mutual funds if any, perform better than their benchmark ETFs."

"So it is as easy as investing in the ETF symbol, such as RSP or IVV, in the same way as investing in a stock symbol such as AAPL (for Apple Inc.) or IBM?" asked Iain.

"It certainly is," I replied.

ETF FEES AND OTHER COSTS

Iain scanned his eye over Tables 9-1 and 9-2 again before saying, "The ETF returns all seem to be slightly lower than the index returns. For example, in the **10 Years** column, the $MID and $MIDTR indices have respective returns of 8.17% and 9.74% compounded per year, whereas the corresponding ETF of MDY has respective returns of 8.15% and 9.41% compounded per year."

"This is due to fees," I replied. "ETF annual fees are substantially lower than active mutual fund fees. Note earlier in Table 9-2 that the **Fees** column shows *fees for index ETFs in the range of 0.07% to 0.25%* with two outliers of 0.40% and 0.48%. In other tables that I have shown you in earlier sessions, *active mutual funds have annual fees in the range of 0.55% to 1.15%*, except Vanguard, which is below this range."

Table 9-3

	Mutual Fund Symbol	Mutual Fund Name	Fees	FuM	Turnover
Index	VFIAX	Vanguard S&P500 Admiral Class	0.05%	219B	3%
Index	VFINX	Vanguard S&P500 Investor Class	0.16%	219B	3%
Index	VTSAX	Vanguard Total US Mkt Admiral	0.05%	404.3B	3%
Index	VTSMX	Vanguard Total US Mkt Investor	0.16%	404.3B	3%
Index	VDIGX	Vanguard Large Cap Div Growth	0.32%	25.4B	23%
Index	VMGRX	Vanguard Mid Cap Growth	0.46%	4.3B	93%
Index	VEXPX	Vanguard Small Cap Growth	0.53%	11B	62%
Sector	VGHCX	Vanguard Health Care	0.34%	52.3B	20%
Index	FUSEX	Fidelity Spartan 500 Index	0.10%	91.5B	4%
Index	FCNTX	Fidelity Contrafund	0.64%	109B	45%
Index	FDGRX	Fidelity Large Cap Growth	0.82%	40.7B	12%
Index	SWPPX	Schwab 500 index	0.09%	21.4B	2%
Index	VADAX	Invesco S&P500 Equal Weight	0.56%	4.9B	21%
Balanced	AOGIX	American Century One Choice Aggr	0.96%	1.1B	29%
Balanced	VASGX	Vanguard LifeStrategy Growth	0.17%	11.5B	13%
Balanced	SFAAX	Wells Fargo Advan. Index Asset All	1.15%	937M	43%
Balanced	LKBAX	LKCM Balanced Fund	0.80%	375M	20%
Balanced	IBNAX	Ivy Balanced Fund	1.11%	2.6B	33%
Balanced	WAGRX	InvestEd Growth Fund	1.05%	150M	29%
Balanced	ABALX	American Balanced Fund	0.59%	83.6B	68%
Balanced	FBALX	Fidelity Balanced Fund	0.56%	29.2B	128%
Balanced	FPURX	Fidelity Puritan	0.55%	25.2B	106%
Balanced	VBINX	Vanguard Balanced Fund	0.23%	26.5B	53%
Balanced	VWELX	Vanguard Wellington Fund	0.26%	86.8B	71%
Balanced	RPBAX	T. Rowe Price Balanced Fund	0.60%	4B	53%

"Let's look at the comparisons in a bit more detail," I said handing Iain Table 9-3. "I have included the **Fees** column in the tables that I provided so far but let's summarize them. Table 9-3 shows the **Fees**, **FuM** (Funds under Management) and **Turnover**, which is the percentage of the fund that is bought and sold over the previous twelve months (100% = total turnover of the FuM)."

"Why are the fees so much lower?" asked Iain. "It seems that ETFs are a fund and hence must have management costs."

"They certainly do," I replied. "But the costs are nowhere near as high as the costs incurred by active mutual funds."

I continued, "As you correctly said, index ETF providers are effectively fund managers. But they do not use discretion and analysis to select stocks or calculate how much capital to invest in a particular stock, or in which asset class to invest to reduce volatility and how much to invest in each asset class. Active fund managers need to employ a highly qualified team to do this or hire third party organizations to do it for them."

"I'm sure that these teams would be expensive," said Iain.

"They certainly are more expensive than having no investment team!" I exclaimed. "**Turnover** gives us an indication of how active the mutual fund is. For example, in Table 9-3 the Fidelity Balanced Fund, FBALX, turned over 128% of $29.2 billion, which equals $37.4 billion; whereas the American Balanced Fund, ABALX, turned over 68% of $83.6 billion, which equals $56.9 billion over twelve months. The processes that precede the decisions to turnover through rebalancing – which requires buying and selling–are expensive to run, let alone the additional execution costs."

I continued, "Active fund managers also have marketing departments; some are large and spend a great deal on marketing and advertising. When did you last see TV ads for Vanguard or an ETF provider such as iShares or PowerShares? They do advertise a little but are drowned out by many of the higher cost active mutual funds."

"In other countries such as Australia the industry Superannuation funds, which are supposed to be low-fee not-for-profit organizations, advertise way more than any of the other active mutual fund providers. Advertising is a cost before calculating the profit!"

I showed Iain Table 9-4 listing the major ETFs showing the **Fees, FuM** and **Turnover**.

Table 9-4

Mutual Fund /ETF Symbol	Mutual Fund Name /ETF Name	Fees	FuM	Turnover
SPY	SPDR S&P500	0.09%	182B	2.8%
IVV	iShares S&P500	0.07%	70.3B	4%
VOO	Vanguard S&P500	0.05%	219B	3%
RSP	S&P500 Equal Weight	0.40%	9.6B	18%
QQQ	PowerShares NASDAQ 100	0.20%	43B	11.4%
VTI	Vanguard Total US Market	0.05%	404.3B	3%
MDY	SPDR S&P400 Mid Cap	0.25%	14.8B	16.7%
IJH	iShares S&P400 Mid Cap	0.12%	26.7B	15%
IJR	iShares S&P600 Small Cap	0.13%	17B	14%
XLV	SPDR Health Care	0.15%	16.5B	3.25%
IBB	NASDAQ Biotech	0.48%	8.05B	33%
VHT	Vanguard Health Care	0.09%	6.7B	4%

Iain commented, "Besides **Fees**, the **Turnover** is much lower with index ETFs than active mutual funds. I notice that you have included the Vanguard S&P500 ETF, VOO, in this table."

"Another reason why mainstream index ETF fees are much lower is that **Turnover** is much lower than active mutual funds. Yes, VOO has been excluded from most of the other tables because it was only listed in September 2010 as an ETF and hence didn't have five years' performance to June 30, 2015."

I continued, "Notice that VOO has the same **Fees** and **FuM** as the index fund VFIAX in Table 9-3, and the same **FuM** as VFINX but different **Fees**. All three are effectively exactly the same fund, just accessed via different buying and selling processes for the investor. Just as VTI, VTSAX, and VTSMX are also all effectively the same fund."

"In reality, what sort of difference in dollars do these fees make?" asked Iain.

John Bogle, the founder of Vanguard and index funds, explained the effect of fees in an interview in November 2012, "*What happens in the fund business is the magic of compound returns is overwhelmed by the*

tyranny of compound costs. It's a mathematical fact. There's no getting around it.'

I showed Iain Table 9-5 with examples of what the dollar difference can be, based on years left to retirement, different amounts of starting capital, contributions, varying fees and rates of growth.

Table 9-5

Starting Capital	Growth Rate	Annual Contributions	Years	% Difference Less in Fees	$ Difference Less in Total	% of Total
$50,000	7.5%	$3,500	35	0.50%	$153,425	12.9%
$50,000	8.0%	$3,500	35	1.00%	$330,652	24.3%
$130,000	11.71%	$6,000	20	1.00%	$243,625	15.0%
$130,000	7.5%	$6,000	35	0.50%	$346,131	13.4%
$250,000	8.5%	$6,000	20	0.50%	$128,657	8.2%
$500,000	9.5%	$10,000	20	1.50%	$841,811	22.6%
$500,000	9.5%	$10,000	20	0.50%	$304,448	8.2%
$750,000	8.0%	$20,000	10	1.00%	$157,209	8.2%
$1,000,000	6.50%	$24,000	10	1.50%	$270,184	12.3%

I explained to Iain, "The second line shows that starting with $50,000, investing $3,500 per year and ***paying just 1% extra in fees per year over the following thirty-five years,*** thirty-year-olds could ***potentially lose a quarter, 24.3%, or $330,652, of their entire retirement nest egg.'***

"The more important number here is the 25%; meaning that regardless of what the **Starting Capital** is, with a 1% differential ***around 25%, or a quarter, will be the amount of the nest egg that will be forfeited purely through the additional 1% in annual fees*** over thirty-five years.

"Why do some rows have 1% and 1.5% in the difference in fees in Table 9-5?"

"The 1.5% could include additional fees for 401(k) Plan fees, and for investment advice fees for those who might use it. In Tables 9-2 to 9-4, the **Fees** column are *only* the annual management fees that are deducted by the fund. These exclude any one-time and annual recurring fees that an investor would pay directly to a separate financial investment adviser or a 401(k) Plan provider."

"How many people actually use an investment adviser?" asked Iain.

"Take a look at Figure 9-1 from ICI Research. It shows that the number of households with an IRA that use a financial adviser as the *primary source* for their retirement strategy is nearly six times more (58% vs. 10%) than the next category; which is friends and family. And almost ten times more (58% vs. 6%) than books or media articles. It appears that avid readers and users of software tools are certainly not part of the herd!"

Figure 9-1[3]

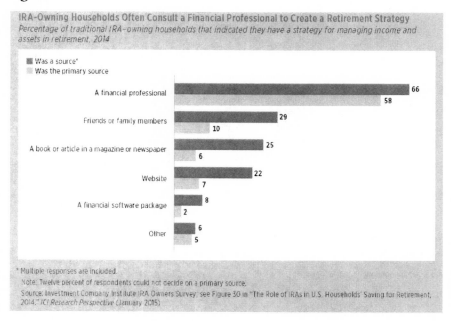

I continued, "The 66% clearly are not do-it-yourself (DIY) investors. Financial investment *advice* will typically carry a recurring annual cost whereas financial *planning* typically has a once-off cost. Minimize paying recurring advice fees, especially when they calculate the fees based on FuM!"

"Vanguard offers an advice service for a minimum investment of $50,000 called Vanguard Personal Advice, which costs 0.3% per year. This fee currently is around the lowest for 401(k) and IRA advice for dealing with a person at Vanguard.

However, obtaining investment advice from an advisor mostly ranges

---

from 0.5% to 1.5% per year in fees, depending on the amount of funds under management with the advisor. These are additional fees that would need to be added to the active mutual fund or ETF fees to calculate an annual total percentage fee cost to the investor."

I concluded, "There are online alternatives where fees are much lower, but you don't get to talk to a person for the investment advice; they recommend a particular asset class mix, or theme, which is similar to the robo-advice that we covered in Chapter 4."

"If I followed your suggestions, would I need to pay your company for any additional investment advice?" Iain asked.

"Not for the simplest strategy that I will show you; but for our active strategies, there is a fixed annual fee regardless of the size of your investing capital to access the strategy and to receive daily stock market data. You would be a fully-fledged DIY investor and would only pay the ETF management fee, which is deducted from the ETF dividend distributions and is, therefore, ***included in the returns shown in Table 9-2***."

"What other costs would I have?" asked Iain.

"Besides accounting costs for tax returns and any ongoing annual IRA or 401(k) costs, the only other fees would be commission fees for buying ETFs and for re-investing ETF dividends by purchasing more of the same ETF. However, it's important to remember these are fixed fees, some of which are one-time, which do NOT scale as your total investment value rises, and hence are not a percentage of FuM costs, which is typically how active mutual funds and financial investment advisors charge."

---

*"Some ETFs can be bought and sold **commission-free** with certain broker-dealers,which means that the reinvesting of dividends and buying more units of an ETF with your monthly 401(k) contributions will incur no additional costs."*

Recurring 401(k) Plan fees[4] can vary between 0.3% and 1.3% per year depending on, amongst many other variables, the size of your FuM that the 401(k) Plan manages.

---

4   Inside the Structure of Defined Contribution/401(k) Plan Fees. 2013 https://www.ici.org/pdf/rpt_14_dc_401k_fee_study.pdf

Forfeited Nest Egg through Fees and Performance

"Can you imagine if the combined forfeited nest egg was more than 2% compounded per year, which some people still forfeit in total fees and worse performance when investment advisors and additional 401(k) Plan fees are involved? What was it that Albert Einstein said about people that don't understand compounding?"

Iain replied, "They are the ones that pay it while those that do understand it, earn it!"

"Exactly, look at it this way, by understanding the effect of the lost compounding from paying additional fees every year and ensuring that you pay as little in fees as possible, **your retirement nest egg will grow by much more**. If you don't pay as little as possible then these dollars might as well be taken straight out of your back pocket and handed to somebody else in the financial industry," I said.

I paused to let this sink in. Then I asked, "Are you going to be someone who pays it or earns it?"

Iain answered, "On the point of fees alone people just have to take some action. They can't know this and do nothing about it!"

"**Fees are only a part of the difference** between the returns that a low-cost index ETF achieves and that a higher cost balanced active mutual fund achieves.

The other part of the difference, of course, which the differentials in Table 9.5 do not include, **is forfeited performance through diversification** over the long term. We have already seen that diversification forfeits lots of compounding without sufficient corresponding benefit of protecting capital enough during severe bear markets."

Table 9-6 shows a few different scenarios with a differential of 2.86% compounded per year in *fees and diversification* for a total compounded annual return (CAR) of 10.93%. 10.93% is the performance achieved by the S&P500 Equal Weighted Total Return index ETF, RSP (**S&P500EW Fund** in Table 9-6) over twenty years to June 30, 2015.

The column with the heading **Average 7.66% CAR** is 2.86% CAR less than 10.93%, which represents an average return from Balanced Funds and Target Date funds over the same period, twenty years. Over this period the following compounded annual return (CAR) was achieved:

- Vanguard LifeStrategy Growth Fund, VASGX, 7.65%.
- Fidelity Balanced Fund, FBALX, 8.97%.
- BlackRock LifePath 2030 Target Date, STLDX, 6.97%.
- IVY Balanced Fund, IBNAX, 5.46%.
- Vanguard Balanced Fund, VBINX, 7.91%.

By the way, the S&P MidCap 400 ETF, MDY, achieved 1.18% CAR better over this period at 11.71% CAR, meaning that the differential could have been even larger, as much as 4% CAR!

The column headed **Retirement Savings at start of Period** is the nest egg size at the commencement of the periods from ten to sixty years. The column headed **Average p.a. Contributions** assumes annual 401(k) contributions over the different periods from ten to sixty years.

The two rightmost columns show the amount of dollars forfeited to *fees and diversification* over the different periods in absolute and percentage terms.

The longer the investment period, the higher is the proportion that a nest egg forfeits to fees and diversification. Another investing principle.

Table 9-6

	Retirement Savings at start of Period	Avg p.a. Contrib.	Average 7.66% CAR	S&P500EW Fund 10.53% CAR	$ Lost to Fees & Diversifying	% Lost to Fees & Diversifying
10 Yrs (57 - 67)	$300,000	$12,000	$801,787	$1,016,826	$215,039	21.1%
20 Yrs (47 - 67)	$175,000	$10,000	$1,219,924	$1,927,844	$707,920	36.7%
30 Yrs (37 - 67)	$80,000	$8,000	$1,412,598	$2,744,046	$1,331,447	48.5%
35 Yrs (32 - 67)	$40,000	$6,000	$1,524,443	$3,259,724	$1,735,281	53.2%
40 Yrs (27 - 67)	$15,000	$6,000	$1,765,445	$4,056,666	$2,291,221	56.5%
50 Yrs (37 - 87)	$80,000	$5,000	$5,839,335	$19,279,131	$13,439,796	69.7%
60 Yrs (27 - 87)	$15,000	$5,000	$6,875,767	$26,365,955	$19,490,188	73.9%

The **40 Years** (age 27–age 67) period shows that a twenty-seven-year-old with forty years to retirement that starts with $15,000 could forfeit **$2,291,221 or 56.5%** of the nest egg that he could achieve if the CAR differential is 2.86%!

For forty-seven-year-olds starting with $175,000 planning to retire at sixty-seven and contribution $10,000 per year, **$707,920 could be**

forfeited, which would come directly out of their nest eggs; or **36.7% of their nest eggs could be forfeited** to fees and diversification if the CAR differential is 2.86% over twenty years!

The thirty-two-year-old could **forfeit over half, or 53.2%, of their nest egg**, if the CAR differential is 2.86% over thirty-five years.

Paying away small amounts in fees annually and forfeiting perfor-mance due to diversification has an enormous long-term effect, due to years of lost compounding that should work for YOU.

By spending a few hours now, just once, to reorganize your investments, you get the benefits for years to come which will add up to of tens of thousands of dollars more in your pocket. If you don't, the active mutual funds will have your money and will benefit from the compounding working for them, rather than for you.

"Iain, I suggest you keep these printouts close at hand for future reference and remember to look at them whenever you are comparing fees for whatever reason. Or, even better, *keep a link to this website http://401kfee. com/how-much-are-high-fees-costing-you/ which has a calculator to help calculate how much retirement nest egg will be forfeited by unneces-sarily paying higher fees.*"

"I certainly will keep them as a reference," said Iain.

I concluded, "It is critical to ensure that the ongoing fees that scale as your nest egg increases in value are kept to an absolute minimum and, if possible, eradicated."

OTHER INDICES THAT CAN BE ACCESSED USING ETFs

"What other ETFs could I consider?" asked Iain.

"The full list of ETFs numbers over 1700 in the U.S. and there are also ETFs on other stock exchanges around the world. That comprehensive list includes non-index ETFs, or 'active ETFs' that use proprietary and other methods to invest their capital. These active ETFs are effectively active mutual funds that are listed on the stock exchange. We are not interested in these, just the index or sector ETFs, such as the Financial or Health sector."

"Is that it?" Iain queried again.

"There is another category that we are interested in, international ETFs. These allow an investor to invest in the German index or Chinese index. Or even the Mexican, Japanese, Australian or Brazilian indices. Just about any stock exchange index in the world!" I exclaimed.

"What's the bottom line?" asked Iain. "How many could I use?"

"You would focus on one to five or six ETFs," I said, "but you will be able to choose from a list of about thirty-five to forty-five index and sector ETFs. The simplest approach would be to focus on a single ETF. However, I acknowledge that many investors may want to have a broader choice or wish to invest more of their time investing for their retirement or otherwise."

"Right I'm ready," said Iain, "show me how."

An important footnote quoted from Warren Buffett[5]:

---

*"**If the investor, instead, fears price volatility, erroneously viewing it as a measure of risk**, he may, ironically, end up doing some very risky things. Recall, if you will, the pundits who six years ago bemoaned falling stock prices and advised investing in "safe" Treasury bills or bank certificates of deposit. People who heeded this sermon are now earning a pittance on sums they had previously expected would finance a pleasant retirement. (The S&P 500 was then below 700; now it is about 2,100.)*

*If not for their fear of meaningless price volatility, these investors could have assured themselves of a good income for life by **simply buying a very low-cost index fund whose dividends would trend upward over the years and whose principal would grow as well** (with many ups and downs, to be sure).*

*Investors, of course, can, by their own behavior, make stock ownership highly risky. And many do. Active trading, attempts to "time" market movements, inadequate diversification, **the payment of high and unnecessary fees to managers and advisors**, and the use of borrowed money can destroy the decent returns that a life-long owner of equities would otherwise enjoy. Indeed, borrowed money has no place in the investor's tool kit: Anything can happen anytime in markets. And no advisor, economist, or TV commentator – and definitely not Charlie nor I – can tell you when chaos will occur. Market forecasters will fill your ear but will never fill your wallet.*

*The commission of the investment sins listed above is not limited to "the little guy." **Huge institutional investors, viewed as a group, have long underperformed the unsophisticated index-fund investor***

---

who simply sits tight for decades. A major reason has been fees:
Many institutions pay substantial sums to consultants who, in turn,
recommend high-fee managers. And that is a fool's game.

There are a few investment managers, of course, who are very good
– though in the short run, it's difficult to determine whether a great
record is due to luck or talent. **Most advisors, however, are far better**
at generating high fees than they are at generating high returns. *In*
truth, **their core competence is salesmanship.** *Rather than listen to*
their siren songs, investors – large and small – should instead read Jack
Bogle's The Little Book of Common Sense Investing."

Emphasis added by the author.

LAST WORD

- Index ETFs are a straightforward way of investing directly in a stock market index.
- The ETF compounded annual returns include annual management fees and are only marginally less than a Total Return index, sometimes as little as 0.08% compounded per year over many years.
- We know from the SPIVA® Scorecard that Total Return indices beat between 82% and 88% of active mutual funds over five years.
- We know from the SPIVA® Persistence Report that Total Return indices beat nearly all active mutual funds the over periods of longer than six years or more.

CHAPTER 10

The Better Way to Beat 88% of Active Equity Mutual Funds

"Simplicity is the ultimate sophistication."

LEONARDO DA VINCI

"Let's go right back to where we started," I said to Iain, "right back to the SPIVA˚ Scorecard."

"I know," said Iain, "if you match the index, you will outperform 88% of active equity mutual funds over five years."

"Correct," I said. "We know that from the 'All Domestic Equity Funds' row in Table 2-1 in Chapter 2. Also, active equity mutual fund performance doesn't persist over periods of longer than five years, as we saw from the SPIVA˚ Persistence Scorecard in Table 2-8, meaning that by matching the index over longer than five years we can outperform nearly every active mutual fund. And Balanced Funds and Target Date funds do worse than the active equity mutual funds and hence than the indices over the long term."

I continued, "The first HOW that I'm going to show you is the simplest strategy that anybody could use. The benefit is massively better returns, as I have just stated, over the long term by simply matching the index."

I continued, "The strategy is:

- **Buy an index ETF and hold it for longer than six years, prefer-ably decades.**
- **When you receive a dividend, reinvest it, typically on a quar-terly basis.**
- **Buy more of the same index ETF with regular retirement contri-butions, typically on a quarterly basis."**

"Is that it?" asked Iain.

"Well, yes," I replied. "That is the total ongoing effort required. Of course, at the outset, you will need to determine and establish the entity through which to carry out the strategy, but that is no different from any other strategy. It should obviously be as low a tax environment as possible. Once the entity is established an initial capital invested *it really shouldn't take more than fifteen minutes a quarter to execute the strategy.*"

I continued, "You will also need to open an account with a broker-dealer that charges less than $8 per transaction, or one that offers commis-sion-free investing for your chosen index ETF(s)."

"I should mention that this strategy could be executed using an index mutual fund if there is a corresponding index mutual fund to the index ETF. However, an improved strategy to this one that we will discuss soon will not be as easy to follow with an index mutual fund, if at all. Also, there are many more ETFs available than index mutual funds that track mainstream indices."

SINGLE INDEX, BUY & HOLD STRATEGY

"Let's imagine that twenty years ago, Jack, was the same age as you are now, in your mid-forties. Jack was twenty years away from retirement and was contributing to an active mutual fund through a 401(k) that used a balanced strategy."

"We'll assume that Jack had a *$162,000 nest egg and was able to contribute $5,500 per year, or $458.33 per month up until he turned 50, and then $6,500 per year, or $541.67 per month to his retirement savings consistently over the twenty years.*"

"We will look at how simply directing the same contributions to an index ETF compares to doing the same with two of the better performing Balanced Funds, one of them Vanguard's VBINX."

"Hey, that's similar to my situation," said Iain.

"I said that I would show you how I calculated the $800,000 difference between your current nest egg investing path and investing via a stock market index."

"The two Balanced Funds that we will use are:

- FBALX, the $29 billion Fidelity Balanced Fund, and
- VBINX, the $26 billion Vanguard Balanced Fund."

"In this twenty-year example starting in July 1995, I will use an ETF that tracks the S&P MidCap 400 Total Return index, the State Street SPDR MDY ETF, rather than the S&P500 Equal Weight Total Return index. Guggenheim only listed its RSP ETF in April 2003. The other option is the iShares MidCap Total Return index ETF, IJH, which iShares only listed in May 2000."

Chart 10-1

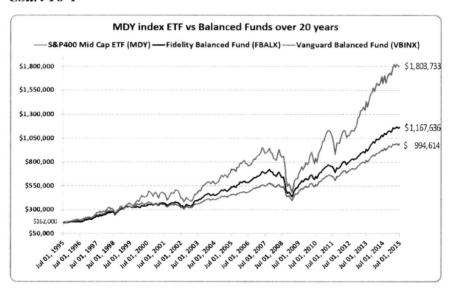

While Iain had a close look at the monthly plotted Chart 10-1 to no doubt start with a few questions, I added, "These returns *exclude* any fees that a 401(k) Plan would charge. Which would make the two Balanced Funds returns worse but not reduce the MDY returns if executed in an IRA or equivalent entity through which you do it yourself (DIY)."

Iain's opening question was, "So, using actual fund data validates the spreadsheet calculation that you did right at the beginning to show the $800,000 differential?"

"That's correct. An $809,119 differential to be more precise."

"So this is how I could potentially end up with over $800,000 more in my retirement savings leading up to my retirement in twenty years' time?" Iain asked while punching away on his calculator. "*That's 81.4% more! Incredible!*" he exclaimed.

"The assumption is that the market, and hence also the Vanguard Balanced Fund, performs in a similar fashion for the next twenty years. Of course, this won't be the case as the future is always different from the past."

I continued, "If the market performs worse in the future then so will a Balanced Fund because the majority of its performance is linked to the stock market. If the market performs better in the future then so will a Balanced Fund, but not as well as a mainstream stock market index and its index ETF."

"The only scenario where the Balanced Fund would possibly do better is if the stock market had a negative return over the entire twenty-year period. This scenario is possible but unlikely."

THE FIDELITY BALANCED FUND OUTPERFORMED THE VANGUARD BALANCED FUND

Iain then asked, "Why did the Fidelity Balanced Fund do nearly 18% better overall than the Vanguard Balanced Fund? Especially when it charges more than double the annual fees at 0.56% compared to Vanguard at 0.23%?"

"It's yet another lesson in asset class mix and how 'balanced' one Balanced Fund is from the next. In a nutshell, Fidelity has invested more in stocks and more in 'investment grade' bonds than Vanguard has. Both of which provide better long-term returns for taking a little more risk. This more than makes up for the higher fees."

I provided Iain with the asset class breakdown for both Balanced Funds as at November 2015.

"Note in Table 10-1 that FBALX weights its bond selections towards lower credit ratings indicating investment grade corporate bonds whereas VBINX is majority invested in AAA-rated government bonds."

Table 10-1

	FBALX	VBINX
Stocks	65.8%	58.0%
Cash	4.7%	2.6%
Other	2.6%	0.0%
Bonds	26.9%	39.4%
AAA	40.2%	69.4%
AA	4.0%	4.0%
A	24.0%	12.6%
BBB	24.0%	14.0%
<=BBB	7.6%	0.0%

"And furthermore, the decline in each of the equity curves in Chart 10-1 in 2002 and 2008 validate this with the Fidelity Balanced Fund experiencing quite a bit more drawdown than the Vanguard fund, especially in 2008."

I showed Iain Table 10-2 which shows the respective drawdowns of the three equity curves in the two major bear markets over the twenty-year period, including re-investing dividends but excluding ongoing monthly contributions.

Table 10-2

	Bear Market Drawdown	
	2002	**2008**
MDY	-32.02%	-55.07%
FBALX	-21.67%	-43.57%
VBINX	-18.14%	-35.97%

"The Fidelity Balanced Fund, FBALX, paid the price for investing more in stocks and riskier bonds by experiencing deeper drawdowns than VBINX but benefitted from the higher stocks exposure and riskier bonds to achieve better long-term growth. An extra $173,000 in retirement savings is nothing to sneeze at."

"I get this growth thing now; there is a direct link between the size of drawdown and size of growth," said Iain. "The growth comes from investing in the riskier assets as defined by how much they can fall during bear markets."

"That's a great way of putting it; however, that principle should only be applied to assets like mainstream stock market indices and developed countries' government bonds, that can't go to zero value. Either of these going to zero value would probably require the collapse of capitalism. That's not impossible, but if it happened then we would all be in the same boat and doomed; there are, however, hedge strategies for such an outcome, but that's a debate for another time. However, individual stocks or their corporate bonds can go to zero value."

Iain then exclaimed, "FBALX got to *within 11.5% of the drawdown that MDY experienced in 2008, but MDY still ended up 47.7%, or over $618,000, ahead of FBALX in final value.*"

"That is a combination of the growth power of stocks in MDY, combined with the handbrake effect of bonds in FBALX in a primary bull market in stocks."

Iain then asked, "Surely investing around 40% in bonds should provide more protection than a -43% or a -36% drawdown in 2008?" He reminded me, "We saw similar drawdowns with the Target Date funds."

"You are probably correct," I answered, adding, "One method of determining whether the risk that is taken to generate the return is better or worse is to use the Sharpe Ratio. The Sharpe Ratio measures the risk relative to the excess return achieved above a risk-free return. While not perfect, it has become one of the accepted measurements of risk-adjusted return."

"Did you do this calculation for these three equity curves?" asked Iain.

"I certainly did," I answered, "Here they are."

Given the period of twenty years, I used a risk-free return of 5% in the Sharpe Ratio calculation. One of the issues with the Sharpe Ratio is what risk-free return to use in its calculation. The Sharpe Ratios for this period, using monthly data, the higher, the better, are:

- MDY: 0.4300.
- FBALX: 0.3928.
- VBINX: 0.3222.

Meaning that, besides returning at least $636,000 more in absolute dollars while experiencing deeper drawdowns than FBALX, the MDY index ETF has the best risk-adjusted return of these three investing journeys. We know that it ends with the most growth and therefore, the highest ending account balance. What the Sharpe Ratio tells us is that the risk taken to achieve this growth is not greater than the risk taken to produce the growth attained by the two Balanced Funds. In fact, the risk is lower relative to the return!

In a low-interest rate environment, the Sharpe Ratio would balance out between the three, but even then the risk-adjusted return doesn't skew favorably enough towards the Balanced Funds.

Also, this is a sample of one. Other samples of buying and holding index ETFs compared to Balanced Funds might show Balanced Funds having closer, or even slightly better, Sharpe Ratios. However, if there isn't a gaping difference in the risk-adjusted return, then investors shouldn't be influenced to suffer returns that can potentially be hundreds of thousands of dollars less.

In a high-interest rate environment, the risk-adjusted return using the Sharpe Ratio skews more favorably towards the stronger growth strategy, the index ETF.

WHAT IF THERE WAS A SEVERE BEAR MARKET RIGHT NOW?

Iain was thinking ahead, "What if the stock market fell -55%, as it did in 2008, after the date of June 30, 2015, which is the end date in Chart 10-1 showing MDY, FBALX, and VBINX?"

He continued, "Some Balanced Funds, like FBALX, and longer dated Target Dated funds fell -40%, and other Balanced Funds, like VBINX, and shorter dated Target Date funds fell -30%? Where would the final values be?"

"Those would be reasonable scenarios given the drawdowns that we have researched for longer and shorter dated Target Date funds and various Balanced Funds. Let's look at some scenarios," I replied.

We used spreadsheets to calculate Table 10-3. Each column shows a different scenario of a 'severe bear market'. Working from the left the first column shows in each row the outcome of MDY falling -45% from June 30, June 2015, FBLAX -30% and VBINX falling 20%. The next column the same for a -50% fall for MDY, -33% for FBLAX and -23% fall for VBINX and the third column -55%, -40% and -30% falls, respectively.

Table 10-3

	Severe Bear Markets		
	45%, 30% & 20%	50%, 33% & 23%	55%, 40% & 30%
MDY & Index ETFs	$992,053	$901,866	$811,680
FBALX & Lng TDFs	$817,345	$852,374	$700,582
VBINX & Shrt TDFs	$795,691	$765,853	$696,230

"Iain, I think you'll agree that the drawdowns used for the Balanced Funds and Target Date funds could actually be deeper given their historical track records, but I would prefer to err on the side of showing these funds more favorably rather than less favorably."

Iain responded, "I do agree and even then *the values for FBLAX and VBINX are still lower than MDY in all scenarios. In each scenario, the index ETF is still better off by at least 10% than VBINX.*"

"And which would grow by more when the market eventually turned and started rising again?" I asked.

Iain nodded in an unassuming way saying, "The MDY index ETF would, of course."

He continued, asking, "What if the active mutual funds changed their asset mix to invest less in stocks, or invested more in government bonds, or invested in other asset classes such as infrastructure or commercial property so that their drawdowns wouldn't be as big in the next severe bear market?"

I responded, "You tell me. You know enough about this now to think through the answer."

Iain thought for a few seconds and then replied, "I suspect their growth would have been less and slower, and they wouldn't have reached as high a value before the drawdown started. That would have left them with lower peaks than they actually reached."

"Exactly correct," I said. "No matter how you look at it, you simply cannot get more growth out of asset classes that just don't grow by as much as the stock market over the long term. That's just the way it is."

"So why don't more investors invest most or all of their retirement capital directly into index ETFs?" asked Iain.

"That's exactly at the heart of the work I do and why I am taking you through this journey right now," I answered. "I am trying to show people, using evidence and logic to counter the propaganda, what opportunity cost they forfeit, or what their potential investing returns can be with some simple stock market strategies. I truly hope to empower people by providing them with simple skills that will enable them to be more successful investors now and during their retirement by breaking free from the herd and by doing it themselves."

WHY DON'T MORE INVESTORS INVEST THIS WAY?

Simply put, the powerful deep-pocketed active mutual fund fraternity would prefer that average investors don't invest on their own. Why? An en masse exit by investors from active equities mutual funds and Balanced Funds into index ETFs would cost them hugely in lost fees revenue over time.

The trend in the U.S. over the seven to eight years to the end of 2014 is that the migration from active mutual funds to index ETFs and even index mutual funds has started in earnest and is growing. Take a look at this research from ICI in Figure 10-1.

Figure 10-1[1]

Some of the Outflows from Domestic Equity Mutual Funds Have Gone to ETFs
Cumulative flows to and net share issuance of domestic equity mutual funds and index ETFs, billions of dollars; monthly, January 2007–December 2015

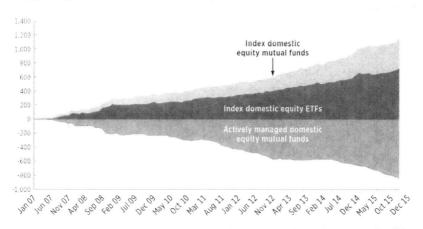

Note: Equity mutual fund flows include net new cash flow and reinvested dividends. Data exclude mutual funds that invest primarily in other mutual funds.

---

1   ICI Fact Book, 2016, Pages 46–47

According to the ICI 2016 Fact Book, "*Index domestic equity mutual funds and index-based ETFs have particularly benefited from the investor trend toward more index-oriented investment products. From 2007 through 2015, index domestic equity mutual funds and ETFs received $1.2 trillion in net new cash and reinvested dividends. Index-based domestic equity ETFs have grown particularly quickly — attracting almost twice the flows of index domestic equity mutual funds since 2007. In contrast, actively managed domestic equity mutual funds experienced a net outflow of $835 billion (despite including reinvested dividends) from 2007 to 2015.*"

The active balanced and equity mutual funds in the U.S., which includes the retirement funds industry such as the Target Date funds, will fight this trend. The Balanced and Target Date funds are — with their biggest weapon of stressing the volatility of the stock market.

Active mutual funds such as the industry and retail Superannuation Funds in Australia and balanced pension funds in Europe and elsewhere face the same challenge. In Australia, the industry Superannuation funds have become marketing machines.

The evidence presented in Tables 4-3 to 4-6 in Chapter 4 and the relatively small 16% of index investment in the U.S. show that Balanced Funds and Target Date funds may well be meeting the challenge so far and actually winning the war against the move to indexing.

Their core messaging through TV advertising, press releases, content in the financial press and online exposure is: "Volatility is bad! If you don't use us, it will get you! It's very difficult not to let it get you, especially if you try to do this investment thing all by yourself. Therefore, use diversification into bonds and infrastructure locally and around the world."

Also, you will seldom see Balanced Funds and Target Date funds compare their fees and performance to index ETFs or index mutual funds.

Nearly all investment advisors are on the same bandwagon. If everyone realized how simple it could be, depending on how active they wish to get, then the entire investment advisory industry could shrink dramatically. Guess what? Regulators don't want a shrinking investment advice industry; they apparently prefer one that continues to create jobs and more importantly, they want a layer of compliance between the everyday investor and various investment avenues and asset classes. Furthermore, en masse migration to the stock market would reduce the demand for bond products which are required to support a government and corporate debt market and borrowing pool.

It's within the industry's interests to say things like, "performance and returns aren't everything," and "too many retirement assets are tied up in risky assets such as the stock market and more should be invested in bonds." This justifies a larger government debt market funded by retirement funds but also ensures less retirement nest egg for retirees in the long term.

"Performance and returns aren't everything" may be the case over a three to seven-year horizon *but over the long run, particularly one to five decades, returns are everything.* Nothing else matters but performance when it comes to growing retirement nest egg; everything else is marketing, irrelevant banter or justification for a customer not to jump off their fee gravy train.

I said to Iain, "Due to this ongoing programming by the industry, ordinary investors have grown to fear volatility to the extent that all too often volatility is mistaken for total and permanent loss. Investors react by selling when the stock market is exhausted at or near its lows and don't re-enter the stock market when it recovers, as it always does, thereby locking in the losses."

"How can ordinary investors like me overcome this fear?" asked Iain.

"Firstly, they can listen to Warren Buffett, perhaps the most successful investor ever, rather than succumbing to the perfidious propaganda of some of the financial industry. As I showed you in one of our sessions, Warren Buffett has publicly stated that when he passes, he has given instructions to invest 90% of his estate into an index fund that tracks an index such as the S&P500."

"You have suggested using the S&P MidCap 400 index ETF MDY or IJH when Warren Buffett has stipulated an S&P500 index fund. Why have you suggested a different index ETF?" asked Iain.

"I'll answer this with a picture," I replied.

I handed Iain Chart 10-2 which plots from the date of inception of MDY in June 1995 compared to the S&P500 index ETF SPY and compared to Berkshire Hathaway A Class shares (BRK.A), Warren Buffett's investment company.

Chart 10-2

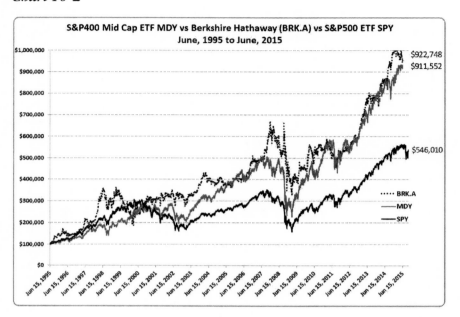

I explained, "There is hardly any difference in the outcome between MDY and BRK over this period, but both are a long way ahead of the SPY ETF."

"I can see why you suggest the S&P MidCap 400 index now," said Iain, "it has nearly matched the performance of the world's greatest investor over the last twenty years and done so much better than the S&P500."

"Exactly," I said, "and investing in the S&P400 since 1995 has been less volatile than investing in Berkshire Hathaway, which had two significant drawdowns, one of -48.95% in 1998 to 1999 and another of -51.4% in 2002 to 2003."

Iain replied, "That's two decent drawdowns. I now understand that volatility and drawdown are very much part of investing especially if the world's greatest investor experiences this kind of volatility with his investing."

I continued, "The S&P400 ETF, MDY, and S&P500 ETF, SPY, graphs *both include dividends being re-invested*; however, the Berkshire Hathaway graph excludes dividends because Berkshire Hathaway has never paid a dividend."

I returned to our discussion about overcoming fear. "There is no doubt that investors' fear of being totally or near totally invested in the stock market is due to that 'volatility thing' that occurs; especially when a severe bear market happens. I offer two options to help overcome this fear:

1. Adopt the single index ETF buy-and-hold strategy presented above and reframe your expectations about how you view your investments, especially during steep market declines, while deploying this strategy. I have provided plenty of evidence to assist with reframing your long-term perspective.
2. Time the market in a near-passive manner to help avoid the majority of any severe bear markets that will inevitably come in the future."

I said to Iain, "I will deal with the first option here and the second in our next few sessions."

"I'm eagerly looking forward to the timing sessions," Iain responded.

The first solution is the strategy at the start of this Chapter; invest 100% of retirement savings in stock index funds, either index mutual funds or index ETFs, and re-invest all dividends. This strategy is applicable for employees aged around fifty and younger who are contributing monthly to a retirement nest egg, or to capital invested outside of a retirement fund.

It's not because the stock market is about to take off like a rocket or because it will never have another decline such as in 2008, 2002, 1990 or 1987, just to mention some of the more recent declines. And it's not because the risk is lower in owning stocks.

It's because you now understand the risk-to-reward equation that I have outlined so far. You should now have realistic expectations of the potential extent of the declines and rises of stock indices and of Balanced Funds and Target Date funds, and know that this strategy is suited to long-term goals of growing retirement nest eggs.

Let's examine the principle of risk or so-called volatility to the downside. The extent of drawdowns that occur during more severe bear markets, such as 2002 and 2008, ultimately determines the level of volatility and hence risk that an investor takes to generate a return.

WHAT IS RISK?

Risk is a word that is overused and misplaced by much of the financial fraternity. It is a powerful word for them because it strikes fear into the hearts of investors causing them to make irrational decisions at nearly every level of investing ranging from why and what, to how to invest. What is risk? How do you define it?

Ask yourself these questions when considering an investment path or strategy:

"Can I lose any of my money?"

If the answer is "No," then this is a poor long-term investment because the odds are very high that returns will be low. If the answer is "Yes," then determine how much can be lost and under what circumstances; then determine how much you are prepared to allocate.

"Can I lose all of my money?"

If the answer is "Yes," then determine the probability of this occurring. If there is a relatively high probability, such as with options, Forex, and binary spreads, then this is a poor long-term investment. If there is a tiny probability, then determine under what circumstances. If there is a high probability of the circumstances occurring, then reject. If a low probability, then make sure that your investment is limited to a small portion of your capital, preferably less than 15%.

If the answer is "No," then determine how much you can lose and under what circumstances; then determine how much you are prepared to allocate.

When you invest in an index ETF that comprises the top twenty, thirty, fifty, 100, 500 or 1000 stocks by market capitalization at any given time, the probability is virtually zero of that investment value going to zero or close to zero. The same doesn't apply to investing in an individual stock, stock option, currency contract or futures contract.

Could your index ETF investments be worth half their value in a few months? Absolutely. But really, how big is that risk if you don't need the money in a few months or even a few years but will need it in twenty years or longer?

The value of your retirement savings will fluctuate up and own over the next two decades. That is certain. They won't go up in a straight line. They won't go down in a straight line. These fluctuations are volatility. There are normal in an index ETF, in active equity funds, in Balanced Funds or Target Date funds.

Is there risk that there will be volatility? Absolutely! It's a dead certainty that there will be volatility. *The **bigger risk** is that you get emotionally sucked into these fluctuations. And because you don't understand, or rather don't completely accept, the big picture of how a stock market index moves over the long term, **you exit near the bottom of a big bear market and don't re-enter to capture the growth that inevitably follows**.*

But if you ***know that you are not going to exit*** because you are going to buy-and-hold the index ETF, re-invest all dividends, and buy more units of the index ETF with monthly or quarterly retirement contributions, *is volatility even relevant to you*?

There is a risk that stocks perform poorly over the next two to three years and achieve a negative return, even including dividends. How much better would Balanced Funds and Target Date funds, with 60% exposure to stocks, have performed under such circumstances? Are you prepared to stick with safe investments such as 100% cash in case such a scenario occurs and endure the poor cash returns *for the entire twenty years* if the adverse stock market scenario doesn't pan out?

Or is a flat to negative return by investing 100% in stocks a risk you are willing to accept? Considering that Balanced Funds and Target Date funds would perform only slightly less poorly with some degree of exposure to stocks. If this occurred, then cash probably wouldn't be much better anyway.

There are other risks too.

There is the risk too that is the flipside of trying to avoid volatility. It is the risk of numerous tiny additional compounding fees, which eat away at returns, like unseen termites inside the woodwork. Beware of any up-front fees, high management expenses, 12b-1 marketing fees, and other charges compounded over decades that can erode tens, or even hundreds of thousands of dollars from a retirement nest egg, as I have already demonstrated.

The even bigger risk over the long term than fees and volatility is the risk of forfeited opportunity through diversifying for decades.

This could ***significantly increase longevity risk***; the risk of not having enough to last through retirement.

Diversifying for decades to protect capital for just one, two or three periods of severe downside volatility isn't a rational approach when it can easily retard growth by many hundreds of thousands of dollars for the long-term investor. I have already demonstrated this cost and the lack of potential benefit of diversification.

WHAT ARE YOUR EXPECTATIONS?

Expectation is nothing more than a projection into the future, positive or negative.

Do you expect your retirement savings to grow by 25% to 30% over the next twelve months? What about 10%? Or 5%? My point is, given that retirement savings are long-term investments, do you need an expectation of what returns you will achieve next year or the year after? Or do you expect instead that there is a high probability that if you don't meddle or sell for twenty years, or more, that your 100% invested index ETF will deliver a better return than the alternatives?

What if it's a rough twenty years in the stock market, as I just raised? Do you think your index ETF will still grow by more than 0%? What if it's a great twenty years in the stock market and you expect it would average 13% compounded per year? Would you be comfortable expecting an average return somewhere in between 0% and 13%?

It is a broad range, I know, but "anything can happen" is one of the fundamental principles of the market as it is about accepting that you have no control over what will occur in the future especially over the next twenty years or longer.

If you expected a 0% to 13% range of returns with an index ETF, then expect a range of returns between 0% and 7% for a Target Date fund and between 0% and 10% for a Balanced Fund.

All you have control over is what and when you buy, how much you buy and when you sell. And you know that if you kept all of the money in cash and term deposits, it wouldn't have any chance of earning the best return available of up to 13% compounded per year.

Build into your expectations that your investments will fall about -8% to -15% in value around every twelve to eighteen months if you have 100% exposure to the market. By the way, with 60% exposure to the market via Balanced Funds and Target Date funds your investments will also fall but not by as much *but also would not have grown by as much leading into the fall.* Why? That's what financial markets do.

Also build into your expectations that between one and four, or even five, times over the next twenty years or longer, your investments may drop between -25% and -55%.

Bear markets are not as rare as people think they are. In the twenty years between June 1901 and August 1921, the Dow Jones Industrial

Average (DJIA) index had one decline of at least -50%, three declines between -45% and -50% and one between -40% and -45%. That's a total of five declines of at least -40% in twenty years!

Can that happen again? Assume that "anything can happen."

It sure can. In just under seventeen years between January 1966 and August 1982, the DJIA ('Dow Jones') index fell between -25% and -30% three times, -33% once and -45% once.

Two of the longest sideways periods on record occurred from 1906 to 1924 and from 1966 to 1982. Two of the biggest bull markets on record followed each of these periods over eight and five years, respectively. With a little research, you discover that there are ***more long-term positive periods than there are long-term negative periods*** with impressive rises such as:

- 261% over 9.5 years,
- 485% over eight years,
- 366% over 4.67 years,
- 125% over four years,
- 503% over 16.5 years,
- 245% over five years,
- 563% over twelve years,
- 175% over six years.

As I have stated before, stock market indices have an upward bias over the long term. By default, indices comprise the biggest and most innovative businesses that over the long run benefit from the inherent principles of capitalism and long-term organic growth.

You might have a negative expectation about the future of capitalism. Or that multi-decade negative growth might eventuate. Either of these might lead to negative growth from the biggest and most innovative business over the long term. If so, you might consider investing a portion of investment capital in a hard asset such as gold or silver as a hedge against such an expectation. But remember, gold and silver don't pay dividends and only rise in value over the long run through demand out of scarcity.

However, even in such adverse scenarios, the listed businesses in mainstream stock market indices have still survived and then prospered over the long term. Even in the 1930's during the depression. If your expectations are in line with this positive reality, then you should be completely comfortable with your choice of investment. In other words, you should be able to "keep your head when all those around you are losing theirs[2]."

Is your expectation, your projection into the future, going to be negative or positive; and will your expectation build in and accept the usual ups and downs that go along with the stock market just as in all other walks of life?

WHAT ARE YOUR GOALS?

At what age do you think that you will retire? Be specific right now. You may change your mind in the future, but you can only plan with what you know and what you expect, not with what you don't know or are uncertain.

Whatever that period is from now to retirement, *your goal over that time should be to generate the highest possible return. Full stop! Period! End of story!*

What goals do you have for your investing journey?

Deciding up until a certain age to invest it all in the asset class that has the highest potential returns on offer provides the highest probability of achieving the goal. And that is stock market index ETFs or index mutual funds which have the best long-term track record.

The goal shouldn't be to get the smoothest equity curve or investing journey up until that particular age.

I fully accept that higher returns in index ETFs are not a certainty. I also know that as you move closer to retirement, you can make changes to the strategy that you use to reduce risk substantially while not reducing returns, in fact even improving them. Then, you will have to put in a little more investing effort and time than merely buying and holding a low-cost index ETF.

What knowledge and skills goals will you work on with respect to investing? Reading this book fits into that the category of skills acquisition. What other books will you read and what training will you undertake?

"This is a great discussion," said Iain. "It certainly has provided perspective for me to ask myself some questions that I need to answer."

I replied, "These questions and more will be asked and answered when we get to the next step of compiling an Investment Plan."

---

2   "If" by Rudyard Kipling

LAST WORD

- The simplest, most productive and most efficient long-term strategy for time-poor investors is to invest in index ETFs or index mutual funds.
- The S&P MidCap 400 index, with dividends reinvested, has nearly matched the returns of Warren Buffett's Berkshire Hathaway over the twenty years to June 30, 2015; and handsomely outperformed the S&P500 index.
- The even bigger risk over the long term than fees and of stock market volatility is the risk of lost returns through diversifying for decades. That has a far greater negative effect than the potential benefits of diversifying.
- The strong trend is that investors are moving from active equities mutual funds to index funds but for newly hired employees Target Date funds are growing in popularity much faster than index investing.

PART 3

Putting Your Plan Into Action

> *"Someone's sitting in the shade today
> because someone planted a tree a long time ago."*
> **WARREN BUFFETT**

THE ACTION PLAN

I love this title, "Action Plan," because it combines both the activities of 'planning' and 'doing.' Of course, the planning must be completed before starting execution, so maybe it should be "Plan Action"!

Either way, action without a plan typically results in unproductive, inefficient, poorly-directed steps that mostly don't achieve the goal. Let's face it, some 'doings' will take place, but will they be the necessary activities to reach the objective?

Planning provides a way out of chaos and disorganization; planning provides hope and light at the end of the tunnel. Only *action* delivers the outcomes and enables you to *reach* the light at the end of the tunnel.

Of course, failure to achieve the goal is usually not apparent until the future time of reaching the goal arrives, by which time it is all too late.

This reality is very relevant to saving and investing for retirement. Someone may have planned to plant that tree, but if nobody took action on the plan, there would be no shade today in that spot. Worse still there may be weeds or just nothing at all. Will you have shade when you get to retirement? Or just weeds, or even barren sand?

In Part 3, I will provide a framework and a real plan, along with practical, easy to follow executable strategies to lay the foundation so that everyday investors can achieve the returns, or better, that I have been discussing in Parts 1 and 2 of this book.

CHAPTER 11

Core Satellite Investment Approach

"When your life or aspects of it are not your problem–then you have a problem."

WARWICK DAVEY, A CLIENT OF THE AUTHOR'S COMPANY, SHARE WEALTH SYSTEMS.

Core Satellite is an investing approach with two key segments: a 'core' portion, which is the larger dollar portion and is passive or near-passive, and a 'satellite' portion, which is more active and smaller in total dollars than the 'core' portion.

The Core Satellite approach provides a framework for investors to allocate their investments across asset classes, investing instruments and strategies.

You may immediately wonder why there should even be a 'satellite' portion. The 'core' portion deploys strategies to at least match the performance of the stock market, while the 'satellite' portion of capital deploys strategies that can provide higher returns than the market, and hence greater than the 'core.' Together, the two portions of your holdings outperform the market while still limiting risk, so the 'risk-adjusted return' is improved.

Having said that, the 'core' can be 100% of your investing capital and the 'satellites' 0% on occasion, or all of the time, depending on your objectives, time availability for investing, your tolerance for risk and the amount of capital that you have to manage.

TYPICAL CORE SATELLITE APPROACH

Core portion

The 'core' portion comprises securities that are typically *passively* managed, such as index ETFs, passive index mutual funds and individual large-cap stocks that usually pay good dividends.

The 'core' portion can use a standard benchmark such as the Wilshire 5000 index or the S&P500 index for stocks, against which to compare performance.

The strategies in the 'core' portion will typically have a strong bias towards investors' goals and objectives, such as large and Mid-cap index funds, large-cap high dividend yield companies, mid/small-cap growth companies or listed real estate investment trusts that pay good quarterly dividends for income.

The use of other asset classes has already been discussed in the context of stock market investing.

In the 'core' the emphasis is on *passive*, or near-passive, investing.

Satellite portion

The 'satellite' portion comprises securities that the investor envisions will do better than an accepted market benchmark. Base these selections on some research rather than hearsay.

Holdings may include *actively* managed stocks, active mutual funds, rotating sector ETFs, international index ETFs or passively managed assets with a particular style that is different from the style aimed at enhancing the bias of the 'core'.

The emphasis is on using an *active* approach that has an edge and hence a higher probability of growing the 'satellite' portion of capital by more than the 'core' portion, or passive portion, in a timeframe that meets the investor's objectives.

Active means that buying and selling, or rebalancing, will occur based on some timing criteria with the option to be 100% in cash, when appropriate, according to the timing model. Timing allows the investor to outperform the market by protecting investment capital during severe bear markets of at least -30% to -55% declines.

The 'satellite' portion may be allocated 100% into domestic and international equities strategies and alternative strategies such as Real Estate Investment Trusts (REITs), bonds, commodities, options, FX or even exotic investments such as vintage cars and art. Deciding which asset classes to include will depend on the investors' interests, capital, time availability, goals, tolerance for risk and investing skills.

The stocks and ETFs in the 'satellite' can be the same as those in the 'core' but using an active strategy rather than a passive, or near passive, strategy.

The 'satellite' portion should improve the return and reduce the risk of the overall portfolio. Achieve this through low-correlated strategies, short and medium-term investment methods, and applying market risk (systematic risk) timing techniques that are typically different from those in the 'core' portion, but still consistent with the mission statement and goals and objectives of the Investment Plan.

CORE SATELLITE CONSIDERATIONS

The Core Satellite investment approach allows investors to construct many strategy permutations. In this short section, I provide various ideas that are not constrained by my personal preferences. Examples could include:

- A long-term stock market focused strategy for the core and more aggressive active short or medium or long-term stocks (also called equities) strategies for the satellites.
  - ◊ The long-term equities core portion could be achieved using index funds (index mutual funds or index ETFs) and/or large-cap 'blue chip' stocks.
  - ◊ Commercial and residential real estate could be used for a portion of the core capital if an investor has experience in this area and sufficient capital.
  - ◊ The satellites could deploy timing on index ETFs/funds or directly in stocks of varying time frames.
- For the core: a long-term combination of passive equities and bonds; for the satellite portion: active commodities, stock market sector strategies, corporate bonds or direct stocks strategies.
- Treasury bond funds, Treasury Inflation Protection Securities (TIPS) and fixed interest could be used as part of the core to ensure

a "safe" level of cash flow and use stock and commodities strategies as satellites for growth.

- The use of some leverage into one or more of the satellite strategies with timing.

The following diagram shows sample Satellite strategies positioned around sample Core strategies.

Figure 11-1

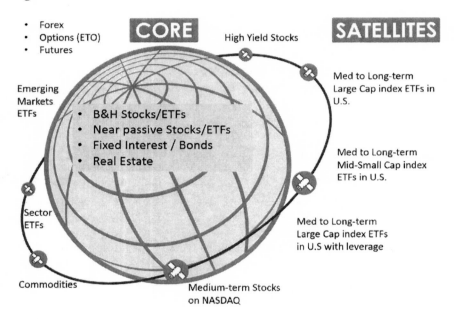

The mix depends on a number of criteria including a person's investment objectives, the amount of capital invested, risk tolerance, age, investing horizon, time availability and investing skills.

The percentage of the portfolio allocated to the core portion is a variable; there is no set percentage except that the core portion must be larger than the total of the satellites, therefore greater than 50%.

There is also no set quantity for the number of satellites except that the investor must be able to monitor the holdings practically. Each satellite should be large enough to play a meaningful role but not so substantial that it can have a large adverse effect on the performance of the core. In other words, the losses in any single satellite should not have the potential to derail the entire portfolio from achieving its long-term investment goals and objectives.

A 'shut-off valve' can be used too; determine the satellite shut-off level by measuring the percentage fall of all or part of the satellites' combined performance from a particular point such as a recent peak in the equity curve of the entire Core Satellite portfolio.

The underlying theme of the Core Satellite approach is to use the satellite portion to take bigger risks for growth with a smaller portion of the portfolio investment capital.

A simple Core Satellite approach may have a significant core, say 80% of the total portfolio, and just one satellite of 20%, or two satellites of 10% each. A more sophisticated approach may use one or two passive strategies for the core portion and multiple active satellites with the satellites differing in size, some even with leverage.

The key to a Core Satellite approach is to have the satellites complement the core without significantly altering either the risk or the growth potential of the portfolio. *The satellites should provide better opportunities for more growth and less correlation to the core.* If the satellites don't potentially offer more growth, then the capital should be transferred back into the core portion.

Complexity and effort for the average investor increase with the number of satellites. Consequently, when determining their Core Satellite structure, investors should be realistic about their skill levels and time availability.

I will discuss each possible strategy that from now on in the context of the *Core Satellite* framework.

SUGGESTED CORE SATELLITE APPROACH

"That all sounds a bit beyond me!" exclaimed Iain.

"I know," I agreed. "At the risk of scaring you off, I provided a more detailed explanation than what you need to **achieve YOUR goals and objectives**."

"At the very least you should aim to **match the returns of a Total Return index over the long term, but preferably you could seek to achieve a few compounded percentage points annually higher returns than a Total Return index**."

"Let's start getting more specific," I said. "This will lead us to structure YOUR Investment Plan, which has to be straightforward and efficient to execute."

"We looked at the preferred way that will beat 84% of all active mutual funds, which includes active equities mutual funds, Balanced Funds and Target Date funds, over five years or more. That means ***buying and holding an index ETF that has a strong growth track record. When you receive retirement contributions and dividends, invest them in that same index ETF.***"

I showed Iain Figure 11-2 that reflected this simple approach and reminded him of Chart 10-1 (in Chapter 10) showing how much the S&P MidCap 400 ETF, MDY, outperformed investing in the Vanguard Balanced Fund, VBINX.

Figure 11-2

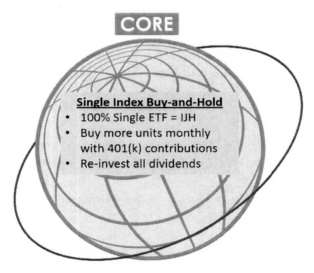

"This *Core Satellite* approach has 100% invested in the S&P MidCap 400 index ETF, IJH, with no satellites. Anyone could use it for any part of a portfolio. However, it ***lends itself very well to employees aged between twenty and fifty-five who make regular contributions to their retirement nest egg via any retirement savings accumulation and growth plan who want to minimize the time they spend managing their investments and maximize their investments growth,*** I explained.

Continuing, I added, "We also know from all our previous sessions and the evidence-based research from the SPIVA Persistence Report that, over periods of six years and longer, merely matching the index has a near 100% chance of beating all active mutual funds. And therefore beating active equities mutual funds, Balanced Funds, Target Date funds and bond funds. And you'll not only beat them; you'll do so by a large margin."

"Agreed," said Iain. "But why have you suggested the IJH ETF instead of the MDY ETF? Which ETF is IJH?"

"IJH is the iShares ETF for the S&P MidCap 400 index whereas MDY is the SPDR ETF for the same index. Both track this index the same way so you could use either ETF. I have used MDY in all the research that I have shown you because MDY was listed in 1995 and therefore has more historical performance data that I could use to show you for the twenty-year period ending in 2015. The listing of IJH occurred only in May 2000."

"Chart 11-1 shows how closely both of these ETFs track the S&P MidCap 400 index. All three of the S&P MidCap 400 index ($MID), MDY and IJH are plotted in Chart 11-1 from June 2000 to March 2016."

Chart 11-1 [Printed with permission from Beyond Charts]

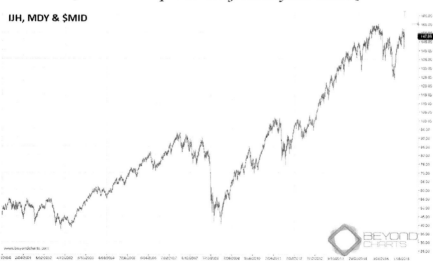

"Are three lines plotted on that chart? I can't notice any difference between them."

"This indicates how closely both MDY and IJH track the S&P

MidCap 400 index. *I suggest that IJH be used going forward because it can be bought and sold commission-free with some broker-dealers whereas MDY cannot."*

"Also IJH's annual management fees at 0.12% are less than half those of MDY at 0.25%," I added. "However, MDY is far more liquid meaning that there are more daily average dollars traded–about three to four times more–than in IJH. But IJH's daily average dollars traded is still healthy at between $100 million and $250 million daily."

"It looks like the lower annual fees and commission-free buying for re-investing dividends and monthly 401(k) (or IRA) contributions decides it for IJH," said Iain.

"We'll cover the commission-free trading in more detail when we get to your Investment Plan."

"If the plotting of Chart 11-1 is over about fifteen years shouldn't the annual ETF management fees cause a gap to open up between the index and the ETFs?" asked Iain.

"They would if the ETF provider deducted the fees from the ETF unit price. But they deduct the fees from the dividends before they are distributed to investors," I responded.

I summarized, "A key theme behind a *Core Satellite* investing approach is to minimize the risk of downside potential while putting capital at risk to earn a high return. As we've discussed, the investing fraternity calls this 'risk management.'"

"By investing in a single index ETF without any satellites or a strategy to manage the core portion, we are not actually doing any risk management, only return maximization. Return maximization of their retirement nest egg, or any other long-term growth needs, is fine for people up to about age fifty-five, but *as people reach within at least seven years of retirement, they should start adopting risk management techniques*, especially if a lot of growth has been achieved up until then."

I continued, "In essence, the *Core Satellite* investing approach is also another way of framing diversification across **different** asset classes that the Balanced Funds use. However, the *Core Satellite* approach also frames capital allocation in a way that supports a logical method of allocating your capital across multiple strategies in the **same** asset class."

"A little later we are going to tackle the 'risk management' issue differently, especially for people aged fifty-five through eighty, or even older. Rather than diversifying into lesser performing asset classes as Balanced

Funds and Target Date funds do, we will make the core portion a larger percentage, even the full 100% of capital, and deploy near-passive TIMING to manage risk, the risk being the downside potential that ensues from severe falls in the equities markets."

"The timing model for index ETFs, while active, requires so little effort it can be called *near-passive.*"

"The satellite portion may not be required. But if investors have different goals and have sufficient time, inclination and skill then they can use other active–meaning 'timing'–stocks strategies in the satellite portion. They could even use the same timing strategy utilized in the core portion but with some leverage. Remember, *the underlying theme is to use the satellite portion to take slightly larger risks with a smaller portion of the portfolio investment capital to achieve more growth for the overall portfolio.*"

"Before we get into the nuts and bolts of YOUR Investment Plan, I would like to share with you the investment philosophy that guides my approach, and hence the approach that my clients use. Hopefully, understanding my beliefs and the market principles to which I subscribe, that many others also have discovered through their research, will help you position YOUR Investment Plan."

LAST WORD:

- The *Core Satellite* approach provides a framework and ground rules by which investors can allocate their capital across different strategies. It provides a simple big picture concept for capital allocation.
- For all 401(k), IRA and retirement investors, the simplest and higher growth *Core Satellite* approach than active balanced mutual funds would be 100% of the 'core' portion invested in the iShares MidCap ETF, IJH.
  - ◊ For residents of other countries, please visit www. blueprinttowealth.com for comparable index ETFs with which to deploy this simple strategy.
- Investing in the iShares MidCap ETF, IJH, would be appropriate for everyone aged twenty to fifty-five who is investing for retirement. It could also be used by those that are older, depending on the age at which they plan to retire. Or by investors that invest monies outside of their retirement savings.
- Leading up to and post-retirement, investors should consider using 'risk management' techniques to reduce the effect of a large bear market, such as near-passive timing.

CHAPTER 12

My Investing Beliefs

"Our performance, relatively, is likely to be better in a bear market than in a bull market ... in a year when the general market had a substantial advance, I would be well satisfied to match the advance of the averages."

WARREN BUFFETT[1]

Warren Buffett's quote from all those years ago is very much part of my investing philosophy. I use timing that requires me to make decisions every few weeks, on average, for my long-term investing with ETFs and large-cap stocks, and to make more frequent decisions for my market-wide stock investing, aiming for potentially better performance through additional compounding.

I believe that investors should be on the sidelines in cash for most of a bear market while they can capture most of an advancing market by engaging the market with all investment capital.

However, with a little more passion, planning, preparation, patience, process, practice, perseverance, principled action, and perspective, active investors can do a lot better than "match the advance of the averages" when they have a "substantial advance"; even though only a little better will do.

To achieve this, I have a predetermined set of simple actions that I

---

1   Warren Buffett from page 2 of his 1957 Annual Letter to Shareholders

execute without any reservation, hesitation, fear, uncertainty or doubt; in a few minutes each day.

My Investment Plan documents the steps that guide everything I think, feel, say and do about investing, including my processes, decisions, attitude, and habits.

How do you reach the point of having such a straightforward, stress-free and easy-to-use process in such an uncertain, opinionated, volatile and complex environment as the financial markets?

What is the source of these simple actions? Why do I follow them as I do? How do I know that the steps of my process will work?

There are methods that I use that are aligned and consistent with my investing beliefs. And, these processes are aligned and consistent with how the market moves over a particular investing time frame.

A principle is an unchangeable and timeless truth that serves as a foundation for a chain of reasoning. Grasp, accept and trust investing principles and the execution of the investing process becomes simple.

You are probably wondering why I invest in this particular way. To answer that, let me talk about my investing journey and then I'll explain the essence of my approach to investing.

MY STORY

Over the years, I have been contacted by traders and investors who have wanted to understand more about my personal investment journey. People who have followed my blog (www.gary-stone.com/my-journal) know that I'm an advocate of technical analysis methods and systems. However, I began my journey as a fundamental analyst. I thought that if I invested capital in fundamentally sound stocks and past robust performers that I was certain to receive a return on both my capital and time. Sound familiar? Fortunately, I learned very early on that this wasn't necessarily the case. Instead, after doing lots of research, I took another path that has been both financially rewarding and personally fulfilling.

In the late 1980's in my late twenties, I found myself with capital to invest during a successful sales career in the computer industry. With no investing experience, I researched the available investment asset classes and decided to pursue investing in the stock market. My first stock market investment around June 1990 was in a company called BTR Nylex. I picked it for the sole reason it had been the best-performing stock in the 1980s!

Well, BTR Nylex didn't do that well. It mainly went down to sideways as I continued to churn through other non-performing stocks. My inconsistent outcomes resounded loud and clear; I needed to change the way that I went about investing. I needed to improve my timing and my basis for selecting stocks.

From 1990 to 1995, I was involved heavily in the study of fundamental analysis and technical analysis. My trading was sporadic and inconsistent, and the overall outcomes continued to be negative, despite a 40% bull market during most of 1991 and a 70% rise in the index from late 1992 to early 1994.

I reacted to tips, newsletters, broker-dealers input, financial magazines, company material and media reports, all of which I now classify as "noise." These were the primary ways I was "called to action" to take positions in the market. Even though I was studying financial market analysis techniques, the "noise" still got the better of me.

I battled to achieve any consistency. I had some good winning outcomes but also had some shock-horror loss trades. The shock-horror losses more than eclipsed the profit trades such as a warrant trade in a stock called WMC that later merged; it turned into a $14,000 loss. In the early 1990s, this was a huge loss that caused much angst and emotional pain! Yes, we remember the big loss trades; they seem to make larger imprints on our subconscious than the big winning trades.

My biggest problem, in hindsight, was not the analysis; it was that my investing decisions were inconsistent and subjective and based on reaction to "noise" from and around the markets. Rather than using my ever-increasing knowledge about fundamental and technical analysis to source an entry to a position objectively, I was using it to justify an idea that emanated from the "noise." This was the complete opposite from how I should have been investing. But I still had to work that out.

Despite thousands of hours of analysis spent over annual reports, hard-copy charts of stock price movement and at the computer screen, I was not able to determine *in advance, for sure,* what a losing trade looked like compared to a profitable one. At this stage, I still believed that I would be able to solve this problem as if it was a scientific equation – just as with my training in a formal university education when I completed a Science degree, majoring in mathematics and computer science.

In 1995, after more than five years of frustrating investing results, I decided there had to be a better way of investing in the markets. After all,

I had a university degree, was successful in the corporate world, had better than average skills as an athlete and other sports and had done pretty well in everything that I pursued. Why not in the financial markets? I had invested in the necessary tools and had five years of solid research under my belt in both technical and fundamental analysis.

After much reading, research, and soul searching, I decided to start working on designing a 'mechanical market system' to improve my investing results. I had been led to believe, although I didn't accept it at the time, that my difficulties had more to do with the way that I thought about the workings of markets rather than the logic that I tried to apply to my market-related decision making.

A 'mechanical market system' is a method that uses unambiguous criteria for precisely deciding when to enter a position, exactly how much money to invest in the position, and precisely when to exit the position.

By definition, unambiguous means that there can be no debate about the existence of an entry or an exit signal. It either exists, or it doesn't on any given day. There is no subjectivity or discretion about the existence of the signal.

The signal, and hence the investing decision, is purely dependent on price movement, not the "noise", outside influence or surmise from magazines, newspapers, TV shows, newsletters, family or colleagues. Or on emotional feelings about what you want to happen.

Market system design is not an easy activity. It is an arduous task that requires technical analysis skills, understanding of price movement concepts, computer programming skills, lots of time, discipline, motivation, rigor, curiosity and persistence to keep moving to a successful end. I know most who start don't finish.

It was during this time of research and design that I am convinced that my previous life experiences – my mathematics, statistics, and computer science training, practicing and playing team and individual sports such as golf, the long distance training and completion of numerous marathons and ultra-marathons–came to the fore. I had done the preparation part of the journey before in other walks of life and had experienced the associated successful outcomes. I had to do the same in the investing arena.

Through 1995 and 1996 the mechanical system started taking shape. At the beginning of 1997, I found myself in a year-long trading contest in *Personal Investor*, a financial monthly magazine. It was now or never. Would I use my volition and discretion, or would I trust the preparation that had gone into the mechanical system that I was creating?

Purposefully, I decided to use my system. It used market price movement to determine when to buy and sell, not my subjective volition. I had taken my first step towards reaching some degree of objectivity and consistency in my investing.

It was a life changing moment in my investing journey and was the next significant step on my journey to believe in, surrender to, and trust a researched process that emanated from the market, not from a discretionary human societal paradigm.

I won the publicly audited trading contest which ended in November 1997, a period that included the tenth anniversary of the 1987 stock market crash. The Australian All Ordinaries index dropped 10.8% in the last six weeks of the contest! The opening paragraph of the final report about the competition in *Personal Investor* magazine said, *"By the length of the proverbial straight, Gary Stone has won the shares investing competition."*

Subsequently, the magazine ran another twelve-month trading contest in 1998 which I won again using the medium-term mechanical investing system that I had been researching.

After a three-year project, I completed the research and design process during 1998 and finalized the unambiguous mechanical rules in precisely defined detail. The mechanical system was formally released as a product in Australia in August 1998 to my then customers. It was called SPA, or Share Profit Advantage ('Sustained' which was later changed to 'Share'), and renamed to SPA3 to reflect a later edition of the product.

In 2001 *Personal Investor* magazine re-introduced the idea of a year-long publicly audited investing contest. Again I was invited to participate, and again I used SPA3; which had become a far more mature product and was now being used by many hundreds of investors to manage their portfolios.

I was again successful in the year-long investing contest which used $100,000 starting capital. SPA3 performed very well in the January 2001 – January 2002 contest, the period in which 9-11 occurred. Despite the extreme volatility in the markets around that event, the audited SPA3 portfolio managed to return 29% over a year in the same period that the Australian All Ordinaries index posted a return of 4.5%.

Throughout this period, I continued to invest mechanically in my accounts, using the SPA3 system, and my investing performance continued to improve, matching and surpassing the results achieved in the trading contests. What was actually happening, as I was later to discover in 2004 when I met Mark Douglas, author of *Trading in the Zone* and an advocate of mechanical trading and investing, was that my investing habits were automatically transitioning from thinking with a societal paradigm to thinking with a market paradigm.

The mechanical system was transforming how I thought about the workings of the market. ***The more mechanical trades that I completed, the more empathetic I became to market price movement and how it behaved.***

I had begun to see the price action objectively from the market's perspective rather than from my own perceived perspective, and how it might potentially hurt or benefit me.

There were no more large-loss-trades as I systematically defined my risk for each trade and mechanically closed the position when called to do so by my objective rules. I started to achieve consistency through objectivity in the moment. I had mostly overcome the 'noise brigade' that surrounds the market, comprised mainly of *commentators who see the market from their perspective; which is pigeon-holed by the limitations of their subjective opinions about the future.*

I no longer reacted with a reflex response to the random short-term volatility of the market; as I now understood that this is a natural part of the ebb and flow of the market, impacted by thousands, even millions, of different variables interacting with stock price movement.

When short-term market randomness caused me to exit from open positions unexpectedly by reaching my unambiguous pre-defined exits, I understood and accepted that this could and would happen just as it had many times in my research of historical data. I knew and accepted that the exit was designed to save me from a possible large loss in an individual position. Despite such exits triggered by short-term randomness, the evidence from my research, and ensuing experience showed the existence of a robust positive edge that would generate net profits from the winning trades that also occurred.

Even though I wasn't conscious of it at the time, I was moving towards investing from a big picture perspective. I was comprehending and accepting that there is a random outcome in samples of one or a few, but over samples of many tens, or even many hundreds, there is a high degree of certainty of success. Provided that I executed according to a probabilistic edge, encapsulated within a structured process, I could have a positive expectation based on using the unambiguous and objective criteria as defined from an evidence-based research process.

I continue to use the SPA3 mechanical investing process as my investment approach for managing ETF and stock portfolios in the U.S. and Australia, both in personal and company open-book 'public portfolios', with the latter available for public scrutiny. It requires minimal effort which has left me plenty of time for my family, running a business, keeping fit, playing golf and writing this book. ***The returns-to-effort ratio is incredibly high.***

Further research over the years since SPA3 was first released, using exploratory simulation to stress test the system, has re-affirmed the methodology as has live execution in the market.

SPA3 supports investing in ETFs and stocks in the U.S. and Australia. It is a stocks/ETFs and cash strategy in which the rules support being entirely invested in stocks/ETFs and then totally in cash according to the Market Risk and ETF timing.

I have found that mechanical investing in ETFs and stocks has worked best for me – it has become the backbone of my investing life. I have been fortunate to have been able to share the SPA3 methodology with thousands of other like-minded everyday investors.

I have managed portfolios in real time in the public eye since 2001. Besides 1997 and 1998, *Personal Investor* magazine also audited and published my portfolio investing results monthly for two years in 2001 and 2002; I beat the market in all four years. Over a twelve-month period from July 1, 2006, to June 30, 2007, one of the four major accounting firms audited the publicly executed portfolio results of the SPA3 mechanical stocks system. Over that twelve-month period, the SPA3 open-book publicly managed and published portfolio achieved a return of 59.55% compared to the index gaining 27.28%.

Since January 2013, I have managed real money open-book publicly executed portfolios using our mechanical systems for stocks on the NASDAQ and for U.S. ETFs. Each transaction has been available for my clients to scrutinize since the early 2000s and is provided from time to time on my company's website (www.sharewealthsystems.com), or upon request from the Share Wealth Systems team.

There is a well-known Chinese Proverb that says; "To get through the hardest journey we need take only one step at a time, but we must keep on stepping." Perseverance has been a tenet of my approach to the markets since I began investing in June 1990 and hope it can be yours. The journey continues ...

My Beliefs about Investing in the Financial Markets

My beliefs about investing get to the core of why I invest via the stock market, why my company exists and why my team and I continue to do what we do so passionately.

At the highest level, I believe:

1. That the primary investing avenues for everyday people, that of active mutual funds and products offered by the 'big guys', need to be challenged, exposed and avoided as mainstream investing avenues in the stock market. This is done, firstly, by substantially outperforming them through the use of simple alternative strategies; and secondly, by making others aware of how to and why they can and should do it.
2. That the "little guys" should take control and do it themselves through the acquisition of knowledge and skills to be able to outperform the 'big guys."

I see myself as one of the "little guys."

-   The following *supporting values* are the foundation for these two *core beliefs*. The values have been cemented and energized in my psyche through personal research and experience, studying others' research and experiences, and mentors:
-   Active mutual funds (also called active managed funds), including 401(k) Plans, Target Date funds, Superannuation funds and pension funds the world over, struggle to match, let alone outperform their respective benchmark indices for periods of longer than five to six years, and sometimes even shorter periods.
-   These outcomes are due to three main reasons:
    ◊   The fees, based on FuM, that active mutual funds charge their investors to manage their fund, to pay their fund management teams, their distributed network of financial planners and advisers and to pay for marketing and advertising.

◊ Balanced Funds and Target Date funds diversify into or invest in *lower* performing asset classes than the stock market.

◊ Mistakes that active fund managers make when being active.

- Distributed networks of financial planners and advisers (and some accountants), who receive a percentage advice fee based on FuM, feed the active mutual fund industry. These fees increase the cost to the everyday investor.

    ◊ Figure 9-1 in Chapter 9 shows that two-thirds of IRA owners in the U.S. consult financial professionals and therefore pay additional fees in some way or another, all of which reduces long-term returns.

- To get sufficient protection and growth for their investments and overcome longevity risk–the risk of running out of money during retirement–average investors need to find a way to outperform the Total Return index by at least 2% compounded per year over any rolling periods of greater than ten years. ***I believe that the ONLY way to achieve this on a consistent basis is to do it yourself using an active growth strategy that also protects your capital from a severe bear market.***

- The biggest threat to any investor's nest egg is the big bear market, such as those that occurred in 2008, 2002, 1987, 1973, 1938 or 1929, in which there were close to or at least -50% declines in stock market indices. Many other bear markets have occurred with losses between -30% and -50%. The problem is that you don't know when the next big bear will appear, and if it occurs at the wrong time in an investor's lifetime, a retirement nest egg can get decimated and not recover in time to meet retirement needs.

- The only way to avoid most of a severe bear market, and thereby protect one's investment capital, retirement savings or otherwise, is by deploying an unambiguous, well-researched set of timing criteria. The process should require minimal vigilance that alerts the investor to exit the market to cash before a baby bear turns into a big bear.

- ALL investment asset classes including the stock market, residential property, commercial property, treasury bonds, corporate bonds or even exotic investments can experience many years of wide-ranging movement where there is little or no advance in asset values. Why do I believe this?

◊ There were five market declines of at least -45% between 1901 and 1921 with no advancement in the Dow Jones Industrial Average (DJIA) over this time. If it happened in the early 1900's, it could happen again.

◊ The DJIA made no gain for nearly seventeen years between January 1966 and October 1982.

◊ The S&P500 made no net gains for nearly thirteen years between March 2000 and February 2013.

◊ As at mid-November 2015, the FTSE100 Index is almost 10% below the peak that it reached on 30th December 1999, nearly sixteen years earlier.

◊ The above measurements all exclude dividends.

◊ Residential and commercial property prices in Japan are still less than 50% of what they were twenty-seven years ago, in 1989.

◊ Property price deflation has occurred multiples times in Europe over the last 400 years.

- Market risk (also called systematic risk) has the most significant potential adverse effect on long-term capital protection and growth. Therefore, market timing to move 100% into cash at times is necessary for a timeframe that is consistent with the investor's lifestyle and tolerance for risk.

- Leaving investment capital in cash for the long term instead of investing it in growth asset classes will remove the risk of loss but will also all but eliminate the potential for growth, which will ensure that longevity risk increases while inflation slowly erodes an investor's nest egg.

- Leverage will do more harm than good to more investors, due to leverage magnifying small mistakes. However, those with the necessary skills and processes can use leverage to their advantage.

- Investors should define their "level of excess" which, when reached, mean they no longer need to continue investing only for themselves but should also do so for others who are needy.

Motivated and inspired by these investing beliefs I have been on an ongoing journey for well over two decades discovering market principles that are consistent with these beliefs.

These beliefs fuel the core purpose of why my business Share Wealth Systems exists—to empower and skill everyday people to achieve a better life and retirement through stock market investing.

PRINCIPLES THAT I HAVE DISCOVERED
ABOUT INVESTING

I have sought principles applicable to the stock market that are consistent with my investing beliefs.

Among the tenets that I have discovered on my investing journey are:

- Price trends exist in the market.
- Price momentum builds and tends to persist, causing these price trends.
- Trends occur in the market in many time frames and in both directions, up and down.
- Trends repeat themselves in very similar but not identical patterns. There are many different types of patterns that repeat and each pattern repeats in large samples over time.
- Trends are caused by numerous and varied reasons and by many different variables. Causes for a trend is not necessarily the same for each in any given stock or traded instrument. Causes include but are not limited to:
  ◊ Breakouts above a previous high/low price.
  ◊ Mean reversion or the tendency to move to an average price over time, from a low/high to a higher/lower price. The average price referred to here can be heading in an up, down or sideways channel.
  ◊ Perceived price anomalies compared to a perceived intrinsic value.
  ◊ Ongoing company fundamental strength/weakness.
  ◊ Peer price pressure caused by, for example, the same sector, perceived similar characteristics (e.g. high yield, defensive, growth), same commodity, same geographical area, etc.
  ◊ News, e.g. government announcements, company announcements, cultural events, stories written about companies, discoveries, inventions, etc.
  ◊ Systematic risk, which is a falling market caused by geopolitical, events, wars, natural disasters, terrorism, economic or company growth, or positive sentiment.
  ◊ Cycles, such as seasons.
  ◊ Human despair, euphoria and emotional over-reaction.
- In any given time frame, trends end when price retracts sufficiently to determine that the trend has reversed direction.

- Trends end for wide-ranging reasons that change for each trend. Knowing the trend end prices in advance, for certain and consistently, can never be achieved.
- Trends can be measured over large samples via the movement in price by determining unambiguous criteria that signal when there is a high probability that a trend has started and that a trend has ended, in a particular time frame.
- Only price movement can measure trends.
- It is impossible for any entity or investor to be aware of all positive and negative causes that hold sway and to what degree at any given moment, in any given time frame, or in advance, for any given stock, commodity or investment instrument. That is, "anything can happen."
- ***It is not necessary to know the particular cause in advance for any given trend when unambiguous and objective criteria are used to determine the start and end of a trend.***
- When measuring trends over large samples, it is possible to determine the statistical edge for a set of unambiguous and objective criteria that define the start and end of the trend. Determining statistical edges has been a cornerstone of the research that we have done over many years at my company, Share Wealth Systems.
  - ◊ The fact that high probability positive statistical edges exist emphatically demonstrates that investors can exploit the price trends that exist in financial markets, and they can generate handsome profits.
- Repeating investment into and out of these trends using the criteria that define a positive probabilistic edge creates compounding of profits through the re-investment of realized profits into newly identified trends that comply with the probabilistic edge.
- The profits generated can be far greater than alternative investment avenues such as fixed interest, bonds, active mutual funds or buy-and-holding stocks or index funds.

Principles guide decision-making. Without principles in any activity, the range of options from which to choose is massively increased to the point of massive confusion and chaos; resulting in poor, inefficient and unproductive decision-making.

Discover principles in the market that are well founded. Do this and narrow your range of options to the point where decision-making will become simple, consistent and objective.

How can you determine whether your principles are sound or ill-founded? Look at the outcomes that they produce over a large sample of events that test your principles. If the results are positive in relation to your objectives, then you'll know that your principles are fundamental, unchangeable and timeless truths. These outcomes, and what you do to achieve them, will simply prove what you believe; leading to trust on a scale that breeds confidence to overcome fears, uncertainty, doubt, and adversity.

The more market principles your discover, the more you will think from and operate from the market's perspective. Your investing goal, therefore, is to discover market principles that are consistent with your investing beliefs, to create a set of values and rules based on those principles and then live your investing life by executing them according to those values and standards. Like life.

ON BUSYNESS

Life is made up of busyness: working, learning, dealing with adversity, recharging our batteries, spending time with family and friends, being challenged, helping others and many other things.

But we also spend plenty of time on not-so-important things that use up our time. Instead of wasting too much time browsing online or watching TV, you can choose to do more valuable tasks first. Prepare for, and focus on the big things such as relationships, development, health (mental, physical and spiritual) and investing for retirement. Then, you can spend time watching videos or commenting on social media posts.

Notice that we all 'spend' time watching TV, or 'spend' time on social media. Why not rather do things that 'save' or 'invest' time.

Saving and *investing* are better for our financial health than *spending*.

We can reuse many resources, such as money and materials but we cannot reuse time. So use time wisely. Do small maintenance things incrementally on your relationships, health, mind, body, spirit and finances rather than putting it off for some big bang project someday. That someday will probably never arrive. And there is only one person who will be responsible. YOU.

What we *invest* our time in is merely a matter of priorities, choice and focus. Where on your list of priorities do you place the big-ticket items in your life? What are the big picture concerns in your life? What matters and what is in your control?

Determine them and then place them near the top of your list of priorities and push the other *spending* items further down the list.

LAST WORD

- There are principles behind the processes that I use that are aligned and consistent with my investing beliefs. And, these beliefs are aligned and consistent with how the market moves in the time frame in which I invest.

- To achieve objectivity and consistency in investing, you must use market price movement to determine when to buy and sell, not your own subjective volition, or outside influence or surmise.

- Trends are simply part of stock market movements. You can never accurately predict when they will start and finish, but you can have a process in place that will tell you, based on pre-determined signals, whether it is time to sell or buy that will generate bigger profits than losses and hence net profits.

CHAPTER 13

Compiling an Investment Plan

"If you fail to plan, you are planning to fail."
BENJAMIN FRANKLIN

"It's such a clichéd quote but so true because few people actually do the necessary planning for anything, let alone their investing. It is very necessary to write an Investment Plan for long-term investing even if it is just one page to start. Do you have an Investment Plan, Iain?"

"No," he replied.

"Well, that is pretty consistent with new clients to my business over the past twenty years. Starting a new planning process for anything requires some degree of research; which is where most people get stuck."

"Do you have investing goals?" I asked Iain.

"Not written down anywhere although I do have a rough idea in my head. I guess this is a 'Maybe' but not a definite 'Yes'!" he said.

"A goal without a plan is just a wish."
ANTOINE DE SAINT-EXUPÉRY

"With most things in life preparation and planning are necessary to thrive and be effective and efficient. It is no different with investing. Stating your purpose for investing, doing the necessary research to determine how, when and in what vehicles you will invest ongoing retirement contributions, and what actions you will take in particular investing conditions, are all part of the essential preparation required to be a successful investor."

"That sounds like a lot of hard work," protested Iain.

"It needn't be. I'll give you a template Investment Plan. Even if your plan is to invest your 401(k) contributions in active mutual funds, *it would be remiss of you not to at least go through this process instead of checking off a box with little consideration for alternatives. Investing, particularly for retirement, is too important a part of your life to pay it so little attention.*"

"Need I repeat it, everybody who is contributing to a 401(k) Plan is an investor. Why not put in a little effort to be successful at it rather than accept an average to poor outcome by doing no planning yourself for YOUR money."

"Ok, where do I start?" asked Iain.

"Have you ever been involved in writing a Business Plan in any of your jobs?" I asked Iain.

"You're right; we had to do market research and product research, among other things, to compile the business plans in which I was involved."

"Correct," I said. "Compiling an Investment Plan is similar. But let me ask, do you think that writing the Business Plan was even necessary in the first place?"

Iain replied, "Yes. In my experience a Business Plan had two main benefits:

1. The first benefit was that it enforced a thought process that demanded you to determine why you were going to do something, what you were trying to achieve and how you would go about it. Part of the 'how' thinking was determining the best way to reach the objective, what obstacles you might encounter along the way and how to overcome them proactively.
2. The second benefit was in the execution phase of the plan; if an event occurred that caused someone to question what action to take, you could reference the Business Plan to determine objectively how to react under the circumstances."

"That's a great answer," I replied. "I assume that the outcomes of the why, what and how were all recorded in a single document?" I asked.

"Absolutely," responded Iain.

"Well then, writing your Investment Plan should be a cinch for you," I replied. "Let's look at the main components, and then we'll compile an actual simple plan for the simple strategy that we have already researched, that of buying and holding an S&P MidCap 400 index ETF."

MAIN COMPONENTS OF AN INVESTMENT PLAN

There are six main elements of an Investment Plan:

Mission Statement

- "Why are you investing?" This statement defines your ***purpose for investing***. It is your inspiration and motivation, particularly to persevere during challenging times.
- The answer may be to accumulate and grow capital for retirement, for your children's education, for income for another purpose, or to make a significant charitable contribution.
- May I suggest that you consider an even bigger mission, such that some or all of the above are merely a subset of your greater vision. Something that requires complete financial freedom, so that you can focus nearly all of your waking time achieving it without *having* to do other regular income generating tasks.

Goals and Objectives Statement

- This section defines the 'what.' It details the amount of starting capital, the period over which investing will occur, and the expected return in both dollar and percentage terms over the entire period and at various stages along the way.
- Achieving these goals will position and support you to work on your mission.
- It also details the necessary investing skills goals required to achieve the financial goals. These may be a higher priority than the financial goals and objectives as skills acquisition are a prerequisite depending on your financial goals and the strategies required to achieve them.

Method for the Strategy

- This section defines 'how' to achieve the 'why' and the 'what'.
- It describes the strategy, precise criteria for opening and closing a

position in the stock market. A method is required for each market strategy whether it's a long-term passive strategy, a long-term active investment strategy or even a short to medium-term trading strategy for, stocks, options, futures or even Forex.

- It defines the exact process for investing regular contributions and how to re-invest dividends.
- Following detailed research, it demonstrates and describes the known edge for the strategy if it is an active strategy – that is, what to expect.
  ◊ An edge, or Mathematical Expectation, or Expectancy is defined as $[(\text{Payoff Ratio} + 1) * \text{Win Rate}] - 1 > 0$, where Payoff Ratio = Average Winner/ Average Loser and Win Rate = Winning Trades/Total Trades. If this calculation is greater than 0 so that the sum of the winning trades exceeds the sum of the losing trades, then an edge exists. Also, include commission fees. The higher the Expectancy, the better.
- It stipulates which broker-dealer will be used to execute the process and what the commissions and fees will be.
- It could also include the entity through which you will execute the Investment Plan.

Risk Management

- Specifies the tools and rules to recognize, assess and manage risk according to your tolerance level for risk. The main risk to manage is 'market risk', also called systematic risk.
- Risk Management can be an integrated part of a particular Method.

Money Management

- Specifies how much capital is managed and allocated to individual asset classes and individual positions within asset classes.
- Money Management can be an integrated part of a particular Method in a given asset class.

Process Management

- This section includes the regular routines and procedures required for adhering to the signals and rules of the Method for buying and selling, the Money Management and the Risk Management.
- Monitoring your investments occurs on an ongoing basis to

determine if action is required and how it is tracking compared to the target benchmark.

All six components are key for consistent and objective execution in the stock market. Most market participants probably practice each element to some degree. Anyone who has participated in the market would have had profitable outcomes at some stage, if only due to randomness. The key to steady growth, however, is to be consistent in approach and process.

Remember, an Investment Plan does not exist until it has been committed to paper in sufficient detail to achieve the desired outcome.

The remainder of this book will address some portion of at least one these six sections of the Investment Plan.

SINGLE INDEX ETF, BUY-AND-HOLD STRATEGY

"We are made wise not by the recollection of our past but by the responsibility for our future."

GEORGE BERNHARD SHAW

"Iain, this sample Investment Plan is specially compiled for this strategy which is almost entirely passive except for the need to buy more ETF units on the stock exchange when:

1. The ETF pays a Dividend.
2. You make your regular 410(k) or IRA contribution." (In other countries these would be regular contributions for retirement, e.g. Superannuation contributions in Australia.)

I continued, "Depending on which index ETF is preferred and which broker-dealer an investor uses to buy more units of the ETF, there may be no need to pay any broker-dealer commission costs. A little homework to find a broker-dealer that supports an Automatic Investment Plan (AIP) or charges zero commission on certain ETFs can help reduce costs over the years."

Iain asked, "If I were to use this strategy I would probably lean towards the S&P MidCap 400 index. Two of the ETFs that you have shown in your research for this index are the State Street SPDR MDY ETF and the iShares IJH ETF. Could I use an index mutual fund? If so, what are the equivalent index mutual funds for this index?"

I responded, "There is a smaller choice of index mutual funds. Vanguard has a MidCap index mutual fund, VSPMX, but for institutional investors only, meaning a minimum of $5,000,000 to invest. There are a few others suitable for ordinary investors for a MidCap index."

Some online exploring found these index mutual funds:

- Vanguard's VIMSX index mutual fund tracks the CRSP MidCap, which is a similar index to the S&P MidCap 400 index.
  - ◊ It is the index mutual fund equivalent of Vanguard's VO ETF.
  - ◊ VIMSX supports an AIP and pays dividends quarterly. (VIMAX is an 'Admiral Class' version of VIMSX, which typically means lower fees but higher initial investment.)
- Northern Trust's NOMIX supports an AIP and a dividend re-investment plan without paying any broker-dealer fees. NOMIX pays dividends annually.
- Columbia Threadneedle NTIAX supports an AIP. NTIAX pays dividends annually.
- Principal Funds PMFNX, but this appears closed to new investors at the moment.

The different MidCap ETFs, their providers, and which of the two MidCap indices that they track, are:

- MDY, State Street SPDR, S&P MidCap 400 index ETF.
- IVOO, Vanguard, S&P MidCap 400 index ETF. It is the ETF equivalent of the Vanguard VSPMX institutional index.
- IJH, BlackRock iShares, S&P MidCap 400 index ETF.
- JKG iShares, MorningStar MidCap index ETF.
- VO, Vanguard, CRSP MidCap index ETF.
- SCHM, Schwab, DJUS MidCap index ETF.
- MDYG, State Street SPDR, S&P MidCap 400 Growth index ETF.
- MDYV, State Street SPDR, S&P MidCap 400 Value index ETF.
- IJK, State Street SPDR, S&P MidCap 400 Growth index ETF.
- IJJ, State Street SPDR, S&P MidCap 400 Value index ETF.
- JKH iShares, MorningStar MidCap Growth index ETF.
- JKI iShares, MorningStar MidCap Value index ETF.

"I have summarized these ETFs in Table 13-1," I said to Iain. "We have discussed **Turnover** as being the percentage of the FuM that the fund sells and buys over the previous twelve months. For example, IJK turns over half of its $5.4 billion of funds under management annually, or around $2.7 billion, which would be relatively small compared to VO's 11% turnover of $6.6 billion."

Table 13-1

ETF Symbol	ETF Name	Fees	FuM	Turnover	Liquidity	Years since Inception to Jun 30 2015
MDY	SPDR S&P400 Mid Cap	0.25%	14.8B	16.7%	500M	20.2
IJH	iShares S&P400 Mid Cap	0.12%	26.7B	15%	150M	15.1
JKG	iShares MorningStar S&P400 Mid Cap	0.25%	529M	55%	1.5M	11.0
IVOO	Vanguard S&P400 Mid Cap	0.15%	1.1B	12%	1.5M	4.8
VO	Vanguard CRSP Index Mid Cap	0.09%	66B	11%	50M	11.4
SCHM	Schwab DJUS Mid Cap	0.07%	1.9B	12%	9M	4.5
MDYG	SPDR S&P400 Mid Cap Growth	0.21%	317M	53%	1.5M	9.6
MDYV	SPDR S&P400 Mid Cap Value	0.21%	156M	44%	.75M	9.6
IJK	iShares S&P400 Mid Cap Growth	0.25%	5.4B	50%	25M	14.9
IJJ	iShares S&P400 Mid Cap Value	0.25%	3.9B	42%	15M	14.9
JKH	iShares MorningStar S&P400 Mid Cap	0.30%	214M	50%	.65M	11.0
JKI	iShares MorningStar S&P400 Mid Cap	0.30%	178M	33%	.75M	11.0

"What does 'Liquidity' mean?" asked Iain.

"The **Liquidity** column shows the average daily traded dollar value and indicates which ETF is the easier to buy and sell on any given day. Liquidity is averaged over three months to smooth out the effect of large volume days. Note that the most **FuM** doesn't necessarily mean the most liquid. Based on liquidity, MDY and IJH would be the two most tradeable S&P400 ETFs."

"Having said that, measuring the liquidity of ETFs is different from stocks. Index ETF providers can access liquidity from the stock constituents of the underlying index that they track."

"Also, some broker-dealers offer commission-free investing in some of these index ETFs. All the ETFs just mentioned pay dividends quarterly. Paying dividends annually, which many index mutual funds do, reduces compounding. Index mutual funds also typically charge slightly higher annual management fees than their equivalent ETF. Therefore, it would be preferable to use index ETFs rather than their corresponding index mutual funds."

I continued, "For example:

- TD Ameritrade offers commission-free buying and selling on over 100 ETFs, including IJH.
- Fidelity offers commission-free ETF trading for around seventy ETFs including the main iShares ETFs and IJH, IJK and IJJ from the list in Table 13-1.
- Schwab OneSource offers commission-free ETF buying and selling for Schwab ETFs and ETFs from other ETF providers, including the SCHM, MDYG, and MDYV ETFs, but not MDY or IJH.
- Firstrade also offers commission-free buying and selling of IJH and other ETFs.
- Other broker-dealers in the U.S. may offer commission-free buying and selling for varying lists of ETFs."

"With all these S&P MidCap 400 ETFs, remind me why you chose to show me the charts using MDY?" asked Iain.

"I used MDY purely because it had the longest set of historical data to show twenty years of performance compared to active Balanced Funds and Target Date funds. State Street was first to market with its ETF, MDY, for the S&P MidCap 400 index."

"iShares IJH tracks the S&P MidCap 400 index just as closely as MDY, as I showed you in Chart 11-1 in Chapter 11. iShares first listed IJH in July 2000. Because IJH can be bought and sold commission-free with a few broker-dealers, this is the ETF that I will suggest in this Investment Plan. Meaning that there will be no additional commission cost for investing regular monthly contributions and for re-investing dividends thereby reducing ongoing fees and increasing compounding over the long term. Also, IJH's annual management fee of 0.12% is half that of MDY of 0.25%."

"Now that we are getting down to brass tacks, through which entity should I execute this Investment Plan?" asked Iain.

RETIREMENT INVESTING ENTITIES

I explained to Iain that there are several ways to do this yourself and that he should seek rules and tax advice before finalizing his decision because there are a number of variables to consider, including one's age, salary, and tax situation.

The guiding principles are that you use an entity that provides you with ***the greatest degree of control over your investment decisions at the lowest cost***. This will:

- Substantially reduce recurring annual fees based on a percentage of the size of your investing capital.
- Use fixed costs wherever possible.
- Maximise growth without the ongoing burden of contributions tax and tax on profits that you make in your nest egg, which significantly limit growth.
- Allow you to follow the strategies that we and others have researched.

Here are the choices of entity, but you should also do your own home-work for your particular situation:

- Choose a 401(k) where your employer matches or partially matches your non-taxed contributions whenever possible since the matching employer contribution is as good as free money.
  - ◊ A traditional 401(k) is the most well-known entity.
  - ◊ A Roth 401(k) where you pay tax on your regular contributions but future withdrawals during retirement will be tax-free.
    - As at 2016, traditional and Roth 401(k) contributions can be up to $18,000 annually if you're aged less than fifty and up to $24,000 if you're aged fifty and older.
  - ◊ Even though investing flexibility may exist, employer 401(k) Plan providers charge fees that may not be obvious to the employee. These fees can range from 0.3% to 1.2% per year; ask your employer's 401(k) Plan provider. You can find additional information on the United States Department of Labor website: http://www.dol.gov/ebsa/publications/401k_employee.html
- The entity which allows the most investing flexibility is an Individual Retirement Account (IRA).
  - ◊ The everyday investor can establish either a traditional IRA or a Roth IRA. A traditional IRA allows tax-free contributions with tax deferred until after retirement while a Roth IRA requires taxed contributions with no tax due on distributions during retirement.
  - ◊ During retirement, a traditional 401(k) or IRA requires minimum annual withdrawals. A Roth IRA does not require minimum annual withdrawals.

Which you use between a 401(k) and an IRA will depend on your circumstances, but a limiting factor with either of these IRAs is the annual contribution limit of $5,500 if you're younger than fifty years old and $6,500 if you're aged fifty and older. There are also other limitations at the higher end of salaries depending on your current salary.

- If you are a sole proprietor, then an Individual (or Solo) 401(k) is an option to achieve high annual contributions limited at $53,000 if you're younger than fifty years old and $59,000 if you're aged older than fifty.
- A SEP IRA is also an option for the self-employed or small business-person. The current annual contribution limit is $53,000.
  ◊ An everyday investor can establish an Individual 401(k) or SEP IRA with most broker-dealers such as TD Ameritrade, and typically have small or no ongoing fees.
- Both a 401(k) and an IRA can be used simultaneously, including traditional and Roth. You should seek tax advice for your particular situation before deciding a way forward.
- Two of the simplest entities with the combination of investing flexibility and higher contribution limits are the SIMPLE IRA and SIMPLE 401(k). The 2016 employee contribution limits are $12,500 if you're younger than age fifty and $15,500 if you're aged fifty or older, and can be even higher with employer contributions. Not all companies can provide a SIMPLE plan; companies must have 100 or fewer employees.

"Which entity you use will also be influenced by the investing flexibility of your firm's current 401(k) Plan provider," I said to Iain. "Some 401(k) Plan providers will allow individual employees the flexibility to execute the Investment Plan that we are about to compile, such as ForUsAll.com. Others not."

I continued, "If your company's 401(k) Plan provider is inflexible it may be difficult to execute the Investment Plan that we are about to write up. The self-employed and small business owners, on the other hand, should have the least problems establishing this investing regime."

"I'll do some research on whether I have this flexibility in my employers 401(k) Plan," said Iain.

He continued, "If the returns over the next twenty years are similar to the last twenty years I should be able to achieve my target retirement savings with the current traditional and Roth IRA contribution limits. I'm sure that the limits will increase a little over the next twenty years too as over ten years ago IRA contribution limits were much lower at $3,000 and $3,500."

"Correct," I said. "To achieve the necessary amount of $1,543,135 for a couple to enjoy a comfortable independent retirement in twenty years' time with the limited annual contributions for an IRA, a compounded annual growth rate of 10.4% would be required. Remember that a typical Target Date fund's growth rate of 6.4% wouldn't let you reach that target even with the maximum annual 401(k) contributions of $18,000 and $24,000 for a single breadwinner in a household."

"Last question before we look at the Investment Plan. If I wanted to use the S&P500 Equal Weight index, which ETF would suit best and are there equivalent mutual funds?" asked Iain.

"This is a simpler choice than for the S&P MidCap 400 index," I responded. "I have mentioned Guggenheim's RSP ETF, which is the only S&P500 Equal Weight index ETF, is commission-free with Charles Schwab only, and it pays quarterly dividends. Its annual management fee of 0.4% is higher than most other index ETFs. The equivalent index mutual fund for the S&P500 Equal Weight index is Invesco's VADAX, which has a higher annual management fee at 0.56% and pays dividends annually."

"I've gone into some detail about entities, commission-free buying of ETFs and reinvesting of dividends. You should be aware of these factors, but I don't want you to get bogged down in the details and distracted from the overall investing strategy and potential associated returns. So let's step back to get some big picture perspective again and write a simple Investment Plan for this strategy."

INVESTMENT PLAN FOR THE SINGLE INDEX ETF BUY-AND-HOLD STRATEGY

This Investment Plan is relevant from January 4, 2016, and supersedes all other versions of this Investment Plan.

This Investment Plan assumes the investment entity to be a traditional IRA, but other retirement entities can also use it as is.

Mission Statement

This Investment Plan only covers investment capital that is focused on *growing retirement savings* by as much as possible over the long term, for a minimum of twenty years.

To grow the current investment capital of $162,000 until December 31, 2035, by between 0% at worst case and 13% compounded per year.

The specific dollar target is $1,543,000 using the Method described in this Plan.

Goals and Objectives

The overall objectives are to:

- Use a simple, efficient and structured process for passive investing using Exchange Traded Funds (ETFs) that **takes no longer than fifteen minutes a quarter** to manage. (Skills goals will take longer if pursued.)
- To accumulate a nest egg and maximize growth for the stakeholders:
  ◊ Invest $162,000 starting capital according to this Plan beginning on January 4, 2016, with no capital withdrawals.
  ◊ The Method will not make use of any leverage.

The **Reward Objective**–nest egg performance goal–is to:

To achieve **2.8% CAR better** *than the CAR of the S&P500 Total Return index. That is, to achieve* **11.71% CAR** *over twenty years.*

The S&P500 Total Return index is the benchmark for this Investment Plan. (This is the comparative reference for the majority of capital invested in active equity mutual funds and Balanced Funds.

[See Method below for an explanation of outperformance.]

To put this further into perspective, based on research over twenty years, and similar market conditions in the future, this Reward Objective could then also be:

- Around 3.8% (11.71% – 7.91%) compounded per year, better than the Vanguard Balanced Fund, VBINX, and
- Around 4.8% to 5% (11.71%–6.9%) compounded per year, better than any of the current 2035 Target Date funds, such as Fidelity's FFTHX and Vanguard's VTTHX, up until that time.

Notes:

1. While 11.71% CAR is the Reward Objective, 10.4% CAR plus

monthly IRA contributions and reinvesting dividends should achieve the Mission of $1,543,000 as of December 31, 2035, for a comfortable independent retirement.

    a.   10.4% CAR without IRA contributions would achieve around $1,162,300.

    b.   10.4% is roughly the same CAR achieved by the MDY ETF with reinvesting dividends.

2.   Achieving 11.71% CAR, plus monthly IRA contributions, would reach $1,915,854, without indexing IRA contributions for inflation.

3.   If the Plan achieves $1,915,854, what to do with the additional retirement savings of $372,854 is considered at the end of Chapter 18.

The **Risk Objective** for the portfolio is:

This portfolio will not have any Risk Objective as it will accept whatever drawdowns result from using the strategy described under Method. The portfolio is a passive one that doesn't include any selling at any stage; unless the Investment Plan is modified to do so.

The **Skills Objective** for the portfolio is:

To achieve investing skills improvements with respect to investing mindset, purchasing additional ETF units, market environment understanding, investing knowledge, journaling, strategy design and any other skills that may be identified to add a Satellite strategy alongside the Core.

Method

Buy and Hold the Applicable ETF, according to the following actions:

- Start the portfolio with $162,000 on January 4, 2016.
- Contribute $5,500 per annum, or $458.33 per month, to retirement savings until the age of fifty (2021 for Iain). After age fifty, contribute $6,500 annually, or $541.67 per month.
  - ◊ Adjust these amounts accordingly as the IRA contribution limits are increased by the government and are affordable.
  - ◊ Contributions will total $125,000 over the twenty years, excluding inflation adjustments.

- Reinvest all dividends by purchasing more units in the Applicable ETF, which pays dividends quarterly.
  - ◊ Use a Dividend Re-Investment Plan (DRIP), if available. A DRIP should be a prerequisite for selecting the broker-dealer if available, combined with the availability of commission-free ETF buying.
- Reinvest all regular IRA contributions.
  - ◊ Buy additional ETF units the next trading day after the quarterly Dividend is received , to the value of the Dividend plus 3 x months of IRA contributions.
  - ◊ Currently, no Automatic Investment Plan (AIP) is available for the Applicable ETF. Monitor this with various broker-dealers to simplify the regular investing process further.
  - ◊ Purchasing quarterly instead of monthly *reduces effort considerably to just fifteen minutes a quarter rather than fifteen minutes a month*.
- The purchase of additional ETF units will use a Market on Open (MoO) order.
  - ◊ The Applicable ETF is a liquid ETF that should attract multiple bids and asks on the Open; this will hopefully reduce the spread for additional purchases.
- Consider TD Ameritrade, Fidelity or Firstrade, which all offer commission-free ETF investing for the Applicable ETF.

[**Explanation of outperformance 2.8% CAR** is the outperformance that the S&P MidCap 400 ETF MDY, achieved, including reinvestment of dividends and payment of ETF fees, over the S&P500 Total Return index, i.e. 11.71%–8.91% over twenty years from 1995 to 2015. The S&P500 ETF SPY achieved 8.8% CAR, including reinvestment of dividends and payment of ETF fees.]

Instruments used

This portfolio will focus on just one ETF, the Applicable ETF:

- IJH

Follow the Method in this Investment Plan as depicted in the Core Satellite diagram in Figure IP-1, i.e. there are no Satellites.

Figure IP-1

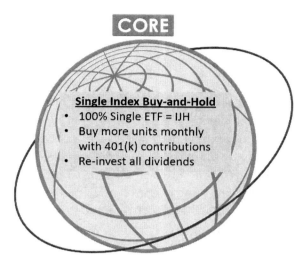

Reviewing Instruments in which to invest

From time to time, or at least every year on July 1, review the Applicable ETF compared to other available S&P MidCap 400 ETFs. Use the following criteria:

- A significant change occurs in the characteristics of the Applicable ETF. For example, the relationship between the ETF and the underlying S&P MidCap 400 index changes and large tracking errors result.
  ◊ Use a chart similar to Chart 9-1 to determine this.
- A significant shift in the business prospects for iShares that may endanger the existence of the Applicable ETF. While this is inconceivable at the moment, "anything can happen."
- The liquidity of the Applicable ETF falls dramatically for a few contiguous months.
- The annual management fees for the Applicable ETF change to be high relative to other S&P MidCap 400 ETFs.
- The Applicable ETF is no longer commission-free, and other S&P MidCap 400 ETFs are.

If any of these conditions arise, the Investment Plan will be revisited in its entirety to find a similar Applicable ETF in which to invest the total funds accumulated to date.

These conditions are no different from investing in any other mutual funds.

Risk Management

Market Risk

- As this is a passive buy-and-hold strategy, no Market Risk management will be considered until January 1, 2031 (which is five years' before the start of retirement). At this time a timing strategy may be considered to assist in reducing a potentially significant drawdown in a severe bear market in relatively close proximity to retirement.
- Review this in light of improved investing skills and knowledge every three years as per the Skills Objective in the Investment Plan.

Definition of Market Risk

The definition of **Market Risk** is: the possibility of an investor experiencing significant portfolio drawdown due to any factor(s) that negatively affect the overall performance of financial *markets*.

Diversification cannot eliminate Market risk, also called "systematic *risk*." There are a number of methods to hedge against and to minimize risk, including going into cash from time to time.

Liquidity Risk

Do not open a position in any ETF whose daily liquidity averaged over the prior three months is less than 25x the Portfolio Value.

Portfolio Value (i.e. the total current value of the retirement nest egg) is used for this calculation because just a single position will be open at any given time in the portfolio. However, it won't be sold for many years since it is a buy-and-hold strategy.

Calculate the liquidity by using the 'Liq xMA' indicator in Beyond Charts. Or thus: the sixty-three-day Simple Moving Average of price is multiplied by the sixty-three-day Simple Moving Average of volume and then plotted daily.

View the example Chart IP-1 where graph one at the top is the IJH price movement, and graph two at the bottom shows that IJH averages US$160 million per day (the thick horizontal line) and oscillates between US$100M and US$250M in traded value per day.

Note: This calculation is an indication of the tradability for the Applicable ETF. The traded value of all the constituents in the underlying index that the Applicable ETF tracks determines the actual liquidity for an ETF.

Chart IP-1 [Printed with permission from Beyond Charts]

Money Management

This Portfolio does not require Money Management as the single ETF position has all the capital invested in it.

Open Positions and Risk Distribution

The planned number of Open Positions will only ever be one.

Money in the Market

The objective is to expose all capital to the stock market at all times.

Position sizing

There is only ever one open position with 100% of capital invested.

Starting the Portfolio

Once the investor deposits the money into the IRA account, invest it straight away by purchasing units in the Applicable ETF. That is January 4, 2016.

This is a passive Investment Plan, so do not attempt timing at any stage (until five years before retirement starts or the Plan is changed to being more active), including when to start.

Process Management

Keep a readily available hard-covered file which will contain all paper records of:

- This Investment Plan and all future versions.
- Account administration such as communications with the broker-dealer, including regular broker-dealer statements.
- Records of regular quarterly Applicable ETF purchases from IRA contributions.
- Records of quarterly dividend reinvestments.

If the investor pursues further skills, consider starting an Investment Journal to maintain as part of meeting the Skills Objectives; though they are not necessary to execute this Investment Plan.

Not any deviation from the Investment Plan in the Journal.

- If the deviation results in a modification to the Investment Plan, it will be formalized in a newer updated version of the Investment Plan.
- Implement Version Control for this Investment Plan.
- If the deviation was an error, action will be taken to ensure that it does not recur, by, for example, journaling or making additional notes in the Process Management section of the Investment Plan.

The Quarterly Process

Step 1 – Dividends reinvested AND buy more ETF units with 3 x monthly IRA contributions

- If a DRIP is not available:
  - ◊ buy more ETF units with a Market on Open order when the dividend is deposited into the broker-dealer account, to the value of the dividend plus 3 x monthly IRA contributions.
- If a DRIP is available:
  - ◊ ensure that the DRIP is executed after the Dividend Date Payable at the end of March, June, September, and December.
  - ◊ place a Market on Open order to purchase additional ETF units in the Applicable ETF on the first trading day after every third IRA contribution is received.

END OF INVESTMENT PLAN

Share Wealth Systems executes and updates the strategy in this Investment Plan monthly. Please visit the webpage www. blueprinttowealth.com to see how it has performed since January 4, 2016, compared to Balanced Funds and Target Date funds.

Australians can refer to the Appendix for the suggested modifications to this Investment Plan for the Australian context.

RECOMMENDED ACTIONS AND LAST WORD ON FEES

Create an Investment Plan similar to this as a potential replacement for using a financial advisor. And potentially to replace the fees you're paying to a 401(k) Plan and any active mutual funds that they may use. Get those fees you would have paid working for you rather than for them. That's right, do it yourself and do better.

Sixty-six percent of IRA investors in the United States (58% as their primary source) use financial advisors, as shown in Figure 9-1 in Chapter 9. If investors continue to use advisors, the difference typically paid in recurring fees is around 1% per year of FuM (for face to face but less for online or robo-advice) for the rest of the everyday investor's investing life. *The combination of advisor fees and active mutual fund fees* WILL potentially cost the investor hundreds of thousands of dollars in direct costs and lost compounding, over a twenty-year period.

Combine this with paying fees to 401(k) Plans (and other retirement nest egg investing institutions around the world) and investors are getting fee-fleeced year in and year out.

Furthermore, "*excessive caution*", as Charles Ellis calls it, leads to diversification of your investments across multiple asset classes by Balanced Funds and Target Date funds. Investment advisers will typically suggest diversification too. Too much diversification leads to further loss of compounded growth over many years.

While the majority of investment advisers will typically recommend diversification across a number of active mutual funds, it amazes me that their advice *could* be as simple as "invest all your retirement savings and future contributions and dividends into a single index ETF." Or "spread your retirement savings and future contributions and dividends across these two or three index ETFs."

Such 'privileged' advice from the investment advisor could cost you around 1% compounded per year for years in *additional direct costs and opportunity cost* if you allow the advisor to execute this straightforward advice through his firm instead of you doing it yourself directly into exactly the same ETFs. Perhaps you should start doing it yourself as per Iain's Investment Plan!

Iain asked, "So what could it really cost me in absolute dollars? We have looked at some scenarios of what it could cost others but show me a table that directly quantifies what I lose if I pay an investment advisor every year to help me?"

"Alright, let's do the calculations," I replied. "But first read part of an interview with John Bogle, the founder of Vanguard, that he did in November 2012[1]."

[Interviewer question] ... I don't have a hard time understanding that it's hard to pick winners, but what I have a hard time understanding is that a 2 percent fee that I might pay to an actively managed mutual fund is going to really have a great impact on my future retirement savings. How do you get that across to people?

*[John Bogle] ... Well, you have to rely on somebody to get out a compound interest table and look at not the impact on the year's return, but **look at the impact over an investment lifetime.***

*You compound 7 percent, let's say as a hypothetical stock market return, and compare it with 5 percent, which is the same stock market return minus 2, and at the end of the investment lifetime, there's a gap of 30 percent for each 100 cents the market delivers. **You get 30 cents, or 30 percent.***

[Author's comment: this should be, "... a gap of 70 percent for each 100 cents..."]

[Interviewer question] ... I've lost two-thirds of my retirement savings?

*[John Bogle] ... Exactly. It's mathematically a certainty. ... So why don't we have people asking what I will call, in all modesty, the Bogle question? Do you really want to invest in a system where **you put up 100 percent of the capital, you, the mutual fund shareholder, you take 100 percent of the risk, and you get 30 percent of the return?** ...*

"That can't be!" exclaimed Iain. "Just 2% per year less in returns and I'll be left with only a third of what my nest egg should have been?"

---

1   Source:http://www.pbs.org/wgbh/frontline/article/john-bogle-the-train-wreck-awaiting-american-retirement/

"John Bogle did say "investment lifetime." Let's do the calculations," I replied.

Iain and I then spent ten minutes or so compiling Table 13-2 with a 2% CAR (compounded annual return) differential with a starting capital of $162,000 and no additional contributions, just raw CAR.

The **% of Potential** shows how much in percentage terms Iain would have had left of his nest egg over the period in the leftmost column.

The left half of Table 13-2 calculates the 2% differential between 7% CAR and 5% CAR; the right half the 2% differential between 5% CAR and 3% CAR. There is not much difference in the **% of Potential**.

Table 13-2

	5% CAR	7% CAR	% of Potential	3% CAR	5% CAR	% of Potential
10 years	$262,811	$316,887	82.9%	$217,174	$262,811	82.6%
20 Years	$428,093	$623,364	68.7%	$291,858	$428,093	68.2%
35 Years	$889,978	$1,719,881	51.7%	$454,690	$889,978	51.1%
50 Years	$1,850,209	$4,745,204	39.0%	$708,370	$1,850,209	38.3%
60 Years	$3,013,805	$9,334,534	32.3%	$951,970	$3,013,805	31.6%

"It turns out that **John Bogle is mathematically correct,** but it will take just over sixty years to qualify as an 'investment lifetime' to get to '30% of the return,' but that's how long Warren Buffett has been at this investment activity. If you think about it, with retirement contributions beginning when an eighteen to twenty-year-old starts working, in some countries like Australia these contributions being compulsory, that's at least how long they will all be investors."

"Sixty years is out of the question for me," said Iain, "but twenty and thirty-five years certainly are in my range. With a 2% CAR difference over twenty years, *I would lose a third of my potential nest egg*, or $195,271 and be left with 68.7%, or $428,093, compared to $623,364."

"Over thirty-five years a 2% CAR differential in total fees paid would *erode nearly half of my potential nest egg*, or $829,903 of $1,710,881! That's incredible!" he exclaimed.

"These days you probably wouldn't get to a 2% CAR differential unless you are also paying an advisor, but not many everyday investors would even know what the total fees are that are being paid away every year."

"Currently, your annual fees paid to the Vanguard Balanced Fund, VBINX, are low. But I doubt you know what the total percentage fees are that you pay to your employer 401(k) Plan provider. You also don't use an investment advisor, but nearly two-thirds of Americans with IRAs do. And last but not least there is the opportunity cost that is 'paid' due to diversification that leads to underperforming a stock market index, such as the S&P MidCap 400 index."

"Add all these up and I'm confident that it will be more than 2% per year that vanishes from your nest egg when you include all these costs."

"How much would I be giving up in lost compounding in percent if the differential was 1.5% CAR or 2.5% CAR?" asked Iain.

We plugged in the numbers which showed that for a differential of 1.5% CAR, in the left half of Table 13-3, over twenty years Iain would be *giving away a quarter of his money in lost compounding, and over thirty-five years nearly 40%*.

Table 13-3

	5.5% CAR	7% CAR	% of Potential	4.5% CAR	7% CAR	% of Potential
10 years	$275,488	$316,887	86.9%	$250,660	$316,887	79.1%
20 Years	$470,576	$623,364	75.5%	$389,268	$623,364	62.4%
35 Years	$1,050,554	$1,719,881	61.1%	$753,345	$1,719,881	43.8%
50 Years	$2,345,349	$4,745,204	49.4%	$1,457,938	$4,745,204	30.7%
60 Years	$4,006,208	$9,334,534	42.9%	$2,264,136	$9,334,534	24.3%

The right half of Table 13-3 shows that he would *give away 37.6% over twenty years and more than half at 56.2% over thirty-five years* for a differential of 2.5% CAR!

Iain replied, "I guess the message is to get the compounding working in my favor rather than for somebody else. Just as Albert Einstein said we should."

"Since we're discussing financial planners, I want to say that financial planners can be useful. A financial plan can help you consider all the parts of your financial life:

1.   Initiating the planning process in the first place.
2.   Relevant insurances appropriate for one's line of work, lifestyle, and phase of career and business interests.

3. Rules and tax efficiency applicable to your age, income, career, investments and tax situation.

4. Assisting with deciding on the most tax-effective retirement investing entity for you."

"However, these can all be achieved by paying a one-time fee-for-service every few years with specialists in each of the related fields. After all, an accountant or a lawyer charges a fixed hourly rate."

I continued, "Most financial planners and investment advisers still typically charge fees year in and year out based on percent-of-FuM, regardless of whether they meet with you or not. A few charge partially fee-for-service and partially percent-of-FuM, and even fewer charge fee-for-service for all fees; that is, for their time only. Fees for time only would typically have very high fixed hourly rates."

"There certainly is no need to be paying a percent-of-FuM in fees every year for the rest of your investing life for investment advice. The absolute size of the fees will continue to scale up as the size of your retirement savings increase, even if only by your contributions, let alone the market growing them for you, and not the investment advisor."

Last Word:

- Compile a DIY Investment Plan to ensure that you do the necessary thinking, research, and planning. Your retirement savings are just too valuable not to make a plan.
- Do this by asking yourself lots of questions. Visit the Resources page on the website www.blueprinttowealth.com for a template of detailed Investment Plan Questions.
- Minimize recurring percent of FuM fees!
- Minimize recurring percent of FuM fees!
- Minimize recurring percent of FuM fees!
- Calculate and set financial goals.
- Then put a plan in place that specifies how you will achieve them.
- Then execute the Plan.
- For Applicable ETFs in Australia see the *Appendix for Australian Readers*.
- This Investment Plan can be ideal for:
    ◊ Younger generations with plenty of time ahead of them and who are time-poor today.
    ◊ Those with small amounts of money to invest, from a few hundred dollars to a few thousand.
- Share Wealth Systems executes and updates the strategy in this Investment Plan monthly. Please visit the webpage www.blueprinttowealth.com to see how it has performed since January 4, 2016, compared to Balanced Funds and Target Date funds.

CHAPTER 14

Risk Management through Timing

"There's a time to make money, and there's a time to not lose money."

DAVID TEPPER

Everyday investors are so afraid of the trumpeted volatility and complexity of the stock market that they end up remaining with the status quo, like a rabbit caught in the head lights of an oncoming car at night. ***In the U.S., eighty-four percent invest their savings and retirement funds in active equity funds, active Balanced Funds, Bond funds, money market funds and Target Date funds. Just sixteen percent invest in index mutual funds and index ETFs.***

Fear freezes them into inaction which leads these investors to give up thousands, potentially millions, in the forfeited growth of their retirement savings. This dread is so debilitating that it will lead most readers of this book to do absolutely nothing different with their retirement investments, despite the overwhelming evidence here and in many other publications.

As I've stated before, this fear has been programmed in by the big players in the financial industry that control billions of dollars of everyday investors' money. People are just too nervous to depart from the herd. They're worried about taking responsibility and being accountable and hence defer to the social default.

If you're caught in the head lights, all I can say is take some action. Take a few steps to the side and do some research to verify the evidence in this book. It may just be the difference between having a luxurious retirement doing everything you've dreamed of doing in your 'golden years', or a stressful one where you have to watch every penny you spend.

At the very least, follow the buy-and-hold strategy of an index ETF as I suggested earlier. If you're feeling more inspired and convinced, keep reading and your returns, and hence your life and retirement and those around you, can be even better, through magnificently magnified returns.

TIMING

Iain started the session eagerly, "We're finally at the timing session!"

"First up I'm going to discuss *why timing is so important* then I'll show you *how the timing works*. Then we'll look at some outcomes from using timing and then determine whether you wish to modify your Investment Plan," I replied.

Why is timing the market so important?

The exercise in Chapter 7 demonstrated that **the best and worst days in the stock market occur in close proximity to each other and that missing the worst days was far more important than being invested for the best days** is a part of the importance of timing. This relates to **general market risk** which obviously affects average compounded returns over the long term.

Related to that, but more important, is **when** bear markets occur in **YOUR investing lifetime**. Meaning that the sequence in which bear markets occur relative to your date of retirement is crucial. Severe bear markets that occur say, fifteen years or more before retirement matter far less than those that take place in the three or so years leading up to retirement and during retirement. The latter has the biggest adverse effect on retirement nest eggs. When severe bear markets occur is called **sequence-of-returns risk**.

Stock market indices recover over time. Particularly Total Return indices, which typically rise to their former levels within six years.

Everyday investors that are *close to retirement* have less time to allow the market to recover their lost wealth before they start drawing down from their retirement nest egg.

For *those in retirement*, wealth can be rapidly depleted by the combination of a bear market and drawing down income from a diminishing nest egg, leaving less nest egg to benefit from a subsequent market recovery. The losses may not be recoverable even if the market offers high returns a few years later because the growth will occur on a lesser sum of money.

And remember from Chapter 5 that the target retirement nest eggs required a return of 5% compounded growth per year *during retirement*, which retirees can probably only achieve with at least 50% exposure to the stock market. The nest egg would have to be 25% larger if expecting 2.5% growth, and 60% greater if expecting 0% growth during retirement, as is shown in Table 5-7.

"What are you telling me? That I need to consider seriously using timing at some stage of my investing career, even if not right now?" asked Iain.

"Correct. The alternative way to reduce sequence-of-returns risk is to invest in Target Date funds," I replied.

"But then I'll be applying a brake on returns every year between now and when I retire. And there is a very high probability that I will have much less nest egg in the future for a severe bear market to affect."

"There is no silver bullet. Decisions have to be made based on probabilities gleaned from researching the past. Which is what we are doing and why I say go with the probability of outcomes from a researched process."

Timing Signals

"How did you come up with this timing?" asked Iain.

"I've shared my background with you so you'll understand that I firmly believe, like countless other investors around the world, that technical analysis is a valid technique to use to determine whether a trend may be starting or ending."

"Yes," said Iain.

"It's important to understand and accept that analysis of any the financial markets is not a perfect science, meaning that there are no 'dead certs,' just probabilities."

I continued, "I've studied technical analysis since 1990 and spent thousands of hours studying charts and conducting manual research of the movement of stock market indices and listed companies, and then programmed many different concepts that capture price trends. Since

1998 I have been able to devise a number of timing systems of differing timeframes to meet different objectives that have been used by investors."

"Are these timing systems unique?" asked Iain.

"The techniques that I have used certainly are not unique; they are concepts that are well understood by market technicians. Precisely how I have used the techniques may be unique, but I haven't looked at every other technician's way of timing the market," I answered. "I have used trend-following techniques, also called momentum analysis, where the aim is to remain invested for the duration of a trend in the timeframe in which you wish to invest actively and then exit the market when there is a high probability that the trend has ended."

I continued, "The first timing system that we will discuss here is designed specifically to alert the start and end of trends in stock market indices and large-cap stocks on the basis that the period from start to end is what I would call a 'longer term trade' in the stock market."

"How long is 'longer term'?" asked Iain.

"The average hold period for each position between the buy signal and a sell signal is about fifteen weeks. Winners average about nineteen to twenty-five weeks, and losers average about six to nine weeks, meaning that losers are sold fairly quickly in case the market continues to fall preventing a little loser becoming a large loser."

"Can you show me what this timing looks like?" Iain asked eagerly.

"Sure," I said showing Iain Chart 14-1 as I started explaining it to him. "As you know, MDY is an ETF that tracks the S&P MidCap 400 index; so effectively by timing MDY you are timing a proxy for a stock market index. The idea is to buy the 'index' – via the ETF – when it is rising and sell it when it starts falling to be 100% in cash."

Chart 14-1 [Printed with permission from Beyond Charts]

"Chart 14-1 shows daily price data that covers the period from February 16, 2010, to September 26, 2012, two years and seven months. A 'bar chart' plots the open, high, low and close price of MDY for each day.'"

"The timing is shown in Chart 14-1 by 'entry' and 'exit' signals and a 'trailing' indicator line that 'trails' the price up and down after each entry and exit, respectively."

"The trailing indicator line (green line below the price in Chart 14-1) cannot fall in value when it is below the price of MDY; it can only remain the same value or rise as the price of MDY rises. If the close price of MDY falls to a level that is below the trailing indicator line at the end of a trading day, it signals an 'exit' and the trailing indicator line moves to above the current price of MDY."

"When it is above, the trailing indicator line (red line above the price in Chart 14-1) can only remain the same value or fall in value as the price of MDY falls. It cannot rise. Another 'entry' signal occurs when the end of a trading day close price of MDY rises above the trailing indicator line."

"I can see that now," said Iain. "But why is the trailing indicator line sometimes close to the price of MDY and at other times far away."

"Good eye," I responded. "It's due to that much maligned 'volatility' again! The middle of Chart 14-1 in the second half of 2011 is a great example."

I continued, "Notice when the price fell sharply and then had wild up and down swings the trailing indicator line remained a long way above the price. There are relatively simple techniques of determining the volatility on a day by day basis by measuring the daily ranges of the price bars from the days' highs and lows and then averaging them over two to four weeks. If the current volatility is high, then the trailing indicator line will remain far away from the current price, and as volatility falls the trailing indicator line will track closer to the current price."

"I get it," said Iain. "That's quite sensible. I can see the trends that you have mentioned. How is the indicator line calculated?" asked Iain.

"The volatility is calculated on a day by day basis and averaged over a rolling month. The volatility is then multiplied by a factor that keeps the trailing indicator line far away from the current close price at the end of each day when the volatility is high and allows it closer to the close price of the ETF or stock when the volatility is low. Each volatility zone has its own multiplying factor."

"So the trailing indicator line sort of self-adapts depending on the current level of volatility?" asked Iain.

"Exactly, that's a great way of putting it," I said. "However, the trailing indicator *only self-adapts as new price data is appended, it doesn't recalculate the indicator on historical data; meaning that all past signals will always occur on the same trading days.*"

I showed Iain Chart 14-2, another chart of MDY; this time zoomed into a different period from the end of 2007 to the beginning of 2010.

Chart 14-2 [Printed with permission from Beyond Charts]

I continued, "You can see the indicator line more clearly in Chart 14-2 during a very volatile period. Notice how during September to November 2008 in the lower middle part of Chart 14-2, the indicator line is a long way above the price action making it difficult for a buy signal to occur."

"How would I get access to these timing signals?" asked Iain. "They appear to be programmed into the chart."

"They are the culmination of years of investing experience and years of research. Rather than having to calculate manually where the signals occur, we have programmed the logic into a technical analysis software tool called Beyond Charts. ***The timing signals are part of a methodology that is called SPA3ETF*** which also provides the signals via ***alert notifications to a Smartphone and tablet App.***"

"Got it," said Iain. He then asked, "How did timing MDY perform compared to just buying and holding MDY during the period February 16, 2010, to September 26, 2012, in Chart 14-1 that you showed me?"

"Chart 14-1 reveals that during this time, the S&P MidCap 400 ETF MDY rose from $133.04 to $178.57, an increase of 34.2%. Including the eleven dividend payments during this time an additional 3.4% would have been added to the return, making a total return of 37.6% from buying and holding MDY over this period."

"However had the timing entry and exit signals been followed, thereby avoiding the substantial market decline in the middle of Chart 14-1 in August to October 2011, the total return would have been 50.9%."

"How was that achieved?" asked Iain.

Table 14-1 shows the six completed trades over this period. An investor would have received only six of the eleven dividends because timing MDY like this would have ensured being in cash with no open position in MDY at the time of recording the other five dividends.

I summarized, "Of the total profit, 48.9% came from profitable timing and 2% from dividends."

Table 14-1

Entry Date	Entry Price	Exit Date	Exit Price	% Change	Weeks Held
Feb 17, 2010	133.04	May 6, 2010	141	5.98%	11
Jul 27, 2010	140.21	Mar 17, 2011	170.53	21.62%	32.4
Mar 31, 2011	179.55	May 24, 2011	175.97	-2.00%	7.4
Jun 30, 2011	177.45	Jul 19, 2011	178.23	0.44%	2.4
Oct 25, 2011	157.15	Apr 11, 2012	174.62	11.11%	23
May 30, 2012	169.01	Sep 26, 2012	178.57	5.65%	16.6

I continued, "This is during a period when the stock market and MDY rose in price. Of course, the market is not always like this but this short period gives an idea how timing an ETF would work."

Iain then asked, "At the top middle of the Chart 14-1 in 2Q 2011, what happened there? There are two quick ins and outs in succession?"

I showed Iain a zoomed in Chart 14-3 of this period.

Chart 14-3 [Printed with permission from Beyond Charts]

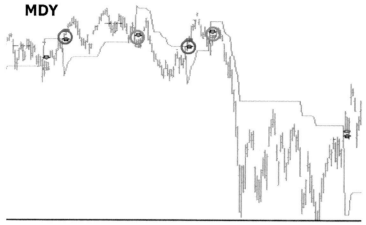

MDY

2011
Mar | Apr | May | Jun | Jul | Aug | Sep | Oct | Nov

"I responded, "This will happen from time to time when 'false break-outs' occur. This occurs when the price advances and gives the same signs as if a trend is developing but doesn't persist because, for whatever reasons, at that time there are more sellers than buyers who cause the price to fall."

"Of course, we don't know at the date of entry that the trend won't develop; we only find that out after the fact. In the bigger scheme of things, short small profit and loss trades do occur. Indeed, loss trades around -10% also occur, but not that often. They are part and parcel of timing the market and an integral part of being consistently successful as perfectly successful doesn't exist and we shouldn't expect it."

"This means that I will experience a short, small loss trade when this happens?" asked Iain.

"Correct, the operative word being 'small,' or better said, a 'limited loss' trade. Limiting a trade to a small loss when the price turns down is of utmost importance. This ensures that the investor is not caught holding the ETF when the price falls from $178 down to $135 as occurred in July to early October 2011 with MDY, a -24% fall, as can be seen in Charts 14-1 and 14-3."

"As it happened, the system signaled to close the trade on July 19, 2011, which was a 0.44% profit trade before MDY declined -24%."

Iain replied, "If investors are taking notice of what is happening in the stock market they wouldn't want to be a stakeholder in something that falls by -24%."

I responded, "That's a key point you make, Iain, 'taking notice of what is happening.' Remember that when stock market indices fall like this so does the unit price of all other active mutual funds that have some exposure to stocks. When you're timing the market, you have regular contact with the stock market meaning that you feel all the up and down bumps in real time. People can become emotionally affected by these up and down bumps depending on how severe the downs are and how high are the ups. It's a case of 'in sight, in mind' instead of 'out of sight, out of mind' as is the case of investing your money in an active mutual fund."

"Just looking at the timing signals on the chart with no money on the line I can feel a degree of excitement," said Iain. "I know that I wasn't even aware that this fall happened in the stock market in 2011, but I'm sure that the value of my 401(k) also fell at the time. Do you know how much it fell?" he asked.

"All Balanced Funds and Target Date funds fell. VBINX fell -12%; which is half of what MDY declined had you been holding a buy-and-hold position in MDY. The Fidelity 2020 Target Date fund fell -13%."

"If I had known I might have become emotionally involved, although I didn't know enough to do anything about it," responded Iain.

"The important thing is not what happens on a trade by trade basis but what happens over the long term. And even *more importantly, what happens when there is a severe fall in the stock markets around the world such as occurred in 2008. Avoiding most of such market declines is THE most important reason to use timing as the key risk management technique rather than diversification.* Recall our session when we discussed *being out for the ten worst days leads to far better performance over the long term than being in for the ten best days.*"

I continued, "As with all things in life, the bigger the perspective that you can have on a given subject, the better your decision making will be."

"Remember what we covered in one of our first sessions; ordinary investors can use timing because we can be agile and flexible and remove all our money from the stock market. We can spend periods on the sidelines, 100% in cash, waiting for the next opportunity. Nearly all active mutual funds cannot do this hence their need to over-diversify."

"How would the timing process have worked over the long term? What is the big picture perspective?" asked Iain.

SINGLE INDEX ETF TIMING STRATEGY

"Now, that I've shown you how the timing works, I'll show you the long-term research results of the effects of timing on a single index ETF. We'll continue using MDY."

"Chart 14-4 plots the equity curves of buying and holding MDY and timing MDY over the twenty-year period from June 16, 1995, to June 30, 2015. It starts with $100,000 and excludes the re-investment of dividends in both equity curves and also excludes 401(k) contributions. The top line shows the up and down journey of timing MDY and the lower line the up and down journey of buying and holding MDY."

Chart 14-4

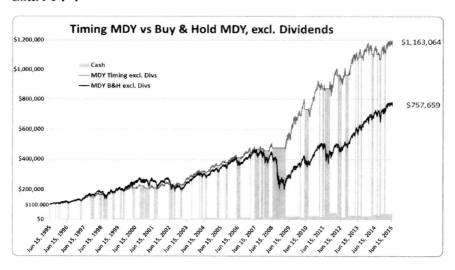

"Notice the effect of this straightforward timing during the 2008 bear market in the middle of the chart. The timing equity curve, which is the top line, tracks sideways in a horizontal line while the buy-and-hold equity curve falls. The light gray shaded areas show when the timing investor is 100% in cash, hence the timing equity curve being a straight line and not moving up or down during most of 2008."

"The greatest benefit of using timing is being in cash during most of a severe bear market."

"Up until 2008 the timing equity curve more or less matched the MDY buy-and-hold equity curve?" Iain questioned.

I answered Iain, "As Warren Buffett said, he would be 'well satisfied to match the advance of the averages' when they 'had a substantial advance' and 'be better in a bear market.' That's precisely what we are doing here *except we are using 'timing' as our core risk management technique rather than diversification into lesser performing asset classes.*"

I continued, "Warren Buffett manages to outperform the S&P500 Total Return index in advancing markets through his investment selections and by using leverage."

"How many gray areas are they?" asked Iain, meaning how many times would an average investor have had to buy and sell over the twenty years.

"There were forty-nine completed closed positions (trades) and one position still open as of June 30, 2015, or fifty buys followed by forty-nine sells, over twenty years. The average is two and a half completed trades a year," I answered.

"Let me see if I understand what's happening here," said Iain. "An investor merely times the index two to three times a year to outperform the same index, instead of spending hours and hours of research and reading copious amounts of newsletters and other 'noise' trying to find individual stocks to manage as a portfolio to outperform the index."

"Absolutely correct," I said.

I added, "*A major index ETF won't go to zero, won't get merged, closed or lose performance because the fund manager retires.* The major index ETFs have the lowest management fees and some broker-dealers even let you buy and sell these ETFs commission-free, unlike stocks."

"That equity curve has up and down bumps in it but not nearly as many as buying and holding the MDY ETF, a Balanced Fund or even the ups and downs that Berkshire Hathaway experienced as we examined in a previous session. What was the worst drawdown?" asked Iain.

"-14.43% in August 2010," I answered. "Compared to the worst drawdown of -56.3% in March 2009 for buying and holding MDY and -29% for the Vanguard Balanced Fund, VBINX."

"Is that the sort of drawdown that I should expect if I do this timing strategy over the next twenty years?" asked Iain.

"Probably not," I answered.

"Why not?" asked Iain.

"Well, if I can make a prediction with any certainty it is that the next twenty years will be different than the past two decades; meaning that the returns and the associated drawdowns will be different," I answered.

"The drawdowns may be better, but the odds are that they will be worse; that's typically what happens in financial markets and, psychologically, worse is what you should expect, so you're not disappointed. However, if financial markets perform worse over the next twenty years, then all returns will relatively adjust downwards. And being in cash for most of a miserable twenty years, using timing, will have the highest probability of a higher ending value than the active mutual fund alternatives even though the worst drawdown may be worse than the previous twenty years."

"I understand the logic, but can you guarantee this?" asked Iain.

"No," I answered, "there are no guarantees with any investing. There are only probabilities, so it pays to use strategies that offer the better probabilities."

"I understand," said Iain. "And what was the compounded return of timing MDY compared to buying and holding MDY?"

Iain indeed had grasped which metrics are important to focus on, and in the right order, wanting to know about the risk before the return.

I answered, "The $1,163,064 outcome over twenty years starting with $100,000 is 13.02% compounded per year compared to $757,659 being 10.63% compounded annually. *The difference is 2.39% better per year than buying and holding MDY achieving 53.5% more retirement nest egg at the end of the twenty years.*"

I continued, "And to keep things in perspective, let's compare this to a Balanced Fund. The *timing of MDY, excluding dividends, is a little over 4% compounded per year better than the FBALX Fidelity Balanced Fund, which is 8.97% compounded per year, including reinvestment of distributions*, with an ending total of $559,334 over the twenty years."

I then showed Iain Chart 14-5 of the same two strategies, timing MDY and buying and holding MDY, this time *including the reinvestment of dividends.*

Chart 14-5

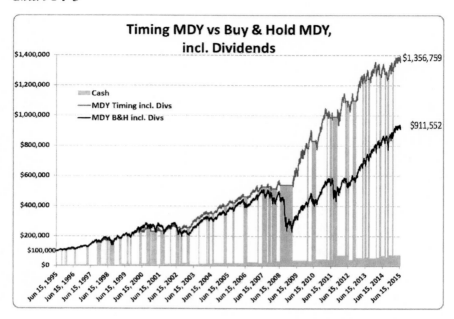

Iain summarized, "The timing strategy is $445,000 better off than buying and holding MDY. Let me ensure I have this right—the Single Index ETF Timing Strategy involves buying MDY when there is a buy signal, and if any dividends are due while that position is open, the dividends are reinvested immediately until a sell signal occurs. Then the entire position, including all the reinvested dividends, is closed, and the strategy will then be totally in cash until another buy signal occurs."

"Correct," I said. "In this example, the money was invested in MDY for 67.3% of the twenty years and was in cash the remaining one-third of the time."

"So that means that the strategy missed about a one-third of the dividends?" asked Iain.

"Yes, of the ninety dividends paid during the twenty-year period, the timing strategy received 57, or 63% of them."

I continued, "Looking at the ending values in Charts 14-4 and 14-5, re-investing dividends added 1.02% compounded per year to the final outcome *for buying and holding MDY*, over the twenty years. The absolute dollar difference was $153,893. Note again how much of a difference the compounding of small amounts makes over the long term. *For the timing strategy*, the difference was 0.88% compounded per year, equating to $193,695 more than excluding the re-investment of dividends."

"The drawdown would have been a little better because dividends can't make it worse. So what was the compounded return?" asked Iain.

"Well, merely add the 0.88% to 13.02% which is 13.9% compounded per year," I responded. "Which is 2.24% compounded per year better than buying and holding MDY with reinvesting dividends from June 15, 1995. And 5.02% compounded per year better than the S&P500 Total Return index over the same period.

Iain checked the performance tables, Table 3-2, and Table 9-2, and continued to put the performance into perspective:

"Compared to the VBINX Vanguard Balanced Fund of 7.91% compounded per year this is 5.99% compounded per year better, which equates to $893,729 better. Even Fidelity's FBALX, one of the best performing balanced funds, would have been $799,395 worse off."

Chart 14-6 shows this, which is the same as Chart 14-5 with the VBINX equity curve also plotted, starting from $100,000.

Chart 14-6

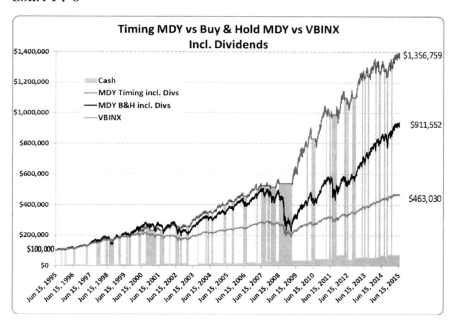

"What about compared to a Target Date fund?" I asked.

Iain dug out the Target Date fund returns from his folder and said, "Ok, let's use 8.26% compounded per year return over a twenty-year period."

"How did you get that?" I asked, as no 2015 Target Date fund has been around for twenty years, so Iain had to improvise to find a proxy.

"I took the 6.94% for the STLDX, which is the longest dataset for a Target Date fund that you have, and then looked at the difference in return between the best performing 2015 Target Date fund and STLDX over the ten years to June 2015. That difference is 1.32% which I added to 6.94%, giving 8.26%."

"I'll go with that even though I think that it would have been in the top echelon of Target Date funds over the period if even achieved," I responded.

We plugged 8.26% compounded per year into our compound growth calculator which gave an ending value of $489,058.

"That is a long, long way behind!" exclaimed Iain looking at Chart 14-6 and pointing out the position of the end value. "$867,000 behind," he added.

"How many of the forty-nine completed trades were profitable when timing MDY?" asked Iain.

"Thirty-three trades, or 67%, were profitable with an average of 9.5% per trade. Hence 33% were losing trades at an average of -2.52% each. There was an upward bias in this twenty-year period leading to a relatively high rate of profitable trades. If prices moved sideways for twenty years, then the rate of profitable trades would decline somewhat, possibly to below 50%."

Iain thought a little more as he looked at Charts 14-5 and 14-6 before continuing, "So timing MDY over the twenty years would have done better than buying and holding Berkshire Hathaway (BRK.A) too?" he asked also looking at Chart 10-2 in Chapter 10 that we had discussed earlier.

"Correct," I said. "Over the same period, *buying and holding BRK.A would have been roughly the same as buying and holding MDY, some $434,000 behind timing MDY*."

"This does not seem like much effort at all," Iain continued.

"Let's see; I would have to do two and a half odd trades a year, on average, a total of five transactions. And another two and a half dividend buy transactions; and also buy more ETF units with my monthly 401(k) contributions."

"When would I do the 401(k) contributions transactions?" asked Iain.

"Well, if your nest egg is in cash because the last timing signal was a sell signal, then you would merely add your 401(k) or IRA contributions to the investment account at your broker-dealer. Then, when the next buy signal occurs you would use all of the investment capital that you have allocated to this strategy to buy the ETF, including your recent 410(k) or IRA contributions."

"The other scenario is that the ETF position is open in the market. In this scenario, your monthly contributions can be used to purchase more units of the ETF as and when your contributions are due each month. Or you could leave them in cash to be used when the next buy signal occurs thereby minimizing effort."

"And that's it," asked Iain.

"Basically, yes," I answered. "You would, of course, need to establish an online broker-dealer account, preferably one that has commission-free ETF investing, and it would be preferable to select an ETF that is on their commission-free list. Not all ETFs are commission-free as we have discussed."

"How would I know when the buy and sell signals occur?" asked Iain.

"The signals are computed using historical price data that resides in a software package called Beyond Charts, which supports the SPA3ETF product. The trailing indicator line logic is programmed into Beyond Charts and supports more than fifty index ETFs, large-cap stocks, and stock market indices."

I continued, "Each Monday to Friday when the stock exchanges are open, the latest prices for every ETF, stock and index are pushed out to Beyond Charts three hours after the end of the trading session. The most recent day's prices are evaluated by the SPA3ETF programmed logic to determine if there is a buy or sell signal. If neither occurs, then there is nothing to do."

"Is that it?" asked Iain. "How long does it take to do that?"

"It shouldn't take more than a minute or two a day to analyze whether a buy or sell signal is present. There is *also a smartphone and tablet App that will alert you if there is a buy or sell signal for any of the ETFs supported which means that you only have to open the Beyond Charts software when the App notifies you. The App reduces the time taken to execute this strategy to potentially a few minutes a month.* Of course, you can use the Beyond Charts software to do other stock market analysis since it is a full technical analysis charting package."

"Wow," exclaimed Iain, "that is efficient. Is it really that easy?" he asked.

"Easy for receiving the signals and information required to decide when and how to act," I said. "The tough part is adhering to the signals. They usually occur amid adverse circumstances that psychologically challenge the investor to act on them. Some people find it simple to adhere to the signals but others have difficulty doing so allowing media and commentary 'noise' to override their decision making."

"You have hinted at this psychological challenge. Will we discuss that in more detail?" Iain asked.

"We will cover this as it is one of my coaching interests and strengths. I was mentored by one of the best, if not the best, trading psychology coaches the world has known, the late Mark Douglas, who authored *Trading in the Zone*. We became good friends."

"What index ETFs would you recommend using with this strategy?" asked Iain.

The following could be used for this strategy to maximize growth:

- Guggenheim S&P500 Equal Weight ETF, RSP,
- PowerShares NASDAQ100 ETF, QQQ,
- iShares S&P MidCap 400 ETF, IJH,
- SPDR S&P MidCap 400 ETF, MDY,
- iShares S&P600 Small-cap ETF, IJR,
- iShares NASDAQ Technology index, IBB".

"Rather than going through the research results for each one now, you can access them on the Resources page under 'Single Index ETF Strategy' on the website www.blueprinttowealth.com."

"Of these, my research shows that only IJH, IJR, and RSP are commission-free at this stage. IJH with TD Ameritrade, Fidelity and Firstrade Securities, IJR with Fidelity and RSP with Schwab."

"I note that you have excluded all S&P500 index ETFs," said Iain.

"I have because, as per the long-term growth we have discussed, the S&P500 index doesn't offer the best growth but has the same risk in a severe bear market as the S&P MidCap 400 index," I answered. "However, if an investor wants to time one of the S&P500 ETFs, such as IVV or SPY, the signals are available in SPA3ETF in Beyond Charts."

"A *Core Satellite* approach for timing a single index ETF might look something like either of Figures 14-1 and 14-2," I said. "Figure 14-1 shows timing the S&P MidCap 400 index ETF IJH with 100% of core capital."

Figure 14-1

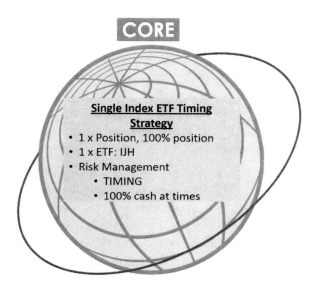

"The *Core Satellite* approach in Figure 14-2 combines using 65% of capital to buy-and-hold a single index ETF in the core with one satellite that uses 35% of capital to time the same ETF."

Figure 14-2

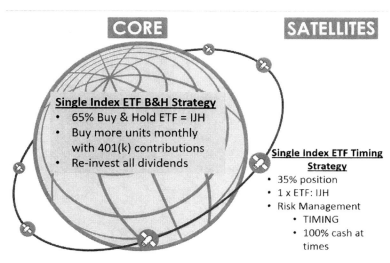

"Why should someone use the 65% / 35% Core Satellite allocation in Figure 14-2 instead of the 100% timing as the Core in Figure 14-1?" asked Iain.

"Because of the difference in the size of the position exposed to the stock market," I answered. "Not everybody would be psychologically comfortable with moving 100% of a large amount of money in and out of a single ETF using timing when it comes to actually clicking the [Commit] button. To start with it may even be better to start with a 95% / 5% allocation until a degree of comfort and confidence is reached with entering and exiting positions."

Revisit FDGRX with timing

"In an earlier session Iain, you asked how the diversified stocks-only active mutual fund, the Fidelity Growth Company Fund FDGRX, had performed from its peak in March 2000 onwards compared to the S&P500 Total Return index and two other balanced funds. Remember that FDGRX was focussed on technology and health stocks and had performed brilliantly from June 1995 to June 2015?"

"Yes," said Iain, "we were going to come back to see how timing works with that scenario. How would it have gone from March 2000 using timing?"

I responded, "This is highly relevant since it will help with the overall when-to-start perspective, as March 2000 just happens to be, with the benefit of hindsight, the exact wrong time for the novice active investor to start."

I showed Iain Chart 14-7 of the same four equity curves that we had researched earlier in Chapter 3 in Chart 3-2, but this time starting from March 6, 2000, when FDGRX reached its highest peak at that point, rather than starting from June 1995. I also added the equity curve of the NASDAQ 100 QQQ ETF. In Chart 14-7 the legend matches the equity curves in descending order.

Chart 14-7

What a different picture; demonstrating that the market conditions that prevail when investors start their journey do indeed make a big difference. If it makes a difference when you start, then why not during the journey? The morals of the story are that **timing does matter,** and you should rather wait for an entry signal to start investing.

"Even though this would have been a worst case scenario in Chart 14-7 by starting right at the highest peak reached, FDGRX still outperformed the buy-and-hold equity curve of QQQ and almost matched IBNAX. But it was well behind SFAAX and the S&P500 Total Return index."

"I wouldn't want that to happen to me," said Iain. "And, imagine novices starting their investing journey with high expectations before the novelty wears off."

"Exactly. It's like falling off your bike as a five-year-old and having to deal with the fear of maybe falling off again," I replied.

I then showed Iain Chart 14-8, this time with timing QQQ and FDGRX using the QQQ timing signals for both.

Chart 14-8

> *"Wow, avoiding most of a severe bear market makes a huge difference,"* said Iain. "FDGRX ends with more than double than it achieved in Chart 14-7!"

"THAT is THE main reason for using timing. There will still be some volatility and down periods since the type of timing being used tries to remain invested, but exits altogether should downside volatility exceed the trailing indicator line, as shown in Charts 14-1 to 14-3."

"It seems that *timing also makes it easier to decide when to start since we will never know what lies ahead of us in the immediate future. It liberates us from the fear of heading straight into a severe bear market,*" said Iain.

"Indeed, QQQ and FDGRX still had enough of a drawdown, and it took until the second bear market of 2008 before both the QQQ and FDGRX equity curves rose above SFAAX and the S&P500 Total Return index."

"This is a great demonstration of how timing can really help," Iain concluded.

Using Leverage

"It would be remiss of me not to mention that one of the biggest advantages of using timing is that an investor can use some degree of leverage."

"Why would you want to use leverage? Isn't it riskier?" asked Iain.

"It is riskier, but many investors use it to boost returns," I answered. "But in increasing returns, you will also experience deeper drawdowns than without leverage."

"I know that more sophisticated active investors that use instruments such as Exchange Traded Options (ETOs) and Futures use leverage because leverage is an integral part of the instrument," said Iain. "But if there is more risk involved, why would an average investor place his retirement savings at risk of worse drawdowns?" asked Iain.

"Well, they don't *have* to," I answered. "It is an option to do so, preferably as a satellite strategy, as part of the *Core Satellite* approach if they wish to. But there's another persuasive reason. **Researchers of Warren Buffett's methods have determined that he uses the leverage of 1.6:1**[1] in his investing which might explain the extra volatility that the Berkshire Hathaway price journey experienced compared to stock indices over the eighteen odd years since 1997."

"What are you saying?" asked Iain. "If Warren Buffett uses leverage, then anybody can? He's arguably the greatest investor that has ever lived, so he knows what he is doing. Most people wouldn't have the skill to use leverage when investing," Iain challenged.

"You are quite right, especially when investing in the stock market," I replied. "Even though many also use leverage to invest in stocks through Reg-T Margin broker-dealer accounts. But that aside, just about everyone who has bought property, residential or commercial, has used leverage to do so."

"That's different; it's bricks and mortar. It seldom loses too much value, and when it does the value always comes back," Iain ventured in reply.

"Maybe it does. But in what time frame? It doesn't mean that because it has for many decades that it will continue to do so in a time frame that fits in our investing lifetime. In Japan, house prices are still less than half the value they were at in 1989. Remember, 'anything can happen.' Do some scouting around the Japan Real Estate Institute website to find out more," I replied.

---

1   Source: "Buffett's Alpha"

"Also, real estate investing starts out at much higher levels of leverage, typically around 2:1 to 5:1 leverage and then over many years, as much as twenty to thirty, the leverage factor continues to decline until there is no leverage," I added.

Iain didn't respond.

I continued, "There is no doubt that using leverage in the stock market is riskier than in real estate because it is more volatile, even with lesser levels of leverage. And people take far more notice of the price of their stock market investments than they do property prices and hence react more emotionally. As a result, they're continuously challenged to make a decision to either hold or sell".

"This is why anyone who does include using leverage as a satellite strategy must deploy risk management techniques such as having well defined and well-researched exit criteria. That ensures that they have sound decision-making criteria on whether to hold or sell. Also that they won't have to endure a deep and long bear market that could wipe out nearly all of their capital when using leverage."

"Okay then, Warren Buffett does it, and I will have exit criteria to protect the worst happening. What sorts of returns are possible with 1.6:1 leverage?" Iain asked.

"Leverage has the potential to improve healthy returns and to worsen poor returns. It is a magnifying agent in both directions. That is why investors should only use leverage in satellite strategies with smaller percentages of their overall investing capital. In this instance of timing MDY over this particular period using leverage, an additional 5.51% is added to the return, to total 18.56% compounded per year, excluding dividends. We know that including dividends would add at least a further 0.88% compounded annually, making a total return of 19.44% compounded per year!" I exclaimed.

I provided Iain with Chart 14-9 and explained the equity curves on the chart and the statistics behind this researched outcome.

Chart 14-9

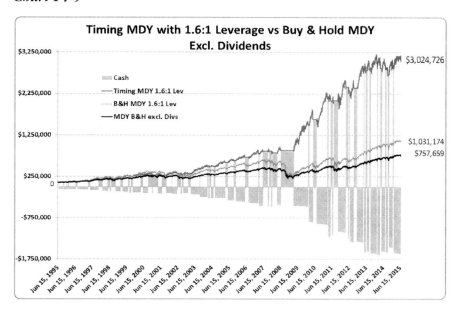

"This nearly triples the final account value over twenty years. That is huge," Iain responded. "So an investor could expect that sort of additional compounded return per year when using leverage?" he asked.

"You shouldn't assume that," I answered. "If the compounded return over the next twenty years of timing an ETF was, say, 7.5% instead of 13.05%, the *additional* return due to leverage might be between 1% to 2.5% compounded per year. Meaning that the leveraged differential to the unleveraged outcomes increases as the unleveraged return increases, and the differential decreases as the unleveraged return decreases."

"What would the size of the borrowings have been at 1.6:1 to achieve that return? And at what interest rate?" he asked.

"The trades that would have been executed using leverage would have been exactly the same as those without using leverage, the only difference being that borrowed money, or 'other people's money,' would have boosted the returns on the investor's own capital."

In Chart 14-9 a borrowing cost of 7.5% interest per year was used for the entire twenty years for borrowing money when needed to execute the strategy at 1.6:1 leverage.

The shaded areas above the zero line indicate periods when the investor was in cash and the shaded areas below the zero line indicate open positions and the amount of borrowed capital for each open position.

Throughout the twenty-year period, the split between the investor's own capital and borrowed money would have been around 62%/38%, respectively, whenever there was an open position. In absolute terms, the most borrowed amount would have been $1,643,000 in April 2014 when the value of the open position at that time was $4,563,900, or 36% borrowed.

Iain was quite amazed at the amount of profit that leverage could generate. "What was the maximum drawdown for timing MDY with leverage?" he asked.

"Just under -23%," I answered. "Compared to -72% for buying and holding the MDY index ETF with leverage, which shows why *not to use leverage for buying and holding an index ETF* as few people would be able to withstand such a deep drawdown mentally. The -72% would also have caused a margin call with most broker-dealers."

I added, "The -72% drawdown did occur during the 2008 bear market, but no one knows when the next severe market decline like that will happen. It may be just around the corner."

"It seems that an active investor that has the time to use satellite strategies in a *Core Satellite* approach should seriously consider using leverage for a small portion of their capital," said Iain.

"They certainly should, but time and inclination aren't the only necessary credentials," I responded. "The chart that I have shown you is a twenty-year chart with a known outcome. Investing with leverage magnifies ups and downs making the psychological challenges tougher during the investing journey on a day by day basis. Let's have a detailed look at a period during 2013 to 2015 where timing didn't outperform with an unknown future that lay ahead of the investor," I added.

I showed Iain Chart 14-10 over the shorter period between May 2013 and June 2015.

Chart 14-10

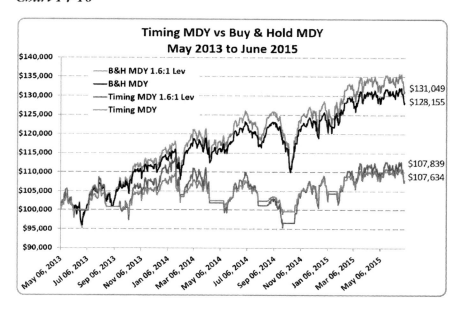

"Buy-and-hold of MDY has performed better over this term of two years than timing MDY, whether using leverage or not!" Iain exclaimed.

"Correct," I said. "And there will be other periods like this. No single strategy does better than another every day of every week or every month or every year. Investing should be at least a twenty-year journey, not a twenty-day, twenty-week or twenty-month stroll."

"So what should I do when I experience a period like this?" asked Iain

"You have to sustain it and not deter from your Investment Plan. That is why you have devised a plan with a big picture long-term perspective. I won't go into too much detail here about how to achieve this mindset since we'll be discussing that in one of our last sessions together. I will cover some important material then," I responded.

"To complete this section on leverage, a *Core Satellite* approach might look something like this," I said.

Figure 14-3

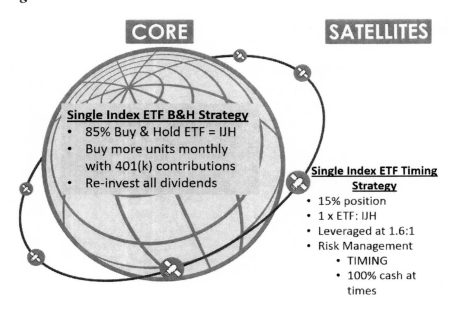

"I would prefer not to use leverage at this stage," said Iain.

"I agree. You can reassess this as your investing skills grow because you must first feel comfortable with your abilities without leverage before starting to invest with leverage," I stressed.

TIMING LARGE-CAP STOCKS

"Just a moment," said Iain, "where are you going with this, talking about including individual stocks now? I thought that you said I wouldn't need to be caught up in the merry-go-round of stock market trading?"

"And you are right; you don't **need** to," I responded. "Bear with me for a few moments, and you can then decide whether it is worth including a few large-cap stocks, or not, in this strategy. Besides it's not trading either, the additional time is negligible."

"Okay, but it will have to be an obvious no-brainer even to think about it after all the index investing material that you have taken me through," Iain said.

"Maybe it will resonate with you and maybe not. *One of the main advantages of using ETFs is the intense focus that you can achieve with just one or a few ETFs rather than trying to pick one or a few stocks at any given time from thousands* and then managing a broad number of stocks in a portfolio," I started.

"Got that," said Iain. "And there's also the benefit I get out of *using timing on a focused short list* of one or a few ETFs. Besides being effective and efficient, *being totally in cash through a severe bear market and not having to endure it with money on the line is also a huge relief.*"

"Correct. But what if you could add just another two or three large-cap stocks to the focused short list of ETFs and potentially boost returns by another few compounded percent per year while still using timing to ensure not being invested in any of these stocks or ETFs during severe market declines? Or if technology disrupts their business, and they get delisted, like Eastman Kodak?"

"Hmmm," Iain was not yet convinced, but it sounded like his mind had been opened to the concept just a little.

I continued, "It's simply broadening the focused list by a few to include a handful of large-cap stocks that are extremely liquid and tend to trend very strongly when they do trend. These stocks might be more volatile than a stock market index but not to the degree of an individual mid or small-cap stock."

"In Chart 14-11 look at the difference between how AAPL, Apple Inc., has moved compared to the S&P MidCap 400 index." I handed Iain a semi-logarithmic chart that compares Apple Inc. to MDY starting with the same relative base on June 1, 1995, through to November 2015.

"Despite the volatility, Apple grew ten-fold compared to the S&P MidCap 400 index and its ETF, MDY, excluding dividends."

Chart 14-11 [Printed with permission from Beyond Charts]

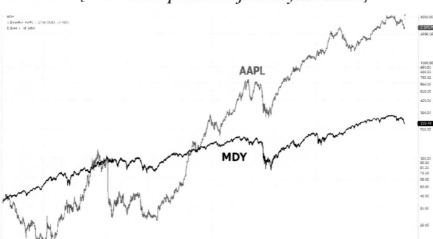

"Which stocks would be on my watch list? Would I have heard of any of them?" asked Iain.

"I'm sure you would have. Apple, Amazon, Microsoft, Morgan Stanley, Fedex, Biogen, Gilead Sciences, Qualcomm, and Freeport-McMoRan. Heard of any of those?" I asked.

"I certainly have," said Iain, "now you've piqued my interest. I've always wanted to invest in stocks like those but have always been too scared, not knowing when the best time would be to buy and when to sell or how many shares to buy in each stock if I did."

"Remember in a previous session we looked at three stocks and Apple was one of them," I said.

"Yes," said Iain, "and if I remember correctly, Apple had a whole bunch of declines of at least 40% including three declines of worse than -70%. I wouldn't want to sit through any of those falls!"

"Don't worry; you won't have to," I said. "Have a look at Chart 14-12 which shows a semi-logarithmic scaled chart of Apple Inc. over twenty years."

Chart 14-12

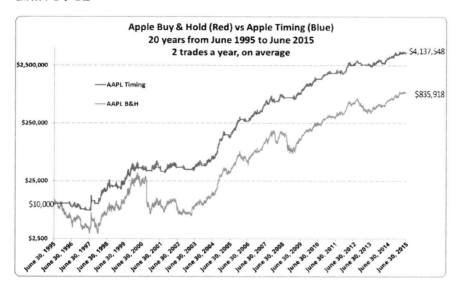

Apple Buy & Hold (Red) vs Apple Timing (Blue)
20 years from June 1995 to June 2015
2 trades a year, on average

"What is this chart telling me?" asked Iain.

"The simple answer is that if you had bought $10,000 worth of Apple Inc. shares on June 30, 1995, and just held those shares, without re-investing the dividends, the $10,000 would have been worth $835,918 twenty years later. The lower line in Chart 14-12 shows the journey of that $10,000."

I continued, "However, if you used the same timing process on Apple Inc. that we've discussed for timing ETFs, the outcome would have been at least $4,137,548. The journey of the equity curve, starting from $10,000, is plotted on the top line in Chart 14-12. Again, this is without re-investing dividends."

"Wow," said Iain, "$3.3 million more in returns than buying and holding after starting with $10,000! I want to know more. What was the compounded annual return, the maximum drawdown and how much effort would have been required to have achieved this?"

"Maybe an extra minute or two a week," I replied. "You would have executed forty-one trades over the twenty years or two trades a year, on average, each lasting around fifteen weeks, on average. This delivered a 34.9% compounded return per year, excluding dividends. You would have invested your capital 68.8% of the twenty years and the rest of the time it would have been in cash. The profits do not include interest income from the cash periods."

"And no leverage was used?" asked Iain.

"No leverage," I answered.

"What about buy and sell commission fees?" asked Iain.

"Believe it or not, investors can buy and sell stocks in the U.S. for a flat commission rate of $4.95 to $8.95, and even less for frequent traders, regardless of how many shares are purchased and at any value!"

"What was the compounded annual growth of buying and holding Apple?" asked Iain?

"24.7% compounded per annum!"

"Wow!" said Iain, "the additional 10.2% compounded per year makes a huge difference."

"With the benefit of hindsight," I said. "Firstly, you don't know in advance that Apple Inc. will enjoy price movement like this in the future, and secondly, remember the drawdowns that Apple Inc. had along the way."

I continued, "Notice that the top equity curve in Chart 14-12, timing Apple Inc., is smoother than the bottom equity curve; however, the top line still had a maximum drawdown during this period of -38% in 1997. That's still a lot less than buying and holding Apple that had a drawdown of -82% twice during this twenty-year period, once in 1997 and another in 2003. Apple was teetering on failure in 1997."

"Not only is the return so much better than the risk taken to achieve this performance, but the risk is also much less than buying and holding Apple Inc. or buying and holding any of the mainstream index ETFs."

Iain added, "Thinking back to the maximum drawdowns we discussed in earlier sessions, *the risk is actually lower than buying and holding some of the Target Date funds and active Balanced Funds, which had drawdowns of at least -40% during 2002 to 2003.*"

"Quite right," I agreed. "That's the benefit of timing."

"Furthermore, understand that 39% of the forty-one trades were losing trades with four of them at least -10% losses, one even being a loss of -16%. Any form of investing will incur losses. It is important to understand that adverse periods will occur regardless of what strategy you use. You must build up resilience to endure such times that occur whether you're using timing or not. Then be prepared to take advantage of the upswings."

I continued, "So you are aware, the last position opened was a $3,561,313 position."

"That is a huge position," said Iain.

"It is for the everyday investor. But it is tiny relative to the average daily dollar turnover in Apple Inc. on the stock market," I replied. "Apple turns over around $5.5 billion a day and has averaged higher. $3,561,313 is 0.064% of Apple's average daily turnover."

"This looks too good to be true," said Iain. "What's the catch?"

I smiled, "That is the past. With the benefit of hindsight, Apple Inc. has proved to be just ideal for this sort of investing with momentum timing. It is also called trend-following. It has trended fantastically in both directions and spent little of its time bobbing along going sideways. And when it has trended, it has done so with some vengeance leading to nice juicy profit trades. The risk is that it loses this strong-trending characteristic and becomes a fuddy-duddy low volatility non-to-hardly-trending stock that bobs along sideways going nowhere for long periods of time."

I answered Iain's question, "So there might be no catch, but there may. That's what risk is, not knowing what the future holds. It makes sense to use the past as a guideline from which to determine probabilities, but there are no guarantees."

"However, the real risk to protect against is that you don't do any worse for the rest of your investing days than you would have, had you left your retirement savings in Vanguard's Balanced Fund; which now becomes your benchmark against which to determine investing success or failure."

"So how do you feel about including a few stocks in your focused short list?" I asked.

"I reckon that I could handle that," replied Iain. "What is the full list of stocks that I could choose from to include in my Investment Plan and how would I go about adding them?"

"They are mainly household names such as Apple Inc., Amazon, Microsoft, and FedEx. The list is somewhat focused on between ten and twenty-five stocks which have the necessary characteristics. Access the latest list and some of the stocks' research results on the Resources page under 'Stocks' on the website www.blueprinttowealth.com ."

"Before continuing Iain, understand that the research that I have shown you with Apple Inc. is to demonstrate how timing can work with individual large-cap, highly liquid, strong trending stocks. *The idea is to use a small, focused list of stocks and ETFs rather than pick a single stock and time it on its own forever.* Banking the future on the characteristics of just a single stock would not be an effective long-term strategy riddled with too much risk."

I continued, "There are a number of ways that stocks can be included, depending on your objectives, tolerance for risk and time availability to execute the strategy," I said. "The investing challenge is always to manage an allocation of capital effectively and efficiently as a portfolio, not in a single stock, with the best possible risk-to-reward-to-effort ratio."

Last Word

- Timing should be the DIY investor's primary approach to risk management.
- The longer the average hold period that results from timing, the simpler it is to be successful at the timing of ETFs and stocks.
- With timing, aim to achieve what Warren Buffet[1] said in this quote: "Our performance, relatively, is likely to be better in a bear market than in a bull market ... in a year when the general market had a substantial advance, I would be well satisfied to match the advance of the averages."
- Leverage can be used to boost returns; however, deeper drawdowns should be expected.
- Leverage should be limited to Satellite strategies.
- Including a small, focused list of individual large-cap, strong trending, highly liquid stocks can also boost returns, with or without using leverage.

---

1   Warren Buffett from page 2 of his 1957 Annual Letter to Shareholders

CHAPTER 15

Simple Active Strategies

*"Creativity is just connecting things. When you ask creative
people how they did something, they feel a little guilty because
they didn't really do it, they just saw something. It seemed
obvious to them after a while. That's because they were able to
connect experiences they've had and synthesize new things."*

STEVE JOBS

Now that I have established that investors can achieve effective risk
management through timing rather than to diversify across lesser
performing asset classes than the stock market, I can introduce some
simple but creative approaches to make an even better return with only a
little extra effort.

STRONGEST SINGLE INDEX ETF STRATEGY

"You now understand how timing a single index ETF works; let's look
at a potentially more efficient strategy that uses timing and a technique
that determines which is the strongest index ETF at any given time from a
small list of index ETFs. The method is called Relative Strength analysis."

Iain asked, "Why would you introduce more work for yourself if you
already have one strategy that holds an outperforming index, such as the

293

S&P MidCap 400 via the IJH or MDY index ETFs, and re-invests their dividends to beat nearly every active mutual fund over the long term. And another strategy that carries out timing on that index to do even better."

"Because there is a risk that the single index ETF that you choose many years in advance may not be the best in the future over the long term," I responded. *"This technique will ensure that you are invested in the best performing index ETF from a short list most of the time in the future."*

I explained the process to Iain.

Select a short list of index ETFs on which to conduct the timing and Relative Strength analysis. There is only ever one ETF position in which you invest capital, the relatively strongest of a short list of ETFs.

Say a list of five index ETFs is selected.

In the process described below an 'open trade' is defined as a Buy signal being the last signal displayed on the chart of an index ETF, i.e. the latest available price data does not generate a Sell signal. The 'open trade' is not necessarily an *open position* in the market with money invested, but an investor could have invested money had capital been available at the time of the Buy signal. A 'closed trade' is one where the last displayed signal on a chart is a Sell signal.

The process is as follows:

1. When there are no 'open trades' in any of the selected ETFs, i.e. on all these ETFs, the last displayed signal is a Sell signal, then analyze each of these ETFs on a daily basis to determine whether a Buy signal occurs on any given day.
   ◊ The Buy signal will occur when the stock market has closed for the trading day and the Close price for an ETF rises from below the trailing indicator line on the previous day to above it today.
   ◊ The SPA3ETF App provides an alert notification when a Buy signal occurs.
2. If a Buy signal occurs in more than one ETF, then open a single position in the ETF with the highest Relative Strength (RS) – see explanation below for the process of *'Analyzing Relative Strength.'*
   ◊ Allocate all the cash assigned to this strategy to that single ETF open position by placing a Market on Close (MOC) or Market on Open (MOO) order for the necessary quantity on the next trading day after the signal.
3. Analyze the open ETF position daily for a Sell signal.

◊ The SPA3ETF App provides an alert notification when a Sell signal occurs.

4. If a Sell signal occurs in the open ETF position, close the position the next trading day after the Sell signal occurs, using either a Market on Close (MOC) or Market on Open (MOO) order.

5. On Fridays, after the market has closed, compare the Relative Strength of the open ETF position to the other 'open trade' index ETFs on the list to determine if there is a higher Relative Strength ETF that is an 'open trade.' This process determines which is the strongest ETF.

◊ The SPA3ETF App provides a list of the 'open trade' ETFs ranked in descending order of Relative Strength.

6. If on a Friday, another ETF on your focused list of ETFs is an 'open trade' with a higher ranked Relative Strength, then Swap out of your existing open ETF position into that highest ranked ETF.

◊ Close the lower ranked ETF position on the Monday (if it is not a trading holiday) using either a Market on Close (MOC) or Market on Open (MOO) order and buy the higher ranked ETF with a MOC or MOO order on the same day.

7. If all the selected ETFs are 'closed trades' according to the SPA3ETF price momentum rules, then all capital allocated to the strategy will be in cash.

8. If a dividend distribution occurs while an ETF is an open position, then deposit the dividend into the investment account and include it in the next ETF position; i.e. all dividends are re-invested into the strategy to maximize growth.

Only conduct Relative Strength analysis on a weekly basis while a current ETF position is open and when one of the remaining selected ETFs are 'open trades.' Therefore, swapping from an open ETF position to another 'open trade' ETF on the list only ever occurs on a Monday after analyzing the Relative Strength for all the other 'open trade' ETFs using Friday's data after the market closes at the end of each week.

'Analyzing Relative Strength' involves setting up a Rate of Change (ROC) indicator with a 126-day period in Beyond Charts. 126 trading days is approximately six months. This measures the highest percentage change of the selected ETFs over a rolling six-month period. The index ETF with the highest ROC 126 after any given Friday's market close is the strongest index ETF at that snapshot in time.

I selected the period of 126 days after conducting extensive simulation research using 21 days (1 month), 42 days (2 months), 63 days (3 months), 126 days (6 months), 189 days (9 months), 252 days (1 year) and weighted combinations of these. Also, I researched ranking on each day of the week and every two weeks rather than weekly. Daily ranking to determine whether a swap was necessary did not add sufficient value for the five-fold increase in effort.

The Beyond Charts desktop software and the SPA3ETF App have a programmed Relative Strength Ranking scan that automatically ranks the supported ETF list using these parameters.

If the five index ETF's selected are IJH, QQQ, IBB, IJR and SPY then these are the five index ETFs that will be analyzed to determine which is the strongest when any of them are 'open trades.'

Figure 15-1 shows a *Core Satellite* diagram for this strategy.

Figure 15-1

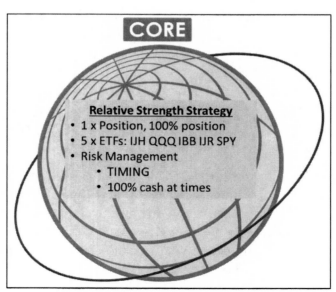

I researched and stress tested the Relative Strength strategy using these five ETFs on historical data. The outcomes of this research, including the equity curve chart, can be found on the Resources page under 'RS Strategy' on the website www.blueprinttowealth.com.

The research was started in February 2001 when the IBB ETF was first listed; the other four ETFs initial listings were before that date. February 2001 was right in the middle of a primary bear market which gathered more downward steam over the ensuing months.

"How did this strategy perform?" asked Iain.

"From February 20, 2001, to May 10, 2016, it **achieved 15% compounded annual return (CAR) with a maximum drawdown of -26%**, excluding dividends, compared to the S&P500 index achieving a maximum drawdown of -56% and overall growth of 3.27% CAR. The S&P500 Total Return index achieved 5.25% CAR over the same period."

I continued, "This means that a starting capital of $100,000 would have grown to $847,000 compared to the S&P500 growing it to $163,000 and the S&P500 Total Return index to $217,901. Vanguard's Balanced Fund, VBINX, did slightly better than the S&P500 Total Return index over this period achieving 5.78% CAR, or $235,219."

"That certainly is great outperformance using the Relative Strength strategy. How active is this strategy?" asked Iain.

"It's more active than timing a single index ETF. The Relative Strength strategy would average around seven to eight completed trades a year, eight each of buys and sells equalling sixteen transactions a year."

"Why would an everyday investor use this approach with the extra effort?" asked Iain.

"To improve returns. It's that straight forward. Using this approach exposes one's capital to other index ETFs that can potentially do better than timing a single index. There is room to include better performing ETFs in the mix such as the NASDAQ 100 ETF, QQQ, and the NASDAQ Biotechnology ETF, IBB; and even others that we'll discuss shortly."

"How did timing IJH perform over the same period?" asked Iain.

"Timing IJH achieved 11.3% CAR with a maximum drawdown of -20% growing $100,000 to $510,000," I replied. "Table 15-1 summarizes the comparison."

Table 15-1

Strategy	Figure	CAR	Max DD	Ending Capital	Exposure	No. of Trades p.a.
S&P500		3.27%	-56.8%	$163,000	100%	0
S&P500 Total Return		5.25%	-55.2%	$217,900	100%	0
Vanguard Balanced Fund		5.85%	-36%	$235,219	100%	0
B&H IJH S&P400 ETF,inc Div		8.36%	-55.3%	$339,313	100%	0
Timing IJH, excl. Divs		11.3%	-20%	$509,950	68.5%	1.9
Core 5x ETF Rel. Strngth,ex Div	15-1	15%	-26%	$847,000	86.6%	7.6

Note:

- CAR = Compounded Annual Return
- Max DD = Maximum Drawdown
- Starting capital was $100,000 on February 20, 2001. Ending Capital was on May 10, 2016.
- Exposure is the percent of time 'exposed' to the market. The remaining time was in cash.
- No interest received is included in this research for the periods in cash.
- No. of Trades Annually: Total no. of buy and sell transactions would be double this number.

I continued, "The future is unknown and never the same as the past, which is why it pays to include a few ETFs and stocks on the list so that at least one can rise to the top using the simple technique of Relative Strength. *That's the beauty and simplicity of using Relative Strength analysis; it determines the relatively strongest* ETF or stock from a list, and we don't mind which one it is. And during adverse stock market conditions, your money will be 100% in cash due to using timing for risk management."

"Let's move to another way of using Relative Strength analysis, by also including individual stocks."

STRONGEST SINGLE STOCK STRATEGY

"You can use the same approach of Relative Strength analysis on a focused list of stocks, or a list can be compiled that includes both ETFs and stocks."

"Using the *Core Satellite* approach with just a Core strategy, the strategy with which to execute the latter Relative Strength strategy is shown in Figure 15-2."

Figure 15-2

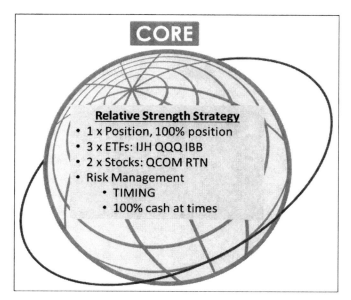

"How did the research for this Core strategy in Figure 15-2 compare to using the Relative Strength approach with the five ETFs in Figure 15-1?" asked Iain.

"The maximum drawdown was worse at -33% but the compounded annual return (CAR) was 17.7%, growing the $100,000 starting capital over the same period from February 2001 to May 2016 to $1,206,000, without re-investing dividends."

"That's $359,000 more than using the Relative Strength Strategy with five ETFs without any stocks. The difference is way more than the entire return of VBINX over this period! Why didn't you include Apple Inc. (AAPL) in the research?" asked Iain.

"Simply because the results become mindboggling with AAPL included. I thought that I'd rather show you what's possible with two lesser performing stocks. However, if you decide to use stocks in your Core Satellite Investment Plan, I'll suggest that you include Apple Inc. (AAPL). By the way, with AAPL included the CAR was 27%!"

"Another approach could be that the Core uses the SPA3ETF Relative Strength strategy with the bulk of investment capital, and a Satellite strategy could use one to ten stocks also using the Relative Strength strategy but with a much smaller amount of capital, as shown in Figure 15-3."

Figure 15-3

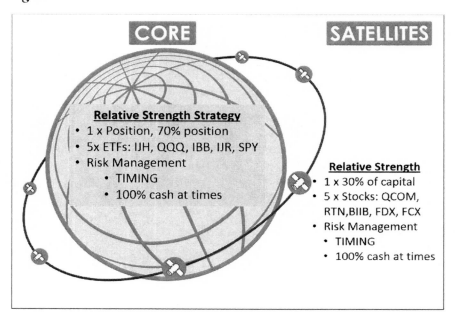

"The selected stocks provide a spread across industries of technology (Qualcomm Inc.–QCOM), industry (Raytheon–RTN), transportation (Fedex–FDX), biotech (Biogen–BIIB) and resources (Freeport-McMoran–FCX)."

"How did this approach perform and how active was it?" asked Iain.

"The ***effort doubled***, compared to the other two Cores without a Satellite, to around nearly eighteen trades a year, or thirty-six buy and sell transactions. The CAR was between the other two at 15.93% growing $100,000 to $948,000 without rebalancing the 70/30 split over the same period. This excluded dividends which would have further improved the returns."

"Why would this approach be used if the return was lower than with the approach used in Figure 15-2?" asked Iain.

"Because the maximum drawdown was better. In this Core Satellite plan, the maximum drawdown was -28% instead of -33%. However, due to the high effort required there may be better ways of growing capital with less effort and less drawdown which we will discuss shortly. Table 15-2 summarizes these three strategies."

Table 15-2

Strategy	Figure	CAR	Max DD	Ending Capital	Exposure	No. of Trades p.a.
S&P500		3.27%	-56.8%	$163,000	100%	0
S&P500 Total Return		5.25%	-55.2%	$217,900	100%	0
Vanguard Balanced Fund		5.85%	-36%	$235,219	100%	0
B&H IJH S&P400 ETF,inc Divs		8.36%	-55.3%	$339,313	100%	0
Timing IJH, excl. Divs		11.3%	-20%	$509,950	68.5%	1.9
Core 5x ETF Rel. Strngth,ex Divs	15-1	15%	-26%	$847,000	86.6%	7.6
Core 3x ETF, 2x Stcks Rel. Strngth	15-2	17.7%	-33%	$1,206,000	92.8%	6.7
Core 5x ETF, Satellite 5x Stcks RS	15-3	15.9%	-28%	$948,000	87.2%	17.6

"Why haven't you shown me how the Core strategy of five stocks on their own performed using the Relative Strength strategy?" asked Iain.

"I would recommend not using this strategy for long-term retirement nest egg investing," I responded. "If you look at the maximum drawdowns in Table 15-2 for Figures 15-2 and 15-3 you will see that the drawdown is markedly higher due to including stocks. And the stocks that can experience greater volatility, such as Apple Inc. (AAPL) and Amazon (AMZN), were not included. If Figure 15-2 has allocated more than 30% to the stocks Satellite, drawdown would have been worse, but with a better return of course."

These Core Satellite plans did not use leverage. Nor did they include dividends, unless indicated. Nor did they include interest received for periods when investment capital was in cash.

MULTIPLE ETF EQUAL WEIGHTING STRATEGY

"Another strategy!" exclaimed Iain. "Do I need to know about more strategies!"

"This is the last one! It would be remiss of me not to provide you with an overview of simple strategies that are well within the reach of everyday investors. It's important that I leave you with some basic knowledge of a small choice of strategies before our sessions come to an end. Rather than be prescriptive about just the two discussed so far, the single ETF strategy and the relative strength of a few ETFs and stocks."

"Well Okay," said Iain reluctantly. "What have you got for me now?"

I responded, "View these as potential strategies to add as Satellites, or even part of the Core in the case of the next strategy, to a Core Satellite approach. This strategy deploys your capital equally across a number of ETFs simultaneously rather than in just one at a time, as we have discussed so far. We call it an ETF Equal Weighting strategy. It uses timing and allocates each equally weighted position to an ETF. If the ETF position is not an 'open trade', then the allocation will be in cash. Of course, stocks can be used too."

"How many positions could be open at any given time using the Equal Weighting strategy, and why?" asked Iain.

"Anywhere from two or three to as many as ten," I responded. "It depends on how much capital you have and to which markets you wish to expose your capital to achieve growth."

I proceeded to explain the strategy to Iain.

Divide the money allocated to this strategy by the number of simultaneously open positions. For example, if there are four open positions then allocate 25% of capital to each ETF or stock, if five then 20%, if six then 16.6% to each position. Assign a single ETF or stock to each of these positions; meaning that the total list of ETFs and stocks equals the number of equally sized positions.

The process is as follows:

1. When there are no open trades in any of the ETFs/stocks, analyze each ETF/stock on the list on a daily basis to determine whether a Buy signal occurs on any given day.
    ◊ The SPA3ETF App provides alert notifications for Buy signals.
2. If a Buy signal occurs for an ETF/stock, then open a position for each ETF/stock that provides a Buy signal. Use either a Market on Close (MOC) or Market on Open (MOO) order on the next trading day.
    ◊ Allocate the equal portion of the portfolio to each ETF/stock for which a Buy signal occurs.
3. Analyze the open positions in each ETF/stock for a Sell signal daily.
    ◊ The SPA3ETF App provides alert notifications for Sell signals.
4. If a Sell signal occurs in an open position, close the position on the following trading day, using either a Market on Close (MOC) or Market on Open (MOO) order.
5. The allocation of capital to that ETF/stock will now remain in cash until another Buy signal occurs for that particular ETF/stock.

6. If all ETF/stocks are closed positions according to the SPA3ETF momentum rules, then all capital assigned to the portfolio will be in cash.
7. If a dividend distribution occurs while an ETF/stock position is an open, then the add the dividend to the cash in the portfolio and divide it equally amongst each equal allocation in the portfolio; i.e. all dividends are re-invested to maximize growth.

"How active is this strategy?" asked Iain.

"It can be a little more active than the Relative Strength strategy. It would average around eight to nine completed trades a year, nine each of buys and sells equalling eighteen transactions."

"Why would an everyday investor use this strategy?" asked Iain.

"From research, this strategy has performed worse than the Relative Strength strategy but has experienced much-improved drawdowns when using ETFs or stocks. A reasonable Risk Objective can be around -15% or -18% maximum drawdown in an Equal Weighting Investment Plan instead of around -25% for an ETF Relative Strength strategy; or lower for a stocks' Relative Strength strategy, around -30%."

"Another reason is that investors with large investment portfolios, relative to their tolerance for risk, might feel uncomfortable placing all their investment capital in a single ETF or stock position when using the Relative Strength (RS) strategy. With the Equal Weighting strategy, making each position, say, a fifth of the size of an RS strategy position, their capital will be spread simultaneously across a few ETFs or large-cap stocks."

"A *Core Satellite* diagram might look like Figure 15-4 using five index ETFs with 20% in each position."

Figure 15-4

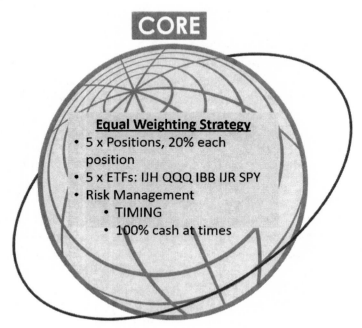

"How did this Core portfolio perform over the same period as the Relative Strength portfolios, between February 2001 and May 2016?" asked Iain.

"It's biggest advantage is the excellent maximum drawdown of -15% compared to the SPY (S&P500 index ETF) experiencing a -56% drawdown in 2008. However, it's CAR is lower at 9% growing $100,000 to $370,000, excluding dividends, from February 2001 to May 2016."

"Why is the growth so much inferior to the ETF Relative Strength strategy, and to timing IJH on its own without re-investing dividends?" asked Iain.

"Firstly, it is lower than timing IJH because IJH on its own performed better than at least two of the ETFs, QQQ and SPY, over this period; both of which would have had some lower performing capital allocated to them. You don't know in advance which single ETF will perform the best."

"Secondly, the Equal Weighting approach exposes your capital to the market for much less time than with the Relative Strength strategy, because capital with this approach spends longer in cash waiting for an entry signal to occur in one of the five ETFs. The 'exposure' of capital to the market with this approach was 67.8% compared to the Relative Strength strategy 'exposure' with these five ETFs over the same period being 86.6%."

"How do you improve returns without also making the maximum drawdown worse?" asked Iain.

I responded, "Now you are starting to think like a strategy designer! You need to increase the exposure by increasing the opportunity to invest capital. There will be times during rising market conditions that one or two of the allocated positions might be in cash because their respective ETFs are not 'open trades' when other ETFs not on your list might be 'open trades'. This would be a poor use of capital and opportunity."

"The list of ETFs or stocks on which you focus can be longer than the number of simultaneously open positions. For example, ten stocks could be on your list competing on a first-come-first-served basis for the five equally weighted positions. And when one position is closed, because a timing exit signal occurred, there will be an opportunity to fill the vacated position from more than one of the other stocks on the list. I prefer this approach as it makes more efficient use of investing capital and opportunity, and it improves exposure and performance."

EXPANDING THE EQUAL WEIGHTING LIST

"We can expand the list to ten ETFs and stocks that vie for five equally weighted positions and act on entry signals on a first-come-first-served basis between the ETFs and stocks. This approach provides more opportunity to get more exposure to the earlier and better performing ETFs or stocks. Figure 15-5 shows that a Core Equal Weighting approach using five ETFs and five stocks can improve exposure and performance through access to more volatility, without increasing drawdown too much."

Figure 15-5

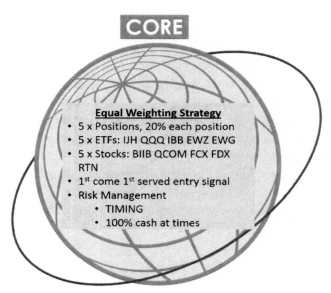

I continued, "*Including stocks immediately improves performance by nearly 5% CAR to 13.91% CAR compared to the strategy in Figure 15-4 but also pushes the maximum drawdown lower to -19.7%.* Given that the additional effort of around one more trade per year compared to the strategy in Figure 15-4 I'm sure you'll agree that including some stocks is worth it. The two more volatile stocks of APPL and AMZN would have further improved performance over this period but would probably also have made the maximum drawdown a little worse."

"What about using only ten *stocks* and no ETFs with the Equal Weighting strategy vying for five simultaneously open positions?" asked Iain.

"**This is certainly a healthy approach,**" I answered. "**A number of things combine to provide an excellent reward-to-risk-to-effort ratio for this scenario:**

- **the lower exposure of the Equal Weighting strategy than the Relative strategy, which leads to an improved maximum drawdown,**
- **the key risk management technique of timing, and**
- **the additional volatility provided by stocks to boost returns.**"

Figure 15-6

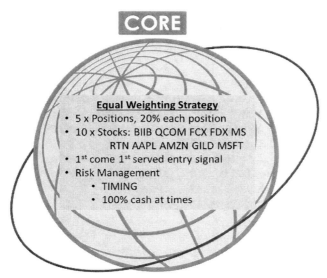

"How did this approach perform?" asked Iain.

"Very well," I answered. "Using only stocks, as shown in the Core diagram in Figure 15-6, **improved the CAR (Compounded Annual Return) by 4.5% compared to Figure 15-5 and improved the maximum drawdown. Effort rose marginally to an average of 11.1 trades per year. Making this the highest return strategy we have discussed so far.**"

"Here's a summary table showing the outcomes of all the approaches discussed in Chapter 15," I said to Iain showing him Table 15-3.

Table 15-3

Strategy	Figure	CAR	Max DD	Ending Capital	Exposure	No. of Trades p.a.
S&P500		3.27%	-56.8%	$163,000	100%	0
S&P500 Total Return		5.25%	-55.2%	$217,900	100%	0
Vanguard Balanced Fund		5.85%	-36%	$235,219	100%	0
B&H IJH S&P400 ETF,inc Divs		8.36%	-55.3%	$339,313	100%	0
Timing IJH, excl. Divs		11.3%	-20%	$509,950	68.5%	1.9
Core 5x ETF Rel. Strngth,ex Divs	15-1	15%	-26%	$847,000	86.6%	7.6
Core 3x ETF, 2x Stcks Rel. Strngth	15-2	17.7%	-33%	$1,206,000	92.8%	6.7
Core 5x ETF, Satellite 5x Stcks RS	15-3	15.9%	-28%	$948,000	87.2%	17.6
5x ETF Equal Weighting	15-4	9%	-15%	$370,000	67.8%	8.6
5x ETFs, 5x Stocks Equal Weight	15-5	13.9%	-19.7%	$725,556	71.7%	9.6
10x Stocks Equal Weighting	15-6	18.5%	-17.6%	$1,321,766	71%	11.1

Variations of the Core in Figure 15-6 can be used too, either as a Core or as a Satellite:

- Ten stocks can vie for four, or even three, simultaneously open positions.
- Use leverage in a Satellite at 1.2x leverage up to 1.6x leverage.

Both of these variations would improve performance but would also make the maximum drawdowns worse.

I concluded, "The Equal Weighting strategy of following multiple ETFs or stocks really suits portfolios of multiple hundreds of thousands of dollars to multiple millions whereas the Relative Strength strategy better suits smaller amounts of capital and preferably Satellites."

International & Commodity ETFs

"Before we finish with strategies I should introduce another set of more volatile index ETFs that could also improve the returns of the Equal Weighting strategy, international index ETFs. These are ETFs that are available on the U.S. stock market but track the main benchmark indices of other international stock exchanges in their local country currency."

"That sounds pretty flexible, but a little scary," said Iain.

"International ETFs provide a great opportunity for ordinary investors to spread their risk into another currency and potentially more favorable international stock market indices by buying an equivalent ETF listed in the U.S. in U.S. dollars just like they can buy a stock. Just about every developed and emerging stock market in the world is accessible."

"You have to be aware of exchange rate movements with international index ETFs because a particular international index could be rising, but if the local currency weakens against the U.S. dollar, this might offset any gain in the index ETF listed in the U.S. in U.S. dollars. However, the SPA3ETF timing logic programmed into Beyond Charts for the index ETFs will take into account both the currency and index ETF movement."

"Which international stock exchanges can everyday investors access?" asked Iain.

"These are the ETFs that the SPA3ETF module supports with signals in the Beyond Charts charting software and the SPA3ETF App:

- Chinese XIN0 Large-cap index iShares ETF, FXI.
- Japanese Nikkei 225 index iShares ETF, EWJ.
- German DAX index iShares ETF, EWG.
- Hong Kong Hang Seng index iShares ETF, EWH.
- Mexican Bolsa index iShares ETF, EWW.
- Brazilian Bovespa index iShares ETF, EWZ."

"Currently, there are four commodity ETFs supported by SPA3ETF. You can include these in the Relative Strength and Equal Weighting strategies to get exposure to either of two commodity indices or directly to Gold or Silver. GLD and SLV both closely follow the Gold and Silver price in U.S. dollars:

- Commodity DB index PowerShares ETF, DBC.
- Continuous Commodity index, Greenhaven ETF, GCC.
- Gold in U.S. dollars, SPDR ETF, GLD.
- Silver in U.S. dollars, SPDR ETF, SLV."

"It is not recommended that these ETFs be used in the single ETF timing strategy, but rather as part of a Relative Strength or Equal Weighting strategy."

"A sample *Core Satellite* strategy might look like this," I showed Iain Figure 15-7.

Figure 15-7

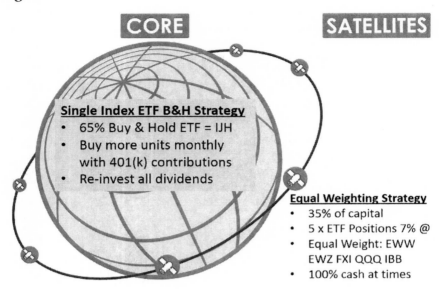

CORE

SATELLITES

Single Index ETF B&H Strategy
- 65% Buy & Hold ETF = IJH
- Buy more units monthly with 401(k) contributions
- Re-invest all dividends

Equal Weighting Strategy
- 35% of capital
- 5 x ETF Positions 7% @
- Equal Weight: EWW EWZ FXI QQQ IBB
- 100% cash at times

"Of course, an investor can compile other combinations using the *Core Satellite* approach to meet their requirements. For example, they could use a combination of Relative Strength, Equal Weighting and buy-and-hold of a single ETF; or include a second Satellite."

"But there's more. Other ETFs that are good candidates for Relative Strength and Equal Weighting strategies are the SPDR sector ETFs."

SECTOR ETFs

The GICS Select Sector ETFs, or SPDRs, comprise additional ETFs that track the GICS stock market sectors, which the average investor can use as part of an active strategy:

- XLB, Basic Materials.
- XLE, Energy.
- XLF, Financial.
- XLI, Industrial.
- XLK, Technology.
- XLP, Consumer Staples.
- XLU, Utilities.

- XLV, Health Care.
- XLY, Consumer Discretionary.

The iShares IBB NASDAQ Biotechnology and iShares IYR U.S. Real Estate ETFs can be added to this list of sectors too that are supported by SPA3ETF by displaying researched buy and sell signals.

The philosophy behind using the SPDR sectors in a strategy is that at least one sector should be relatively stronger than the overall market index at any given time and hence be outperforming the overall market. This happens as investment capital moves in cycles between different industries and sectors of the market.

Just a single sector ETF, or more, of the eleven, can be invested in at any given time using the SPA3ETF Relative Strength strategy. Of course, if all are falling and none are an 'open trade' then a strategy would be 100% in cash. Alternatively, the top two or three 'open trade' ETFs, using Relative Strength, can be invested in at any given time and rotated on a regular basis, say, monthly or every two weeks.

To determine the relatively strongest, perform a regular ranking of a user-selected list of ETFs or stocks. Beyond Charts and the SPA3ETF App provide this Ranking functionality.

Figure 15-8 shows the Ranking on a given day in descending order of the OPEN and CLOSED ETF trades, and the last signal that occurred each ETF.

Figure 15-8[1]

Code	Security Name	Action	Ranking ▽	Close	Last Signal Date
EWZ	iShares MSCI Brazil Capped	OPEN	31.354	28.53	6/8/2016
SLV	iShares Silver	OPEN	27.239	16.91	6/24/2016
GLD	SPDR Gold Shares	OPEN	22.538	125.32	1/6/2016
XLU	Utilities Select Sector SPDR	OPEN	17.612	51.22	6/3/2016
DBC	PowerShares DB Commodity Index Tracking	OPEN	15.303	15.22	4/12/2016
GCC	WisdomTree Continuous Commodity Index	OPEN	10.790	20.33	4/19/2016
XLE	Energy Select Sector SPDR	OPEN	9.909	66.44	3/3/2016
IYR	iShares US Real Estate	OPEN	6.953	80.45	3/1/2016
QCOM	Qualcomm Inc	CLOSED	5.910	52.51	6/13/2016
RTN	Raytheon Co	OPEN	5.355	132.99	7/13/2015
XLP	Consumer Staples Select Sector SPDR	OPEN	4.961	53.32	1/29/2016
AMZN	Amazon.com Inc	OPEN	4.850	707.95	1/28/2016
XLB	Materials Select Sector SPDR	CLOSED	2.397	44.85	6/27/2016
MDY	SPDR S&P MidCap 400	CLOSED	2.148	262.419	6/24/2016
IJH	iShares Core S&P Mid-Cap	CLOSED	2.143	143.96	6/24/2016
XLI	Industrial Select Sector SPDR	CLOSED	1.237	54	6/27/2016
RSP	Guggenheim Invest S&P 500 Eql Wght	CLOSED	0.753	77.63	6/24/2016
IJR	iShares Core S&P Small-Cap	CLOSED	-0.108	111.43	6/27/2016
FDX	FedEx Corp	CLOSED	-0.209	148.1	6/24/2016
DIA	SPDR Dow Jones Industrial Average	CLOSED	-0.663	173.82	6/27/2016

"Iain that's it for the strategies and ETF list that we need to cover. I have provided further discussion on more active stock strategies that can do as much as seven to ten trades a month in the Appendix. I know that this doesn't appeal to you right now but they may in years to come."

"It's now time to review the first Investment Plan that we compiled to determine whether you wish to expand it by including a timing strategy, or not."

---

1   Source: Beyond Charts technical analysis software with the SPA3ETF module

LAST WORD

- Relative Strength is a powerful technical analysis price momentum technique that allows the cream of the crop to filter to the top.
- Long-term index ETF timing using relative strength can improve returns, reduce risk and still be executed in less than fifteen minutes a week.
- Consider using large-cap, highly liquid, strong trending stocks in a focused, efficient investing process to boost returns further.
- Using a small, targeted list of ETFs – mainstream U.S. indices, international, and sector – an average investor can invest in a broad range of financial markets within the stock market asset class.
- An Equal Weighting strategy can provide a lower risk approach to using a focused short list of ETFs or stocks than the Relative Strength strategy, which hugely outperforms the S&P500 benchmark index and hence all active mutual funds over the long term.
- Combinations of the two timing strategies with various ETFs and stocks can provide many creative approaches to managing large amounts of capital for the everyday investor.

CHAPTER 16

Iain's Final Investment Plan

With this new knowledge, Iain was keen to revise the first Investment Plan that we compiled to incorporate the techniques of using timing with Equal Weighting or Relative Strength.

"After much consideration, I would prefer having one Core and one Satellite strategy," said Iain. "The Core will be to focus on timing one index ETF, IJH, and the Satellite will be an Equal Weighting strategy of five positions but using ten stocks, without leverage."

"Why have you come to this conclusion?" I asked.

"I believe it offers the best risk-to-reward-to-effort ratio, especially compared to where my nest egg is currently invested, in a Balanced Fund. Others may wish to include an ETF Relative Strength strategy as their Satellite, may be leveraged; others may wish to include stocks in an Equal Weighting Core; others may wish to include sector, commodity, and international ETFs. I recognize that there are many possible and flexible combinations."

Iain continued, "I also believe that I can fit this into my busy life if I have a structured, researched and rigorous process. I understand that you have done all the hard work and can provide me with a shortcut to a robust process that is backed by rigorous research. From the evidence I have seen, there is a very low probability, even with some mistakes, that I will do worse than where I would have invested my retirement nest egg for the next two decades."

"Okay, let's prepare a revised Investment Plan for your chosen Core Satellite approach," I concluded.

Iain and I then spent an hour or so revising the first Investment Plan that we had devised and then made the necessary modifications.

The mission statement was revised to achieve a 50% better outcome than buying and holding IJH for twenty years and reinvesting all the dividends.

Visit www.blueprinttowealth.com for a copy of this Plan and for updates on how both of the Investment Plans are performing compared to Iain's prior investment avenue, Vanguard's Balanced Fund, VBINX.

Iain's Final Investment Plan, as updated at this website, uses real money; it is not just an academic plan.

IAIN'S INVESTMENT PLAN

This Investment Plan is relevant from January 4, 2016, and supersedes all other versions of this Investment Plan.

This Investment Plan assumes the investment entity to be a traditional IRA, but other retirement entities can also use it as is.

Mission Statement

This Investment only covers investment capital that is focused on **growing retirement savings** by as much as possible over the long term, for a minimum of twenty years.

To grow the current investment capital of $162,000 by between 0% at worst case and 15% compounded per year until December 31, 2035.

The specific dollar target is $2,332,000 using the Method described in this Plan.

Goals and Objectives

The overall objectives are to:

- Use a simple, efficient and structured process for long-term active investing using Exchange Traded Funds (ETFs) and large-cap stocks that **takes no longer than fifteen minutes a week to execute and manage**. (Skills goals will take longer if pursued.)
- To accumulate a nest egg and maximize growth for the stakeholders:

◊ Invest $162,000 starting capital according to this Plan beginning on January 4, 2016, with no capital withdrawals.

◊ The Method will not make use of any leverage.

The **Reward Objective,** or performance goal, for the portfolio, is to:

*To achieve **4% CAR better** than the CAR of the S&P500 Total Return index. That is, to achieve **12.91% CAR** over twenty years.*

The S&P500 Total Return index is the benchmark for this Investment Plan. (This is the comparative reference for the majority of capital invested in active equity mutual funds and Balanced Funds. [See Method below for an explanation of outperformance.]

To put this further into perspective, based on research over twenty years, and similar market conditions in the future, this Reward Objective could then also be:

- Around 5% (12.91% – 7.91%) compounded per year better than the Vanguard Balanced Fund, VBINX, and
- Around 6% (12.91%–6.9%) compounded per year better than any of the current 2035 Target Date funds, such as Fidelity's FFTHX and Vanguard's VTTHX, up until that time.

Notes:

1. While 12.91% CAR is the Reward Objective, 10.4% CAR plus monthly IRA contributions and reinvesting dividends should achieve the comfortable independent retirement of $1,543,000 as of December 31, 2035.
    a. 10.4% CAR without IRA contributions would achieve around $1,162,300.
    b. 10.4% is roughly the same CAR that the MDY ETF achieved with reinvesting dividends.
2. Achieving 12.91% CAR, plus monthly IRA contributions, would reach $2,332,000, without indexing IRA contributions for inflation.
    a. With indexing of IRA contributions or contributing at a higher rate through, say, a SIMPLE or SEP IRA, or Solo 401(k), a much larger financial goal could be achieved.
3. If the Plan achieves $2,332,000, consider what to do with the

additional retirement savings of $789,000 as discussed at the end of Chapter 18.

The **Risk Objective** for the portfolio is:

This portfolio has a Risk Objective of a maximum of -25% drawdown as a result of using the strategy described under Method.
Calculate the -25% drawdown from the highest peak reached by the portfolio.
[Everyday investors could add this rule to the Risk Objective:
If a -25% drawdown occurs, then execute a portfolio 'shut-off valve' by closing all positions, going 100% into cash and await the next Buy signal to restart the strategy.
Calculate the -25% drawdown from the highest peak reached by the portfolio, or from the most recent entry signal for the Applicable ETF]

Notes:

1. Based on research, this Risk Objective should be around half of a severe bear market and suffer less drawdown, and hence less risk, than a balanced active mutual fund, such as a relevant Target Date fund, which can suffer drawdowns of between -25% and -45%.
2. The real money portfolio that Share Wealth Systems executes that strictly follows this Investment Plan will not operate with a 'shut-off valve,' which will allow investors to see what an unrestricted drawdown can be for this strategy.

The **Skills Objective** for the portfolio is:

To achieve skills with respect to investing mindset, purchasing additional ETF units, market environment understanding, investing knowledge, journaling, strategy design and any other skills that may be identified to potentially add another Satellite strategy, or to potentially use a little leverage similar to Warren Buffett.

Method

- Use SPA3ETF as the timing and risk management methodology to execute this Investment Plan.
- Start the portfolio with a Portfolio Value of $162,000 on January 4, 2016.

- The Core strategy is the Single Index ETF Timing strategy. Only one position in the Applicable ETF will be open at any given time based on being:
  ◊ An open trade according to SPA3ETF.
  ◊ When the SPA3ETF entry/exit signal occurs for the Applicable ETF, the Applicable ETF Position Size *must* be invested/closed.
- The Satellite strategy is a large-cap stock Equal Weighting strategy. Five positions in any of the Applicable Stocks will be open at any given time based on being:
  ◊ An open trade according to SPA3ETF.
  ◊ Fill the five Satellite positions on a first-come-first-served basis using SPA3ETF entry signals.
  ◊ When a SPA3ETF entry/exit signal occurs for any of the Applicable Stocks, the Applicable Stocks Position Size *must* be invested/closed.
- Contribute $5,500 per annum, or $458.33 per month, to retirement savings until the age of fifty (2021 for Iain). After age fifty, contribute $6,500 annually, or $541.67 per month.
  ◊ Adjust these amounts accordingly as the IRA contribution limits are increased by the government and are affordable.
  ◊ Contributions will total $125,000 over the twenty years, excluding inflation adjustments.
- The monthly IRA contribution is to be deposited directly into the IRA broker-dealer account. Leave the cash there until SPA3ETF signals to open a new position. Use the cash according to the Money Management rules in this Investment Plan.
- After the Applicable ETF or Applicable Stocks deposit dividends as cash into the IRA broker-dealer account, leave the cash there until SPA3ETF signals to open a new position. Use the cash according to the Money Management rules in this Investment Plan.
- Purchase Applicable ETF units or Applicable Stocks on the next trading day after a SPA3ETF Buy signal occurs using a Market on Open (MOO) order.
- Sell Applicable ETF units or Applicable Stocks on the next trading day after a SPA3ETF Sell signal occurs using a Market on Open (MOO) order.

[**Explanation of outperformance: 4% CAR** is at least the outperformance that the Single Index ETF timing strategy with IJH achieved, including reinvestment of dividends and payment of ETF fees, over the S&P500 Total Return index in stress-tested simulation research of ETFs, as did the Equal Weighting strategy with stocks, over periods of around fifteen years. The S&P500 ETF SPY achieved 8.8% CAR, including reinvestment of dividends and payment of ETF fees.]

Instruments used

This portfolio will focus on one Applicable ETF and ten Applicable Stocks:

- IJH is the Applicable ETF.
- AAPL, AMZN, BIIB, GILD, FCX, FDX, MS, MSFT, QCOM, and RTN are the Applicable Stocks.

Follow the Method in this Investment Plan as depicted in the Core Satellite diagram in Figure IIP-1.

Figure IIP-1

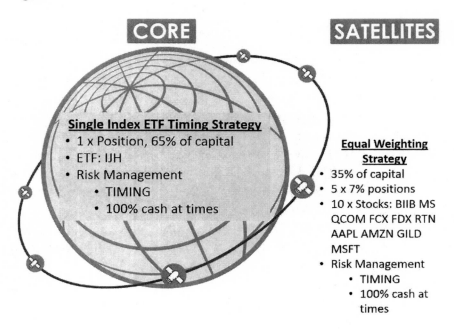

CORE

SATELLITES

Single Index ETF Timing Strategy
- 1 x Position, 65% of capital
- ETF: IJH
- Risk Management
  - TIMING
  - 100% cash at times

Equal Weighting Strategy
- 35% of capital
- 5 x 7% positions
- 10 x Stocks: BIIB MS QCOM FCX FDX RTN AAPL AMZN GILD MSFT
- Risk Management
  - TIMING
  - 100% cash at times

Reviewing Instruments in which to invest

From time to time, or at least every year on July 1, review the Applicable ETF/Stocks compared to other available ETFs/Stocks. Use the following criteria:

- A significant change in the characteristics of the Applicable ETF. For example, the relationship between the ETF and its underlying index changes and large tracking errors result.
  - ◊ Use a chart similar to Chart 9-1 to determine this.
- A significant shift in the business prospects for the ETF providers, e.g. iShares, PowerShares and Guggenheim, which may endanger the existence of an applicable ETF. While this may be inconceivable at the moment, "anything can happen."
- The liquidity of the Applicable ETF/Stocks falls dramatically for a few contiguous months.
- The annual management fees for the Applicable ETF change to be high relative to other available ETFs.
- The characteristics change of an Applicable Stock, such as it is merged, becomes illiquid or loses its trending capabilities.
- The list of available ETFs or stocks supported by SPA3ETF changes.
- The investing skills of the investor improve or more time is available to extend the lists of Applicable ETF and Applicable Stocks.

If any of these conditions arise, the Investment Plan will be revisited in its entirety to find similar Applicable ETF/Stocks in which to invest the total funds accumulated to date.

These conditions are no different from investing in any other mutual fund.

Fees and Costs

- Commission-free ETFs are preferred where there is a choice, e.g. IJH and MDY; and use flat fee commissions for stocks, not cents per share.
- Choose from TD Ameritrade, Fidelity or Firstrade, which offer commission-free ETF investing for IJH.
- Minimize all percentage costs that scale on a FuM basis and seek fixed costs wherever possible to execute the Investment Plan.
- An ongoing fixed cost of $900 paid annually (or $85 paid monthly) will be paid to continue accessing SPA3ETF signals and functionality.

Risk Management

Market Risk

- Monitor Market Risk at all times with the SPA3ETF timing of the Applicable ETF and Applicable Stocks.
- Adhere to SPA3ETF exit signals such that when the Applicable ETF and Applicable Stocks are all 'closed trades,' the portfolio will be 100% in cash.

Definition of Market Risk

The definition of **Market Risk** is: the possibility of an investor experiencing significant portfolio drawdown due to any factor(s) that negatively affect the overall performance of financial *markets.*

Diversification cannot eliminate Market risk, also called "systematic *risk."* There are a number of methods to hedge against and to minimize risk, including going into cash from time to time.

Liquidity Risk

Do not open a position in any ETF whose daily liquidity averaged over the prior three months is less than 25 multiplied by 65% of the Portfolio Value.

Do not open a position in any Stock whose daily liquidity averaged over the prior three months is less than 25 multiplied by 7% of the Portfolio Value.

Portfolio Value is the total current value of the retirement nest egg.

Calculate the liquidity by using the 'Liq xMA' indicator in Beyond Charts. Or thus: the sixty-three-day Simple Moving Average of price is multiplied by the sixty-three-day Simple Moving Average of volume and then plotted daily.

View the example in Chart IIP-1 where graph one at the top is the IJH price movement, and graph two at the bottom shows that IJH averages US$160 million per day (the thick horizontal line) and oscillates between US$100M and US$250M in traded value per day.

Note: This calculation is an indication of the tradability for the Applicable ETF. The traded value of all the constituents in the underlying index that the Applicable ETF tracks determines the actual liquidity for an ETF.

Chart IIP-1 [Printed with permission from Beyond Charts]

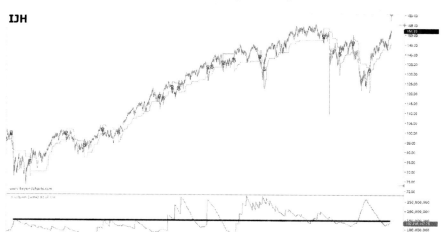

Money Management

- Allocate 65% of the initial capital to the Core strategy.
- Allocate 35% of the initial capital to the Satellite strategy.
- From time to time, the entire portfolio will be 100% in cash–due to there being no open trades in either the Core or the Satellite. If one strategy has performed better than the other, which has resulted in the 65%/35% changing, reallocate the capital to the 65%/35% split.
- The 65%/35% split between Core and Satellite can be reviewed depending on improvements in the investing skills of the investor and on portfolio performance.
- If a stakeholder wishes to add a Satellite, the necessary research must be presented as evidence to support the change to this Investment Plan.

Open Positions and Risk Distribution

The planned maximum number of Open Positions will be six, one for the Core strategy and five for the Satellite strategy.

Money in the Market

The objective is to expose all capital to the market as much as possible. However, research of the timing strategies deployed shows that capital will be in the market around 68% to 71% of the time and the remaining time the capital will be in cash during potentially adverse market conditions.

The Reward Objective has not included the receipt of interest for periods when the portfolio is in cash.

Position sizing

There will be just the two position sizes, measured as a percentage of the total portfolio value:

- Applicable ETF Position Size: this Plan allocates 65% of the Portfolio Value to the Core strategy.
- Applicable Stocks Position Size: this Plan allocates 7% each to five open positions, totaling 35% of the Portfolio Value to the Satellite strategy.

Starting the Portfolio

Once the stakeholder deposits the initial capital of $162,000 into the IRA account invest it by purchasing units in the Applicable ETF and shares in the Applicable Stocks, according to the following criteria:

- Core: Open a position in the Applicable ETF using the Applicable ETF Position Size when the next entry signal occurs after the start date of the Investment Plan.
- Satellite: Open positions in the first five entry signals that occur for the stocks on the list of Applicable Stocks after the start date of the Investment Plan, using the Applicable Stocks Position Size.

Maximum Brokerage Percentage Rule

If the commission for any transaction, for whatever reason, is equal to or greater than 0.5% of the position value, then do not execute the transaction until the position is large enough to reduce the commission at most to this percent level.

Process Management

Keep a readily available hard-covered file which will contain all paper records of:

- This Investment Plan and all future versions thereof.
- Account administration such as communications with the broker-dealer, including regular broker-dealer Statements.
- Records of regular receipts of IRA contributions.
- Records of quarterly dividend receipts.
- Records of Applicable ETF and Applicable Stock buys and sells.

Use a Portfolio Management software tool to:

- Record all buy and sell transactions.
- Record all re-invested dividends.
- Record all IRA contributions.
- Monitor annual and to-date growth statistics.
- Plot a portfolio equity curve for comparison against the S&P500 Total Return index.
- Use the SPA3ETF Portfolio Manager or a separate tool such as Excel if preferred.
- The SPA3ETF Portfolio Manager will automatically update the following statistics on which to conduct analysis on a quarterly basis:
  ◊ Total profit trades versus loss trades, i.e. winning rate.
  ◊ Average profit/loss per trade
  ◊ Average hold period
  ◊ Profit/loss percentage
  ◊ Maximum Drawdown %
  ◊ Compounded Annual Return % (CAR%)

Start and maintain an Investment Journal as part of meeting the Skills Objective.

- Document every transaction noting whether the stakeholder followed the Investment Plan process, or not.
- Note any deviation from the Investment Plan in the Journal.
  ◊ If the deviation results in a modification to the Investment Plan, formalize it in a newer version of the Investment Plan with the changes tracked.
  ◊ If the deviation was an error, take action to ensure that it does not recur. For example, journaling or additional notes will be made in the Process Management section of the Investment Plan.
  ◊ Report deviations to an Accountability Buddy, typically a spouse.

The Daily Process

- **Step 1** – Await an alert notification from the SPA3ETF App for the Applicable ETF or Applicable Stocks. Preferably, also conduct this analysis in Beyond Charts by scanning or viewing each chart individually in the list of Applicable Stocks:
  ◊ Buy or Sell according to the *Method* and *Money Management* rules.

- **Step 2** – Close and Open a new position, if applicable.

If a Sell signal occurred in the Daily Step 1, then a new Applicable Stock position must be sought to be opened.

The current open position for which the Sell signal occurred must be closed on the next trading day after the Sell signal occurred, using a MOO (Market on Open) order.

If there is a replacement trade, then open that position on the same trading day as the previous position was closed, using a MOO (Market on Open) order.

The Monthly Contributions Process

- **Step 1** – Automatic deposit of monthly IRA contribution into broker-dealer account.

Only deploy this cash injection in the market when the next Buy signal occurs for either of the Core or Satellite strategy.

Maintain the 65%/35% split between the Core and Satellite strategies. If an imbalance has resulted from market price action, then this cash can be used to help restore the 65%/ 35% balance.

The Dividend Process

- **Step 1** – Deposit of dividend into the IRA account.

The cash should remain in the broker-dealer account until the next Buy transaction.

Maintain the 65%/35% split between the Core and Satellite strategies. If an imbalance has resulted from market price action, then this cash can be used to help restore the 65%/35% balance, i.e. the dividend from the Applicable ETF or Applicable Stock does not have to apply to that ETF/stock, apply to the overall Core Satellite portfolio.

END OF INVESTMENT PLAN

LAST WORD

- Download a copy of Iain's Investment Plan from: www.blueprinttowealth.com
- Follow the journey of Iain's Investment Plan on the same website. Share Wealth Systems executes this Plan with real money. View the Plan's progress, warts and all.
- The research for Iain's Investment Plan, complete with equity curve and closed trades can be viewed or downloaded from the same webpage.
- Achieving a potential 2035 Target Date fund return of 6.9% CAR over the next twenty years could grow a nest egg to only $868,986, including unindexed IRA contributions and reinvested distributions.
- Achieving a potential Balanced Fund return of 7.91% CAR over the next twenty years could grow a nest egg to only $1,025,741, including unindexed IRA contributions and reinvested distributions.

CHAPTER 17

The Traits of a Consistently Successful Investor

"Life is one big transition."

WILLIE STARGELL (HALL OF FAME BASEBALL PLAYER)

*"The secret to change is to focus all of your energy, not
on fighting the old, but on building the new."*

SOCRATES

"Depending on how active you wish to be with your investing you may need to go through a transition process."

"What do I need to transition from and why?" asked Iain.

"You may not need to transition at all. But I have discovered in my many years as an active investor, a financial markets researcher and an active investing coach that the degree to which active investors deny the need to change how they think with respective to active investing, is the degree to which they will need to transition their thinking."

"If you decide to use the simplest of the ETF strategies suggested and merely follow a buy-and-hold strategy in an index ETF, invest all retirement contributions and re-invest all dividends into that index ETF pre-retirement, then you will probably not need to transition the way you think."

"When you need to make more decisions, you will make more mistakes if you do not align how you think with how you need to execute your Investment Plan. Active investors do not check off a box on a form and then forget about it for the rest of their working life."

"As you have decided to use timing, more decisions will need to be made in the pressure cauldron of the financial markets. The more decisions presented to an investor, the more challenging active investing can become; your thinking then needs to be more in tune with the fluctuations of the market."

"You ask from what and to what you need to transition. It is what I call thinking from a societal perspective to thinking from a market perspective."

"What do you mean by societal and market perspectives?" asked Iain. "What's the difference?"

"How society programs us to think is very different from how you need to think to prosper as an active investor in the financial markets. My view is that if you can change the way that you think to become consistently successful in the markets, this way of thinking will help you excel in other aspects of your life too."

"Are you saying that investing successfully in the market can teach us to become better people?"

"Yes, the skills required to become a consistently successful investor can lead to you becoming a better person."

"That's a big call," said Iain. "Tell me more."

PLANNING AND PREPARATION

"I'll start with planning. All ventures and endeavors in which you desire some degree of success begins with proactive planning and preparation. Sustained success rarely occurs through irregular impulsive reaction."

"The primary step in planning is determining your purpose; in this case, for investing. We did this as part of devising the mission statement of your Investment Plan; which in turn plays the major role in determining what your financial goals and objectives are for building a nest egg for retirement, or for other investment goals for other aspects of yours and your family's life."

"Are planning and preparation doing what is necessary to complete all the sections of the Investment Plan?" asked Iain.

"Yes. In essence, what we have done in our time together is the important first step, that of planning and preparation, which includes knowledge acquisition and evidence gathering, for the venture of becoming and continuing to be a successful investor."

"As your level of investing activity will need buying and selling decisions, there are a number of traits, or thinking patterns, and ways of conducting yourself with respect to becoming a consistently successful active investor, that you should transition to."

"I'll deal with each leading into the transition exercise. Let's now prepare for that process."

EMPATHY

"To be successful in the markets you need to learn to think from the market's perspective. Effectively this means ***that the more empathetic you are to seeing things from the market's perspective, the way that it behaves and moves, the smoother and less stressful your active investing journey will be***. You will be more accepting and understanding of both the inevitable ups and downs that will occur."

"What is the market's perspective?" asked Iain.

"Well, you tell me. Does the market always rise? And if not, how does it move?" I asked.

"It goes up, and then it goes down," Iain responded. "Come to think of it, it seems to go up and down in smaller cycles while it's *going down* in a bigger cycle, and also goes up and down in those smaller cycles while it's *going up* in a bigger cycle."

"Correct, it goes up and down whether it's going up or down! In different time frames! Those up and down moves are called cycles, swings or trends. Indeed, there are trends within trends of various time frames. That's what makes the market so random and tricky to trade in the short term."

We looked at Chart 17-1 of Apple Inc. in my Beyond Charts charting software and applied a fifty-two-week (big outside looped swings), thirteen-week (large inside swings) and four-week swings (smaller inside swings), which are annual, quarterly and monthly swings.

Chart 17-1 [Printed with permission from Beyond Charts]

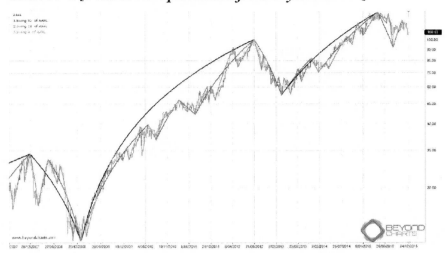

I explained, "The monthly and quarterly trends can be rising while the annual trend can be falling. If I had also added the weekly and daily swings, then the current direction in all time frames would be even more confusing. Indeed, there are also intraday swings measured in ticks, or in one, five, ten, fifteen and thirty minutes; and one, two, four and six hours. Opportunities exist in all these timeframes in any given moment; in fact, there is an endless stream of opportunities across all time frames."

"This is what makes the market; there are so many views of the current direction of the market in so many different time frames. And there are so many variables that interact with the market in a way that each one, or collectively, can have a positive or negative effect on the market at any given moment. Add all this together and it produces random price movement in the short term that nobody can *predict* on a sustained basis, and therefore must just be accepted."

"Understanding, accepting and having empathy that markets rise and fall, and can do so randomly in the short term while moving in a steadfast longer term direction, is one of the principles of the market. It is almost like the ebb and flow of the tide – waves still roll in and out whether the tide is coming in or going out. Meaning that you must accept that the value of your investments will also rise and fall in a similar way."

"Having total empathy means that you shouldn't feel despair when the value of your nest egg falls as that is just the market doing what it does.

It also means that you should not feel euphoria when the market rises sharply as that too is just what the market does."

"You imply that empathy is not a societal perspective. Why?" asked Iain.

"It would be nice if it were, but unfortunately society programs us to see everything regarding how it affects us personally. We are a 'me, myself, I' society that determines good from bad by what effect it will have on each of us as an individual. We then react to that negatively when we perceive the market is hurting us when it is merely doing what it does."

"We are self-absorbed and struggle first to understand others before imposing our views and opinions. While you might argue that we need to be self-absorbed to protect ourselves from harm, I would contend that we have been programmed more and more by a selfish and greedy collective narrative to look after 'numero uno' almost to the total exclusion of looking out for others."

"We justify this type of thinking and carry it into our endeavors in the market where we don't first seek to understand before imposing ourselves on the market, and it doesn't work. The market is just not going to change its modus operandi to how we think individually."

"We all want a better world, thinking that the world must change around us, but the paradox is that if more people changed themselves to practice real empathy, the world would become that better place. As will your investing world if you become empathetic with the market."

"Becoming genuinely empathetic requires shutting down your outward bound transmitters and assigning all their bandwidth to your inbound communications receivers to maximize inbound bandwidth. This takes effort and discipline initially. It requires asking valid questions of the market, followed by intense listening. Be still and listen. Maybe that's why the word ***listen is an anagram of silent***.

Be silent and listen to the market, not to commentators who are influenced by biases. Listen to your completed Investment Plan, not the 'noise' and gossip that surrounds the market."

"The transition process attempts to retrain the budding active investor to become an inbound communications expert, through all senses, and hence to be empathetic."

THINK IN PROBABILITIES

"However, even with total empathy for how the market works, when it does fall, the risk still exists that the value of certain instruments can fall to zero or to levels that may not be recoverable. Or the use of leverage at the wrong time can wipe out large portions of capital."

"All this creates massive uncertainty in the minds of investors," I said.

"It is important to understand the pitfalls as well as the peaks that can occur with active investing. Those who embark on an active investing journey in the stock market, rather than a passive one, and persevere will learn more about themselves than from just about any other journey in life."

"There are degrees of challenges that the active investor will need to endure. The shorter the average holding period per trade, the more decisions the active investor will need to make and the tougher the challenges will be along the way. The longer the holding period per position in the market, the fewer decisions that will be faced and the simpler the investing journey will be."

"It's a numbers and probabilities game. More choices and decisions means a greater likelihood of making a terrible mistake and of making more errors."

"If the market is a melting pot of uncertainty with random short-term price movement, then a 'probability of one' just does not exist over a large sample of outcomes. Meaning that only *probabilities of less than one* exist; meaning that winning 100% of outcomes cannot be attained; meaning that there WILL BE positions that will lose money. But experiencing losing positions doesn't mean over many trades over the long term that losing overall is the only final outcome. In fact, despite experiencing many losing outcomes, money can be multiplied, as I have demonstrated in many charts and tables in our sessions."

"Therefore, understand and accept that the market offers an endless stream of opportunities and that these opportunities occur in a probabilistic environment where not every event turns out to be a winner. The main reason for this is the randomness that occurs with short-term price movement caused by the almost limitless number of variables that interact with the market, the vast majority of which are totally out of investors' control."

"The challenge is to tap into the endless stream of opportunities in a timeframe that meets your objectives."

"The way to do that is to think in terms of probabilities because 'probabilities' is how the market presents itself to the investor; meaning it doesn't present itself as a certainty on any single interaction that an investor has with the market."

"How do I do that?" asked Iain.

"***Devise a robust 'timing edge'*** that has a researched positive statistical probability of being successful when executed in the market. The statistical probability can be called mathematical expectation, or expectancy, the formula for which we initially discussed in the session on compiling an Investment Plan in Chapter 13. Table 17-1 is the 'timing edge' for timing MDY over the twenty-year period."

Table 17-1

Number of Trades	49
Winning Trades	33
Winning %	67.35%
Avg Profit %	9.52%
Losing Trades	16
Losing %	32.65%
Avg Loss %	-2.27%
Payoff Ratio	4.194
Expectancy	2.498

The formula for expectancy is [(Payoff Ratio + 1) * Winning %] − 1 where Payoff Ratio = Avg Profit % / Avg Loss % = 9.52%/2.27% = 4.194 and Winning % = 33/49 = 67.35%.

Therefore, the expectancy = [(4.194 + 1) * 67.35%] − 1 = 2.498.

"If the expectancy were less than zero, then there would be a negative mathematical expectancy meaning that the timing criteria don't work for MDY, and hence there is no edge."

"It is far easier to determine a 'timing edge' for a stock market index which has a bias to rise over the long term because of its innate characteristic of 'survivorship bias.'"

"We use the same timing criteria for the other ETFs that we have discussed, but the edge metrics will differ for each ETF and stock because the price movements for each are unique and different."

View the 'timing edges' for other ETFs and stocks on the Resources page under ETF Edges on the website www.blueprinttowealth.com.

"With the example of MDY in Table 17-1, thinking in terms of probabilities means thinking that every time an investor opens a new position in MDY there is a 67% chance, on average, of a 9.52% advance in the price of MDY, and a 33% chance of a -2.27% fall in MDY. Even though these are averages and every outcome will be different, it gets your expectations better aligned with the probabilistic environment rather than expecting a positive outcome for every position and then feeling despair when it doesn't happen."

"I can see that now," said Iain. "But what if I had a string of three or four losing outcomes in a row?"

"That certainly does happen," I responded. "The distribution of wins and losses is also random because price movement is random in the short term. But trends will eventually form, and that's when the 'timing edge' will come to the fore and work in your favor. The edge through its precise definition of risk via pre-defined exit signals will protect your capital when the market trends down strongly by being in cash most of the time and will grow your capital when the market rises strongly by being in the market most of the time."

"And what about when the market tracks sideways?" asked Iain.

"That's typically when most of the losing outcomes occur. The active everyday investor simply must close out of a small losing position when the exit criteria of the method occur in case that position turns into a large losing position if the investor does not act upon the exit signal and the sideways move turns into a strong long down trend. Remember, *every large loss outcome starts out as a small one*."

"The 32.65% of all trades being losing outcomes in MDY is quite a low losing rate. The number of losing trades can often exceed 50% meaning that there are more losers than winners. But *overall the 'timing edge' is still profitable because the average size of the winners is much larger than the average size of the losers achieved through limiting the size of the losers by executing the exit signals of the method*."

"That's what leads to a positive expectancy."

"*Researching historical data demonstrates that the key to long-term investing success is not doing something outstandingly brilliant. The key is not to do something outstandingly stupid* by compounding mistakes such as hanging onto large losing positions for extended periods of time, or breaking the rules of one's finalized Investment Plan."

"This is the sort of empathy and probability thinking that an active investor requires, especially when there has been a string of losing trades resulting merely from the distribution of winners and losers being random."

"Nearly all novice active investors fear experiencing a losing outcome because it is negative feedback. People hate negative feedback, taking it personally as a direct reflection of their ability. The losing outcome bruises their pride. They see themselves as a failure because their self-absorption sees everything in terms of themselves."

"Society trains us to fear failure in one-off events rather than truly accepting failure as a natural part of becoming and being successful over a large number of events. Probabilistic thinking helps put individual losing outcomes into perspective."

Iain asked, "Understanding the probabilities may help accept the losing outcome but how do active investors overcome the fear of experiencing a losing outcome before it occurs?"

TRUST

"By trusting and believing in their edge which defines their probabilities of success. Which is why thinking in probabilities and having a robust edge is so important," I replied. "When you think in terms of the probabilities of your edge, you move to *fully accepting that losing is part of the probabilities which then liberates you before the event to be able to execute* and to transition to not personalizing each losing outcome as you being a failure."

"How would I build trust in my edge?" asked Iain.

"You would access provable evidence and have a big picture perspective. I have provided you with plenty of evidence that over a large sample of timing decisions over many years that you will be much better off timing an index ETF than by buying and holding it. This is the edge that has to be trusted."

"*Trust builds confidence and commitment. You cannot trust and fear at the same time*. If you are fearful of executing the next buy signal, especially straight after a losing outcome or when market conditions are jittery, then you are not trusting your edge."

"But it takes so long to build trust, and one bit of negative feedback can break it in a flash," said Iain.

"This is true, and that is why trust alone is not sufficient to think from the market's perspective. You must build trust in conjunction with:

- **empathy** of how the market ebbs up and down in different timeframes,
- the **belief** that favorable trends will develop again in the future, which the probabilities of your edge will take advantage of, and
- that **setbacks are inevitable but temporary** over the long term."

"I have also provided you with evidence that buying and holding an ETF and reinvesting all dividends will provide far better returns over the long term than buying and holding an equities mutual fund, Balanced Fund or Target Date fund. This is the edge that the stock market has over other asset classes."

"How can I totally trust this?" asked Iain.

"How can you totally trust that a Balanced Fund or Target Date fund will provide you with the necessary retirement nest egg to last all your retirement years?" I answered his question with a question to get him thinking.

"I can't," he answered.

"Well, you have to trust something going forward from here. Which will you trust? The evidence of performance from lower fees and focusing on a single performing asset class that I have presented to you in our sessions; or will you trust the evidence provided by the active mutual fund industry via active equities mutual funds, Balanced Funds and Target Date funds as researched by the SPIVA˙ Scorecard?"

"*There is no doubt that those that don't seek to understand defer to the social default*" and suffer the long-term consequences. Whereas those, like yourself, that do strive to understand can reap the fantastic benefits of their deeper gained knowledge."

I asked, "Why is the onus on me, and many others like myself who question the status quo, to provide evidence and there is no onus on the status quo operators to provide proof? Yet they continue to blast marketing messaging misinformation around the airwaves and continue to get away with it."

Iain chose not to answer his question.

I answered it for him, "Because you have been programmed by the industry to fear to do it yourself. That's why. Life is about overcoming fears to grow to a new level of knowledge, understanding, and skill. When you do this, you can break free from deferring to the social default."

"How do I trust that the market will provide positive opportunities and outcomes in the future?" asked Iain.

PERSPECTIVE

"A societal paradigm keeps reminding us how people break trust. With people, there is no way of knowing that who breaks your trust will revert to the way that they were before they broke your trust in them."

"That is because many people aren't guided by principles even though they should be. Markets move to the rhythm of unfailing steadfast principles. One market principle, just like life, is that it will provide an endless stream of opportunities from which to grow. Therefore, trends aligned to your 'timing edge' will occur again and again in the future. Your task is to be skilled and vigilant to recognize these opportunities and to engage them when they occur."

"But how do I know that they will?" asked Iain.

"***Big picture perspective allows the active investor to visualize the procession of outcomes in the market over many executions and many years.*** It sees long lasting up trends, and it sees large down trends. It sees the sideways movement going nowhere. It sees winning, and it sees losing. Of varying degrees. It gains a feeling of experience before actually experiencing the event in real life. It trains the subconscious to know how to feel as the market does what it does. It paints pictures in the minds-eye before the eye has seen them in real life. A perspective such as this helps overcome fear, uncertainty, and doubt during trying times, and euphoria in times of plenty. It helps build confidence and commitment."

"Perspective comes from doing preparation through due diligence and research, and then from real life experience. I have endeavored to provide you with a shortcut by doing this research on your behalf to save you hundreds of hours compared to doing the research yourself. Hopefully, I have achieved this by communicating this due diligence and research to you in our time together."

"I certainly do have an entirely different knowledge and view of investing now," said Iain.

"Big picture perspective is gained by having an insight into how stock market indices and simple stock market strategies have journeyed over the long term. Allowing the active investor to ***visualize the big picture's long-term procession of outcomes when challenged by the short-term randomness and volatility*** of the market."

Iain chipped in, "I can see what you mean when I look at the long-term equity curve performance of MDY when using timing, and even when not using timing when compared to active stocks-only mutual funds and Balanced Funds."

"This is the long-term big picture that you must visualize when feeling challenged by the market. An analogy I sometimes use is to imagine you are a bird flying high above a ticker tape parade moving through the main street of a city. You can see the beginning and the end of the procession, and at your whim, you can see any particular part or outcome of the parade that you wish by swooping down on that section."

"Compare that view to a person standing in one spot along the side of the street in the parade that can only see a tiny part of the procession at any given moment in time. They can't see what is coming until it arrives. They only have a partial snapshot contextual view. Big picture perspective has an insight of what may come, positive and negative, and is prepared to embrace it rather than fear it."

PROCESS

> *"No institution can possibly survive if it needs geniuses or supermen to manage it. It must be organized in such a way as to be able to get along under a leadership composed of average human beings."*
>
> ### PETER DRUCKER

"When we compiled your Investment Plan the express purpose for doing so was to define an efficient and profitable process that anybody can follow. If the Investment Plan is planned, prepared and documented in the necessary detail, a complete novice could execute it after a short explanation."

"This can be called 'McDonaldizing' the investing process," I responded. "And, yes, your spouse or anybody you trust with your money should be able to follow the plan after a short demonstration and without assistance from you."

"Process is defined as executing a series of actions or steps to achieve a particular outcome. But process is more than this; it is about ensuring that the 'right thing' is done and that the 'right thing' is done right."

"If effectiveness is doing the right thing and efficiency is doing the thing right, then correct process makes you both effective and efficient. Meaning the process is easy, practical and highly repeatable."

"Proper process breeds **consistency**, and to be consistent you need to be *objective*. If there is no objectivity, and subjectivity reigns, then there is no consistency, nor is there process as what to do in any given situation will be made up on the fly. If there is no process, then ineffectiveness and inefficiency become the modus operandi and chaos reigns."

"Trusting and executing your positive statistical 'timing edge' in a proper process ensures consistency."

"What's more, following process, and doing the right thing right, is not determined by the outcome of one, two or a few events turning out how you wanted them to. In the case of active investing, everybody would want a position that is bought and then sold to have been a profitable outcome. However, a profitable outcome does not equal right, and a losing outcome does not equal wrong."

"What does then?" asked Iain.

"Doing the right thing is determined by how closely the investor follows the right process," I responded.

"What is the right process?" Iain continued with his prying.

"To use corporate terminology, it is the process that you have documented in your execution 'policies and procedures manual;' your Investment Plan. You prepared and wrote your Plan outside of investing hours, away from the pressure of live execution, uninfluenced by an emotional reaction to 'noise' or surmise to ensure that you incorporated as much objectivity as possible into the plan."

"Therefore, your Investment Plan defines what is right and what is wrong, in the context of what you are trying to achieve."

"If you don't have an Investment Plan and therefore have no defined active investing 'policies and procedures' then you can do no wrong as there is no definition of wrong. By definition, you will always be doing the right thing, which will be your discretion of what you want 'right' to be in any given moment. You will find yourself justifying your action after the fact by distorting actual events and rationalizing the outcome as favorable in some way to you."

"This is why so many people have difficulty completing their Investment Plan. Subconsciously, they simply do not wish to be held accountable and responsible for having done the wrong thing, which are the mistakes that they will inevitably make; so they resist defining what 'wrong' is in the first place."

"How do you define a mistake?" Iain was quick to ask.

"Ah, great question. With no Investment Plan and no definition of when, what and how much to buy, hold or sell, then there is no such thing as a mistake. Human beings have a natural tendency to abhor being wrong, making mistakes, losing and missing out. With no Investment Plan, you have total freedom to do what you like… until the pain threshold of losing comes home to roost."

"An investing mistake is taking any action that is contrary to what you document in your Investment Plan."

"For example, if an exit signal occurs and you decide to ignore it, that is a mistake. The exit signal has been researched to precisely and objectively define and limit your risk. Not following it is breaking process and doing the wrong thing. It's the equivalent of the McDonald's staff member deciding on the spur of the moment to add mayo instead of ketchup when ketchup is part of the documented process."

"Operating without an Investment Plan, which defines right from wrong, will lead to never overcoming frustration and fear because losing outcomes will ALWAYS be part of the range of outcomes. Randomness will ensure that all on its own!"

"If there is no Investment Plan, losing outcomes, by definition, will always feel as if you have done the wrong thing. Which will invariably lead to frustration and fear of executing the next call to action, even when the variables that caused the losing outcome were probably totally out of your control."

"I now fully understand that losing outcomes are a certainty, if only due to short-term randomness and the seemingly infinite number of variables that interact with the markets," Iain added.

"Yes! However, with an *Investment Plan that reframes right from wrong not by the outcome but by the process, and whether it was followed correctly or not,* there is a way of overcoming frustration and fear and hence of achieving peace of mind with all outcomes. Which leads to being liberated just to follow the process unhindered by doubt, hesitation or reservation. *You will NEVER be wrong if you adhere to the process because the definition of being right is to follow the process."*

"There will always be variables that are outside the control of the executor that cause outcomes of every kind. But if the process is followed then over a large sample of executions, many tens or even hundreds, investors will have an edge that will be profitable and fruitful but will still have negative outcomes along the way, even when they follow the process. *If investors follow the process, these losing outcomes will still constitute doing the right thing."*

"This is the way of accepting losing outcomes without beating yourself up," Iain recognized.

"Precisely. Every time that a favorable outcome occurs when investors override the Investment Plan with their own discretion and do not follow the process, they are rewarded for doing the wrong thing. Being rewarded for doing the wrong thing will re-enforce the dysfunctional habit of doing the wrong thing again and again."

"Consistency and objectivity can never be achieved with such behavior. It will ensure a never-ending cycle of inconsistency, subjectivity, frustration, hesitation, reservation, doubt, uncertainty, and fear. Decisions will continue to be highly discretionary, random and whim-led. Which will guarantee an unsuccessful investing journey over a large sample of outcomes over the long term, but most likely also lead to at least one great devastating outcome from not following the process."

"How do you know for sure that it will lead to being unsuccessful over the long term?" asked Iain.

"Because a person's discretion has an unknown edge as do random decisions that are impulsively whim-led. The probability of an unknown edge based on no research being positive is extremely tiny, maybe zero. Imagine the McDonalds hamburger process being random on each occasion by each burger maker? Would there be a consistent burger from one franchise to another?"

"I get it," said Iain.

"Tested and evidence-backed process leads to repeatedly doing the 'right thing' right with confidence and commitment."

GRATITUDE

"Another important trait of consistently successful investors is gratitude. Being grateful means being thankful for and accepting of what you have, not envious of what you don't have."

"With respect to investing, we have discussed how the stock market ebbs up and down in cycles in numerous time frames; and how losing is a natural part of winning over the long term. When the market ebbs down, portfolio values also decline, sometimes quite significantly. At such times being grateful means focusing on and being thankful for what you have, not focusing on what you don't have. Otherwise, you can become frustrated by not now having what you had before the recent fall."

"Frustration and envy for what you don't have can lead to feeling sorry for yourself and even feeling like you are a victim; a victim of that mean stock market and all it represents. Self-pity and victimhood can be comforting because it allows you to abrogate responsibility by **blaming external forces for our current lot**. Self-pity justifies not taking an action that requires effort and doing something that may be outside of your comfort zone. It freezes you into inaction instead of continuing to execute in the face of adversity."

"Practicing gratitude every day by being thankful for the current value of your investments, regardless of whether the market has had a recent massive decline or significant run-up, overcomes feelings of envy, self-pity, and victimhood. An attitude of gratitude, having big picture perspective and trusting your process helps keep you grounded and neutral in the moment. The action that requires effort is to execute your process without hesitation or reservation."

NEUTRALITY

"Talking of neutrality, this is the following trait," I said continuing.

"What do you mean by being neutral? We are all biased in some way or another," Iain suggested.

"We certainly are, it's part of the societal paradigm. Neutrality means having no expectations of what the next outcome will be. 'Let it be' as the Beatles famously sang, when you have established all the actions that comprise your process; let the process play itself out in its target environment without you meddling on the fly with un-researched discretion or whim-led knee-jerk reactions."

"Easier said than done. I know that I have problems just following a recipe without my special discretionary touch of adding an ingredient here and there that is not in the recipe," Iain responded with a smile.

"It sure is. But while the current process is your chosen process you should merely expect an outcome, not whether it will be a profitable or a losing outcome. Unmet expectations cause a subjective and unsubstantiated action that is not in the process; that is doing the wrong thing. Don't project your self-centered wants into the future; instead, have a genuinely open mind to whatever happens in the present."

"Be mindful of the process in the present moment, not what has happened in the past or might occur in the immediate future. Mindfulness of the process keeps you focused on what you have to execute now and prevents self-sabotage from your mind wondering off to associate itself with past poor outcomes or an exaggerated future hope, both of which would typically cause a breaking of the process."

"Your reactions should be the same, neutral; regardless of what happens because you already know from your edge, perspective and probabilities that losing outcomes are factored into the process and will absolutely happen. Adverse results occur in a random distribution; just as positive results do."

"No amount of additional research, analysis or reading will remove the principled fact that losing outcomes will occur. Be neutral and just allow them to happen. You can do this because you trust that your 'timing edge' will deliver if you adhere to the entry and exit signals of the process over the long term."

"How will I know when I have achieved neutrality?" asked Iain.

"Your process will become effortless to execute without hesitation, reservation, fear, uncertainty or doubt; and you will be at peace with all outcomes."

"Wow, that sounds like a cool, calm and contented place to be!" Iain exclaimed.

"It sure is and should be," I assured Iain. "Otherwise, the outcome of a previous event could cause you to experience an extreme emotion of some kind, potentially either emotional pain from losing or overjoyed euphoria from a big win. Each, in turn, will put you in a frame of mind that will inevitably cause you to make mistakes in the next execution by breaking your process; either by not taking a trade that you should, or by risking less or more than you should."

"Regardless of what has happened, developing a neutral frame of mind prepares you best to handle the current and the next execution. You can't change the past, but if the past affects your present state of mind, this can affect how you execute the next imminent event."

"The past cannot be cured."

Queen Elizabeth I

HONESTY

"The market is completely honest and brutally objective with its participants. It says it like it is, loud and clear without distortion. It does this by communicating the net aggregate feelings of all its participants–the whole spectrum from extremely negative to extremely positive–objectively through price movement at any given moment."

"To be successful in the market, which is ruthlessly honest with its feedback through price action, you also need to be totally honest. First and foremost with yourself. You do this by executing your Investment Plan as you have prepared it. See your Investment Plan as a contractual arrangement with yourself. Which means being accountable to your Plan and dealing objectively with the numbers that the market communicates to you, whether they be positive or negative. Which means that you can't justify mistakes after the fact, distort outcomes or twist your way out of the truth."

"If you are dishonest with others how can you be honest with yourself; and vice versa? You are either honest, or you are not; and being dishonest in one part of your life will infiltrate another. The same applies to all the other traits."

"Wow, operating with a market paradigm sets a high bar," said Iain.

"The way I see it, humans thinking with a market paradigm as I'm describing should be the norm; it's the societal paradigm that sets a low bar," I replied.

SURRENDER

"Surrender!" exclaimed Iain. "Surely you don't mean surrender as in fly the white flag and 'give up' investing?"

"Certainly not. I mean surrender as in give up control. Control is handed over to the process. Do not try to control the market or anything else in the environment. This will merely lead to frustration since control of the market is not possible."

"I thought that not being able to control the market would be obvious to anyone," Iain offered.

"To the logical mind away from the heat of the market, it is obvious," I responded. "But the logical mind is not always what determines how we think, say, feel and do in the moment; it is the subconscious mind that does our bidding, especially when the pressure is on. **Pressure makes all the difference.** People who are typically in control in their respective societal and work environments will try to find ways to control the market environment without even being aware they are trying to do so. They will subconsciously bring their business or work 'behavior' and 'mindset' to their active investing which will mostly be disastrous. They self-sabotage themselves without even knowing that they are doing so."

"Will this happen to me?" asked Iain.

"It could if you started investing with the more active medium-term methodology, SPA3 NASDAQ (see details in Appendix) straight away," I responded. "You would need first to complete the transitioning exercise that I'm about to take you through. However, it shouldn't happen to you with the rather inactive method that is currently in your Investment Plan since that only requires a few decisions a year. But if you sense that it is happening with you, then continue doing the transitioning exercise that I am about to take you through."

"Okay," Iain confirmed. "But an ordinary investor must take control at some stage."

"You take and have control when you prepare your process and document it in your Investment Plan ***before*** you start executing. That's what we did together. Once the planning and preparation are complete, it is time to execute, not to continue 'preparing' on the fly as you go. In execution mode, the role of investors is to surrender to the process that they planned and prepared, and to follow it."

"There are only three things that any investor *can* control themselves: these are–***what*** to buy, ***how much*** to buy and ***when*** to execute, i.e., buy and sell. Everything else is outside of the investor's control. So surrender to the process."

"By surrendering and giving up control of the market, you gain control, self-control of your focused process. Another paradox."

PRACTICE

"While practice doesn't necessarily make perfect, it does allow the active investor to learn how to execute the ins and outs of the process and to gain execution skills. Like training wheels on a bike that reduces the risk of falling while learning how to balance and operate the brakes and pedals."

"***The idea is to start practicing the process with little or no money at risk.*** Which is akin to net practice for baseball or standing on the driving range for a golfer. Practice allows the sportsperson to acquire skills without the pressure of a costly outcome from a poor shot; removing the risk of a costly outcome frees the mind to focus on learning key competencies. The objective of practice, therefore, is to gain skills in a pressure-free environment before executing in the pressure of the real environment where the outcomes of the shots and the score count."

"Then, when the steps and actions that comprise the process have been learned and can be executed error-free without risk, start executing in the real environment, where the score matters, with a small amount of money so that the dangers of making an unintentional error are small. The skills goal at this stage is to become comfortable with a little pressure derived from doing the real thing. Remember, pressure makes all the difference."

"Another analogy that I like to use is that of a trainee tightrope walker. When first beginning to acquire skills, the trainee starts with a wide slackline. The wide slackline is close to the ground because the stakes are small for falling thereby liberating the trainee from the fear of poor execution and removing the pressure associated with the high risk of potentially feeling physical pain. In the case of the non-transitioned everyday active investor, the pain from losing is emotional."

Figure 17-2

"As skills are acquired and confidence is gained to execute according to the plan, the stakes can gradually be raised, literally in the case of the tightrope walker as the tightrope is raised higher from the ground."

"Execution is exactly the same at all heights; the only change is what is at risk in the event of a mistake or poor execution."

"This is precisely how the active investor should acquire investing skills, by gradually increasing the absolute stakes at risk through committing more money to the strategy."

"In effect, with an Investment Plan, the percent risk is precisely the same regardless of the size of the capital. However, the absolute stakes at risk are larger for more significant amounts of money. In theory, the capital size shouldn't matter when thinking is terms of percent risk, but in reality, everyday investors that haven't transitioned their thinking are hugely affected by the absolute size of dollars at risk."

"How will I know when I have acquired the skills to execute with the *Core Satellite* strategy for growing my retirement savings?" asked Iain.

"When you can continue to execute the process flawlessly without reservation, hesitation, fear, uncertainty or doubt about how much money in absolute terms is at risk; which is objectively defined by your method as the potential loss, should the next closed position be a loser. Your mind and body will tell you. You won't lose sleep thinking about the possibility of a losing outcome, or get grumpy with those closest to you when you do lose."

"For example, assume that your next position in an index ETF is $100,000, and the trailing indicator line is 5.5% away from the current price, meaning that if the price fell straight to that line without the line rising, then $5,500 would be the loss. If losing $5,500 causes you to break out in a sweat and get heated under the collar, then the tightrope is too high. Lower it by using less capital until you are comfortable with the risk; otherwise, your discomfort or frustration will cause you to take actions that are not in your Investment Plan; these are execution errors."

"The Core Satellite approach suits this technique of acquiring skills. *A suggested 'training wheel' method of starting 'Iain's Final Investment Plan,'* if you are initially uncomfortable, would be to allocate most of your retirement savings in an IRA, say 90% to 98% depending on your capital base, to the IJH buy-and-hold strategy, the Core. And allocate the remaining amount to timing, the Satellite, and *then gradually increase the Satellite portion as your comfort levels improve in line with your skills*. Then migrate the Core from buying-and-holding to timing IJH."

"Initially the exercise for having the Satellite strategy is one of skills acquisition operating under minimal pressure, not necessarily growing

capital. Then as your skills, confidence and commitment grow and improve, the objective becomes improving returns; the Satellite could even then become the Core."

PATIENCE

"I've heard the saying that patience is a virtue but why do investors need patience in the stock market?" asked Iain.

"The market cannot be forced or controlled. If it is declining and your process stipulates that you should be in cash, then don't get impatient, override your process and open a position on the basis that you think the market has fallen enough, maybe buoyed on by contrarian commentators or an intuitive feeling that it cannot fall any further. Be patient and wait for the signal when the market has turned up. The signal is there to alert you to take action."

"But that means I would have missed out on some of the run-up from the bottom," said Iain.

"That's right. Remember, we researched the signals on years of historical data meaning that the edge and the probabilities in which you place your trust already has the 'missing out' of an initial run-up built in. Trust the edge."

"Likewise, if you feel that an open position has yielded enough profit, have the patience to wait for the exit signal. Sure, there is a high probability that the price will retrace at some stage and give back some of the profit, but that may still be a lot higher than the current profit level."

"And this means that I would have given some back by not getting out earlier and locking in profit," said Iain.

"*Oh, so you would have known in advance that the price was going to fall?*" I asked and got a blank gaze back from Iain. "It may have continued much higher, and you would have left lots of money on the table, causing frustration from the opportunity cost and from not following the process. Again, the retracement is built into the edge. And the right thing to do is to follow the process, not try to be a hero by predicting the exact top of a trend!"

"The point is that you don't know. Surrender to not having to know; fully accept that you don't need to know. Because nobody knows and can know what will happen next in the market."

"Have the patience to follow your process and let the market do what it will do. Research supports a robust edge that will produce consistent outcomes if you have the patience to surrender to it and follow it."

"In fact, the less patient you are and the more that you try to second-guess the process of your edge, the more time it will consume and the more frustration you will experience. Frustration can turn into anger and anger makes you stupid – scientific research has proven this. Lack of composure and calmness makes for poor decision making."

"Have patience and don't allow the randomness of the market to consume or overcome you."

RESILIENCE

"Like so many other things in life, active investing is essentially about handling adversity. The more active you are as an investor, the more adversity you will face and hence the more resilient you will need to be to prosper. Resilience is the capacity to recover quickly from setbacks and adversity. This ability can be learned–investing in the stock market in a certain way that the transition exercise explains will develop resilience."

Iain interrupted, "Having listened intently to this material I now understand what you meant when you said that becoming a successful active investor could lead to me becoming a better person."

I smiled, "Resilience requires a mindfulness of reality in the moment. *It requires a staunch belief that your life is meaningful, backed by values and principles and the ability to confidently create and apply researched solutions in advance to deal with the adversity that you can face.* It requires gratitude for what you have, not envy for what you don't have."

"How much adversity do DIY investors face on a day to day to basis?" asked Iain.

"Let's put it this way, even when stock markets rise strongly, there is still plenty of negative feedback. Take the last two bull markets. In 2002 to 2007 the S&P500 index rose 101% from start to finish. Yet 45% of the trading days were days that the S&P500 declined. In the 2009 to 2015 bull market, the S&P500 rose 215% from trough to peak, yet 44.3% were down days. On nearly all the negative days, investment nest eggs would have fallen in value."

"Wow, that's a lot of down days for two strong bull markets," said Iain. "I'm sure that the value of my house wouldn't jump up and down like that!"

"During bear markets when the S&P500 can fall between -20% and -55% the negative feedback is, of course, worse and more draining. That's the reality of the stock market. And of the news feeds that we hear every day about what's going on in the world, a steady stream of negative feedback."

"Resilience and the structured Investment Plan that we have prepared are needed to overcome the adversity and noise that inevitably comes with negative input; not to subjectively knee-jerk react out of fear and uncertainty about the future."

"Yet amongst all this negative feedback, positive progress can be and is being made in your nest egg. I have unfolded a blueprint for you that details some simple solutions for growth, of you and your money. *The certain way to build investing resilience, in my experience, is to use a plan and a mechanical market timing system such as I have unveiled in this blueprint.* A big picture perspective with a researched and prepared objective plan sees right through the fog of adversity and builds confidence and resilience to overcome negative feedback."

"But above all, resilience has as its foundation stone an unshakeable belief that your life is meaningful, and hence your investing is meaningful too. In the first instance, it is the duty and responsibility for each one of us to create a resilient platform of financial security and stability. From this platform, we can launch ourselves to perform meaningful acts or service for those close to us and then others beyond our immediate circle that need our talents and resources of time and money far more than we do."

PERSEVERANCE

"Once the Plan is set and ready for execution, then engage the environment. As I have said before, investing is a twenty-year and more endeavor, not a twenty-day, twenty-week or twenty-month endeavor."

"There is no doubt that your mettle and plan will get tested along the way. Every journey in life tests us. Adversity, trials, and tests under pressure are what help us grow. That's how we improve and rise to higher levels of understanding and execution. And how we build further resilience."

"It's no different with investing. In fact, active investing can be more testing that any other endeavor because of the high degree of value that we place on money. Rightly or wrongly we do."

"Remember, it's not what happens that matters; it's what we do about it that counts. We cannot control what happens, but we can control how we react. Liberate yourself by not having to know in advance what will happen in the future. Let it be; be confident in your ability and trust your process to handle come-what-may; even within the bounds of its imperfection defined by its probabilities, not its certainty."

"Expect to be tested; in fact, look forward to being tested in adversity and when you are, embrace it rather than fear it, because it is when we get tested that we have the potential to learn and grow the most. ***Don't just GO through it GrOw through it.*** Persevere through the tough times. Seek inspiration from your mission statement. Keep on keeping on."

"Perseverance is about just that, keeping on keeping on in the face of adversity. It's easy to persevere in the middle of a steady stream of positive outcomes; it's a lot tougher when it feels like the whole world is pit against you. ***Perseverance breeds a mindset that believes with every part of who you are that failure only happens when you quit altogether.***"

LAST WORD

- As an active investor your thinking needs to be aligned with how the market moves, that is, you must become empathetic with the market. Listen to it; let it provide what it has to offer.
- There are traits that we need to become better at to become a consistently successful active investor. Devise a process and step into it to acquire and improve these skills and traits, with respect to investing:
  ◊ Planning, empathy, probabilities thinking, trust, perspective, process, gratitude, neutrality, honesty, surrender, practice, patience, resilience, perseverance.

CHAPTER 18

A Transition Exercise

"Why should we look to the past in order to prepare for the future? Because there is nowhere else to look."

JAMES BURKE

"I guess it can only be good for anyone to develop these traits," said Iain.

"There is nothing new in these traits. Anyone who's been alive for a few decades should be familiar with them. What's more, these characteristics apply to many other endeavors in life, not just investing. They certainly apply to business, golf, other individual and team sports, relationships, and probably many other activities."

"It's just that people have difficulty using them most of the time, let alone all the time. ***Most of us know what to do but have difficulty doing what we know.*** That's why it is important to step into a process to start transitioning towards what you really want to do."

"Many people struggle with such processes, examples of which include giving up smoking or losing weight. They fear to fail and then face the decision of whether to continue the process or quit. So they struggle to start the journey in the first place."

"What is the exercise that I should do to acquire these active investing skills, just in case I need them, or to improve them?" asked Iain.

"The best exercise that I have come across in all my years of actively investing and in coaching others is the exercise explained in the late Mark Douglas's book *Trading in the Zone*. Near the end of the book, Mark asks his readers to complete twenty trades, forty executions in the market, with a ***mechanical investing system***. And with every execution, document in a journal everything that you think, feel, say and do."

"Find and use methods that will assist in this transition. Use repetition. Compile affirmations and read them out aloud just before every buy and sell transaction when you do your journaling. I suggest two fantastic affirmations: Mark Douglas's Five Fundamental Truths, and his Seven Principles of Consistency, which you can find in his book *Trading in the Zone*."

"Write up other affirmations about how you want to think and feel when you execute in the market and record them with your own voice on your smartphone. Do this using binaural beats and listen to the affirmations through headphones when falling asleep, or at other times when relaxing."

"Find tools, such as Apps that can train you to remain mindful of what you must do right now in the moment. Apps such as 'buddhify' or Smiling Mind."

"Isn't this taking it a bit far?" asked Iain.

"Professional athletes continuously do these sorts of drills and exercises. If you want to rise above average and become a consistently successful active investor, then you should consider taking actions that stand an excellent chance of getting you there," I responded.

"What is a mechanical investing system? You have mentioned this a few times before," asked Iain.

"A mechanical investing system is a set of interconnecting procedures that precisely define the unambiguous criteria under which a buy or a sell signal exists. There is no discretion or subjectivity about the presence of the signal. It is exact and objective. There can be no debate. Ed Seykota, the author of *The Trading Tribe* and well-known investor, describes a mechanical investing system as *"an agreement you make between yourself and the markets."* It is the Method in the Investment Plan.

"It also contains mechanical risk and money management rules to determine when to engage the market and when not to and precisely with how much money of the overall portfolio to invest in each individual position."

I continued, "You have heard me mention the SPA3 NASDAQ and SPA3ETF products now and then. Well, these are mechanical investing systems that include the unambiguous buy and sell signals, risk management, and trade size calculations. There is more information on these on the website www.blueprinttowealth.com."

"How do I know that the mechanical system will be profitable?" Iain asked.

"Well, you don't know for certain. Can you know for sure what will happen in the future?" I asked.

"Death and taxes, as the cliché goes!" Iain answered.

"Are you sure about that? Let me put plenty of doubt into your cliché answer. Around 80% of people in western democracies receive more in direct and indirect benefits than the taxes they pay each year and consequently are net tax receivers, not net taxpayers. And as for death, there are multiple billions of people across more than one faith who believe in life after death. Many people may not believe this, but no one really knows for sure!"

"So you are saying that there is nothing that is certain!" exclaimed Iain.

I continued, "If there is no certainty in the future, then, as I have said before, the next best thing in which we can place our trust and belief is probabilities. With a mechanical investing system, the likelihood of what may happen in the future can be determined based on researching how the identical unambiguous and objective criteria performed in the past. If the research shows that the mechanical system has a robust edge, then there is a high probability, not a dead certainty, that using the same criteria in the future will also be profitable to some degree."

"These are the probabilities that you said I have to think in terms of, and to trust?" asked Iain.

"Yes! The gap between a 'dead cert' and probability is risk!"

"That R-word again, I can't get away from it," said Iain.

"The bigger the difference between a probability of one, a 'dead cert,' and the probability of success, the bigger is the risk. If you don't know what the difference is because you don't know the probability of the success of your edge, then the risk is immeasurable. That's not a good place to be."

"This is why it is important to think in terms of probabilities. A mechanical investing system gives us a high probability, not a certainty, of indicating what may happen in the future. What else is there to research but the past?" I asked.

"Why is it important to do the drill with a mechanical investing system?" was Iain's next question.

"Because the decision-making criteria of *the mechanical system will be unambiguous, objective and subscribe to the market's perspective of the past rather than your societal perspective, thereby creating a clash of thinking paradigms*."

Iain was listening intently, his mind trying to reconcile his current knowledge with what I was telling him.

I continued, "The objective of the exercise is to transition your thinking from a societal paradigm to that of a market paradigm with respective to investing in the market. The transition process ensures that the two worlds of societal perspective and market perspective will clash and that the conflict will be resolved between the two paradigms one way or the other."

"The clash of the titans! How long will it take to resolve how I will continue to think?" asked Iain.

"It's not necessarily a function of time; it's a function of the number of times that the conflicting paradigms clash and how well energized your current societal paradigm is to resist change. During the process, a conscious decision must be made to resolve the conflict. Every time that there is a clash of paradigms and investors decide to follow the mechanical investing system, the less energized their societal-like thinking becomes and the more energized their market-like thinking becomes. This is the process of transitioning to becoming a consistently successful investor with respect to investing in the stock market."

"Understand that making a decision *to exit a losing position is a part of being a consistently successful investor* even though that exit in that particular trade locks in a losing outcome. The primary function of exiting that losing position is to ensure that it doesn't become a larger losing outcome. Just as in other walks of life failing is a part of being successful to make sure that a lesson is learned."

"I can see how losing is part of being successful," Iain added. "I've read the quotes about Thomas Edison failing thousands of times before he invented the light bulb. And even the best sporting teams have losses but still win the competition because they have an edge."

"Precisely. *You know this. Now you have to believe it as a natural part of who you are with respect to active investing so that at the subconscious level you can do what you know.* The transition process using journaling helps achieve this belief."

"How do I go about keeping a journal?" Iain asked.

"Use a tool such as Microsoft Word, a Journal booklet or an App like Evernote. You need to organize and arrange the journaling of everything that you think, feel, say or do before and after each buy and sell execution. YOU record in writing what YOU are thinking, feeling, saying and doing. This repeated activity links your head, heart, and soul in such a way that you can transition your old dysfunctional habits and ways of thinking about and doing things to new functional practices of operating in your chosen environment."

"It's like reprogramming my mind with the new way that I would like to function with respect to my investing?" Iain questioned.

"Absolutely correct," I replied. "To assist with this exercise, I have prepared a procession of charts that will take you through ten years of investing decisions in a short studying period of adhering to a mechanical investing system. I will endeavor to explain how to think at each decision point to illustrate how the consistently successful investor with the necessary traits thinks when thinking from the market's perspective."

"Okay, let's do it," said Iain.

"While we go through this procession of charts, practice what you might think, feel, say and do when each position is opened and closed. I will prompt you along the way."

For this exercise, the charts that follow include leverage at 1.6:1 to magnify the testing of adversity and euphoria. They exclude regular contributions and re-investing dividends. They, therefore, focus on the timing decisions of buying and selling MDY when mechanical signals occur. Upward facing arrows for 'buy signals' followed by downward facing arrows for 'sell signals' point out where all the signals occur.

Chart 18-1 covers a two-year period from August 1999 to August 2001. There were five trades (five buys and five sells, i.e. ten executions in the market) over this period of two years. A 'trade' is a buy signal to open a position followed by a sell signal to close the position.

Chart 18-1

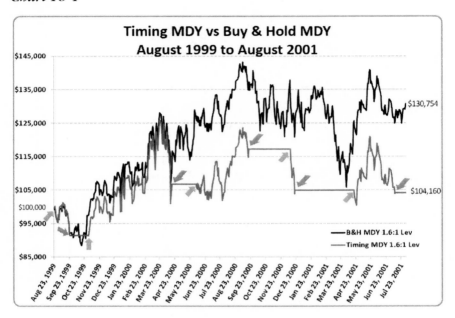

Chart 18-1 shows the five trades on the 'Timing MDY' equity curve (lower line). The upper line is the 'buy-and-hold (B&H) MDY' equity curve.

Given how the market moved over this period and how the mechanical timing system aligned with the market price movement, the timing system underperformed the buy-and-hold of MDY by some 26% over the two years.

The second and third trades of the five marked trades in Chart 18-1 were profitable outcomes, and the first, fourth and fifth trades were losing outcomes with the fourth being a -10% losing trade.

Five trades over two years are just ten decision-making days. The effort required to be vigilant for signals is just minutes a week, if that when you're receiving alerts via a smartphone App and using Beyond Charts that displays buy and sell signals when they occur. The effort required is not one of time but of psychological acceptance and surrender, trust in the system, empathy with how the market communicates its opportunities to investors and believing that the probabilities of the mechanical investing system will play out while you're patient and stick to the process.

What would an everyday investor have thought and felt at this stage after two years of monitoring their investment process? What would he have been saying about his situation? Would he have been impatient and done something to break his process? And hence make a mistake.

"Remember, Iain, what I said about being tested?"

Iain responded, "I'm sure that the investor would have been inclined to pack it in and withdraw from the process."

Maybe feelings of frustration, betrayal, despair and doubt would have prevailed. If he was self-absorbed, seeing only how the world works by how it affects him, he might have been too emotionally hurt and unable to accept the situation.

After all, being $26,000 behind than merely buying and holding MDY is a serious difference after two years. We'll see in a moment how the Vanguard Balanced Fund fared to this point. However, as I've stressed so often, you must subscribe to the belief that "anything can happen" as a fundamental truth in the market and that trust in a robust provable edge eventually has a high probability of prevailing.

In Chart 18-2, exactly one more year is appended to the right of the vertical dotted line, and one more trade (opened and then closed position) occurs during that additional year, as shown with the up and down arrows.

As the legend shows, the top line at the end of the plot area in Chart 18-2 is now the 'Timing MDY' equity curve. Remember, "Anything can happen."

Chart 18-2

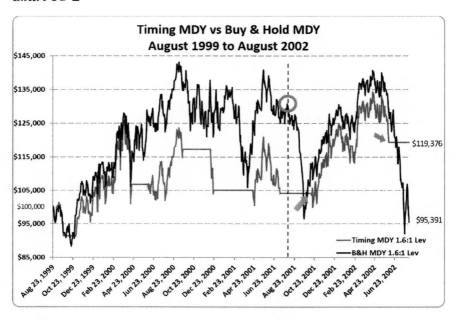

At the point of the dotted line (marked by the magenta circle), buying and holding MDY fell from $130,754 to around $96,000 at the end of September 2001.

The 'Timing MDY' strategy was in cash during this period as shown by the horizontal equity line. Lest we forget, most of this decline was caused by the terrifying 9-11 events in New York.

MDY then rose again to around $140,000 early in 2002 before falling back to $95,391 in August 2002, below where MDY started three years earlier.

Over this additional year to August 2002 the equity curve for 'Timing MDY' improved to $119,376 with the strategy being 100% in cash as at August 2002, as shown by the equity curve being a horizontal line where the exit signal is.

If the stock market had continued to fall beyond August 2002, then the timing strategy would have remained at $119,376. What would your thoughts have been now? How would that have felt? I can assure you; this situation feels great–like being dry, safe and secure alongside a warm crackling fire in a sturdy log cabin in the mountains during a raging storm of hail, rain, lightning, and thunder.

However, the stock market didn't continue to fall. Chart 18-3 appends the next year to August 2003. Over this period there were three rallies with two of them proving to be 'false rallies' when the stock market fell away immediately after the rise. 'False rallies' are a normal part of how the stock market moves; the traits to be neutral and patient are required when these occur.

Remember, "anything can happen." Good things can happen too! The market can rally upwards strongly. It did, starting in March 2003 from a lower point than MDY was at nearly four years earlier at the commencement of the data in the chart.

Chart 18-3 shows two and a half trades (five buy and sell executions in total) in the next appended year after the vertical dotted line through to August 2003.

Chart 18-3

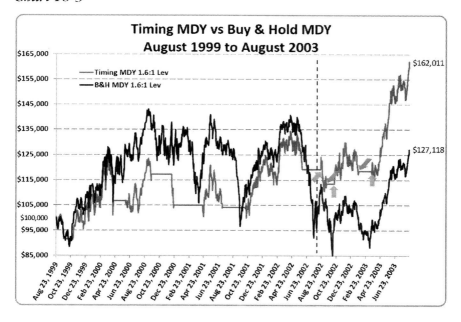

The third trade in Chart 18-3 shows only the buy signal because it was an open profitable position where the chart ends as at August 2003. At this time, the equity curve for 'Timing MDY' (upper line) was almost $35,000 ahead of the buy-and-hold equity curve for MDY.

How would this have felt compared to being $26,000 behind two years earlier? What would you have recorded in your Journal compared to two years earlier? Elation? Euphoria? Would you have bragged to your colleagues, family or friends? Remember, neutrality and being at peace with all outcomes is required.

A consistently successful investor should have recorded that he had followed the process; that he had done the 'right thing' right, effectively and efficiently.

I understand that it will take some time to achieve being at peace with all outcomes and that humans are emotional beings, so some degree of despair and joy, respectively, would be felt along the way. But the journey should be aimed at minimizing emotions. When Neil Armstrong stepped onto the moon after he had completed his first famous statement he reportedly then said, calmly and collectively under his breath to himself, "Just like training, just like training."

Chart 18-4 appends another year after the dotted line, to August 2004. The sell signal for the open trade in Chart 18-3 is the first exit signal at top right in Chart 18-4 followed by two small losing trades, ending the appended year in cash and nearly $40,000 ahead of the buy-and-hold equity curve over the five years since August 1999.

Chart 18-4

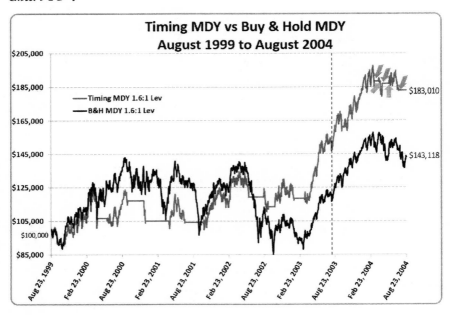

The last two trades in Chart 18-4 to August 2004 were both losing closed positions over a period of three and a half months. A novice DIY active investor just starting and immediately experiencing two losing closed positions would have felt like the active investor who began in August 1999.

Your perspective at this point, having been on this plan for five years and outperforming all market indices and balanced funds would have been very different than the novice's feelings after two losing outcomes. ***My challenge as a mentor and coach is for both these active investors to gain the same big picture perspective over the long term and feel and think the same way at this point having experienced different journeys, purely because their starting times were different.***

Before moving on, how would the Vanguard Balanced Fund, VBINX, have performed relatively to this point? Chart 18-5 shows its performance, some $71,500 behind the timing MDY equity curve, $31,450 behind the buy-and-hold MDY equity curve, or just $11,550 total profit over five years, including VBINX distributions. And after the first two years, as we questioned earlier, it was below the 'Timing MDY' equity curve as at August 2001.

Chart 18-5

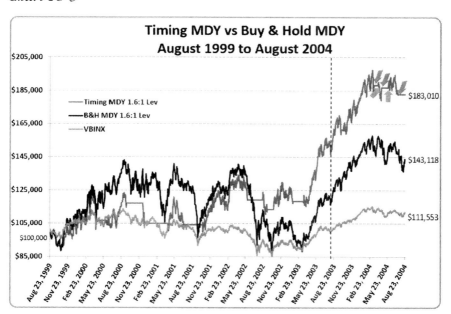

Chart 18-6 appends another three years onto the previous chart, to August 2007 and an additional five profitable trades during a period of strong growth in the stock market. The gap between the two approaches has now widened to more than $100,000 with the benefit of timing and leverage.

At this stage, VBINX would have been valued at $146,012, including distributions and excluding leverage.

This period to August 2007 ends with the equity curve of mechanically timing MDY 100% in cash and the stock market having started a decline.

Chart 18-6

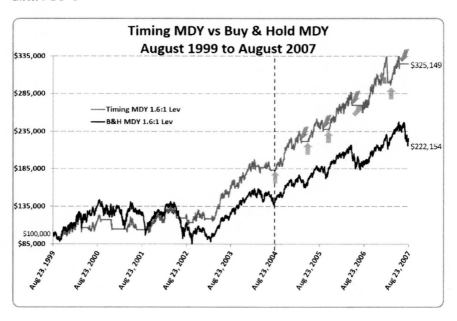

Chart 18-7 advances a little over a year to November 2008 to the bottom of the 2008 bear market. The appended fifteen months sees the completion of an additional three trades with two of the trades registering losses.

Chart 18-7

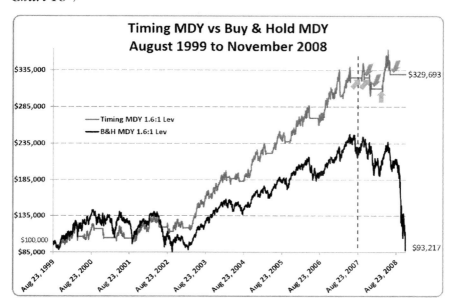

The last exit signal in Chart 18-7 is an important one as it takes the strategy 100% into cash just before a significant stock market decline. At the time the signal occurred it was ***NOT a prediction*** of the impending significant decline. None of the indicators, nor the average or professional investor, knew with any certainty that the market would suffer such a decline. We do know, however, that ***all significant declines start out as a small decline***.

The start of this particular downward price movement looked like any of the other minor corrections that had generated exit signals in the past, sometimes causing losing outcomes when the market reversed upwards again, possibly frustrating uninitiated everyday active investors.

Sure, many doomsayers had been predicting and writing about such a decline, some since the 1990s. ***There are always doomsayers adding to the noise and gossip, regardless of the prevailing market conditions.*** If an investor who used subjective decision-making criteria had fallen victim to the doomsayers' incessant noise, he would probably not have enjoyed the brilliant run-up that occurred before the 2008 bear market.

The -56% decline was a severe bear market, as we now know with the benefit of hindsight, which took the buy-and-hold equity curve of MDY to nearly 7% below the starting value of August 1999.

The equity curve of timing MDY is now nearly a quarter of a million dollars ahead of the buy-and-hold leveraged equity curve. And VBINX, you ask? It ended this period with a value of $105,033.

Chart 18-8 shows the period to August 2009 and the bounce off the trough of the 2008 bear market. The S&P MidCap 400 ETF MDY rose 73% while the leveraged timing equity curve for MDY increased 53.4%, having missed the first three weeks of the rise from the trough of March 2009 to allow the buy signal to meet its criteria before the signal appeared.

Chart 18-8

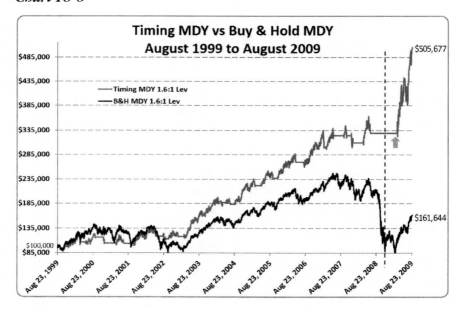

The difference between the buy-and-hold of MDY and 'Timing MDY' equity curves has now reached $344,000 ($505,677–$161,644) from a $100,000 start. And VBINX reached $131,582 to this point.

The main strength of a timing strategy comes home to roost when it protects investors' capital from a large fall in the stock market. In doing so, it keeps the equity curve at a much higher plateau than it otherwise would have been from which to launch its next rise when the stock market next starts a rising trend. This is risk management through timing.

Diversification does an average to potentially poor job of risk management over the long term.

That's probably why Warren Buffett set out in 1957 to beat the market when it fell and match it when it rose. Diversification into lesser performing asset classes will never match the stock market during its long, strong rising trends.

I could show many other examples of periods such as this with other ETFs such as the PowerShares NASDAQ 100 QQQ ETF or the Guggenheim S&P500 Equal Weight RSP ETF. The point is that *investing is not a weeks or months long venture; it is at least a twenty-year venture and if you're age thirty-five or younger, more like a forty-year venture.* And with the building of a retirement nest egg being a defined contribution system, everybody has to take responsibility to become a consistently successful investor, whether they like it not.

CONCLUDING THE TRANSITION PROCESS

What would you have recorded in your Journal about what you were thinking, feeling, saying and doing on this compressed ten-year journey? To be a consistently successful active investor takes patience, trust in process, belief in probabilities, consistent execution of strategy, objectivity, self-control, empathy for how the market ebbs up and down, feeling at peace with all outcomes, perseverance, and resilience in the face of adversity and a big picture bird's eye perspective of what can happen over the long term.

Being successful doesn't mean winning all the time. It also means losing and knowing how to deal with loss, how to frame it so that you grow from it and embrace it with an expectant attitude rather than fearing it and cowering from it.

Being successful means doing better than average. Anybody can do average. Average is leaving your money in a Balanced Fund, or a Target Date fund. And average will, in turn, provide an average to not-so-comfortable dependent retirement. The herd does average or status quo. It's time to break free and go your own investing way to grow and become a better person. And to achieve financial freedom.

Being successful means making the most of what is available – while still being able to "*walk with Kings–nor lose the common touch[1].*" Stock market index-type returns, and better, are readily available. We know from all the research discussed and provided in this blueprint to wealth that

---

1   "If" by Rudyard Kipling

index-type returns will do far better than nearly all active mutual funds over the long term.

"But if everyone becomes aware of this evidence and does it this way, it will become the way of the herd!" Iain ventured.

"No, it won't," I replied. "Most people will continue their busy lives and not change their investing path in the slightest. Evidence can only take people so far because most are more guided by emotions and their currently programmed habits and subconscious than to new evidence."

"However, a select few—those who desire to do better and who take responsibility for their futures—will cross the threshold of change and overcome deferring to the social default. Those that make things happen rather than watch things happen. The former are players, and the latter are spectators. When it comes to investing to build a nest egg, the spectators may join that third category of people on this planet when they reach retirement and wonder what happened."

"Iain, there is nothing more to know. Before you knew what we have covered, you had an excuse of insufficient knowledge and skill. That excuse is no longer valid. Now that you know what to do, *are you up to doing what you now know* and stepping into a new and exciting journey and process?"

ONE LAST CONSIDERATION – YOUR LEVEL OF EXCESS

May I humbly suggest that in your Investment Plan, you set a 'level of excess,' a dollar number, which is the level above which you don't need to acquire any more wealth to live the life that you dreamed and planned. Indeed, you may already have the vision to do things that are only possible with wealth that surpasses your 'level of excess'.

Your 'level of excess' sets a threshold above which that wealth is not for your use but for the use of others whom you can help, others who are needier than you, others who weren't blessed with your lot in life, with your tenacity and talents to achieve better than average. Above this threshold, you move to sharing your wealth and time with and for others.

Once set, this 'level of excess' becomes an investing objective in its own right, not only to achieve but to surpass.

Choose in advance, when you set your 'level of excess' goal, who you would like to invest in, rather than what, with the resources that you have at your disposal. Perhaps deploy to this cause too, the wealth building systems and skills that you have honed. And the life skills that investing and striving in life will have taught you, skills such as empathy, trust, preparation, surrender, perspective, patience, process, practice, perseverance, resilience, consistency, objectivity, self-control, calmness, persistence, gratitude and probabilistic thinking.

Achieving your 'level of excess' also defines reaching your realm of financial freedom. Financial freedom, by definition, is not achieved through relying on a state-provided pension; it is accomplished through you providing for yourself and family through the exertion of your talents, abilities, skills and experiences with which you have been blessed.

Strive to build a platform of financial freedom, from which you can humbly yet assertively, calmly yet passionately, quietly yet confidently, share your wealth and time to touch the lives of those who need help to survive and grow so that they can, in turn, share their wealth and time with others.

I commend to you this do-it-yourself blueprint to wealth to achieve a comfortable and independent retirement; and financial freedom.

LAST WORD

- Complete the active investing skills acquisition exercise to go through a transition process to gain these necessary mental skills.
- Maintain a journal recording all that you think, feel, say and do while completing the skills acquisition transition process.

Appendix for everyday investors who wish to be more active

S hare Wealth Systems (SWS) has designed and developed other active investing methodologies. The methodologies to consider for those wishing to be more active are SPA3 NASDAQ and SPA3 ASX. These are both medium-term active investing methodologies first used by customers in 1998. They are around five to seven fold more active than the methods and strategies discussed in this book for ETFs and large-cap stocks.

MEDIUM-TERM TRADING

You can find further details and past performance for these two methodologies at the author's website, www.blueprinttowealth.com or www.sharewealthsystems.com .

Appendix for Australian Readers

W here relevant, comments and complementary research is provided in this Appendix for the Australian retirement nest egg and investment landscape.

The research provided in the main body of this book uses examples of United States listed equites mutual funds, Balanced Funds and Target Date funds. Similar research using industry Superannuation funds and retail Superannuation funds is provided in similar detail here and on the author's book website, www.blueprinttowealth.com. The research evidences that outcomes and themes are very similar between the fund managers in the U.S. and Australia. This should not surprise readers as investing principles transcend geographic borders.

AUSTRALIAN BALANCED FUNDS ASSET MIXES AND PERFORMANCE *(Discussed in Chapter 3)*

In Australia, AustralianSuper[1] says that 75% of their clients are invested in their Balanced Fund option:

---

1   http://www.afr.com/brand/chanticleer/australiansuper-cracks-100b-and-says-big-will-get-bigger-20160711-gq2vlk

---

"Silk told Chanticleer that AustralianSuper had net inflows of $6 billion in the year to June [2016], excluding the impact of investment returns. Over the same period, the balance option, which holds 75 per cent of member assets, delivered a return of 4.5 per cent."

As the research in this book shows this means that millions of Australians will end up with far smaller nest eggs than they could have.

Investigation of Australian industry Superannuation Balanced funds shows that 'balanced' is very different from one Balanced Fund to another. Figure A3-1 shows the asset allocation of the QSuper industry Super Balanced Fund as at Q2 2015. The asset mix for each Balanced Fund in Australia changes regularly depending on financial market conditions.

Figure A3-1

	Asset allocation[3]	Ranges[4]
Cash	15.4%	0 - 25%
Fixed interest[5]	19.5%	5 - 35%
Property	7.4%	0 - 20%
Australian shares	12.1%	5 - 30%
International shares	19.5%	5 - 45%
Alternative assets	15.0%	0 - 25%
Infrastructure	11.0%	0 - 20%

Figure A3-2 shows the asset allocation for the Colonial First State (CFS) Balanced Fund as at Q2 2015. Both these Balanced Funds have a low asset allocation to the equities asset class when compared to U.S. Balanced Funds. In fact, wider research reveals this to be a consistent trait amongst Australian Super managed funds and Balanced Funds.

Figure A3-2

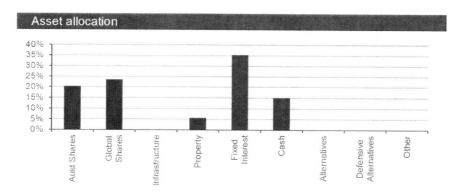

The empty columns in Figure A3-2 indicates 0% investment.

Chart A3-1 shows a seventeen-year comparison of performance between the All Ordinaries Accumulation index and three well known Balanced Funds where long-term everyday investor Superannuation nest eggs are invested.

Chart A3-1

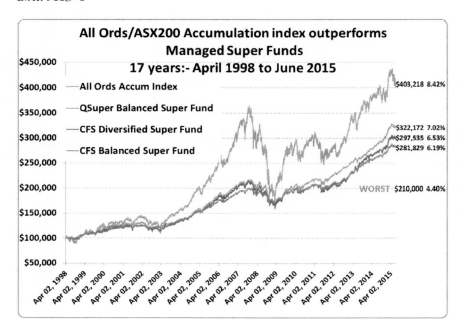

All Ords/ASX200 Accumulation index outperforms Managed Super Funds
17 years:- April 1998 to June 2015

The QSuper Superannuation Balanced Fund has been a top-ten performer for many years amongst all Superannuation managed funds in Australia. The evidence provided here clearly shows that the research revealed in Chapter 3 for the U.S. context is 100% applicable in the Australian context.

The range of performance outcomes from the hundreds of Superannuation managed funds available to long-term Australian retirement nest egg investors also varies greatly making it a lottery in Australia for how much retirees will eventually retire with.

Figures A3-1, A3-2 and Chart A3-1 are provided to whet the research appetite of Australian readers. Further research reveals that *the median returns of Superannuation managed funds trails the All Ordinaries and ASX200 Accumulation indices by around 2.75% compounded annual return (CAR) over twenty-three years to December 2015*.

By now you will know very well that the main reasons for this ongoing long-term underperformance by retail and industry Super funds are fees and diversification into lesser performing asset classes.

Notice how much higher the industry Super Funds fees are than index ETFs in Figures A9-2 and A9-3 below.

TARGET DATE FUNDS IN AUSTRALIA *(Discussed in Chapter 4)*

The phrase 'Target Date funds' is scarcely heard in Australia, however, the trend in Australia is also towards Target Date funds. But most Australian retirement savers probably wouldn't be aware of this. It might pay to do your own research to determine this.

"There are 5.3 million member accounts with the eight retail funds that have adopted a TDF/cohort fund [TDF = Target Date fund] solution according to APRA statistics published in January [2015]. Graeme Mather, head of investment consulting at Mercer, says if one assumes that 80 per cent of these are in the default then over 4 million member accounts will be in TDF/cohort funds in Australia. This figure does not include QSuper members or other lifecycle offerings that implement the de-risking on a member by member basis (by switching members from one fund to another).

ChantWest breaks down this estimate further. By its estimates there are 1.9 million people in what it describes as 'cohorts lifecycle', where a member is part of a group based on age and growth assets reduce progressively as the member gets older. That there is a further 1.2 million in switching lifecycle, where a member is switched from one option to another at a certain age and lastly a further 1 million using 'smooth switching' lifecycle, where members gradually switch from one option to another over a number of years. This latter option is used by Sunsuper and the Aon Master Trust."[2]

ROBO-ADVISORS IN AUSTRALIA *(Discussed in Chapter 4)*

The highest profile robo-advisor in Australia appears to be Stockspot. They use ETFs for all their investing. Whilst they make a big deal about fees, their fees are still a lot more expensive than investing directly with ETFs or even via an industry Superannuation fund, depending on the amount of capital that you have to invest. The picture is not so rosy compared to doing it yourself directly with ETFs.

Their business model compares well to using a financial advisor or

---

2 Source: http://investmentmagazine.com.au/2014/03/target-date-funds-the-start-of-a-big-adventure/

financial planner who charges an annual percent of FuM (Funds under Management). However, it compares poorly to doing it yourself, especially for Self-Managed Super Funds with account balances of greater than $50,000 that can invest directly with ETFs.

As at the time of writing in July 2016 Stockspot had recently reduced their fees. Their fees previously favored balances of less than $10,000 now they incentivize customers with less than around $8,000 not to invest with them.

For account balances of less than $10,000 that have been open for greater than six months, **annual fees range from 7.92% for $1000 to 0.792% with $9,999**, excluding ETF annual management fees.

For account balances of greater than $10,000 and less than $50,000, **annual fees are 0.792%**, excluding ETF annual management fees.

For account balances of greater than $50,000 and less than $500,000, **annual fees range from 0.77% down to 0.671%**, excluding ETF annual management fees.

For account balances of greater than $500,000, **annual fees range from 0.539% to 0.53%**, excluding ETF annual management fees.

Another robo-advisor that is rapidly gaining a profile in Australia is the American micro-investing robo-adviser Acorns. They also use ETFs for all their investing themes.

Acorns fees are lower than Stockspot for account balances of greater than $5,000 at 0.275% per year. This is in addition to the annual ETF management fees. While relatively low, these fees are still higher than doing it yourself with larger account balances.

For account balances of less than $5,000, Acorns charges a monthly fee of $1.25. This may sound low but being a micro investing company Acorns will accept investments of as low as $5. Unless you intend rapidly increasing your investments with Acorns, be careful as the fees could eat away your entire account balance in a matter of months.

For example, on an account balance of $100, $1.25 per month is 15% per year in fees. Nice for Acorns but not for the micro investor who will not achieve sufficient growth on that $100 to cover the fees. Micro investors really want to get their account balances above $1,000 otherwise they will be paying fees that are way too high relative to their potential returns. Below $1,000 it would probably be wiser to open an online savings account with a bank that charges $0 in fees.

How much do you need to retire?
(Discussed in Chapter 5)

The answers to this question provided in Chapter 5 for residents for the United States apply exactly to Australian residents, in terms of the lump sums required. In fact, with impending changes to the Superannuation rules at the time if writing, the tax burden may be higher for retirees that can retire independent of the governments' 'age pension', meaning that the target retirement nest egg will probably have to be higher to account for paying more taxes during retirement in Australia.

In any case, these online articles provide excellent input for assisting in determining what your lumps sum target should be for your retirement nest egg.

http://www.superguide.com.au/boost-your-superannuation/comfortable-retirement-how-much-super-need

http://business.time.com/2013/02/11/sizing-up-the-big-question-how-much-money-do-you-need-to-retire/

Chapter 5 uses research provided by EBRI and ICI for the United States. Such excellent and detailed research is not as readily available in Australia. However, Tables A5-1 and A5-2 provide an insight into the latest available Superannuation account balances in Australia.

They indicate that using $130,000 as the current average Superannuation balance for a forty-five-year-old and $217,000 for a couple as per the discussion in Chapter 5, might be just a little high for Australia, and so growing one's Superannuation in Australia will be a little more challenging if starting from a lower base. You can check the comparable figures for the country in which you live.

Both of Tables A5-1 and A5-2 are sourced from The Association of Superannuation Funds of Australia Limited March 2014 report entitled "An update on the level and distribution of retirement savings" by Ross Clare.

Table A5-1

Table 1: Mean superannuation balance, 2011-12

Age	Male	Female	Persons
	Mean superannuation balance ($)		
15 to 19 years	603	398	503
20 to 24 years	5,533	4,403	4,981
25 to 29 years	18,899	13,399	16,168
30 to 34 years	32,819	22,765	27,772
35 to 39 years	53,221	36,142	44,592
40 to 44 years	66,503	43,826	55,020
45 to 49 years	102,358	60,618	81,231
50 to 54 years	136,707	71,661	103,613
55 to 59 years	203,909	91,216	146,663
60 to 64 years	197,054	104,734	150,321
65 to 69 years	172,767	90,185	130,990
70 to 74 years	142,790	65,121	102,781
75 to 79 years	55,291	24,027	38,708

Table A5-2

					Superannuation account balance group						
	Nil	$1 to $99,999	$100,000 to $199,999	$200,000 to $299,999	$300,000 to $399,999	$400,000 to $499,999	$500,000 to $599,999	$600,000 to $799,999	$800,000 to $999,999	$1,000,000 and over	Total
					Number of persons ('000)						
Persons											
25 to 29 years	262,382	1,379,210	*18,377	n.p	-	*	n.p	n.p	-	-	1,664,293
30 to 34 years	210,339	1,301,259	37,572	n.p	**2,741	-	n.p	n.p	-	-	1,561,548
35 to 39 years	223,172	1,153,812	143,561	22,245	*6,639	*7,777	n.p	n.p	-	-	1,558,470
40 to 44 years	242,458	1,091,255	178,438	51,572	16,347	*5,528	n.p	n.p	n.p	n.p	1,592,706
45 to 49 years	217,907	951,760	214,710	73,566	32,706	22,969	*10,279	*7,772	n.p	n.p	1,539,070
50 to 54 years	254,809	813,262	214,501	82,484	46,323	26,016	16,737	16,010	*12,426	*11,349	1,493,919
55 to 59 years	293,513	580,115	181,722	95,251	64,470	39,553	18,232	34,694	12,608	25,507	1,345,666
60 to 64 years	390,687	424,281	122,837	86,987	53,669	44,575	27,536	35,536	20,841	23,454	1,230,402
65 to 69 years	493,882	189,336	93,052	65,858	32,878	26,085	17,002	24,414	*6,615	25,156	974,278
70 to 74 years	478,990	106,650	47,351	29,281	18,519	*5,369	*7,564	*8,906	*2,050	16,242	725,922
75 years and over	1,008,207	122,203	45,680	21,893	16,796	*9,624	14,878	*4,766	**1,904	**2,010	1,247,961
TOTAL	**4,076,348**	**8,113,143**	**1,297,801**	**541,036**	**291,088**	**187,496**	**115,449**	**136,510**	**64,638**	**110,677**	**14,934,186**

ACCESSING THE INDICES *(Discussed in Chapter 9)*

FEES

These are a sample of annual management fees in Australia for using retail managed funds, Figure A9-1, or industry Superannuation Funds, Figure A9-2; and do it yourself investing (DIY) via directly investing in index ETFs, Figure A9-3. These fees exclude any fees paid directly to financial planners and advisers.

Figure A9-1

Managed Fund	Minimum Annual Fees Jun 30 2005
CFS Balanced	1.83%
CFS Diversified	1.93%
CFS Cash	1.12%
CFS Future Leaders	2.03%
CFS Imputation	1.89%
FirstChoice Australian Shares	1.88%
FirstChoice Growth	2.04%
FirstChoice Diversified	1.78%
FirstChoice Balanced	2.05%
BT Active Balanced	1.93%
UBS Australian Shares	1.90%
Perpetual Australian Shares	1.91%
BlackRock ASX300	1.89%

Figure A9-2

Industry Super Fund	Minimum Annual Fees Jun 30 2005	Plus Admin	Plus
REST Super Australian Shares	0.74%	$57	
REST Super Balanced	0.68%	$57	
REST Super Diversified	0.83%	$57	
QSuper Balanced	0.57%	$77	0.20%
QSuper Aggressive	0.61%	$81	0.20%
CareSuper Balanced (MySuper)	0.86%	$78	0.15%
CareSuper Growth	0.89%	$78	0.15%
Hostplus Balanced (MySuper)	0.92%	$78	
NGS Super Balanced	0.64%	$65	0.10%
NGS Super Diversified (MySuper)	0.77%	$65	0.10%
NGS Super High Growth	0.80%	$65	0.10%
VicSuper Balanced	0.40%	$78	0.28%
VicSuper Growth (MySuper)	0.44%	$78	0.28%

Figure A9-3

ASX Index ETF	Annual Fees	Code
SPDR ASX200	0.19%	STW
SPDR ASX50	0.286%	SFY
iShares ASX20	0.24%	ILC
Vanguard ASX300	0.14%	VAS
iShares S&P500	0.07%	IVV
Vanguard Total U.S. Market	0.05%	VTS
iShares S&P400 Mid Cap	0.12%	IJH
iShares S&P600 Small Cap	0.12%	IJR
SPDR REITs	0.40%	SLF

SINGLE INDEX ETF, BUY-AND-HOLD STRATEGY
(Chapter 13)

Exactly the same Investment Plan can be used in the Australian context except for the following modifications:

1. The Applicable ETFs can be chosen from:
   a. STW, the ASX200 State Street SPDR ETF, annual fee = 0.19%.
   b. SFY, the ASX50 State Street SPDR ETF, annual fee = 0.29%.
   c. ILC, the ASX20 iShares ETF, annual fee = 0.24%.
   d. VAS, the ASX300 Vanguard ETF, annual fee = 0.14%.
   e. U.S. indices available on the Australian Stock Exchange:
      i. VTS, the Vanguard CRSP US Total Market ETF, annual fee = 0.05%.
      ii. IVV, iShares S&P500 ETF, annual fee = 0.07%.
      iii. IJH, iShares S&P MidCap 400 ETF, annual fee = 0.12%.
      iv. IJR, iShares S&P SmallCap 600 ETF, annual fee =0.12%.
2. The entities could be:
   a. A Self-Managed Superannuation Fund (SMSF).
      i. www.esuperfund.com.au is one organisation that establishes and charges annual fees for SMSF tax returns and audits for under $1,000. There are others.
   b. The self-investment option that is offered by some industry Superannuation funds. Additional annual fees are applicable.
3. The Super Guarantee rate is currently a 9.5% contribution of annual salary, paid by the employer and taxed at 15%. However, up to $25,000 can be contributed taxed at the concessional rate of 15%.

Bibliography

These are some of the books, that the author has read, some studied, that have played a role in his research, investing, experiences and forming his approach to, and perspective on, investing as an everyday investor for the long-term.

BOOK	AUTHOR
Trading in the Zone	Mark Douglas
The Little Book of Common Sense Investing	John Bogle
Winning the Loser's Game	Charles D Ellis
What Works on Wall Street	James O'Shaunessey
The Misbehavior of Markets	Benoit Mandelbrot
The Mathematics of Money Management	Ralph Vince
Portfolio Management Formulas	Ralph Vince
The Trading Game – Playing by the Numbers to make Millions	Ryan Jones
Market Wizards	Jack Schwager
The New Market Wizards	Jack Schwager
The Little Book that Beats the Market	Joel Greenblatt
Fooled by Randomness	Nicholas Taleb
Technical Analysis Explained	Martin Pring
Investment Psychology Explained	Martin Pring
Breaking the Black Box	Martin Pring

BOOK	AUTHOR
Smarter Trading	Perry Kaufman
Trading Systems that Work	Thomas Stridsman
Technical Analysis of the Financial Markets	John Murphy
Technical Analysis of Stock Trends – 8th Edition	Edwards and Magee
New Concepts in Technical Trading Systems	J. Welles Wilder Jr
Trading Systems - Secrets of the Masters	Joe Krutsinger
The Trading Systems Toolkit	Joe Krutsinger
New Market Timing Techniques	Thomas R. DeMark
DeMark Indicators	Thomas R. DeMark
The Definitive Guide to Position Sizing	Van K Tharp
Trade Your Way to Financial Freedom	Van K Tharp
Super Trader	Van K Tharp
The Three Skills of Top Trading	Hank Pruden
Inventing Money	Nicholas Dunbar
McMillan on Options	Lawrence G. McMillan
Options as a Strategic Investment	Lawrence G. McMillan
Option Volatility and Pricing	Sheldon Natenberg
The New Options Advantage	David L. Caplan
The 100% Return Options Trading Strategy	Jon Schiller
The Secret of Writing Options	Louise Bedford
Investment Secrets of a Hedge Fund Manager	Laurence A. Connors & Blake E. Hayward

BOOK	AUTHOR
Connors on Advanced Trading Systems	Laurence A. Connors
PPS Trading System	Curtis Arnold
More Than You Know	Michael J. Mauboussin
Predictably irrational – the hidden forces that shape our decisions	Dan Ariely
How to Make Money in Stocks	William J. O'Neil
24 Essential Lessons for Investment Success	William J. O'Neil
High Probability Trading Strategies	Robert C. Miner
The Master Swing Trader	Alan S. Farley
The New Money Managers	John Train
The Quants	Scott Patterson
Way of the Turtle	Curtis M Faith
Long-term Secrets to Short-Term Trading	Larry Williams
The Nature of Trends	Ramon Barros
The Evaluation and Optimization of Trading Strategies	Robert Pardo
Come into my Trading Room	Dr. Alexander Elder
Trading Chaos	Bill Williams PhD
Trend Qualification & Trading	L.A. Little
Getting Started in Global Investing	Robert P. Kreitler
Currency Trading	Philip Gotthelf
Think and Grow Rich	Napoleon Hill
Enjoy Investing on the Stock Exchange	Dr Karl Posel

BOOK	AUTHOR
ETF Investment Strategies	Aniket Ullal
The IVY Portfolio	Mebane Faber
Profiting from ETF Rotation	Leslie N. Masonson
Buy - Don't Hold	Leslie N. Masonson
Investment without Tears	Richard Cluver
Charting Secrets	Louise Bedford
The Secret of Candlestick Charting	Louise Bedford
Trading Secrets	Louise Bedford
Share Trading	Daryl Guppy
Unholy Grails – A New Road to Wealth	Nick Radge
Mastering Risk	Mike Lally
The art of Trading	Christopher Tate
Modeling Trading System Performance	Howard Bandy
Mean Reversion Trading Systems	Howard Bandy
The Profit MAGIC of Stock Transaction Timing	J.M. Hurst
Manias, Panics, and Crashes – History of Financial Crashes	Charles P. Kindleberger
The Bear Book- Survive & Profit in Ferocious Markets	John Rothchild
The Great Reckoning	James D. Davidson & William Rees-Mogg
Numerous books on property investing and others on stock market investing	

CPSIA information can be obtained
at www.ICGtesting.com
Printed in the USA
LVOW12s0851120417
530493LV00002BA/66/P